ENCYCLOPAEDIA OF INDIA, PAKISTAN AND BANGLADESH

ENCYCLOPAEDIA OF INDIA, PAKISTAN AND BANGLADESH

(In 9 Volumes)

(Volume 2)

OM GUPTA

ISHA

ISHA BOOKS

Delhi-110033

Encyclopaedia of India, Pakistan and Bangladesh
(In 9 Volumes)

ISBN : 81-8205-389-7 (Set)
ISBN : 81-8205-391-9 (Vol. 2)

Rs. 6300 (Set)

Published in 2006 in India by
Isha Books
D-43, Prithviraj Road,
Adarsh Nagar, Delhi - 110033
e-mail : ishabooks@hotmail.com

Laser Typesetting : Vinayak Printers, Delhi
Printed at : Salasar Imaging Systam, Delhi

Preface

According to Oxford dictionary Encyclopaedia is a book or aset of books that gives information on many subjects or many aspect of one subject. This encyclopaedia does that on India, Pakistan and Bangladesh. It is the first work of its kind. There have been anthologies on India but there is no compendium of information in an alphabetical order. Even Britannica could go as far as four-volume encyclopaedia on Indian history.

Encyclopaedia is an extension of a dictionary. The latter gives you meanings of words while the former gives facts about people, places and events. No one can claim to compile all the facts and that of a sub-continent called India. But then it is the prerogative of the editor to pick up his entries that he considers would be useful to his reader. Generally we soon find our comfort levels in a language. And rarely consults a dictionary and lesser an encyclopaedia. But those who dare, find the experience worth it. It can be easily compared to a human body. In our daily life we tend to be our own quacks and medicate on the basis of common sense. If we refer to a doctor we come to know the actual cause of the symptom and get relieved on knowing the gravity of the situation or the absence of it. One would realize that encyclopaedia reveals the fundamentals of any situation, person or the event and we feel at home with that information.

A dictionary and an encyclopaedia can easily enlarge the process of learning even to an uninitiated person. It is truer in case of humanities. Popular myth about encyclopaedia is that it is meant to be referred to in a library only. The librarians, the world over keep encyclopaedia in such zealously guarded protection that the generally refrain from asking for it. Since the advent of internet in our life, the bulkiness of encyclopaedias has disappeared. That is why we have divided this enterprise in nine volumes. Encyclopaedias are generally global in its expanse. Even subject-related encyclopaedias give the global perspective.That is why country-specific encylopaedias have never been seriousy attempted. We hope that this effort will fill that volume. Traditionally encyclopaedias don't deal with factual data e.g. Indian exports, population figures, GDP. That is the job of annual reference books. They are also different from alamans in as much as that they don't give dated entries. That will become texts on history. Encyclopaedias need to be updated. A country is alive and kicking. People and events continue to play role in various aspects of life. Hence they need to be added. That is why either annual supplements or updation needs to be done in encyclopaedias. We would strive for that.

Regarding its contents only those entries have been included that continue to influence the life of a nation. There are historical figures who might have played a significant role in their times but if those deeds have no relevance to the present they have been excluded. Another example is literary awards. They always create controversies because their selection at times is subjective. Hence only universally accepted meritorious work has found place in these volumes. In this context a debatable point need to be stated. Who is more important book or the author. Conventionally work is an end product and only that is a measure of the author's importance but then a prolic writer might have produced a large body of creations. Hence to save space the author is entered with all his important work.That is also an international practice.

Lastly, why India, Pakistan and Bangladesh have been clubbed together. Before India's independence they were one nation. They share a common heritage and composite culture. Their post-independence history is different but 22their foundation is undivided. In order to appreciate the historical context better it is necessary to cross-refer and that was possible when they are juxtaposed.

Om Gupta

A

A1 Team Pakistan : A1 Team Pakistan is the Pakistani entry in the A1 Grand Prix, an international racing series dubbed as the world cup of motorsport. The launch of A1 Team Pakistan was one of the most spectacular, with the A1 Grand Prix Car being presented infront of the Lahore Fort, a world heritage site. President General Pervez Musharraf was the star guest at the event hosted by A1 Team Pakistan Chairman Arif Hussain and its Managing Director Chaudry Salik Hussain.

Aalankrita : Aalankrita is the Ethnic Gateway in Hyderabad. Spread over an area of 10 acres, Aalankrita blends the convenience of a 5-star resort, the ambience of a heritage site and the ethnicity of the times gone by.

Aamir Liaquat Hussain : Dr. Aamir Liaquat Hussain is a minister of state for religious affairs in the government of Pakistan. He is an active member of the Muttahida Qaumi Movement or MQM, the 3rd largest political party of Pakistan. He gained swift popularity in South Asian muslim households due to his anchoring of a creative and revolutionary program called 'Aalim Online' broadcast on GEO, a Pakistani news and documentary channel. The program broadcast almost daily, brings together Islamic scholars from the two main schools of thought, Sunni and Shia, who answer questions via live telephonic calls from various corners of the world. The program has achieved overnight popularity and is well-established as a good source of Islamic knowledge.

Abahani Krira Chakra : Abahani Krira Chakra (Abahani Sporting Club) is a sports club in Bangladesh. It was established at Dhaka in 1972 through reorganisation of Iqbal Sporting Club. Within a short time, the club gained fame through commendable performances in hockey, cricket and football tournaments. Abahani introduced junior coaching camps on its own initiative and employed foreign trainers in them. Abahani also did a lot to improve football in Bangladesh through new experiments.

Abahattha : Abahattha the stage after Abhrangsha, which was the final stage in the evolution of the central Indian Aryan language Prakrit. The new Indo-Aryan languages developed from Abahattha. Some peculiarities of Abahattha are the loss of affixes and suffixes, the absence of gender variations, an abundant use of short vowels, nasalisation at the end or in the middle of words, the substitution of h for s, etc. The first compositions in this language were perhaps the Doha, or religious verses, composed by the Buddhist Tantriks and Saivite yogis, such as Sarhapa and Kahnapa, and subsequently collected in the Dohakos. Bangali as well as non-Bangali poets composed Doha in Abahattha.

Secular literature was also written in Abahattha. In the 10th century, when Bangla was just developing, there was some rivalry between the two languages. However, poets often wrote in both languages; for example, they composed charyapada in Bangla and Doha in Abahattha. Dakarnava, a Buddhist classical text ascribed to Dak, was also written in Abahattha. For some time there also existed a pidgin, combining vocabulary drawn from other contemporary languages and Abahattha. Abahattha continued to be cultivated right up to the 15th century. Most shlokas of

Prakritapaingala, composed around the 15th century, were in Abahattha. Vidyapati (15th century) was among the last well-known poets who used Abahattha. His autobiography, Kirtilata, in prose and verse, was composed in Abahattha. Shubhankarer Arya, slokas containing folk wisdom, are examples of Abahattha still current today.

Abanindranath Tagore : Abanindranath Tagore (August 7, 1871 - December 5, 1951), was the principal artist of the Bengal school and the first major exponent of swadeshi values in Indian art. He was also a noted writer. Tagore sought to modernize Moghul and Rajput traditions in order to counter the influence of Western models of art, as taught in Art Schools under the British Raj. Such was the success of Tagore's work that it was eventually accepted and promoted as a national Indian style within British art institutions. Tagore was a member of the distinguished Bengali family, and a nephew of the poet Rabindranath Tagore. His grandfather and his elder brother Gaganendranath Tagore were also artists. Tagore learned art when studying at Sanskrit college in the 1880s.

Tagore believed that Western art was "materialistic" in character, and that India needed to return to its own traditions in order to recover spiritual values. Despite its Indocentric nationalism, this view was already commonplace within British art of the time, stemming from the ideas of the Pre-Raphaelites. Partly for this reason many British arts administrators were sympathetic to such ideas, especially as Hindu philosophy was becoming increasingly influential in the West following the spread of the Theosophy movement. Tagore believed that Indian traditions could be adapted to express these new values, and to promote a progressive Indian national culture.

Abaya : The abaya is an overgarment worn by some Muslim women. It is the traditional form of hijab, or Islamic modest dress, for many countries of the Arabian peninsula. It is sometimes adopted in other parts of Islamic world. Traditional abaya are black, and may be either a large square of fabric draped from the shoulders or head, or a long black caftan. The abaya should cover the whole body save face, feet, and hands. It can be worn with the niqab, a face veil covering all but the eyes. Saudi Arabia requires women to wear abaya in public; the niqab is optional. Abaya-wearing is enforced by the religious police, the mutaween. Contemporary abaya are usually caftans, cut from light, flowing fabrics like crepe, georgette, and chiffon. They are now made in colors other than black.

Abbas Uddin : Abbas Uddin Ahmed (27 October 1901-30 December 1959), popularly known by his first name, was a Bangla folk singer. He was born at Balarampur in Tufanganj subdivision in the district of Cooch Bihar. His father, Zafar Ali Ahmed, was a lawyer at the Tufanganj Sub-divisional Court.

Abbasuddin's interest in music grew through attendance at cultural functions at school and college. He was largely self-taught, except for a brief period when he learnt music from Ustad Jamiruddin Khan in Kolkata. He sang different types of songs such as folk songs, modern songs, patriotic songs, as well as Islamic songs. He also sang Urdu songs. But Abbasuddin became renowned mainly as a singer of folk songs. Abbasuddin wrote an account of his life as a singer in Amar Shilpi Jibaner Katha (1960). For his invaluable contribution to music he was posthumously honoured with the Pride of Performance Award in 1960, Shilpakala Academy Award in 1979 (posthumously) and Swadhinata Dibas Puraskar in 1981 (posthumously).

Abbas Uddin Ahmed : Abbas Uddin Ahmed (27 October 1901-30 December 1959), popularly known by his first name, was a Bangla folk singer. He was born at

Balarampur in Tufanganj subdivision in the district of Cooch Bihar. His father, Zafar Ali Ahmed, was a lawyer at the Tufanganj Sub-divisional Court. Abbasuddin's interest in music grew through attendance at cultural functions at school and college. He was largely self-taught, except for a brief period when he learnt music from Ustad Jamiruddin Khan in Kolkata. He sang different types of songs such as folk songs, modern songs, patriotic songs, as well as Islamic songs. He also sang Urdu songs. But Abbasuddin became renowned mainly as a singer of folk songs.

Abbasuddin stayed in Kolkata from 1931 to 1947. Initially, he worked temporarily as a clerk in the DPI office and then in the Department of Irrigation in a permanent post. When A. K. Fazlul huq was Chief Minister, Abbasuddin was given a Government job as a recording expert. In the 1940's, Abbasuddin's songs played a significant role in raising the Muslim public opinion in favour of the Pakistan movement. In 1947, after partition, he joined the Department of Information and Broadcasting as an additional song organiser. As a representative of Pakistan, he participated at the South East Asia Conference in Manila in 1955, at the International Folk Music Conference in Germany in 1956 and at the Bengali Cultural Conference in Rangoon in 1957.

Abbottabad : Abbottabad is the principal city of the Abbottabad District in the Northwest Frontier Province of Pakistan. It is 4120 feet (1256 m) above sea level, and is located 63 miles (101 km) from Rawalpindi, and is undoubtedly one of the cleanest, the most beautiful cities of Pakistan. The city is much like a valley with scenic beauty and beautiful romantic weather at its peak.

Abdul Alim : Abdul Alim (1931-1974), a Bangladeshi folk singer, was born on 27 July 1931 in the village of Talibpur in Murshidabad district. His father was

Mohammad Yusuf Ali. He did not have much formal education. While at elementary school he heard a gramophone record and became attracted to music. He took music lessons from a local instructor, Syed Golam Ali, and earned a reputation as a singer while quite young.

Abdul Alim also sang on television and for films and recorded about five hundred songs. He was highly regarded for his mystic murshidi songs. He received a number of national awards, such as the Ekushey Padak, Purbani Chalachchitra Puraskar, and Bangladesh Chalachchitra Sangbadik Samiti Puraskar.

Abdul Gani : Abdul Gani (1919-1957) was born in village Nagaish of Burichang upazila, Comilla in 1919. He was the founding father of the famous East Bengal Regiment. Gani received his early education in Comilla and graduated from Calcutta Islamia College in 1940. In 1941, he passed the King's Commission to join the British Indian Army as a lieutenant and fought on the Burma Front for two years. For his valour shown in the Burma Front of the Second World War, he was called 'Tiger Gani'.

Major Abdul Gani played the leading role in founding a Bengali Army Unit in 1945. After the partition of 1947, he opted East Bengal with his army unit. In 1948, Gani became a major and was authorised to establish the First East Bengal Regiment, which he formed on 15 February 1948. Abdul Gani retired in 1954 and entered into politics. He was elected to the Provincial Assembly as an independent candidate. He proposed in the Assembly the foundation of a Cadet College and military school in the then East Pakistan. Gani was vice-president of the Pakistan 'Sabuj Sena' and a member of the Islam Leauge. Abdul Gani died on 11 November 1957 in Frankfurt where he had gone to lead the Pakistan delegation at World Veteran Soldiers' Conference. He was buried at the Mainamati Cantonment graveyard in full military honour.

Abdul Hakim : Abdul Hakim was a poet in medieval Bengal. He was born on the island of Sandwip in 1620. Hakim's most famous work perhaps is Nurnama (Story of Light), a depiction of the life of prophet Muhammad in lyrical Bangla. This work can be considered as an important step in creating a Bengali Muslim identity. However, what Nurnama is arguably more well known for is Hakim's great patriotism and specially his love for the Bangla language. In medieval ages, Persian and Arabic tended to be court languages all over the South Asia and perceived by some as the language to do literary work in.

Abdul Hamid's Mosque : Abdul Hamid's Mosque situated at village Goaldi in sonargaon thana of Narayanganj district, the mosque is located north of Goaldi mosque. It was built in 1705 AD as evidenced by an inscription, and attributed to one Abdul Hamid Shah who lies buried close by. It was originally a single domed square structure with four engaged octagonal corner towers, built in the Mughal style. The mosque measures 5.02m square inside and 6.75m square outside. The mosque has been renovated several times with a permanent Pucca extension on the east and has been further enlarged by temporary tin shed verandahs on the east, north and south sides. There are three entrances in the east, of which the middle one is the largest, and one entrance each on the south and north sides. Renovation and extension have given the mosque a modern look. It is presently being used as a Jami mosque.

Abdul Jabbar : Abdul Jabbar (1919-1952) is a martyr of Language Movement. Abdul Jabbar was born at village Panchua in Gafargaon thana of Mymensingh district on 26 Aswin 1326 BS (1919 AD). He had his primary education in a local pathsala, but could not continue his studies due to poverty. He left the school and was engaged in helping his father in agricultural work. While a boy of fifteen Abdul Jabbar left home unnoticed and reached Narayanganj by train in search of fortune. There he came in contact with an Englishman who helped him in getting a job in Burma. He earned some proficiency in English language there. He returned home after twelve years of service in Burma.

In 1952, Abdul Jabbar came to Dhaka (20 February) with his mother-in-law and wife for the medical treatment of his mother-in-law, a cancer patient. He got her mother-in-law admitted into the Medical College Hospital. On 21 February 1952, there was an assemblage of the students and the public at the premises of the Medical College Hostel demanding recognition of Bangla as one of the state languages of Pakistan. Abdul Jabbar joined the rally. The police fired on the rally, and Abdul Jabbar was severely struck with a bullet. He was admitted into the Medical College Hospital where he breathed his last on the night following. In recognition of his sacrifice, Abdul Jabbar was awarded the Ekushey Padak (posthumously) in 2000 AD.

Abdul Kardar : Abdul Kardar or Abdul Hafeez Kardar was the first Test captain of the Pakistan cricket team. He is widely regarded as Pakistan cricket's father figure. Born in Lahore, Punjab in 1925, Kardar domestic cricket for teams like Oxford University, Northern India and Muslims, under the name Abdul Hafeez. He was one of the few players of that generation who played for India, the national team in Tests against England, and following the Partition of India, representing the Muslim state of Pakistan. He was a left-handed batsman and a slow left-arm orthodox spin bowler, scoring 6,832 runs and taking 344 wickets in first class cricket. He averaged 29.83 in batting, and 24.55 in bowling. Kardar played for the Pakistan team from 1948 to 1952, in the years before Pakistan was granted Test status. Kardar also played for Warwickshire, and Pakistan Services.

Abdul Latif Nawab : Luteef, Nawab Abdool (1828-1893) a prominent personality of mid 19th century Bengal, the pioneer of Muslim modernization and the architect of the Muslim Renaissance, was one of those great men who appeared as saviours of their frustrated, humiliated, demoralized and disorganised fellow countrymen under colonial rule.

Nawab Abdool Luteef came from a very good Muslim family of the district of Faridpur. Abdool Luteef started his career as a teacher in Dhaka Collegiate School. Afterwards, he joined Calcutta Madrashah as a professor of English and Arabic. In 1849 he was appointed Deputy Magistrate and promoted to the post of Presidency Magistrate in 1877. He retired from government service in 1884 and died on 10 July 1893.

In recognition of his feelings for his co-religionists, his merit in public services, and benevolent activities, he was made the first Muslim member of the Bengal Legislative Council in 1862. A year later, he was nominated Fellow of Calcutta University. He was awarded the title of Khan Bahadur in 1877 and was invested with the dignity of the title of a nawab in 1880. He was honoured with the Order of CIE in 1883 and invested with the higher dignity of Nawab Bahadur in 1887.

His chief contribution was in the field of education. He was among the first to understand that young Bengali Muslims should receive modern education. Abdool Luteef's efforts to start an Anglo-Persian Department in the Calcutta Madrasah and to also teach its students Bengali and Urdu were remarkable. His undaunted efforts convinced the Government of the need of higher education for Muslims. As a result, Hindu College was turned into presidency college and made open for all in 1854. Among his other contributions towards Muslim education were 'A Minute on the Hooghly Mudrussah' and 'A Paper on

Mahomedan Education in Bengal'. The latter, was in effect, a report on the Hughli Madrasah. On its basis, the Anglo-Persian Department was opened and scholarships for its students announced. Through the Mohammedan Literary Society, he advanced the cause of Muslim education. At the same time he took an active part in contemporary Muslims politics. Through his efforts the Mohsin Endowment Fund was set apart for Muslims.

Abdul Qadeer Khan : Dr. Abdul Qadeer Khan (born 1935, Bhopal, India) is a Pakistani engineer widely regarded as the father of Pakistan's nuclear weapons programme. (His middle name is also occasionally rendered as Quadeer, Qadir or Gadeer and his given names are often abbreviated to A.Q.). In January 2004, he confessed to having been involved in an international network of clandestine nuclear proliferation from Pakistan to Libya, Iran and North Korea.

On February 5, 2004, General Pervez Musharraf announced that he had pardoned Khan. In an August 23, 2005 interview with Kyodo News Musharraf confirmed that Khan had sent gas centrifuges and centrifuge parts to North Korea, and possibly an amount of uranium hexafluoride.

Abdul Qadir Khan : Abdul Qadir Khan (born September 15, 1955 in Lahore, Punjab) was a Pakistani international cricketer and latterly commentator. He is universally regarded as one of the finest leg spin bowlers in the history of the sport. He made his first-class debut in the Pakistani local competition during the 1975/76 season and within two years had worked his way into the national team. Qadir made his Test debut on his home ground in Lahore against England in December 1977. Natural talent combined with aggression and passion made Qadir one of the most successful bowlers of his time, and without a doubt the finest leg spinner at the time. He is credited with keeping leg spin bowling 'alive' through the 1970s and 1980s when there were very few bowlers of that variety in the game, perhaps indirectly resulting today in modern leg spinners such as Australia's Shane Warne and fellow Pakistani Mushtaq Ahmed.

Abdul Rashid : Sir Abdul Rashid the first Chief Justice of Pakistan was born on 29 June 1889. He received his early education at Central Model School Lahore, and got his BA from Forman Christian College and Masters from Christ's College Cambridge. He started practicing Law at Lahore in 1913. He was appointed Assistant Legal Remembrancer in March 1925. From 1927 to 1931 he officiated as Government of Punjab's Advocate. He was appointed as Judge Lahore High Court in 1933. In 1946, he was made Chief Justice of Judicature at Lahore. Sir Abdul Rashid was elevated as the Chief Justice of Pakistan on 27 June 1949. Sir Abdul Rashid remained Chief Justice till 29 June 1954. He acted as the President of Khuro Inquiry Commission from 28 May 1948 to 11 February 1949. He also acted as Governor General for 9 months, from April 1953 till December 1953.

Abdul Sattar Edhi : Dr Abdul Sattar Edhi, or Maulana Edhi, as he is often known, is one of the most active philanthropists of the world. He is head of the Edhi Foundation. His wife Bilquis Edhi, heads the Bilquis Edhi Foundation. They both received 1986 Ramon Magsaysay Award for Public Service. He is also the recipient of the Lenin Peace Prize. Maulana Edhi, as he is often referred to, is of the Memon community.

Today Edhi Foundation continues to grow. Edhi, looking to the future, has stated that he aims to build a hospital every 500km in Pakistan. Although he is given the title Maulana out of respect, he himself dislikes the title. He has never been to a religious school and he is not an Islamic cleric. Recently he was given an honorary doctorate. He is also famous for being very shy about his popularity and when people personally praise him for his work. He also refuses to accept donations from governments or formal religious organisations, because according to him they set 'conditions'. Both General Zia-ul-Haq and the Italian government sent him generous donations, which he sent back.

Abdullah Abu Sayeed : Abdullah Abu Sayeed is a writer, organizer and activist from Bangladesh. Sayeed was a professor of Bengali language in Dhaka College for many years. In 1975, he founded the Bish-wo Sha-hitto Kendro or World Literature Centre to promote the study of literature. It remains one of the most important cultural institutions in the nation.

Abdullah Kirmani : Abdullah Kirmania medieval saint. He lies buried at Khustigiri in the district of Birbhum, West Bengal, India. According to tradition, he came from Kirman, a town in Persia. He left his native place as a boy, came to India, visited various places and ultimately became a disciple of Shah Arjani in Patna. The teacher ordered his disciple to go to Bengal. Before his departure the Pir gave him a toothpick of Chambal wood and asked him to stay at the place where he would find the toothpick fresh and green. Shah Abdullah Kirmani traversing several places ultimately came to Birbhum and settled at Khustigiri.

According to the Tazkirah-i-Auliya-i-Hind, a book written in Urdu, a very different story is given about Shah Abdullah Kirmani. According to this book the saint was a Bengali by birth and he was a disciple of Shaikh Muinuddin Chishti of Ajmer. It is difficult to say which of the above accounts is correct, because both the sources are of later origin. It is also not clear why did he call himself Kirmani if he were a Bengali. Large number of people venerates his tomb at Khustigiri. He is especially renowned for the powers he had over the serpents.

Abdur Rahim : Sir Abdur Rahim(1867-1952) was a jurist, scholar and politician of Bangladesh. Born in a Zamindar family of Midnapur district Abdur Rahim received his early education in Midnapur and then joined Presidency College, Calcutta. On the completion of his post-graduate studies in English Literature he went to London and joined the Middle Temple for the Bar-at-Law degree and was called to the Bar in 1890. Abdur Rahim quickly established himself as a lawyer in Muslim and Criminal Law. He was appointed as Deputy Legal Remembrancer and later held the post of the Presidency Magistrate for three years (1900-1903) before he resumed his High Court practice in 1904.

Abdur Rahim resigned from the office of Chief Justice of Madras High court in 1920 and joined the Bengal government as a member of the governor's Executive Council (1920-25). From 1925 onward Rahim became increasingly involved in sectarian politics. But despite being a Muslim leader of great learning and authority he was not able to make his public life a source of inspiration for activists of the Muslim community. In the faction-ridden politics of the 1920s and early '30s one may notice several political groupings amidst the Muslim leadership. Every leader seemed to have floated one or another group and the main purpose appeared to be to form ministries.

Abdur Rahim too led a group called Bengal Muslim Party. In the Council elections of 1926 his group emerged as the strongest electoral faction. Rahim was thus made a minister in 1927 but he had to resign within a couple of days, because he failed to enlist majority support in the Council in his favour. He organised a confederate party, Muslim United Party, in 1928, taking all Muslim groups into its fold. Its object was to take the question of Muslim representation to the Simon Commission unitedly. Rahim also organised a peasant party called Nikhil Banga Praja

Samiti, the precursor of the Praja Party in 1929, and became its first president. He retired from public life in 1934 when he was made President of the Indian Legislative Assembly.

Abdur Rahman Biswas : Abdur Rahman Biswas(born 1 September 1926) is a Bangladeshi politician. He was the President of Bangladesh between 1991 and 1996. Biswas was born in Shaistabad of Barisal District, Southern Bangladesh.

He has a BA & MA degree in History as well as LLB from the University of Dhaka. He served as acting president of Bangladesh following the resignation of BNP led government in 1996. That time, in front of ' 96 parliament election, he sacked then Chief of Army, Lt.General Nasim and some other high Army officials. He accused them of conspiring to stage an Army led coup with support of Awami League. Biswas completed his full term as president on 8 October 1996. Abdur Rahman Biswas was not selected for 2001 perliament election by BNP and since then he remains as a private citizen. There are allegations that Biswas was involved in collaboration with the Pakistan Army during the Bangladesh Liberation War of 1971.

Abdur Rasul : Abdur Rasul (1872-1917) nationalist leader and lawyer. Abdur Rasul was born in 1872 in a landed family of Guniauk, a village in Brahmanbaria district. He lost his father Golam Rasul in his childhood but his mother raised him well. He was sent to England for higher studies after he had passed the Entrance Examination in 1888. He took the BA degree in 1896 and the MA degree in 1898. Abdur Rasul was called to the Bar at the Middle Temple in 1898. While in London, he became acquainted with noted Indians like Ali Imam, Syed Hasan Imam, Aurobindo Ghosh and others. Returning to India he got himself enrolled at the Calcutta High Court in 1899.

Abdur Rasul was made an honorary lecturer in International Law at the university of Calcutta.

Abdur Rasul was opposed to the partition of Bengal, 1905. He presided over the Bengal Congress Conference held at Barisal in 1906. In collaboration with Abdul Halim Ghaznavi, Abul Kashem and Mujibur Rahman Khan he published the Weekly Mussalman in 1906. In 1909 Abdur Rasul joined the Bengal Provincial muslim league and in 1912 presided over the Bengal Provincial Conference at Chittagong. He attended the annual session of the All India Muslim League at Lucknow and presided over the annual session of the Bengal Presidency Muslim League at Burdwan. He was elected to the Bengal Legislative Council from the Muslim Constituency of Chittagong division. In 1917 Abdur Rasul was elected the secretary of the Bengal Presidency Muslim League but he died in the same year at the early age of 45.

Abdur Razzak: Abdur Razzak (born 23 January 1942) is a famous Bangla movie actor. He became famous first as a Television actor, then as film hero in the mid 1960s. Throughout the rest of the decade, as well as 1970s, Razzak was considered as the top actor in Bangladeshi movies. Like most other actors in Bangladesh, he became known by his last name, Razzak.

Razzak was born in Kolkata, Bengal. He migrated to erstwhile East Pakistan in early 1960s. Initially, Razzak became a favourite of the viewers of Pakistan Television. He went on to make more than 300 appearances in Bangla and Urdu movies. He also directed around sixteen movies.

Abdus Salam : Abdus Salam (1925-1952) was martyr of the Bengladesh Language Movement. Abdus Salam was born in the village of Luxmipur under Feni district in 1925. Deprived of the opportunity to receive a good education, he used to serve as a peon in the Department of Industries of the government, and had his living quarters at 36B Nilkhet Barrack in Dhaka. On 21 February 1952, students and common people defied official ban on assemblage of people imposed under Section 144, and staged a demonstration in front of Dhaka Medical College Hostel demanding recognition of Bangla as one of the state languages of Pakistan.

Abdus Salam took part in the demonstration and was shot when the police fired on the crowd. He received treatment at Dhaka Medical College Hospital for over a month but passed away on 7 April 1952. He was awarded the Ekushey Padak posthumously in February 2000.

Abdus Salam : Emiritus Prof. Abdus Salam, Nobel Laureate was a Pakistani theoretical physicist who received the Nobel Prize in Physics in 1979 for his work in electroweak theory which is the mathematical and conceptual synthesis of the electromagnetic and weak interactions, the latest stage reached until now on the path towards a unification theory describing the fundamental forces of nature.

Salam, Sheldon Glashow and Steven Weinberg arrived at the theory independently and shared the prize. The validity of the theory was ascertained through experiments carried out at the Super Proton Synchrotron facility at CERN in Geneva, particularly through the discovery of the W and Z bosons.

Abdus Samad Azad : Abdus Samad Azad (January 15, 1922 – April 27, 2005) was a diplomat and politician from Bangladesh. Azad was born in Bhurakhali village, Sunamganj district, in what is now Bangladesh. He was an important member of the Awami League and an assistant to Sheikh Mujibur Rahman by 1970 when he became the chief representative of the Bangladeshi independence movement in exile, helping the movement get international support while Mujibur Rahman was imprisoned. When independence for Bangladesh was achieved in 1971 Azad became foreign minister in the Mujibur Rahman government. He served in that position until 1972 and then became agriculture minister.

Azad did not support the 1975 military coup in which Mujibur Rahman was killed. He was imprisoned until 1978. In 1996, when the Awami League came back to power under Mujibur Rahman's daughter, Sheikh Hasina, Azad was appointed foreign minister again. He served in that position until 2001 when the Awami League lost elections. Azad died at a hospital in Dhaka, Bangladesh's capital, of stomach cancer. He had undergone medical treatment in India but became ill again after returning to Bangladesh and remained in hospital from February 2005 until his death.

Abdus Sattar : Justice Abdus Sattar repatriated from Pakistan at the end of 1973 and joined in government service. He was the chairman of the Board of Directors of Bangladesh Jiban Bima Corporation (1973-74), chairman of Journalist Wage Board (1974-75) and chairman of Bangladesh Institute of Law and International Affairs. Abdus Sattar was appointed special adviser to the President and Chief Martial Law Administrator Abusadat Mohammad Sayem (1975), and was vested with the charge of the Ministry of Law and Parliamentary Affairs. In 1977, he was appointed Vice President of Bangladesh by President Ziaur Rahman. Under the patronage of President Ziaur Rahman a political party called Jatiyatabadi Ganatantrik Dal was floated in 1978 of which he was the convenor.

Within a few months he abolishhe party only to include himself as vice president into a newly floated political party called Bangladesh Nationalist Party headed by President Ziaur Rahman. After the assassination of

Ziaur Rahman in 1981 Abdus Sattar took over as Acting President of the country. He was elected President of Bangladesh in 1981, and chairman of Bangladesh Nationalist Party in 1982. President Sattar was removed from power by a coup-d'etat led by the army chief Hussain Muhammad Ershad on 24 March 1982. He died in Dhaka on 5 October 1985.

Abhayatisya Mahasthavir : Abhayatisya Mahasthavir (1884-1974) the seventh supreme Buddhist patriarch of Bangladesh, was born in May 1884 at Mijritala in banshkhali, chittagong. He was the only son of Nabin Chandra Barua and Kuleshwari Barua. He studied at Jaldi Primary School and in 1893 entered the novitiate under Vaishnava Mahathero. He was ordained in 1903. He studied the Tripitaka with Prajnalankar Mahathero. He went to Akyab where he was reordained by Keyyaru Seyada. Returning to Chittagong, Abhayatisya Mahasthavir was appointed chief abbot of Santi Vihara at Satbaria. During his stay at this monastery, he established Prajnalankar Pali Vidyalaya in 1938. In 1958 he founded Sasana Kalyan Pali Parisad. At a general meeting of the Bangladesh Sangharaja Bhikkhu Mahasabha held on 18 April 1956, he was selected Sangharaja (Supreme Patriarch) of Bangladesh. During his tenure as Sangharaja he did much for the revival of Buddhism in the subcontinent and for unifying the Buddhist communities. He breathed his last at Santi Vihara on 1 July 1974.

Abhaynagar Upazila : Abhaynagar Upazila (jessore district) with an area of 247.19 sq km is bounded by jessore sadar upazila on the north, Dumuria, Khan Jahan Ali, Dighalia and Phultala Upazilas on the south, Narail Sadar and Kalia Upazilas on the east and Jessore Sadar and Manirampur Upazilas on the west. Main river is Bhairab; tank 7; Baor 6. Singra, Beel Dakatia and Kurakhali Beel are notable. Abhaynagar (Town) consists of three mouzas. The area of the town is 10.34 sq km. It has a population of 28597; male 53.67%, female 46.33%; density of population is 1895 per sq km. Literacy rate among the town people is 39%. The town has one Dukbangalow.

Abhedananda Swami : Abhedananda Swami (1866-1939) exponent of Hinduism, was born in Kolkata on 2 October 1866. His original name was Kaliprasad Chanda. He began his education at a primary Sanskrit school and passed the Entrance examination from Oriental Seminary. Religious from childhood, he studied the Hindu scriptures to enhance his knowledge of the religion. He also came in close contact with several Christian missionaries including Kalicharan Bandyopadhyay and became attracted to Christianity. He was also attracted to Brahmoism after listening to the lectures of keshab chandra sen, Pratap Chandra Majumdar and others. His interest in Hindu philosophy grew after hearing the discourses of the eminent philosopher Shashadhar Tarkachuramani. He started practising Hathayoga and Rajayoga after studying Patanjali's Yogasutra. In 1884 he met Sri Ramakrishna at Dakshineshwar. After the death of Ramakrishna in 1886, Abhedananda became a Sannyasi and visited several places sacred to Hinduism through the length and breadth of India. This helped enhance his knowledge of Hinduism and its rites.

At the suggestion of Swami Vivekananda, Abhedananda went to England in 1896. There he met eminent intellectuals including Max Muller and gave several lectures on Rajayoga, Jnanayoga and Vedanta. In 1897 he went to the United States and took charge of the Vedanta Ashram in New York. In 1898 he met the famous philosopher, William James. Abhedananda returned to India in 1906 but subsequently travelled to the United States, Canada, Mexico, Japan and Hong Kong to propagate Hinduism and Indian philosophy. He returned to India after attending the Pan-Pacific Education Conference in Honolulu in 1921. In 1922, while on his way to Tibet from Kashmir, he discovered materials relations to a part of Christ's hitherto unknown life at a Buddhist temple and published this discovery in Kashmir and Tibet. In 1923 he established Sriramakrishna Vedanta Society in Calcutta and, a year later, the Sriramakrishna Vedanta Ashram at Darjeeling. He died at this Ashram on 8 September 1939.

Abhijnanasakuntalam : *Abhijnanasakuntalam* is a well-known Sanskrit play by Kalidasa. It is written in a mix of Sanskrit and the Maharashtri Prakrit, a dialect of Sanskrit. Its date is uncertain, but most scholars place Kalidasa in the period between the 1st and 4th centuries AD. Although Kalidasa makes some minor changes to the plot, the play elaborates upon an episode mentioned in the Mahabharata. The protagonist is Shakuntala, daughter of sage Vishwamitra and the apsara Menaka. Abandoned at birth by her parents, Shakuntala is reared in the secluded, sylvan hermitage of sage Kanva, and grows up a comely but innocent maidan.

Abida Parveen : Abida Parveen, a Pakistani singer, is one of the foremost exponents of Sufi music. Her forte is the kafi and the ghazal, though she has also ventured into traditional male territory and sung qawwalis. Abida was born in Larkana (Sindh province, Pakistan) in 1954. She received her musical training initially from her father, Ghulam Haider, and subsequently from Ustad Salamat Ali Khan. She embarked upon her professional career from Radio Pakistan, Hyderabad, in 1973. Her first hit was the Sindhi song "Tuhinje zulfan jay band kamand widha". This song had been sung by many other Sindhi singers before her, but Abida brought her own unique style to it, rooted in classical music.

ABM Habibullah : ABM Habibullah (1911-1984) was a historian and a writer. Abu Mohamed Habibullah was born in Burdwan district of West Bengal. His father Abdul Latif was an Inspector of Schools of Burdwan Division, while his grand father was a teacher of Arabic and Persian languages. Habibullah started his career as the Librarian of the Calcutta University in 1938 and the following year joined as lecturer in History Department of the Calcutta University.

In 1940 he joined the newly created Department of Islamic History and Culture of the university. Professor Habibullah joined Dhaka University in 1950 and became the Head of the Department of Islamic History and Culture, and continued to serve the department till his retirement in 1973. He was Dean of the Faculty of Arts (1961-63), President of Dhaka University Teachers' Association (1968-72), chairman, University Grants Commission (1976-77) and Curator, Dhaka Museum. He was one of the founders of the Asiatic society of Pakistan. Habibullah made very significant contribution to the medieval historiography of India. His Foundation of Muslim Rule in India is still a standard study for the early medieval history of the subcontinent. Among his other works the Descriptive Catalogue of the Persian, Urdu and Arabic Manuscripts in the Dhaka University Library, Bilayet Nama, Tarikh-i-Assam and a translations of Alberuni's work are best known.

ABM Mohiuddin Chowdhury : Mohiuddin Chowdhury is the mayor of Chittagong, the second largest city in Bangladesh, and a veteran politician associated with the Bangladesh Awami League. He has held the mayoral position since 1994. In 2005, he won a landslide victory, his 3rd term, against his opponent, a minister of the ruling party Bangladesh Nationalist Party.

Abohar : Abohar is a city in Firozpur district in Punjab (India), located on the Ganganagar to Delhi railway route, nearly 50 Km from Ganganagar. Its population as of 2001 is 124,303. This city is also known as the California of Punjab for its rich soil, good irrigation sources, and particularly for 'Kinoo,' a fruit of orange family.

Abrar-ul-Haq : Abrar-ul-Haq is a Pakistani bhangra singer. On his first album "Billo De Ghar" his name appears as simply "Abrar". His best-known work is the song "Billo De Ghar". Before becoming a singer, he was a teacher at Lahore's Aitchison College. He primarily sings in Punjabi which is the main language of bhangra genre, language of most populated province of Pakistan and Abrar's native language. He sings in Urdu too. His popular single "Sanu Tere Nal" is in English and Punjabi.

Abu Sadat Mohammad Sayem : Abu Sadat Mohammad Sayem (1916 1997) was the president of Bangladesh between 6 November 1975 and 21 April 1977. He had his school education at Rangpur Zila School, College education at Carmichael College, Rangpur, and Presidency College, Calcutta. He became a law graduate from the University Law College, Calcutta. He was enrolled as an advocate of the Calcutta High Court in 1944. After partition of India in 1947 and setting up of a high court in Dhaka he shifted his practice to the Dhaka High Court and worked as a junior of veteran advocate Sher-e-Bangla Ak Fazlul Huq.

Sayem was elected secretary and subsequently vice-president of the Dhaka High Court Bar Association. He was a sponsor member of the East Pakistan Lawyers' Association and was elected secretary, general secretary and vice-president of the said organisation for different terms. He was also elected a member of the local Board of the State Bank of Pakistan, Dhaka. He was a member of the East Pakistan Bar Council till his elevation to the Bench.

On 3 July 1962, Sayem was appointed a judge of the High Court of judicature in East Pakistan. In 1967, he was appointed a member of the Commission of Enquiry for finding out the causes of exodus and eviction of the members of the minority community. He was again appointed a member of the new Enquiry Commission formed for the same purpose. He was a member of the Delimitation Commission (1970) for delimitation of the constituencies, and had subsequently been a member of the Election Commission.

After liberation of the country Justice AM Sayem was appointed the first Chief Justice of the High Court of Bangladesh on 12 January 1972, and after the formation of the Supreme Court of Bangladesh on 17 December 1972, he was appointed the Chief Justice of Bangladesh. Justice Sayem assumed the office of President and Chief Martial Law Administrator on 6 November 1975. He relinquished the office of the Chief Martial Law Administrator on 29 November 1976 and office of the President on 21 April 1977.

Abu Sayeed Choudhury : Abu Sayeed Choudhury (1921-1987) was a jurist and President of Bangladesh (1972-73). Abu Sayeed Choudhury was born on 31 January 1921 in a landed family of Nagbari in Tangail district. His father Abdul Hamid Choudhury was the speaker of the East Pakistan Provincial Assembly. Abu Sayeed Choudhury did his graduation in 1940 from the Presidency College in Calcutta, obtained his Masters (1942) and Law degrees from Calcutta University and Bar-at-Law from London. He joined the Calcutta High Court Bar in 1947, and after the partition of India he came over to Dhaka and joined the Dhaka High Court Bar (1948).

Justice Choudhury was appointed vice-chancellor of Dhaka University in 1969. In 1971, while in Geneva he resigned from his post as vice-chancellor as a protest against the genocide in East Pakistan by the Pakistan army. From Geneva he went to London to work as special envoy of the provisional Mujibnagar Government and achieved considerable success in mobilising world opinion in favour of War of Liberation.

After liberation, Justice Choudhury returned to Dhaka and was elected the President of Bangladesh on 12 January 1972. On 10 April 1973, he was again elected the President of Bangladesh, and in the same year (December) he resigned to become special envoy for external relations with the rank of a minister. On 8 August 1975, he was included in the cabinet of Sheikh Mujibur Rahman as minister of Ports and Shipping. After Sheikh Mujib was assassinated he became the minister for Foreign Affairs in the cabinet of President Khondakar Mostaq Ahmad (August 1975), a position which he held till 7 November 1975.

In 1978, Justice Choudhury was elected a member of the United Nations Sub-committee on Prevention of Discrimination and Protection of Minorities. In 1985, he was elected chairman of the UN Human Rights Commission. He was honoured with the insignia of 'Deshikottam' by Visvabharati University. Calcutta University awarded him the honorary degree of Doctor of Law. His book Probasey Muktijuddher Dingooli (1990) is a valuable contribution to the understanding of Bangladesh War of Liberation. He died in London on 2 August 1987.

Abu Taher : Abu Taher (1938-1976) was a famous Bangladeshi freedom fighter, a sector commander in Bangladesh Liberation War, and a left-leaning radical activist. For his gallantry in Bangladesh Liberation War, he was awarded the Bir Uttom award.

Taher was born in his Badarpur, Assam in British India on 14 November 1938. In Pakistan Army, Abu Taher joined the elite Special Service Group of the Commando Force in 1965. Following the start of the Bangladesh Liberation War in 1971, Taher defected from the Pakistan Army to join the war. One month before the end of the war, Taher was seriously wounded during a battle near Kamalpur on 14 November 1971. His left leg had to be amputated. He was taken to India for treatment.

Following his treatment in India, Taher returned to independent Bangladesh in April, 1972. He was appointed as the Adjutant General of the newly-formed Bangladesh Army. Later, he was appointed as the commander of the 44th Battalion at the Comilla Cantonment. However, his left-leaning ideas of forming the Bangladesh Army in the model of the Chinese army was not accepted by others, and he left Bangladesh Army and joined Jatiya Samajtantric Dal (National Socialist Party) in late 1972.

Following the assassination of Sheikh Mujibur Rahman on 15 August 1975 in a bloody coup, there were a string of coups and counter coups in the army, which created a sense of dissent among common soldiers. Abu Taher organised a socialist uprising of the soldiers on 7 November 1975. Colonel Taher freed Ziaur Rahman and restored him to the post of army chief. Zia proclaimed himself Chief Martial Law Administrator (CMLA) on 7 November 1975. Abu Taher was arrested on 24 November 1975, because of possible fears of revolt. He was tried by a military tribunal inside the Dhaka Central Jail and was sentenced to death. He was executed by hanging on 21 July 1976.

Abu-Al-Asar Hafeez Jullandhuri : Abu-Al-Asar Hafeez Jullandhuri (1900-1982) was a Pakistani Muslim poet who authored its national anthem, the Pak sarzamin shad bad in 1951. He lived in Lahore, capital of Pakistan's Punjab province.

Abul Barkat : Abul Barkat (1927-1952) is a martyr of Language Movement. Abul Barkat nicknamed Abai was born in 1927 at village Babla in Bharatpur thana of Murshidabad district. He passed the Matriculation examination from Talibpur High School in 1945, and the Intermediate examination from Bahrampur Krishnanath College in 1947. After the partition of India he came to Dhaka in 1948. He obtained BA (Hons) degree in Political Science from Dhaka University in 1951.

In 1952, when the Language Movement demanding recognition of Bangla as one of the state languages of Pakistan was at its height, the government clamped Section 144 of Criminal Procedure Code in Dhaka city in order to contain student agitation. Abul Barkat was in the procession that students mobilised on the premises of the Dhaka Medical College hostel on 21 February. When the police fired on the gathering, Barkat was shot dead. He was laid to rest in Azimpur graveyard. In recognition of his sacrifice, Abul Barkat was awarded Ekushe Padak (posthumously) in 2000 AD.

Abul Fazal : Abul Fazal (1903-1983) was a Begali educationist and writer. He was born on 1 July 1903 in the village of Keochia in the satkania upazila of chittagong district. His father, Moulvi Fazlur Rahman, was imam of Chittagong Jame Masjid. After initial schooling at a madrasah, Abul Fazal completed the BA from Dhaka University in 1928. In 1931, he did his BT from Teachers' Training College in Dhaka. He completed a Master's degree in Bangla Language and literature from Calcutta University in 1940. Abul Fazal initially began his career as an imam before starting to teach. In 1941 he joined Krishnanagar College as a lecturer of Bangla. In1943 he was transferred to chittagong college from where he retired as a professor in 1956. In 1973 he was made Vice-Chancellor of chittagong university. In 1975 he joined the advisory council of the Government of Bangladesh as member in charge of education and culture, but resigned on 23 June 1977.

Abul Fazal was associated with the founding of the muslim sahitya samaj (1926), Dhaka, and became its secretary in 1930. The Samaj was liberal in outlook, and its purpose was to liberate people from social and religious prejudices. The progressive outlook of this movement is reflected in Abul Fazal's writings. Abul Fazal was a fearless and socially committed writer, whose works reflect patriotism, secularism, and humanism. He was known as 'the Nation's conscience' for his bold stand at moments of national crises. In 1967, he strongly protested when the Pakistan government banned tagore songs from radio and television programmes.

Abul Kashem Fazlul Huq : Sher-e-Bangla ('The Tiger of Bengal') Abul Kashem Fazlul Huq (born 26 October 1873-died 27 April 1962) was a famous Bengali statesman in the first half of the 20th century. He was the Mayor of Calcutta (1935), Chief Minister of undivided Bengal (1937-1943) and of East Bengal (1954), Home Minister of Pakistan (1955) and Governor of East Pakistan (1956-1958). He presented the Lahore Resolution of 1940 that established Muslim League's demand for a homeland for Muslims, that ultimately resulted in the nation of Pakistan.

Abul Quasem : Abul Quasem(1920-1991) is a Language Movement activist, educationist and writer. He was born in 1920 at village Chhedandi in Patia thana of Chittagong district. He joined the Dhaka University in 1945 as a Lecturer in Physics, a position which he held till 1953 AD.

Abul Quasem was the founder of Tamaddun Majlish (1947), a literary and cultural organisation which pioneered the demand for recognition of Bangla as the state language of Pakistan through a booklet entitled Pakistaner Rastra bhasa: Bangla na Urdu published in 1947. He took active part in the Language Movement as a member of the Rastra-bhasa Karma-parisad. Abul Quasem was one of the founders of the Khilafat-e-Rabbani Party (1952). He was elected a member of the East Bengal Provincial Assembly in 1954 from the Patia-Boalkhali constituency in Chittagong as a nominee of United Front. He felt the need of introducing Bangla as medium of higher education in colleges and universities. With this end in view he established the Bangla College in Dhaka in 1962 and served the college as Principal till 1981. He devised a model for the reorientation of spelling of Bangla words and the pattern of Bangla scripts.

Abul-Fazel : Abul-Fazel (also Fazal, Fazl, etc.), the vizier of the great Mughal emperor Akbar, and author of Akbarnama, an account of Akbar's reign. He also led the Mughal imperial army in its wars in the Deccan. He was assassinated in 1602 in a plot supposedly contrived by Akbar's son, Prince Salim, who became the Emperor Jahangir.

Achaemenid Empire : Much of the northwestern Indian Subcontinent (present day Eastern Afghanistan and most of Pakistan) was ruled by the Persian Achaemenid Empire from c. 520 BC during the reign of Darius the Great, up intil its conquest by Alexander the Great. Lands in present-day Punjab, the Indus river from the borders of Gandhara down to the Arabian Sea, and some other parts of the Indus plain, became a satrapy of Alexander's empire. According to Herodotus of Halicarnassus, it was the most populous and richest of all the twenty satrapies of the empire. Achaemenid rule lasted about 186 years. The Achaemenids used the Aramaic script for the Persian language. After the end of Achaemenid rule, the use of Aramaic in the Indus plain diminished, although we know from inscriptions from the time of Emperor Asoka that it was still in use two centuries later. Other scripts, such as Kharosthi (a script derived from Aramaic) and Greek became more common after the arrival of Alexander the Great.

Achanakmar Wildlife Sanctuary : Achanakmar Wildlife Sanctuary in Chattisgarh was established in 1975 Under Wildlife Protection Act of 1972 and biogeographical province 4.8.4 (Indus-Ganges Monsoon Forest). Moreover the area of the sanctuary is 551.55-sq.km mainly a hilly country. Altitude ranges from 200-1000m. Mainly tropical sal forests with other species at higher altitudes are the vegetation of this region. Leopard, Gaur, Chital, Wild Bear, Tiger Panthera tigris, leopard, stripped Hyaena, Jackal Canis Aureus, Sloth Bear Melursus Ursinus, Indian wild dog Cuon Alpinus, Chital, Sambar Cervus unicolor, Nilgai Boselaphus Tragocamelus, four-horned Antelope Tetracerus Quadricornis, Chinkara (mountain gazelle) Gazella Gazella, Blackbuck Antilope Cervicapra, Munyjac Muntiacus Muntjak, wild boar Sus Scrofa and others.

Achar : Achar is the Hindi word for the variety of spicy pickled side dish or condiment popular in the Indian Subcontinent, in Southeast Asia, and in many other areas among ethnically South Asian communities. There are a wide variety of different achars made and each is usually made with a mixture of fruits or vegetables which are chopped and marinated in a liquid and a variety of different spices and salt. Almost all sorts of fruits vegetables found in south Asia are pickled in this manner, including pumpkins, palm hearts, mango slices, limes and rose petals, along with vegetables more conventionally pickled in the west. Some of the most popular achars are lemon pickle, lime pickle, mixed pickle, mango pickle, onion pickle, and garlic pickle. Some achars may even contain fish as their main ingredient. The pickle serves as a flavor enhancer and is eaten typically in small pieces with the rest of the meal.

Acid Survivors Foundation : The Acid Survivors Foundation is a Bangladeshi organisation dedicated to raising awareness and preventing acid attacks. It was founded in 1999 with support from UNICEF and the Canadian International Development Agency. In 2005 the co-founder Monira Rahman was granted the Human Rights Award of Amnesty International. It was able to reduce number of acid attacks about 40% since 2003

Adalaj Wav : 19km north of Ahmedabad, Adalaj Wav is one of the finest of the Gujarati step wells with carvings depicting intricate motifs of flowers and birds. It was built by Queen Rudabai in 1499 and provided a cool and secluded retreat during the hot summer months. The entire structure is underground and it has storeys one above the other and chambers one behind the other.

Adam Motor Company : Adam Motor Company is an automobile manufacturer based in Karachi, Pakistan. Adam developed Pakistan's first own manufactured car, called Revo. Initially Adam Motor was involved in manufacturing light trucks followed by a 4x4 off road vehicle. The Revo was only introduced in recent years.

Adamjee Jute Mills : Adamjee Jute Mill was established in Narayanganj, Bangladesh in 1951, immediately after Bawa Jute Mills (the first jute mill in Bangladesh). Gradually, the mill became the largest jute mill in the world preceding the jute mills of Calcutta, India and Dundee, Scotland. Adamjee Jute Mills was established to utilize the relatively finer jute fibers of the East Pakistan (now Bangladesh) region. Narayanganj's economic activities were largly contributed by Adamjee Jute Mills and it was also called the Dundee of the East. During the start of 1970s, the polypropylene products start to substitute traditional jute products and the fall of Adamjee Jute Mills start. However, it has managed to survive 1980s with nominal margin. The death of Adamjee Jute Mills started during the 1990s. After a strong battle for survival, Adamjee Jute Mills was officially declared dead in 2002.

Adhunik Gaan : Adhunik songeet literally means "modern songs". Although, to outsiders, this may seem an extremely ambiguous way of nomenclature, it has particular motivations. Bangla music traditionally has been classified mainly by the region of origin and the creators of the musical genre, such as Nazrul geeti, ghombhira, etc. However, this prevented the ability to classify any music that failed to fit into any of the classes.

In the period just before Indian independence (Bengal, under British rule, was made a part of one massive India that does not exactly correspond to the India of current day), several new minor musical groups emerged, mainly as playback songs for movies. These songs failed to fit into any particular genre, but seemed to be tied together by common theme of "music for the masses". Most of the music tended to be mainstream, commercial, voice-based with simple words and catchy tunes that were far moved from the classical ragas (modes). Hence, a miscellaneous category, Adhunik songeet, was created, since, at that time, this music was "modern".Although over time these so-called "modern" songs have become fairly old, they continue to be called by the same name. Interestingly, this group of song has grown faster than any other, since it is, well, a miscellaneous category that can accommodate anything that fails to fit elsewhere. The common theme continues to exist. So, although the nomenclature itself might not be as insightful, the genre itself is still well-defined.

Adi : The Adi (also Abor) is a major collective tribe living in the Himalayan hills of Arunachal Pradesh, and they are found in the temperate and sub-tropical regions within the districts of Siang, Subansiri and Dibang. The older term Abor is a dispreferred exonym from Assamese meaning 'those who cannot be controlled'. Of Proto-Austronesian and Tibetan stock, they speak a language belonging to the Tibeto-Burman family. However, their traditions believed them to be the lost descandants of the Tatars and Abo-Teni. They live in over 50 hill villages, traditionally each keeping to itself (many never leave it), under an elected chief styled gam who moderates the village council, which acts even as traditional court.

Owing to cultural isolation and economic insignificance, the Adi culture only elaborated simple manifestions and was spared major disturbance. However, since the late 20th century the people themselves are gradually opting for modernisation, e.g. road connecting them to the outer world, metal roofs, etc. Dormitories play an important role among the Adi tribe, and certain rules are observed. For example, a male can visit the dormitory of a female, although he is not allowed to stay overnight. At times, guardians will have to be around to guide the youngsters. The large majorty loyally followed the animist Donyi-Polo religion, which involves the worship of the sun, moon and the ancestral god Abo-Teni; the shaman, called miri, can be a female, but is losing influence with the younger generations. A growing number converted to Christianity, apparently mainly dissatisfied with traditional shamanistic healing.

Adi Granth : The Adi Granth, literally "the first book" is an early compilation of the Sikh scriptures by Guru Arjan, the fifth Sikh Guru. Often, the term is used to refer incorrectly to the Guru Granth Sahib. In actual fact, the Guru Granth Sahib is an expansion of the Adi Granth which was written in 1604.

Adi Shankara : Adi Shankara, reverentially called Bhagavatpada Acharya (the teacher at the feet of the Lord) was the most famous advaita philosopher, who had a profound influence on the growth of Hinduism through his non-dualistic philosophy. He advocated the greatness and importance of the important Hindu scriptures, the Veda (most particularly on the Upanishads), spoke to a spirituality founded on reason and without dogma or ritualism, and gave new life to Hinduism at a time when Buddhism and Jainism were gaining popularity. He is considered the founder of the Dasanami sannyasin.

The first person to consolidate the principles of Advaita was Adi Sankara. He is also known as Sankaracharya. Continuing the line of thought of some of the Upanishadic teachers, and also that of his own teacher's teacher Gaudapada, (Ajativada). Sankara expounded the doctrine of Advaita — a nondualistic reality. According to Advaitins (followers of Advaita), Sankara exposed the relative nature of the world and established the supreme truth of the Advaita by analysing the three states of experience — being awake (vaishvanara), dreaming (swapna), and being in deep sleep (sushupti). The supreme truth of the Advaita is said to be the non-dual reality of Brahman, in which atman (the individual soul) and Brahman (the Supreme Consciousness) are identified absolutely. (Brahman is not to be confused with Brahma, the Creator and one-third of the Trimurti along with Shiva, the Destroyer and Vishnu, the Preserver.)

Adilabad : Adilabad is a town in Adilabad District in the state of Andhra Pradesh in India. It is the headquarters of the district of the same name. The district occupies an area of 16,105 km² and has a population of 2,479,347 (according to the 2001 census). The district is situated on the northern boundary of Andhra Pradesh, forming a border with the state of Maharashtra. It belongs to the relatively underdeveloped Telangana part of the state. The rivers Godavari, Penganga and Wardha drain the region.

Adilabad derives its name from the erstwhile ruler of Bijapur, Ali Adil Shah. It was created out of a sub-district named Sirpur-Tandur in 1905. Historically, Adilabad has been home to a variety of cultures. Owing to its position at the border of central and southern India, it has been ruled by North Indian dynasties like the Mughals and the Mauryas and South Indian dynasties like the Satavahanas and the Chalukyas. The current culture of the district incorporates significant elements of the neighboring Marathi culture into the native Telugu culture.

Aditya Birla Group : Aditya Birla Group is one of India's largest business groups. The corporate management outfit of the group is called Aditya Birla Management Corporation. The group headed by Kumarmangalam Birla and runs operations in more than 15 countries like Malaysia, Australia and Canada. The corporate website is www.adityabirla.com and gives full details.

Adivasis : Adivasis or tribal peoples comprise a substantial indigenous minority of the population of India. Tribal peoples are particularly numerous in the Indian states of Orissa, Bihar, Jharkhand, and in extreme northeastern states such as Mizoram. Officially recognized by the Indian government as "Scheduled Tribes" in the Fifth Schedule of the Constitution of India, they are often grouped together with scheduled castes in the category "Scheduled Castes and Tribes", which is eligible for certain affirmative action measures. During the 19th century, substantial numbers converted to Christianity.

Tribal peoples constitute roughly 8 % of the nation's total population, nearly 68 million people according to the 1991 census. One concentration lives in a belt along the Himalayas stretching through Jammu and Kashmir, Himachal Pradesh, and Uttaranchal in the west, to Assam, Meghalaya, Tripura, Arunachal Pradesh, Mizoram, Manipur, and Nagaland in the northeast. In the northeastern states of Arunachal Pradesh, Meghalaya, Mizoram, and Nagaland, upward of 90 % of the population is tribal. However, in the remaining northeast states of Assam, Manipur, Sikkim, and Tripura, tribal peoples form between 20 and 30 % of the population.

Another concentration lives in the hilly areas of central India (Chhattisgarh, Madhya Pradesh, Orissa, and, to a lesser extent, Andhra Pradesh); in this belt, which is bounded by the Narmada River to the north and the Godavari River to the southeast, tribal peoples occupy the slopes of the region's mountains. Other tribals, including the Santals, live in Jharkhand and West Bengal. Central Indian states have the country's largest tribes, and, taken as a whole, roughly 75 % of the total tribal population live there, although the tribal population there accounts for only around 10 % of the region's total population.

There are smaller numbers of tribal people in Karnataka, Tamil Nadu, and Kerala in south India; in western India in Gujarat and Rajasthan, and in the union territories of Lakshadweep and the Andaman Islands and Nicobar Islands. About one percent of the populations of Kerala and Tamil Nadu are tribal, whereas about six percent in Andhra Pradesh and Karnataka are members of tribes. Apart from the use of strictly legal criteria, however, the problem of determining which groups and individuals are tribal is both subtle and complex. Because it concerns economic interests and voting blocs, the question of who are members of Scheduled Tribes rather than Backward Classes or Scheduled Castes is often controversial.

A number of traits have customarily been seen as establishing tribal rather than caste identity. These include language, social organization, religious affiliation, economic patterns, geographic location, and self-identification. Recognized tribes typically live in hilly regions somewhat remote from caste settlements; they generally speak a language recognized as tribal. Since independence, however, the special benefits available to Scheduled Tribes have convinced many groups, even Hindus and Muslims, that they will enjoy greater advantages if so designated. The schedule gives tribal people incentives to maintain their identity. By the same token, the schedule also includes a number of groups whose 'tribal' status, in cultural terms, is dubious at best.

Adnan Sami Khan : Adnan Sami Khan (born August 15, 1973) is a Pakistani singer, musician, pianist, actor and composer. Born and educated in the UK, where he first studied at the Rugby School, this graduate of the University of London, started his music career in Pakistan, now lives in India, where he is an extremely popular singer and composer. Adnan's talent was spotted by Asha Bhosle at an R D Burman concert in London, when he himself was 10 years old. She encouraged him to take up music as a career. When Adnan worked his first massively popular album, Asha Bhosle sang the title duet with him.

Adoni : Adoni is a commercial town in the Andhra Pradesh state of southern India; 140 miles (225 km) from Hyderabad and 307 miles (494 km) from Madras by rail. It has a population of about 164,000 (2005). Once a stronghold of the medieval Vijayanagar kingdom, today it has a substantial textile industry. The hill-fort above, now in ruins, was an important seat of government in Islamic times and is frequently mentioned in the wars of the 18th century. Adoni was under the rule of yadavas for in 16th century. At that time Adoni was known as Yadavagiri. Yadavagiri changed into Adavani under the Islamic rule.Later Adavani changed into the now called Adoni. Under British rule Adoni was in Bellary district of Madras presidency. It is known as the grain market of the south.

Adoor Gopalakrishnan : Adoor Gopalakrishnan is a director of Malayalam cinema, India with international repute. Four of his films have won the National Award and he won the International Film Critics Prize for five consecutive films of his. He has been awarded the Dadasaheb Phalke Award for the year 2004, the highest award for a person connected with films conferred by the Government of India. He is also a recipient of the Padma Vibhushan, the second highest civilian award from the Government of India in 2006, apart from receiving the Padma Shri in 1983.

Apart from nine feature films, he has over 30 short films and documentaries to his credit. All the nine films he directed, from Swayamvaram to Nizhalkkuthu, were screened at several International film festivals and won him several National and International awards. He won the British Film Institute award for Elepathayam. He is an alumnus of FTII.

Apart from his films, Adoor's major contribution towards introducing a new cinema culture in Kerala was the constitution of the first Film Society in Kerala, 'Chalachitra'. He also took active part in the constitution of 'Chitralekha', Kerala's first Film Co-operative Society for film production. These movements triggered a fresh wave of good films, called 'art films' by directors like Aravindan, P A Becker, K G George, Pavithran, and Raveendran. At a time this movement was so strong that even the popular cinema had to make synthesis with art cinema to create a new genre of films.

Advaita Vedanta : Advaita Vedanta is probably the best known of all Vedanta schools of philosophy of Hinduism, the others being Dvaita and Vishishtadvaita (total six). "Advaita" literally means "not two", and is often called a monistic or non-dualistic system which essentially refers to the indivisibility of the Self (Atman) from the Whole (Brahman). The key texts from which all Vedanta (lit., end or the goal of the Vedas) texts draw are the Upanishads (twelve or thirteen in particular), which are usually at the end of the Vedas, and the Brahma Sutras (also known as Vedanta Sutras), which in turn discuss the essence of the Upanishads.

Aero Asia International : Aero Asia International is a private airline based at Karachi, Sindh, Pakistan at the Quaid-e-Azam International Airport. It was the first low cost airline to start services in Pakistan and operates to many destinations in Pakistan and the Gulf states. Its main bases are the Quaid-e-Azam International Airport, Karachi and Dubai International Airport, Dubai.

A F M Abul Fateh : AFM Abul Fateh (born May 16, 1924) is the Bangladesh diplomat and statesman who became that country's first Foreign Secretary when it gained its independence in 1971and its highest ranked / most senior foreign service officer. Abul Fateh was born in Kishorganj on 16 May 1924 in a landowning family, to Abdul Gafur and Zohra Khatun; he passed his Matriculation exams from Ramkrishna High English School in Kishorganj in 1941. After passing his Intermediate exams from Ananda Mohan College in Mymensingh in 1943, he undertook higher studies in English Literature at Dhaka University where he also excelled in sport, for a time captaining the cricket team and becoming the table-tennis champion. Abul Fateh is fluent in English, French, Arabic, Bengali, Hindi and Urdu and has a good knowledge of other South Asian Subcontinental languages. Fateh played a significant role at the time of the Bangladesh Independence War in 1971.

A F M Ahsanuddin Chowdhury : AFM Ahsanuddin Chowdhury (1915-2001) was the president of Bangladesh. Born in 1915 at Bokainagar in Mymensingh district Ahsanuddin Chowdhury was graduated and obtained his BL Degree from Dhaka University. He joined the Bengal Civil Service (judicial) in the year 1942, and subsequently served as district judge in Sylhet, Rangpur and Dhaka. He was appointed Justice of the Dhaka high court in 1968, and Justice of the Appellate Division of the Supreme Court in 1973. He retired from service in 1977. Following a military coup d'etat in March 1982 the army chief of staff Hussain Muhammad Ershad assumed power as the chief martial law administrator, and Justice Ahsanuddin Chowdhury was made President of the People's Republic of Bangladesh on 27 March 1982, a position which he held till 10 December 1983.

Justice Ahsanuddin was associated with various social and welfare institutions. He was the chairman of Bangladesh Scouts, chairman of the management board and trustee board of Dhaka Child Hospital, chairman of National Foundation of Mental Health, chairman of the managing committee of Dhaka Law College, chairman of anjuman-i-mufidul islam, and chairman of Dhaka High Court mazar committee. He died on 30 August 2001.

Afrasiab Khattak : Afrasiab Khattak is a former student leader, Pakistani politician, writer and prominent human rights activist. He has been the president of Human Rights Commission of Pakistan (HRCP), which is believed to be the largest human rights organisation in the country.

Aftab Ahmed Chowdhury : Aftab Ahmed Chowdhury (born 10 November 1985 in Chittagong) is a Bangladeshi cricketer, and widely judged to be one of their best batsmen. He made his international debut at the 2004 Champions Trophy, and, despite scoring a thirteen-ball duck was persisted with owing to good performances at Under-19 level for Bangladesh. He made somewhat of a name for himself when Bangladesh toured England in 2005, scoring his first Test fifty with 82 not out as Bangladesh made 316 in the second innings of the second Test, and also made 51 in the first ODI against England in the 2005 NatWest Series. He led Bangladesh to a 3-2 series victory with an unbeaten 81 in the final match against Zimbabwe in 2005.

Aftab ul Islam : Aftab ul Islam, FCA, is the President and CEO of International Office Equipment (IOE) and the former President of the IT Association of Bangladesh. He was the president of the Dhaka Chamber of Commerce and Industry (DCCI) in Bangladesh and also became the first ever non-American president of the forum of the American Chamber of commerce in Bangladesh (AMCHAM). He has 27 years of field experience in marketing office automation products, 16 years as Country Manager of the multinational American company NCR. He participated in various conference and training throughout the world.

Aftab ul Islam was instrumental in establishing the BCS Computer city in Bangladesh. He has been widely recognised at home and abroad for persuading the government of Bangladesh to use information technology for its efficiency and competitiveness and making it duty free for wider use.

Aga Khan III : Aga Khan III, PC (November 2, 1877 – July 11, 1957), also known as Sultan Mahommed Shah, was born in Karachi and was the only son of Aga Khan II, and succeeded him on his death in 1885, becoming the head of the family.

Under the care of his mother, a daughter of the ruling house of Persia, he was given not only that religious and oriental education which his position as the religious leader of the Iasmailis made indispensable, but a sound European training, a boon denied to his father and grandfather. This blending of the two systems of education produced the happy result of fitting this Muslim chief in an eminent degree both for the sacerdotal functions which appertain to his spiritual position, and for those social duties required of a great and enlightened leader which he was called upon to discharge by virtue of his position.

Aga Khan University (AKU) : The Aga Khan University (AKU) is the first private university in Pakistan, chartered in 1983, it is located in Karachi, Sindh, Pakistan. Aga Khan University was founded by His Highness the Aga Khan, under the auspices of the charitable Aga Khan Foundation of the Aga Khan Development Network. AKU's objective is to promote human welfare in general, and the welfare of the people of Pakistan in particular, by disseminating knowledge and providing instruction, training, research and service in the health sciences, education and such other branches of learning as the University may determine. It is Pakistan's largest private medical institute and hospital.

Agama Hindu Dharma : Agama Hindu Dharma is the formal name of Hinduism in Indonesia. It is practised by 93% of the population of Bali, but also in Sumatra, Java (especially by the Tenggerese people on the east), and Kalimantan. Although only about 3% of Indonesian population is officially Hindu, Indonesian beliefs are too complex to classify as belonging to a single world religion. In Java in particular, a substantial number of Muslims follow a non-orthodox, Hindu-influenced form of Islam known as Abangan, while across the archipelago the Hindu legacy, along with the older mystic traditions, influences popular beliefs.

The advent of Soeharto's 'new order' resulted in an increasing Indonesianisation of both Hindu Dharma and Parisada Hindu Dharma, partly due to the fact that every Indonesian citizen was now required to be a registered member of one of the five acknowledged religious communities (Islam, Christianity [i.e. Protestantism or Catholicism], Hinduism and Buddhism). Inspired by the Hindu Javanese past, several hundred thousand Javanese converted to Hinduism in the 1960s and 1970s. When the adherents of the ethnic religions Aluk To Dolo (Sa'dan Toraja) and Kaharingan (Ngaju, Luangan) claimed official recognition of their traditions, the Ministry of Religion classified them as Hindu variants in 1968 and 1980. The Parisada Hindu Dharma changed its name to Parisada Hindu Dharma Indonesia in 1984, in recognition of its national influence.

Agartala : Agartala is the capital of the Indian state of Tripura. It lies on the Haora River and is located 2 km from Bangladesh. It has several temples and palaces. The population in 2004 was about 200,000. Agartala became the new capital of the Royal Tripura Kingdom in the late 19th century after the Tripura kings shifted their capital first from Udaipur to Puran Agartala in the early 19th century and then to the present site of the city.

Agastyakoodam : Agastyakoodam or Agastya Malai is a peak of 1868 m in the Western Ghats. This mountain falls in the Kollam and Thiruvananthapuram districts of Kerala and the Tirunelveli and Kanyakumari districts of Tamil Nadu, south India. It is a pilgrim centre, where devotees come to worship sage Agasthyar. Agasthyar was a Dravidian sage, and is considered to be one of the seven Rishis (Saptarishi) of Hindu mythology. The Tamil language is considered to be a boon from Agasthyar. There is a full-sized statue of Agasthyar at the top of the peak and the devotees can render poojas themselves.

Agatti : Agatti island is the only island in the Union Territory of Lakshadweep, India that has an airstrip. The island has only one hotel and supplies are delivered by ship once a week. It is connected to Cochin airport on the mainland. Indian Airlines and private airline Deccan airlines operate to this airfield. Other islands are linked by a helicopter or boat service.

Agha Hasan Abedi : Agha Hasan Abedi (1922—1995) was the leading banker from Pakistan. He founded the Bank of Credit and Commerce International (BCCI) in 1972. BCCI was known to have assets worth $20,000 million US dollars by 1980. The bank, with its Head Office nominally in Luxembourg but effectively run from London, had 400 branches in 72 countries and was the seventh largest private bank in the world at the time of its glory. He passed away in Karachi, Pakistan on Saturday 5 August 1995 after a prolonged illness.

Aghori : The Aghori are a Hindu sect believed to have split off from the Kapalika order (which dates from 1000 A.D.) in the fourteenth century. Both Kapalika & Aghori sects are worshipers of Lord Shiva. Aghori means non-terrifying in Sanskrit, and may refer to how members of the sect view death. This extremely secretive community is known to live in graveyards, wear the ash from the pyre, and use human bone from the graveyards for the rituals.

Members of the Aghori drink from human skulls and practice cannibalism in the belief that eating human flesh confers spiritual and physical benefits, such as prevention of aging. The Aghori are widely censured in India for their use of human remains. The sect is said to practice human sacrifice, however this has not been confirmed and many believe it to be unlikely. It is also believed that Aghoris perfrom Tantric ritual involving sex with a lower caste, menstruating woman during which the aghori becomes Shiva and his partner shakti. Their history of cannibalism was attested by a sixteenth century persian and nineteeth century British accounts. The main akhada of Aghoris is Kina Ram's Ashram in Varanasi. Kina Ram's samadhi is a centre of piligrimage for aghoris and aghori devotees.

Agra : Agra is an ancient city on the Yamuna River in India, within the state of Uttar Pradesh. It achieved prominence as the capital of the Mughal sovereigns from 1526 to 1658 and remains a major tourist destination because of its many splendid Mughal-era buildings, most notably the Taj Mahal and the Agra Fort. Agra is situated on the bank of Yamuna river, situated between 27°11' North latitude and 78°0' degree to 78°2' East longitude, at 169 meters above sea level. On the north it is bounded by Mathura, on the south by Dhaulpur, on the east by Firozabad, and on the west by Bharatpur.

Agra Fort : Agra Fort is located in Agra, India. The fort is also known as Lal Qila, Fort Rouge and Red Fort of Agra. It is about 2.5 km northwest of its much more famous sister monument, the Taj Mahal. The fort can be more accurately described as a walled palatial city. By most estimates, the fort was taken over from the Lodis by the Moghuls in the late 16th century, by Akbar the Great. During his reign, he shifted the government of his empire from Delhi to Agra. Because of this, much of Agra flourished and the site of the old Lodis fort began changing into more of a royal estate. Akbar tended to build from red sandstone, often inlaid with white marble and intricate decorations.

It was only during the reign of Akbar's grandson, Shah Jahan, that the site finally took on its current state. Legend fortells that Shah Jahan built the beautiful Taj Mahal for his wife. Unlike his grandfather, Shah Jahan tended to have buildings made from white marble, often inlaid with gold or semi-precious gems. He destroyed some of the earlier buildings inside the fort in order to make his own.

At the end of his life, Shah Jahan was imprisoned by his son, Aurangzeb, in the fort. A punishment which might not seem so harsh, considering the luxury of the fort. It is rumored that Shah Jahan died in Muasamman Burj, a tower with a marble balcony with an excellent view of the

Taj Mahal. This was also a site of one of the battles during the Indian rebellion of 1857, which caused the end of the British East India Company's rule in India, and led to a century of direct rule of India by Britain. The fort attained World Heritage Site status from UNESCO in 1983.

Agror : Agror is a frontier valley in the Mansehra district of Hazara Division, North-West Frontier Province of Pakistan, lying between 34° 29' and 34° 35' N. and 720 58' and 75° 9' E. It consists of three mountain glens, 10 miles in length and 6 m in breadth. The lower portions contain a mass of luxuriant cultivation, thickly dotted with villages, hamlets, and groves, and surrounded by dark pine-clad heights, whose depressions occasionally disclose the snowy peaks of the main range in the distance. These valleys are alike in their nature; they have no strictly level spaces, but consist rather of terraced flats which descend from the hills. Water is abundant and perennial, so that failure of crops seldom occurs.

Aguada Fort : Built by the Portuguese in 1609-1612, to command the entry into the river Mandovi, in order to protect Old Goa from potential enemy attacks. A spring within the fort provided water supply to the ships that called there. The fort houses presently the central jail. A lighthouse is situated nearby, the visiting hours for it being 16.00 to 17.00 hrs.

Ahilya Bai Holkar : Ahilya Bai Holkar was the ruler of Indore and the adjoining regions from 1767 to 1795. She ruled from her palace located in a fort, called Ahilya Fort at Maheshwar, situated on the northern bank of the Narmada River. During her reign, Indore grew to be a powerful city of Malwa region. She also built and renovated a number of Hindu temples, including the Vishwanath Temple of Varanasi, and the Vishnupad Temple of Gaya. A commemorative stamp was issued in her honor on 25th August 1996 by the Republic of India.

Ahir : Ahir (a corruption of the word Abhir, "fearless") is a subgroup of the Yadav caste of India. According to tradition, the Abhiras had the distinction of founding the first recorded kingdom on the banks of the sacred river Saraswati. On the other side of the river was the kingdom of the Suras. The Sarswati gradually went underground, and the Suras were blamed for the mishap and charged with sins with which the river was burdened. Both the Suras and Abhiras had to migrate away from their kingdom and were alienated from the rest of society.

Hindu writers have described the Ahirs as living in the north and west, the quarter varying according to the locality of the writer. Some translators have confused them with the Suras, with whom they are generally associated, and have called them Surabhiras. It is sometimes suggested that the native country or city of the Abhiras is Ophir, mentioned in the Bible. According to Markandeya Purana, all the kshatriya (warrior caste) were killed in a holocaust led by Parshuram. Only the Abhiras survived by escaping into the craters between mountains. The sage Markandeya remarked that "all Kshatriya have been killed but Abhira have survived; they will surely rule the earth in Kaliyuga." Vatsyayana also mentions the Abhira kingdoms in the Kama Sutra.

Ahmad Hassan Dani : Ahmad Hassan Dani (born 1920) is a Pakistani archaeologist and linguist, and is considered to be one of the foremost authorities on South Asian archaeology and history. He is Professor Emeritus at the Quaid-i-Azam University and the director of Taxila Institute of Asian Civilizations. He was the first Muslim graduate of the Banaras Hindu University. He is also the recipient of one of the highest civil awards in Pakistan, the Hilal-i-Imtiaz.

Ahmad Nadeem Qasmi : Ahmad Nadeem Qasmi (Born 20 November 1916) is an Urdu language Pakistani poet, journalist, literary critic and short story writer. With some 50 books of poetry, fiction, criticism, journalism and art to his credit, Qasmi is a major figure in contemporary Urdu literature. He stands out among his contemporaries due mainly to his unflinching humanism.

Qasmi is considered second only to Prem Chand in mastefull depiction of rural culture in Urdu short story. Several collections of poetry reveal his love for humanity in all forms. For the past 40 years, he has published and edited the prestigious literary journal "Funoon", which has groomed more than one generation of new writers.

Ahmadi : Ahmadi, arc followers of Mirza Ghulam Ahmad. They comprise two subsects, the Ahmadiyya Muslim Community (sometimes called the 'Qadiani' community, after Qadian, India, though this term is considered offensive by some) and the Lahore Ahmadiyya Movement (Ahmadiyya Anjuman Ishaat-i-Islam). Ahmadi Muslims' beliefs are considered heretical and outside of Islam by most mainstream Muslims, though an exception may be made by some in the case of the smaller Lahore Ahmadiyya Movement.

Ahmed Ali : Ahmed Ali (1908 in New Delhi – 14 January 1954 in Karachi) was a Pakistani novelist, diplomat and scholar. Born in Delhi, India, he was involved in progressive literary movements as a young man. He contributed to Aangarey (Red Hot Embers, 1933), a collection of short stories that caused an uproar among fundamentalist Muslims. The book was banned in March 1933, the publisher was raided by police, and copies of the book were burnt in the streets.

Ahmed Faraz : Ahmed Faraz (January 14, 1931) is considered one of the great modern Urdu poets. He was jailed, and later exiled, during the Zia-ul Haq regime, for writing poems against the military government.

Ahmed Rashid : Ahmed Rashid (b. 1948) is a Pakistani journalist and best-selling author. He was born in Rawalpindi in 1948 and was educated at Malvern College England, Government College Lahore and Cambridge University. He serves as the Pakistan, Afghanistan and Central Asia correspondent for the Far Eastern Economic Review and the Daily Telegraph, London. He also writes for the Wall Street Journal, The Nation (Pakistan), Lahore and academic journals. He appears regularly on international TV and radio such as CNN and BBC World.

Ahmed Rushdi : Ahmed Rushdi was a very important contributor to the Golden Age of Pakistani film music. Born in Hyderabad Deccan in 1938, he migrated to Pakistan after Independance. His first major break was singing "Bunder Road se Keemari" on Radio Pakistan. During his time as a leading play back singer, he lent his vocal talent to major heroes of his time including Waheed Murad, Darpan, Nadeem, Shahid and Ghulam Mohi-ud-Din to name a few. He suffered from poor health during later part of his life and died on 11 April 1983 of a major heart attack, at the age of 45. He will always be remembered as singing vocals for Waheed Murad in hit films like Doraha and Armaan along with other numerous hit songs.

Ahmed Sharif : Ahmed Sharif (1921-1999 CE) was an educationist, philosopher, critic, writer and scholar of medieval Bangla literature. Born in Chittagong, Sharif retired as a Professor from University of Dhaka in 1983. Sharif is widely recognized as one of the most outspoken and radical thinkers of Bangladesh.

Ahmedabad : Ahmedabad or Ahmadabad is the largest city in Gujarat and the 7th largest city in India, with a population of 5 million. The city is also sometimes called Karnavati, an older name and known as Amdavad in colloquial Gujarati. Ahmedabad is the administrative center of Ahmedabad District, and was the former capital of Gujarat State from 1960 to 1970, when Gandhinagar replaced it. The city was founded in the 15th century by Sultan Ahmed Shah on the Sabarmati river, and served as capital of the Sultanate of Gujarat. The historic center of Ahmedabad is presently a thriving business district. Ahmedabad is mainly divided in two parts, the old city, and new city. The old city has developed rather haphazardly, and most of the roads are narrow and crowded during business hours. The new city has well-structured, wide and smooth roads. A wide variety of shops and businesses exist in the city.

Ahoms : The Ahoms ruled parts of present-day Assam (in India) for nearly 600 years: from 1228 to 1826. Historical documents do not call the kingdom "Ahom". They call it "Asam" (or Assam), and the subjects of this kingdom "Assamese" or "Asamiya". After the advent of the British, the meanings of these categories changed. "Ahom" as a term appears in the Buranjis to denote the collection of civil and military officers under the Ahom king, all of which were non-hereditary offices.

In early 13th century, Sukaphaa, a Shan (Mong Mao) prince began his journey with about 9000 followers. He crossed the Patkai hills, fought and defeated the Nagas and reached the Brahmaputra valley in 1228. He moved from place to place, searching for a seat. He decided not to attack the Morans and Borahis but befriend them instead. His followers, much depleted from the original 9000, married into the Borahi and the Mataks. He finally established his capital at Charladeo near present day Sibsagar in 1253 and began the task of state formation.

The Ahom kingdom then consolidated its powers for the next 300 years or so. The first major expansion was at the cost of the Chutiya kingdom, which was annexed in 1522 under Suhungmung. The expansion was not just a success of Ahom military prowess, but also a result of changes in the Ahom social and political outlook. For example, Suhungmung was the first Ahom king to adopt a Hindu name: Swarga Narayan. The Chutiya region was placed under the Sadiyakhowa Gohain a new position that was created. In 1536 the Kacharis were uprooted from their capital at Dimapur. Thus by the middle of the 16th century, the Ahoms were in control over eastern Assam.

In early 17th century, the Ahoms came into conflict with the Mughals over the control of Koch Hajo. In the battle of Itakhuli in 1682 the Mughals were finally removed and the Ahoms got control over most of the Brahmaputra valley. Their power declined in later half of the 18th century. The capital city was taken for a short period during the Moamoria rebellion. In the first part of the 19th century, the Burmese army invaded their kingdom who set up a puppet Ahom king. The Burmese were defeated by the British in the First Anglo-Burmese War resulting in the Treaty of Yandaboo in 1826, which paved the way for the British to convert the Ahom kingdom into a principality and which marked the end of the Ahom rule.

The Tai Ahoms who came into Assam followed their traditional religion and spoke the Tai language. They were a very small group numerically and after the first generation, the group was a mixture of the Tai and the local population. Over time the Ahom state adopted the Assamese language and kings and other high officials converted to Hinduism. Except for some special offices (the king and the raj mantris), other positions are open to members of all tribes and religion. They kept good records, and are known for their chronicles, called Buranjis. One of its greatest achievements was the stemming of Mughal expansionism. In the celebrated battle of Saraighat, the Ahom general Lachit Borphukan defeated the Mughal forces on the outskirts of present day Guwahati in 1671.

Ahsan Habib : Ahsan Habib, (1917-1985) apoet and journalist, was born on 2 February 1917 in the village of Shankarpasha in Pirojpur district of Bangladesh.

Ahsan Habib started writing while still a student. His first poem, 'Mayer Kabar Pade Kishor', was published in the school magazine in 1934 when he was student of class X. Subsequently, his poems were published in various journals and magazines such as Desh, Mohammadi, Bichitra, etc. Ahsan Habib was a poet of urban society, both in language and sensibility. His poems reflect the social reality of his times and focus on the concerns of the middle class. He received several awards for his literary achievements.

Ahsan Manzil : Ahsan Manzil, was the official residential palace and seat of the Nawabs of Dhaka. It is situated on the banks of the Buriganga River. The palace is now a museum. The palace has enjoyed a varied history, starting from being Rang Mahal (of Sheikh Enayetullah, a Zamindar of Jamalpur pargana (Barisal) during the time of the Mughals) to a French trading centre. Khwaja Alimullah bought it from the French in 1830 and converted it into his residence, effecting necessary reconstruction and renovations. The final reconstruction was done by Martin & Company, a European construction and engineering firm, at the behest of Nawab Khwaja Abdul Ghani, who converted this house into the official Nawabi residence.

Ahsan Manzil is one of the most significant architectural monuments of Bangladesh. Established on a raised platform of 1 metre, the two-storied palace measures 125.4m by 28.75m. The height of the ground floor is 5 metres and that of the first floor 5.8 metres. There are porticos the height of the ground floor, both on the northern and southern sides of the palace. An open spacious stairway comes down from the southern portico, extending onto the bank of the river through the front garden. There was once a fountain in the garden in front of the stairs, that does not exist today. The spacious north and south verandas of both the floors rest on semicircular arches. The verandas and rooms are covered with marble.

Recognising the historical and architectural importance of the Ahsan Manzil, the government of Bangladesh took the initiative to renovate it. In 1985 Ahsan Manzil and its surroundings were acquired. After the completion of the renovation work in 1992 under the supervision of the Directorate of Public Works and Architecture, it was brought under the control of Bangladesh National Museum (20 September 1992). A museum has been established there.

Ahsania Mission : Ahsania Mission, Dhaka, an NGO, was established by Khan Bahadur ahsanullah (1873-1965) on 9 February 1958 at 9 Armenian Street, Armanitola, Dhaka. The organisation was in fact first formed in 1935 with its local office at Nalta of Satkhira district where Ahsanullah was born. The main objective of the institution is 'prayer to the creator and service to its creatures' and with this motto the organisation carries out its different welfare activities.

The mission is managed by a 21-member executive council comprising president, one executive secretary, three vice-presidents, one treasurer, one general secretary, one joint-secretary and thirteen members, all elected by the general members of the mission. Ahsania Mission has eight working divisions: administration, finance and accounts, planning, research, training and material development, programme, public relations, and international affairs, each having a director as its divisional chief.

Ahuna : In Nagaland, ahuna is a traditional post harvest festival of the Sumis. Ahuna signifies the celebration of the seasons harvest's in thanksgiving, while evoking the spirits for good fortune in the New Year

Tuluni is a festival of great significance. the festival is marked with feast as the occasion occurs in the bountiful season of the year. Drinking rice beer indispensably forms a part of the fest. This wine is called TULUNI. It is celebrated in mid July every year.

Aihole : Aihole is now in the Bagalkot district of Karnataka, India. Aihole has its own historical significance and is termed as cradle of Hindu rock archtecture. Many temples and caves of historical importance can be found at Aihole. It is a very popular tourist spot in north Karnataka. Aihole was the first capital of the early Chalukyas. Here they built over 140 temples in various styles and is said to be a laboratory of experiments in rock cut architecture. Aihole is to the west of Badami, along the Malaprabha river, while Pattadakal is to the east. Pulakesi I, one of the greatest rulers of this dynasty, moved the capital to Badami nearby. Badami was then known as Vatapi.

The first phase of temple building in Aihole dates back to the 6th century CE, the second phase to the 12th century. The Ravanaphadi temple is a rock cut temple, with a rectangular shrine, with two mandapams in front of it and a rock cut Shivalingam. This temple dates back to the second half of the 7th century. The prominent temple groups here are the Kontigudi group and the Galaganatha group. A group of three temples is referred to as the Kontigudi group of temples. One of these is the Lad Khan temple, named after a mendicant that lived in this temple in the 19th century, another the Huchiappayyagudi temple and the Huchiappayya math.

Air India : Air India is the national flag carrier airline of India with a network of passenger and cargo services worldwide. It is one of the two state-owned airlines in the country, the other being Indian Airlines. Its main base is Chatrapati Shivaji International Airport, Mumbai, with hubs at Indira Gandhi International Airport, New Delhi and Chennai International Airport. The airline connects 44 destinations around the world, including 12 gateways in India.

Air University : Air University is located at Islamabad, Pakistan. Air University was established by Pakistan Air Force in 2002. The Air University is open to all classes and segments of the society. Air University offers degree programs in Engineering, Computer and Management Sciences, Humanities, Education, and Aerospace & Avionics.

Airblue : Airblue is a private airline based at Quaid-e-Azam International Airport Karachi, Sindh, Pakistan. It was the first private carrier to operate the Airbus A320 when it initially started. Airblue has been expanding even after experiencing competition from the other three airline operators in Pakistan. The airline mainly flies on most domestic routes including Dubai International Airport but is planning to go international to many destinations including the United Kingdom and USA.

AirTel : AirTel is a brand of cell phone services in India operated by Bharti Televentures. The AirTel brand has been one of the highly successful Telecom brands in India. Bharti Televentures owns the AirTel brand and provides the following services under the brand name AirTel: Mobile Services (using GSM Technology), Broadband & Telephone Services (Fixed line and Internet Connectivity), Long Distance Services and Enterprise Services (Telecommunications Consulting for corporates). Bharti Tele-Ventures is India's leading private sector provider of telecommunications services based on a strong customer base consisting of 11 million total customers which constitute, 10 million mobile and 1 million fixed line customers, as of February 2005. AirTel has ambitious plans to provide 25 million connections by mid-2006. There is fierce competition among local telecommunications companies to provide better service and AirTel is regarded as one of the top communications service provider in the Asian region too.

Aishwarya Rai : Aishwarya Rai (Ash to fans and media) was born in Mangalore to Krishnaraj and Vrinda Rai, in the South Indian state of Karnataka, on November 1, 1973. She is a supermodel and an award-winning actress from India, and Miss World 1994.

As a professional model, Rai has appeared in many Indian fashion magazines. Rai is an international star; she is acting for both Bollywood and Hollywood. She has been nominated four times in the Best Actress category and once in the Best Supporting Actress category at the Filmfare. She has also won three IIFA Awards, three Z-Gold Awards, four Screen Awards, an EU's Global Diversity Award, three Zee Cine Awards and a Rajiv Gandhi Award.

Aizawl : Aizawl is the capital city of the state of Mizoram in India. Aizawl (Pop:260,000), the capital city of Mizoram which lies at the southern side border, is a beautiful place that offers plenty of tourist attractions to tourists and habitants alike. The city is situated on top of a hill and its surrounding slopes and valleys. Besides its breathtaking beauty, Aizawl is the business centre and storehouse of all important Government offices, State assembly house and civil secretariat. It also enhouses different communities of Mizos wherein they maintain peaceful coexistence as the main theme. Various varieties of jungle products, monuments and memorials connected with legends and folklores are also avalilable. This lively and bustling city is the headquarter of Aizawl District is definitely enchanting and worth visiting.

Aizawl is connected with the rest of the country by NH 54 through Silchar in Assam. The city is also served by Lengpui Airport(1hr drive) which connects the city with daily Indian Airlines flights to and from Kolkata(Calcutta), Imphal and Guwahati. Foreigners and visitors from other Indian states needs to have permit to visit Aizawl or Mizoram which can be applied at Indian Mission at respective countries or Immigration/Home Office in all major cities and airports.

Ajaigarh : Ajaigarh, or Adjygurh, is town in Panna District of Madhya Pradesh state in central India. Ajaigarh was the capital of a princely state of the same name in British India. Ajaigarh was founded in 1765 by Guman Singh, a Bundela Rajput who was the nephew of Raja Pahar Singh of Jaitpur. Ajaigarh was captured by the British in 1809, and became a princely state in the Bundelkhand Agency of the Central India Agency. It had an area of 771 mile^2, and a population of 78,236 in 1901. The rulers bore the title of sawai maharaja. He commanded an estimated annual revenue of about £15,000/-, and paid a tribute of £460/-. The chief resided at the town of Nowgong, at the foot of the hill-fortress of Ajaigarh, from which the state took its name. This fort, situated on a steep hill, towers more than 800 ft (244 m) above the eponymous township, and contains the ruins of several temples adorned with elaborately carved sculptures. The town was often afflicted by malaria, and suffered severely from famine in 1868-1869 and 1896-1897.

The state acceded to the Government of India on January 1, 1950; the ruling chief was granted a Privy purse of Rs. 74,700, and the courtesy use of his styles and titles. All of these were revoked by the government of India in 1971, at the time when these privileges were revoked from all erstwhile princes. The former princely state became part of the new Indian state of Vindhya Pradesh, and most of the territory of the former state, including the town of Ajaigarh, became part of Panna District, with a smaller portion going to Chhatarpur District. Vindhya Pradesh was merged into Madhya Pradesh on November 1, 1956.

Ajanta Caves : The 30 rock-cut Buddhist caves at Ajanta arc of two basic designs called 'Chaitya grihas' and 'Viharas' in Maharashtra. Five of the caves are Chaityas (Buddhist cathedrals) while the other 25 are Viharas (monasteries). Chaitya grihas were halls of worship—large, rectangular chambers separated by rows of pillars into a central nave, surrounded by aisles on three sides, for circumambulation during prayer, with a sanctuary opposite thc entrance. The Chaityas are decorated with sculptures and murals depicting the many incarnations of Buddha. Viharas or monasteries are rectangular shaped halls with series of small cells attached on two sides. The side opposite the entrance contained an image of Buddha or a votive stupa.

The Ajanta caves include the epic in visual form, recalling the life of the Buddha and illustrating tales from Jatakas (Buddhist fables). Cave 1 has a most popular painting of Bodhisattva Avalokitesvara and Bodhisattva Padmapani (one with the lotus in his hand). Cave 2 is remarkable for its ceiling decorations and murals narrating the birth of Buddha. Cave 4 is the largest vihara in Ajanta and depicts a man and woman fleeing from a mad elephant and a man giving up his resistance to a tempting woman.

Ajatashatru : Ajatashatru was a king of the Magadha empire that ruled north India. There is not a great deal known about Ajatashatru. What is known that he became a King of Magadha and the adjoining areas by murdering his father, Bimbisara. Also, he was a contemporary of Lord Buddha, was a patron of the then-new religion of Buddhism, and he let the Sangha function in his Kingdom. Some details of him are given in the earliest Buddhist scriptures.

Ajatashatru's Fort : Ajatashatru's Fort in Bihar built by Ajatashatru (6th century B.C.), the king of Magadha during the Buddha's time. The 6.5 sq. metre Ajatashatru's Stupa is also believed to have been built by him.

Ajay Devgan : Vishal Devgan (born April 2, 1967, Bombay, India), popularly known as Ajay Devgan is one of the best Indian actors working in the Hindi film industry (Bollywood). His debut film was a hit. He then went on to do films which required a lot of action. His intense look and persona made him a favourite with the audience.

He twice garnered the National Award for Best Actor for the movies Zakhm and The Legend of Bhagat Singh.

Ajmal Khattak : Ajmal Khattak is a Pakistani politician, writer and Pashtun poet and close friend of the late Khan Wali Khan. He has had a long career in both the anti-imperial movement against the British in the North West Frontier Province of Pakistan as well as part of the National Awami Party(NAP) in it's various incarnations in Pakistan. His early political career began during the Quit India movement after he came under the influence of the Khudai Khidmatgar movement. He was forced to leave the school due to his involvement in the Quit India Movement. As a writer he served as editor of various Newspapers and periodicals, including Anjam, Shahbaz, Adal and Rahber as well as script writer for Radio Pakistan.

Ajmal Mian : Ajmal Mian was a Chief Justice of the Supreme Court of Pakistan from December 23, 1997 to June 30, 1999. Born July 4, 1934 in Delhi, India Mr. Justice Ajmal Mian son of Mr. Muhammad Mian took the Bachelor's Degree in Economics and Political Science from the University of Karachi in 1953.

Ajmer : Ajmer, or Ajmere, is a city in Ajmer District in India's Rajasthan state. Its population was approximately

500,000 in 2001. The city gives its name to a district, and also to a former province of British India called Ajmer-Merwara, which, after India's independence, became the state of Ajmer until November 1, 1956, when it was merged into Rajasthan state.

A K Antony : Arackaparambil Kurian Antony, was the Chief Minister of Kerala during 1977-78, 1995-96, and 2001-2004. When he became Chief Minister in 1977, he was the youngest Chief Minister of the State. Still he holds that record. He was the Leader of Opposition in Kerala Legislative Assembly during 1996 to 2001. Born on 28th December 1940 as the son of Arackaparambil Kurian Pillai and Elikutty at Cherthala in Alappuzha District, he did his primary education in Government High school, Cherthala and took his B.A. degree from Maharajas College, Ernakulam and BL from Government Law College, Eranakulam.

At present A.K. Antony is a member of Rajya Sabha. Earlier he was the member of the House from 1985 to 91 and 1991 to 1995 and was the Minister for Civil Supplies, Consumer Affairs and Public Distribution in Narasimha Rao ministry in the latter period. As a chief minister he imposed a ban on arrack (country liquor) in 1996. This is one of the famous decisions made by him.

A K Fazlul Huq : Sher-e-Bangla (The Tiger of Bengal') Abul Kashem Fazlul Huq (born 26 October 1873-died 27 April 1962) was a famous Bengali statesman in the first half of the 20th century. He was the Mayor of Calcutta (1935), Chief Minister of undivided Bengal (1937-1943) and of East Bengal (1954), Home Minister of Pakistan (1955) and Governor of East Pakistan (1956-1958). He presented the Lahore Resolution of 1940 that established Muslim League's demand for a homeland for Muslims, that ultimately resulted in the nation of Pakistan.

A K Gopalan : A. K. Gopalan popularly known as AKG, was a communist leader and an Indian politician. He was born on 1 October 1904 in Kannur District of Northern Kerala and educated in Tellichery. By the time he became a teacher, India's independence movement was becoming energized by Mahatma Gandhi. Gopalan took part in the Khilafat Movement which prompted a marked change in his outlook, transforming him into a dedicated fulltime social and political worker. In 1927 he joined the Indian National Congress and began playing an active role in the Khadi Movement and the upliftment of Harijans. He was arrested for participating in the salt satyagraha in 1930.

While in prison he became exposed to leftist thinking and became a member of the Congress Socialist Party and later the Communist Party of India when it finally took shape in Kerala in 1939. He led the hunger march from Malabar to Madras in 1937 and the Malabar Jatha in support of the movement for responsible government in Travancore. The outbreak of the Second World War in 1939 prompted an upsurge in activism against British domination, and Gopalan was again arrested. But in 1942 he escaped from prison and remained at large till the end of the war in 1945. He was arrested again shortly after the end of the war and was still behind bars when India became independent on August 15, 1947. He was released a few weeks later. Thereafter he was a member of Lok Sabha for 5 consecutive terms till his death on March 22, 1977. He also wrote extensively. His autobiography In the Cause of the People has been translated into many languages. His other works include For Land, Around the World, Work in Parliament, and Collected Speeches, all in Malayalam.

In 1964 when CPI split he become an important leader of the Communist Party of India (Marxist). A. K. Gopalan was a staunch freedom fighter, a social reformer and an outstanding leader of the communist movement in Kerala. He sacrificed personal comforts for cause of freedom during British Rule. After independence he continued his struggle for upliftment of the downtrodden particularly the Dalits.

Aka : The Aka, also known as Hrusso, are found in the Thrinzo area in West Kameng and East Kameng of the Indian state of Arunachal Pradesh. Their language belongs to the Tibeto-Burman family Of Tibetan and Assmaese origin, the Aka are a Southeast Asian-looking people of fair-complexion. Well built, the Aka are generally flat-nosed and prominent cheek-boned. They inhabit at regions around Thrinzo, situated at an elevation from 3000 to 6000 feet, living on the immediate west to the Sherdukpen and east to the Nishi. For the convenience of administration, the Aka people elects a chief, who often acts the role of the village headman. Polygamy is widely practiced in their patrilineal society, and the social factor of cross-cousin marriages are accepted. Like most tribes, the Aka have an elementary caste system, the aristocrat Kutsun and the commoner Kevatsum.

The Aka practice shifting cultivation and rear domestic animals such as the Mithun. Temporary huts, accommodated by young boys, are built near the field to guard the crops from the animals. The staple food of Akas is maize and millet. They plant leaves, pulses, potato and rice. Drinks locally made from fermented maize and millet include Lao pani, Mingri and the Aarah.

Akal Takht Sahib : Sri Akal Takht Sahib is the second holiest shrine of the Sikhs. It sits directly in front of the Golden Temple. Sri Akal Takht Sahib was made by the Sikhs' 6th Guru, Guru Hargobind Ji. Sri Akal Takht Sahib is made so that the Sikhs can discuss temporal issues whereas Sri Harmandir Sahib (Golden Temple) is for spirituality. The Head Priest or Jathedar of the Sri Akal

Takht is recognized as the highest spiritual authority in all of Sikhdom. The present Head Priest is Sardar Joginder Singh Vedanti. Sri Akal Takht Sahib is one of five sacred takhts in the Sikh faith.

Akbar : Jalaluddin Muhammad Akbar, also known as Akbar the Great (Akbar-e-Azam) was the ruler of the Mughal Empire from the time of his accession in 1556 until 1605. He is considered the greatest of the Mughal emperors. Akbar "The Great" was one of the greatest rulers in Indian history. He was born when Humayun and his first wife, Hamida Bano, were fugitives escaping towards Iran. It was during these wanderings that Akbar was born in Umerkot, Sindh, on November 23, 1542. Legend has it that Humayun prophesied a bright future for his son, and thus accordingly, named him Akbar.

Akbar was raised in the rugged country of Afghanistan rather than amongst the splendor of the Delhi court. He spent his youth learning to hunt, run, and fight and never found time to read or write. He was the only great Mughal ruler who was illiterate. Despite this, he had a great desire for knowledge. This led him not only to maintain an extensive library but also to learn. Akbar had his books read out to him by his courtiers. Therefore, even though unable to read, Akbar was as knowledgeable as the most learned of scholars.

Akbar came to throne in 1556, after the death of his father, Humayun. At that time, Akbar was only 13 years old. Akbar was the only Mughal king to ascend to the throne without the customary war of succession; as his brother Muhammad Hakim was too feeble to offer any resistance. During the first five years of his rule, Akbar was assisted and advised by Bahram Khan in running the affairs of the country. Bahram Khan was, however, removed and for a few years Akbar ruled under the influence of his nurse Maham Anga. After 1562, Akbar freed himself from external influences and ruled supreme.

During his reign, Akbar managed to subdue almost all of India, with the remaining areas becoming tributary states. Along with his military conquests, he introduced a series of reforms to consolidate his power. Akbar practiced tolerance aimed at Hindu-Muslim unification through the introduction of a new religion known as Din-i-Ilahi. He appointed nobles and mansabdars without any religious prejudice. Akbar's religious innovations and policies, and deviation from Islamic dogma, have been a source of debate and controversy. Akbar was a great patron of literary works and scholars. His court had numerous scholars of the day who are well known as "Nauratan". Akbar had three sons Prince Salim, Murad and Daniyal. Prince Murad and Daniyal died in their prime during their father's lifetime. However, Akbar faced problems with Prince Salim and the last four years of Akbar's life were consumed in crushing Salim's rebellion. Akbar fell ill and died of slow poisoning on October 27, 1605. With him ended the most glorious epoch in Indian history.

Akbarnama : The Akbarnama, which literally means History of Akbar, is a biographical account of Akbar, the third Mughal empreror. It includes vivid and detailed descriptions of his life and time. The book was commissioned by the Great Mughal, and written by Abul Fazl, one of the members of Navaratans of Akbar's royal court. It is stated that the book took seven years to be completed and the original manuscripts contained a number of paintings supporting the texts, and all the paintings represented the Mughal school of painting.

Akhanda Bharatam : Akhanda Bharatam (literally "undivided India") is the historic homeland of the Hindus, before Islamic conquest and colonial partition, which resulted in the subsequent conversion of a significant number to Islam and Christianity. It includes all of present day Afghanistan, Bangladesh, Bhutan, India, Nepal,

Myanmar, Pakistan, Sri Lanka, and Tibet. The geographic frontiers of this region range from the Himalayan region in the north to the ocean in the south. This is derived from the Vishnu puranam text of India. This socio-cultural region is now part of the modern nations of: Iran, Pakistan, Afghanistan, India, Nepal, Bhutan, the trans-Tsangpo and Yunnan regions of China, Sri Lanka, Bangladesh, Myanmar, Maldives, Laos, Cambodia, Thailand, Brunei, East Timor, the Philippines, Malaysia, Indonesia and Singapore, the Mauritius, Maldives, Seychelles, Comoros and other islands of the Indian Ocean.

Akhanda Bharatam is the Sanskrit name for this region. Hinduism and Buddhism are the predominant religions. The Indonesia-Malaysia region, the Pakistan-Afghanistan region and the Sistan-Balochistan region later were converted to Islam. Akhand Bharat is largely based on the concepts of religious or ethnic nationalism rather than a political state. It is an important part of the irredentist ideology of Hindutva subscribed to by Hindu nationalist organizations such as Rashtriya Swayamsevak Sangh (RSS) and political parties such as the Bharatiya Janata Party (BJP).

Akhil Bharatiya Hindu Mahasabha : Akhil Bharatiya Hindu Mahasabha, a Hindu nationalist organization, was originally founded in 1915 to counter the Muslim League and the secular Indian National Congress. The president of Hindu Mahasabha was V.D. Savarkar. K.B. Hedgewar, served as vice president of the organisation. Hedgewar, who became inspired by events in Europe and developments of fascism there, left the Mahasabha to form Rashtriya Swayamsevak Sangh.

Soon after India's Independence, and the subsequent assassination of Gandhi, a good number of Hindu Mahasabhaites joined Bharatiya Jana Sangh under the leadership of S.P. Mukherjee, who had left Hindu

Mahasabha and joined hands with the RSS to float a political party under the control and supervision of RSS. Mukherjee had left Mahasabha after his proposal to allow Muslims to gain membership was turned down by the followers of V.D. Savarkar. The relationship between Savarkar's Mahasabha and RSS was strained mainly because the then chief of RSS, M.S. Golwalkar, felt overshadowed by the influence of Savarkar over the Hindu populace. Officially Mahasabha is still a distinct political entity but its election symbol has been witheld as it has not been getting enough votes. So now the party fights elections on different symbols in different constituencies.

Akhtar Abdur Rahman : General Akhtar Abdur Rahman was the Director of Inter-Services Intelligence (ISI) of Pakistan during the 1980s and was the mastermind behind the Afghan Jihad against the Soviet Union with the support of USA.He was a close friend of CIA chief William Casey.

On promotion to the rank of General, he was appointed Chairman, Joint Chiefs of Staff Committee, Pakistan. His successor as Director General ISI was Lt Gen Hameed Gul. He died in a plane crash that also killed Zia-ul-Haq and top generals of the Afghan war, alongwith an American general and American ambassador to Pakistan. It is suspected that the assassination was a co-ordination agreed by Washington and Moscow and carried out by the elements known specially to CIA due to their network capability in Pakistan.

Akhtaruzzaman Elias : Akhtaruzzaman Elias was a notable Bangladeshi author. Though he wrote only two novels, it has been enough for him to be considered by many critics among the pantheon of great Bengali novelists. Khowabnama depicts the pre-partition rural socio-political scenario in Bangladesh while Chilekothar Sepai is a phsychological journey of a man through the turbulent times of people's uprising in the then East Pakistan during 1969. This latter novel also contains what is arguably the most authentic description of life in Puran Dhaka, the old and distinctive part of Dhaka.

Akleem Akhtar : Akleem Akhtar popularly know as General Rani, was close friend of Yahya Khan during his reign. She lovingly call Yahya Khan as Agha Jani. Due to her close association with Yahya Khan and powers she exercises due to this relation, she was known as General Rani. It is said that during that time, she was the most powerful person after General himself. She held no official position, but she was given full protocol. She refute that she was second to the Yahya Khan and claims that they were just friends.

Akola : Akola is an important Historical, Cultural, Political, Religious, Industrial and Agricultural city in the state of Maharashtra located in the Vidarbha region in central India. It is located around 600 km east of the capital city of Maharashtra state, Mumbai and 250 km west from the city of Nagpur. Akola is the headquarters of Akola District located in Amravati Division. Akola district forms the central part of Amravati division, which corresponds to the former British Raj province of Berar.

Akola is renowned for its cotton production and is the largest cotton producing district in India. The city is also famous for its Pulse or Dal, Oil and Textile mills. It is a rapidly developing and growing Market center with recently announced "Mahanagarpalika" in the Vidarbha region. "Dainik Deshonnati" one of the leading Marathi Newspapers in Maharashtra originated from Akola.

Akram Khan Durrani : Mr. Akram Khan Durrani was elected as the 23th Chief Minister of NWFP on November 29, 2002. He was born in Bannu District. He holds a Degree in law and is a prominent member of the Jamiat-

Ulema-Islam (F) of Maulana Fazlur-Rehman as well as a member of the religo-political alliance the Muttahaida-Majlis-e-Amal.

In his student life he was a member of the Pakhtun Student Federation, the student wing of the Awami National Party. Subsequently he joined the JUI-F and was elected several times to the provincial assembly from his home constituency of Bannu.

Aksai Chin : Aksai Chin is a region located at the junction of the People's Republic of China, Pakistan, and India. It is administered by China and claimed by India. Aksai Chin is one of the two main border disputes between India and China, the other being Arunachal Pradesh. Aksai Chin ('desert of white stones') is a vast desert of salt. This land is also called the Soda Plain. The region is almost uninhabited. One of the proximate causes of the Sino-Indian War of 1962 was India's discovery of a road China had built through the region, which India considers its territory. The road, which connects Tibet and Xinjiang, passes through the settlement of Tianshuihai, the only sizeable town in the region, with about 1600 inhabitants.

Akshay Kr Dutta : Akshay Kr Dutta (15.7.1820-18.5.1886). Born in West Bengal (Chupi-Burdwan). Father was Pitambar Dutta. Published "Tatwabodhini Patrika" as editor first time in 16.8.1843. He was first language scientist of India. He published "Bharatbarshya Upasak Sampradaya in 1870 and also published Charupath (1852), Padarthabidya (1856). He was called the "crownless monarch of Barishal."

Akshay Kumar Maitreya : Akshay Kumar Maitreya (1861-1930) is one of the most important historians and social workers in Bengal. He was born in Nadia (now in West Bengal), but much of his education was in Kolkata and Rajshahi (in Bangladesh). He was a friend of Rabindranath Tagore, but famously engaged with him in an argument about whether history based fiction should necessarily represent historical facts correctly. Maitrya, being a historian, called for historical correctitude, while Tagore declared that an artist has freedom to bend historical facts. Maitreya was instrumetal in creating the Barendra Museum, Rajshahi and also credited for disproving the Black Hole of Calcutta theory used by the colonial British to discredit Siraj Ud Daulah.

Akshaya Trutiya : In Orissa, this festival is celebrated on the third day of the bright fortnight of the lunar month of Vaishakha. This important festival is held in every farming household. It is characterised by the ceremonial sowing of paddy in the field. Oblation is offered to the goddess of destiny, 'Shathi'. This is the most auspicious day to start the construction of house buildings, digging of tanks and wells. This is the day on which the construction of the chariots for Ratha Jatra of Lord Jagannath and his brother and sister starts.

Al Azam Ltd : Al Azam Ltd. was a Pakistani construction company that pioneered low-cost housing for the general public. It was formed during the early 1960s by the former Rehabilitation Minister, Sardar Amir Azam, and his business associate, Muhammad Ali Khan of Rampur.

Alai Minar : Ala ud din Khilji started building the Alai Minar, which was conceived to be two times higher than Qutub Minar. The construction was abandoned, however, after the completion of the 24.5 meter high first storey; soon after death of Ala-ud-din. The first story of the Alai Minar still stands today.

Alaknanda : The Alaknanda is a tributary of the Ganges. It arises from the Satopanth glacier in Uttaranchal, and merges with the Bhagirathi river near Deoprayag after flowing for around 200 km. Following this merging, the river is then known as the Ganga. The Alaknanda contributes a significantly larger fraction to the flow of the Ganga. In mythology, the Alaknanda is believed to have split off from the celestial Ganga when it landed from heaven. The Hindu pilgrimage centre of Badrinath lies along the banks of the Alaknanda river.

Alamgir : Alamgir is a famous Pakistani pop singer of the 1970s, who is in fact the pioneer of the Urdu pop music in Pakistan. Alamgir was born in 1954 in East Pakistan, which is now Bangladesh. He left home at the age of 16, in search of his destiny. He brought with him his guitar and an extra shirt and a small tape recorder. He started singing on the Pakistani Television at the beginning of the 1970's when the people in Pakistan were not familiar with the modern Urdu music and when western music was generally considered as modern music in Pakistan.

Alamgir's first song Albela Rahi, was an Urdu translation of a foreign language song. It proved a hit in 1973 among the youth of the 70's. There was a time during the 70's when the music loving boys and girls gathered regularly on the streets near the Karachi Jheel Park to get a glimpse of this pop singer as he used to travel along in his red sedan in evening. Alamgir's second pop song Pyar hai zindagi ka gehna was also an Urdu translation of a foreign song. He soon became popular among the younger generation in the country. Alamgir is also known for his many renditions of Bengali music. The most notable Bengali song he is known to sing is Aamay Bhashaili Rey.

Alamgir made a dash on the Pakistani music scene. He sang for the Pakistani television in the very beginning of his career but later as the time passed he started singing for the Pakistani music industry. He also performs abroad.

Alamgir always keeps physically fit and is currently residing in Virginia, USA. He is respected by the music lovers everywhere and still performs in live concerts in America.

Alamgir Hashmi : Alamgir Hashmi (also know as Aurangzeb Alamgir Hashmi) (born November 15, 1951) is a major English poet of the latter half of the 20th century. Considered avant-garde, both his early and later works were published to universal critical acclaim and widespread influence. His was a remarkable new voice since the 1970s; each of his successive books attested to an expanding world of cultural discernment and harmony, which he created in poems of peerless beauty.

Alamgiri Gate : The Alamgiri Gate, built in 1673 A.D., is the main entrance to the Lahore Fort in present day Pakistan. It was constructed to face west towards the Badshahi Mosque in the days of the Mughal Emperor Aurangzeb. The monumental gateway is an imposing vestibule flanked by two semi-circular bastions that have boldly fluted shafts and lotus petalled bases and are crowned with domed pavilions. The huge arched entrance in the centre was designed to allow the emperor's elephant mounted caravan to pass through. It leads to the central square hall having deep arched recesses on the east and north and a staircase leading to the upper storey buildings. The archway on the south leads to interior of the fort.

Alang : Alang is a coastal town in the State of Gujarat in India. It is a center of the ship breaking industry. The shipyards at Alang recycle about 50% of the ships salvaged in the world. The yards are located on the Gulf of Khambat, 50 kilometers southeast of Bhavnagar. Before shipbreaking began there in June 1983 the beach at Alang was pristine and unspoiled. It is now seriously contaminated with toxic substances and asbestos. Large supertankers, car ferries and container ships are beached during high tide, and as the tide recedes, hundreds of manual laborers dismantle each ship, salvaging what they can, and reducing the rest into scrap. Tens of thousands of low-paid jobs are supported by this activity, and millions of tons of steel are recovered. The salvage yards at Alang have generated controversy about working conditions, workers' living conditions, and the impact on the environment. One major problem is that despite many serious work-related injuries, the nearest full service hospital is 50 kilometers away in Bhavnagar. Alang itself is served by a small Red Cross hospital which offers only limited services.

Alaol : Alaol (1607-1680 CE) was a medieval poet in Bengal. He is thought to be born 1608 in Faridpur, Bangladesh. Perhaps his most well known work is Padmavati, which depicts the story of the Sri Lankan princess Padmavati. There is an important literary prize named after him in Bangladesh, the Alaol Puroshkar. He is widely believed to be one of the most talented of Bengali medieval poets.

Alappuzha : Alappuzha is one of the 14 districts in the state of Kerala in India. It was formed as Alleppey District on August 17, 1957. The name of the district was officially changed to Alappuzha in 1990. The district is a widely known tourist destination, and is well-known for its coir factories. Most of Kerala's coir industries are situated in and around Alappuzha. The district is also known for its communist traditions. It is home to the Punnapra Vayalar strikes against the British and also the revolt against feudal raj. Alappuzha is strongly connected by waterways to various other parts of Kerala, including the famous tourist destination, Kumarakam. It has the highest population density among all districts of the state. Alappuzha, the district headquarters, is a town with picturesque canals, backwaters and lagoons, was described as the "Venice of the East" by Lord Curzon.

Alauddin Jani : Alauddin Jani (1231-1232) governor of Bengal under Delhi Sultan iltutmish. Alauddin Jani got the Bengal assignment in 1231. He was a Shahjadah (Prince) of Turkistan. Being unable to face the terror of the Mongols, he fled to India and took service under Iltutmish in Delhi. He possessed princely qualities and was conscious of his high lineage. He remained faithful to Iltutmish. Alauddin Jani paid attention to the subjugation and administration of the country. He ruled Bengal for a period of one year and a few months.

Ala-ud-din Khilji : Ala-ud-din Khilji was the second and greatest Indian ruler of the Khilji dynasty. He reigned from 1296–1316 and was the first Muslim to rule the entirety of what is today India. Ala-ud-din was the nephew and son in law of Jalal-ud-din. In first, Jalal-ud-din appointed Ala-ud-Din as the governor of Kara. In 1296 Ala-ud-Din killed his uncle. But Malika Jahan, the widow of Jalal-ud-din, put her younger son Rukun ud din Khilji to the throne. Ala-ud-din quickly marched on Delhi from Kara. He entered Delhi with his uncle's head on a pike and on October 3, 1296, proclaimed himself the King of Delhi. Arkali Khan, Jalal-ud-din older son, and Rukun ud din were blinded. Malika Jahan was imprisoned. A few months later his general Zafar Khan defeated invading Mongols near Jalandhar in 1297 to secure his throne.

Very soon he went about despoiling the wealth of nobles, frequently blinding, imprisoning or killing them. In 1297 Allauddin sent an army to plunder Gujarat, under the generalship of Ulugh Khan and Nusrat Khan. This army looted the temple of Somnath and Shivalinga was broken into pieces and was being carried back to Delhi. Kanhad Dev Songara, ruler of Jalore attacked and defeated Ulugh Khan and captured the broken Shivalinga which was washed in Ganga-jal and the fragments were established in various temples in Jalore. Muhammad Shah a neo-Muslim helped Kanhad Dev Songara. Muhammad was a general in Khilji's army. Muhammad Shah after this war went and stayed with Hammir at Ranthambore. Ulugh Khan went and apprised Allauddin who ordered him and Nusrat Khan to conquer Ranthambore. In 1299 they started out with 80,000 cavalry and a large infantry to attack Hammir.

Hammir's army repulsed the attack and killed Nusrat Khan. Ulugh Khan escaped and reached Delhi. Khilji was taken aback by this defeat and wanted revenge. He finally came himself in 1301, and there was a long siege. Hammir was very well prepared. When the fort would not fall after repeated bloody skirmishes khilji resorted to diplomacy. Hammir was very suspicious but he heeded to his councillors who told him that sword is not always the best recourse. Ratipal and Ranmal, who were close confidants of Hammir, were sent to the khilji camp. Ranmal's father was hung by Hammir for treachery and his property was confiscated. Ranmal earned the trust of Hammir by being brave in battles that Hammir fought but perfidy was in his blood. Khilji bribed these two generals of Hammir's army and consequently Ranthambore fell. After the annexation of Gujarat, he took to the practice of making the innocent families of rebels against the government suffer. In 1299, a horde of 200,000 Mongols entered India with the intention of conquest. His general Zafar Khan showed desperate valor in battle. The Mongols were defeated, but Khan did not survive.

Ala-ud-din Khilji described himself as the Second Alexander on his own coinage and dreamt of founding a world-wide religion. Though not a man of learning himself, one of the great Persian poets of Indian history, Amir Khusro, was his poet laureate. He died in January, 1316 of edema. It is believed that his lieutenant Malik Naib hastened his death.

Al-Badr : Al-Badr a paramilitary force formed during the liberation war of Bangladesh in 1971 under the patronage of Pakistan government which was aimed at creating public opinion in favour of the integrity of Pakistan and also imparting active assistance to the occupation army in East Pakistan. Al-Badr was constituted in September 1971 with the spirit and zeal of the mujahids of the historic battle of Badr under the auspices of General Niazi, chief of the eastern command of the Pakistan army. The Pakistan army had to provide security support to the cadres of al-Badr. The razakar force formed earlier aimed at opposing the freedom fighters while al-Badr's objective was to create panic among the people by political murder. The members of Al-Badr are alleged to have been involved in the murder of distinguished intellectuals at Rayerbazar badhya-bhumi (place of execution) in Dhaka. Al-Badr as a force disintegrated with the surrender of the Pak-army on 16 December 1971.

Albert Ekka : Albert Ekka (1942-71) was a soldier in the Indian army who dies in action during the Bangladesh Liberation War of 1971. For his heroic deeds performed during that war, Albert Ekka was posthumously awarded India's highest wartime gallantry award, the Param Vir Chakra.

Albert Ekka was born on 27 December 1942, in Zari village of Ranchi tehsil of Gumla district in the Indian state of Jharkhand. His father's name was Zuluis Ekka and he hailed from a Christian family of tribal heritage. On 27 December 1962, at the age of 20, Albert was enrolled in the 14 Guards of the Indian army.

Alexander Invasion : Alexander the Great was born in Pella, Macedon, in July, 356 BC, died in Babylon, on June 10, 323 BC, King of Macedon 336–323 BC, is considered one of the most successful military commanders in world history, conquering most of the known world before his death. With the death of Spitamenes and his marriage to Roxana to cement his relations with his new

Central Asian satrapies, in 326 BC Alexander turn his attention to India. King Ambhi, ruler of Taxila, surrendered the city to Alexander. Many people had fled to a high fortress called Aornos. Alexander took Aornos by storm. Alexander fought an epic battle against Porus, a ruler of a region in the Punjab in the Battle of Hydaspes in (326 BC). After attaining victory, Alexander made an alliance with Porus and appointed him as satrap of his own kingdom. Alexander continued on to conquer all the headwaters of the Indus River.

East of Porus' kingdom, near the Ganges River, was the powerful empire of Magadha ruled by the Nanda dynasty. Exhausted by years of campaigning, his army mutinied at the Hyphasis (modern Beas), refusing to march further east. Alexander, after the meeting with his officer, Coenus, was convinced that it was better to return. Alexander was forced to turn south, conquering his way down the Indus to the Indian Ocean. He sent much of his army to Carmania (modern southern Iran) with his general Craterus, and commissioned a fleet to explore the Persian Gulf shore under his admiral Nearchus, while he led the rest of his forces back to Persia by the southern route through the Gedrosia.

Discovering that many of his satraps and military governors had misbehaved in his absence, Alexander executed a number of them as examples on his way to Susa. As a gesture of thanks, he paid off the debts of his soldiers, and announced that he would send those over-aged and disabled veterans back to Macedonia under Craterus, but his troops misunderstood his intention and mutinied at the town of Opis, refusing to be sent away and bitterly criticizing his adoption of Persian customs and dress and the introduction of Persian officers and soldiers into Macedonian units. Alexander executed the ringleaders of the mutiny, but forgave the rank and file. In an attempt to craft a lasting harmony between his Macedonian and

Persian subjects, he held a mass marriage of his senior officers to Persian and other noblewomen at Opis, but few of those marriages seem to have lasted much beyond a year.

His attempts to merge Persian culture with his Greek soldiers also included training a regiment of Persian boys in the ways of Macedonians. It is not certain that Alexander adopted the Persian royal title of shahanshah ("great king" or "king of kings"). However, most historians believe that he did. Alexander let it be known that he intended to launch a campaign against the tribes of Arabia. After they were subjugated, it was assumed that Alexander would turn westwards and attack Carthage and Italy. After traveling to Ecbatana to retrieve the bulk of the Persian treasure, his closest friend and possible lover Hephaestion died of an illness. Alexander was distraught and on his return to Babylon, he fell ill and died.

Alexander the Great : The interaction between Hellenistic Greece and Buddhism began when Alexander the Great conquered Asia Minor and the Achaemenid Empire, reaching the north west frontiers of the Indian subcontinent in 334 BC. There, he defeated King Puru in the Battle of the Hydaspes (near modern-day Jhelum, Pakistan) and conquered much of the Punjab. However, Alexander's troops refused to go beyond the Beas river, and he was forced to march his army southwest. Alexander created garrisons for his troops in his new territories, and founded several cities in the areas of the Oxus, Arachosia, and Bactria, and Macedonian/Greek settlements in Gandhara and the Punjab. The regions included the Khyber Pass — a geographical passageway south of the Himalayas and the Hindu Kush mountains — and the Bolan Pass, on a trade route connecting Drangiana, Arachosia and other Persian and Central Asian kingdoms to the lower Indus plain. It is through these regions that most of the interaction between South Asia and Central Asia took place, generating intense cultural exchange and trade.

Ali Akbar Khan : Ali Akbar Khan (born April 14, 1922) is one of today's most accomplished Indian classical musicians and known for his mastery of the sarod, a 25-stringed Indian instrument. Ali Akbar Khan's family traces its gharana (ancestral tradition) to Tansen, a 16th century musical genius and court musician of Emperor Akbar. Ali Akbar Khan's father, the late Padma Vibhushan Acharya Allauddin Khan, was acknowledged as one of the greatest Hindustani musicians of the 20th century.

Born on 14 April 1922 in Shibpur, Bengal, British India (now in Bangladesh). Ali Akbar Khan began his studies in music at the age of three. He studied vocal music from his father and drums from his uncle, Fakir Aftabuddin. His father also trained him on several other instruments, but decided finally that he must concentrate on sarod and vocal.

In 1956, he founded the 1967 the Ali Akbar College of Music in Calcutta. In 1967, he founded another school of the same name in Berkeley, California; it moved to its present location in San Rafael, California a year later. In 1985 he founded another school in Basel, Switzerland. In 1997 he received the National Endowment for the Arts' prestigious National Heritage Fellowship, the United States' highest honor in the traditional arts.

Ali Azmat : Ali Azmat born in 1970 in Lahore, Pakistan is the lead vocalist of the band Junoon. Currently, he's pursuing a solo career, and has released an album, Social Circus. Recently The Alanis Morissette Music Company has also signed up Ali Azmat.

Ali Haider : Ali Haider is a Pakistani singer and actor. He has had numerous hits in the early 90's such as Purani

Jeans and Qarar. He also had a big hit later in the 90's with Chand Sa Mukhra. Besides singing, he has acted in numerous TV serials on PTV. Among the successful dramas was Chand Sa Mukhra, which used his hit song as the theme music. He also sang the theme music for the serial Chandni Raatein. He has a large fan following in Pakistan and India and with South Asian expatriates around the world.

Ali Zafar : Ali Zafar is a popular singer based in Lahore, Pakistan. His last album Huqa Paani caused a stir in the Pakistani pop-scene and brought about the breakthrough for Ali, though he had been visible earlier on the showbiz scene having acted in a string of television serials and some music videos. The track Channo was a major hit and copies of the album Huqa Paani were sold out at the record stores in a matter of days.

Aligarh : It is a city in Uttar Pradesh state of India. Aligarh is the administrative headquarters of Aligarh District, and has a population of half a million. It is most famous for ancient lock industry. The city is located about 90 miles south-east of New Delhi. The city was originally established as a fort in the 12th century, and was known as Kol. The name was changed to Aligarh in 1776 upon the building of an important fort there. It was taken by the British in 1803. Its garrison mutinied in 1857. The remains of the ancient fort still stand 3 km north of the town. Many railway lines pass through the city connecting it to most of the important destinations in the region. Aligarh Muslim University is also located here. The city is located on a plain between the Ganges and Jumna Rivers. The Grand Trunk Road passes through the city.

Aligarh Movement : Aligarh Movement, was the movement led by Sir Syed Ahmed Khan, to educate the Muslims of the Indian subcontinent after their defeat in the freedom struggle of 1857. It had enormous success and had profound impact on the future of subcontinent. Its most significant achievement was the establishment of Muhammadan Anglo-Oriental College at Aligarh, which later became Aligarh Muslim University. This institution of excellence provided the essential man power for Pakistan Movement.

Aligarh Muslim University : Aligarh Muslim University is located in Aligarh, Uttar Pradesh, Northern India. It was among first institutions of higher learning set up in British India. Many prominent Muslim leaders, and Urdu writers and scholars of the subcontinent have attended the University. Arguably, no other educational institution in the 20th century has contributed more to the shaping of the history of the Indian sub-continent than Aligarh. The movement for creation of Pakistan was spearheaed by this University. Currently the University has almost thirty thousand students, and over two thousand faculty members with over eighty departments of study. It continues to function as an important education institution in India, and draws many foreign students.

Alinagar Treaty : Alinagar Treaty was concluded between the Bengal Nawab sirajuddaula and the English east india company on 9 February 1757. The nawab sacked the English settlement at Calcutta (18-20 June 1756) and drove them out of the city when they refused to redress his genuine grievances against them. He renamed the city as Alinagar. The reinforcement from Madras, sought by the English, arrived under the leadership of robert clive and charles watson and recaptured Calcutta. The nawab on his part marched to Calcutta but retreated when the English surprised him in an early dawn attack near Calcutta. The English asked him to sign a treaty, which he did as advised by his principal advisers and ministers. The main provisions of the treaty were: a) the nawab will allow the English all the privileges sanctioned to them by farrukh siyar's farman of 1717; b) all the English goods passing through Bengal with the company's dastak will be exempted from customs duties; c) the nawab will permit the English to fortify Calcutta without any hindrance; and d) the English will have the liberty to coin money in Calcutta.

Alisagar Deer Park : Alisagar Deer Park is located in Nizamabad district of Andhra Pradesh. The Alisagar was constructed in 1931 by the Nizam. The park is flanked by natural hillocks and lovely flower gardens, the lake and its surrounding vegitations.

Alivardi's Tomb : Alivardi's Tomb situated within a garden complex known as Khushbagh in murshidabad, West Bengal. It is one km away from the bank of the Bhagirathi and stands opposite Lalbagh Sadarghat. alivardi khan died at the age of about eighty on 9 April, 1756 (9 Rajab, 1169 AH) and was buried first within a small elevated enclosed platform near his mother's grave in the centre of the outer enclosure at Khusbagh, or the garden of Delight. Sirajuddaula, his grandson, built a mausoleum here for Alivardi and his family and thus increased the area of Khusbagh. The body was disinterred from the grave and laid in its present tomb. The magnificent garden compound consists of three walled enclosures; in the central one of which stands the mausoleum containing the tombs of Alivardi Khan, his grandson Sirajuddaula, and the principal members of their family.

Alkap Gan : Alkap Gan a regional folk performance, somewhat similar to jatra, popular in rajshahi as well as in Murshidabad, Birbhum and Maldaha, west bengal. It is a composite performance comprising acting, dancing, singing, recitation. An alkap group consists of ten to twelve artistes, led by a sarkar (master) or guru. The group also includes two or three young men called chhokras and one or two gayens or singers. The rest comprise dohar, choristers, and musicians. Alkap performances take place at night on an open stage, which is lit by lanterns, popularly known as hyajak bati. The audience stand or sit around the stage, leaving a narrow passage for the performers.

Al-Khair University : Al-Khair University is has several campuses in Pakistan. The University has established Faculty of Engineering and Faculty of Management Science at Abbottabad, which will gradually be followed by other disciplines. It has established faculties at Mirpur in Azad Kashmir, Lahore, Islamabad and Peshawar. Now the Faculty of Business Administration & Computer Science has been started at Karachi, Sukkur, and Larkana.

All India Anna Dravida Munnetra Kazhagam (AIADMK) : All India Anna Dravida Munnetra Kazhagam (AIADMK) is a regional political party in Tamil Nadu state in India. The party is headed by J. Jayalalithaa, the present chief minister of the state. The party was founded in 1972 by MG Ramachandran (popularly known as MGR), a veteran star of the Tamil film industry, and a popular politician, as a breakaway outfit from the DMK led by M Karunanidhi, the then chief minister, owing to differences between the two. The relations between the two parties have since been heavily tempered with mutual contempt.

All India Council for Technical Education (AICTE) : AICTE is the statutory body established for proper planning and co-ordinated development of the technical education system in India. It was established in November, 1945. The AICTE has its Headquarters in Indira Gandhi Sports Complex, Indraprastha Estate, New Delhi, which has the offices of the Chairman, Vice-Chairman and the Member Secretary.

All India Engineering Entrace Examination (AIEEE) : AIEEE stands for All India Engineering Entrace

Examination. It is held by the CBSE in India for admisssion to various Under-graduate courses in engineering and architecture. Entrance to top ranked colleges in India like National Institutes of Technology are through this exam.

All India Forward Bloc : The All India Forward Bloc is a leftwing nationalist political party in India. Forward Bloc was formed on 3 May 1939 by Netaji Subhash Chandra Bose who resigned from the Congress Party. During Second World War Netaji Subhash Chandra Bose led the Indian National Army against the British colonialists. The British outlawed the Forward Bloc and ransacked their offices. After the war, AIFB was reorganized. Early there was a split in the Bloc, leading to the existence of FB (Ruiker) and FB (Marxist). The party today known as AIFB is the FB (Marxist). The party should, however, not be confused with the Marxist Forward Bloc. MFB is a break-away group led by Pratim Chatterjee.

AIFB struggles for socialism in India but they consider that their ideology differs from that of Communist Party of India (Marxist) and Communist Party of India, as they build their socialism on foreign ideologues as Marx and Lenin, whereas the socialism of AIFB is the Indian socialism of Netaji. AIFB has branches throughout the country, but the main strength of the party is concentrated in West Bengal. It is part of the Left Front government in there, and Forward Bloc has various ministers in the state government. The party is also part of Left Front in Tripura, but since they've failed to win any seat in the State Assembly they don't have any minister in that government. Notably though AIFB is cooperating with CPI(M) in West Bengal, Tripura and on the national level, AIFB is not part of the Left Democratic Front in Kerala.

All India Home Rule League : The All India Home Rule League was a national political organization founded in 1916 to lead the national demand for self-government, termed Home Rule, and to obtain the status of a Dominion within the British Empire as enjoyed by Australia, Canada, the Irish Free State, South Africa, New Zealand and Newfoundland at the time Between 1916 and 1918, when the war was closing, prominent Indians like Mohammad Ali Jinnah, Bal Gangadhar Tilak and the leader of the Theosophical Society, Annie Besant decided to organize a national alliance of leagues across India, specifically to demand Home Rule, or self-government within the British Empire for all of India. Tilak founded the first League in the city of Pune, Maharashtra. Mohammad Ali Jinnah headed up the Bombay League. With its national headquarters in Delhi, the main cities of activity were Bombay, Calcutta and Madras.

The move created considerable excitement at the time, and attacted many members of the Indian National Congress and the All India Muslim League, who had been allied since the 1916 Lucknow Pact. The leaders of the League gave fiery speeches, and petitions with hundreds of thousands of Indians as signatories were submitted to British authorities. Apart from firing up college students, educated Indians and people in the cities, the Leagues elicited little response or enthusiasm from India's masses and the British government. It was often divided upon whether to follow up with public demonstrations, or compromise by contesting elections to the legislative councils that were criticized as little more than rubber stamps for the Viceroy.

Its further growth and activity were stalled by the rise of Mohandas Gandhi and his Satyagraha art of revolution: non-violent, but mass-based civil disobedience. In 1920, the All India Home Rule League elected Mahatma Gandhi as its President. In a year, the body would merge into the Indian National Congress to form a united Indian political front.

All India Institute of Medical Studies (AIIMS) : All India Institute of Medical Studies (AIIMS) is a premier medical college located at New Delhi in India. It was ranked the top medical college in India in 2001, 2003, 2004 and 2005 by India Today. Founded on the recommendations of the Bhore committee and funded by a grant from the government of New Zealand, the All India Institute of Medical Sciences (AIIMS) was established as an institution of national importance by an Act of Parliament in 1956.

The amount of sevices provided by AIIMS is truly staggering, with 1.5 million patients treated in its outpatient departments every year, and another 80,000 being treated as inpatients. Over 100,000 surgeries major and minor are performed every year. Some of India's best physicians, surgeons, researchers and young minds, with an academic environment that actively encourages free thinking, make up a stimulating milieu at AIIMS. Despite its immense contributions to India's scientific self sufficiency, increasing politicisation, fluctuant policies, inadequate nurturing of researchers and declining focus on teaching along with a dilution of its tertiary status have bogged down its progress. Given these hurdles, that many medical innovations, pioneering diagnostic and surgical interventions have come from the institution is a remarkable achievement. The Government of India plans to set up 6 institutions in all regions of the country which will function on the lines of AIIMS.

All India Majlis-e-Ittehadul Muslimeen : All India Majlis-e-Ittehadul Muslimeen (All India Council of the Union of Muslims) is a Muslim political party India. The stronghold of AIMIM is the old city of Hyderabad. In the Lok Sabha elections of 2004 the party won the seat of Hyderabad. The seat has been held by the AIMIM since 1984. In the year 2004 Lok Sabha elections AIMIM received 132807 votes (74,6%) in the Charminar area. 1984-2004 the MP of AIMIM was party president Sultan Salahuddin Owaisi, but ahead of the 2004 elections Owaisi stepped down in favour of his son Barrister Asaduddin Owaisi.

All India Muslim League : The All India Muslim League was a political party in British India and was the driving force behind the creation of Pakistan as a Muslim state from British India on the Indian subcontinent. After the independence of India and Pakistan, the League continued as a minor party in India, especially in Kerala, where it is often in government within a coalition with others. In Pakistan, the League formed the country's first government, but disintegrated during the 1950s following an army coup. One or more of factions of the Muslim League have been in power in most of the civilian governments of Pakistan since 1947.

All India Radio : All India Radio (AIR) is the radio broadcaster of India and a division of Prasar Bharati (Broadcasting Corporation of India), an autonomous corporation of the Ministry of Information and Broadcasting, Government of India. It is the sister service of Prasar Bharati's Doordarshan, the national television broadcaster. All India Radio is one of the largest radio networks in the world. The headquarters is at Akashwani Bhavan, on the Parliament Street next to the Indian parliament. Akashwani Bhavan houses the drama section, the FM section and the National service. The Doordarshan Kendra (Delhi) is also located on the 6th floor of Akashwani Bhavan.

Broadcasting house is an old building next to Akashwani Bhavan. The New Service Division of All India Radio under the Director General (New functions) from this building. Built during the British rule, it is a very popular location and easily recognised building in New

Delhi. Radio broadcasting began in India in 1927, with two privately-owned transmitters at Mumbai and Calcutta. These were nationalised in 1930 and operated under the name Indian Broadcasting Service until 1936, when it was renamed All India Radio (AIR). Although officially renamed again to Akashvani in 1957, it is still popularly known as All India Radio.

AIR covers 99.37% of India's populace, the largest democracy in the world with over one billion inhabitants. AIR maintains approximately 200 broadcasting centres around the country and transmits in 24 different languages. In spite of recent penetration by other media such as Cable TV, AIR remains the most common means of gaining access to information and entertainment, as the radio receivers are relatively cheap and affordable.

All Parties Hurriyat Conference : The All Parties Hurriyat Conference (formed March 9, 1993) is a political front formed by the alliance of 26 political, social and religious organizations in Kashmir. It is a political front created to further the cause of Kashmiri separatism. The Hurriyat is regarded widely as the representative of Kashmiri people, an organisation trying to put the Kashmiri view on the table. It includes parties like Yaseen Malik's Jammu and Kashmir Liberation Front (JKLF), Shabir Shah's People's Democratic Front etc.

Allah Rakha : Ustad Allah Rakha (April 29, 1919 - February 3, 2000) was a master of the tabla, a classical Hindustani percussion instrument. Ustad Alla Rakha is considered one of the great tabla players of the 20th century. His legendary and spellbinding performances with Ravi Shankar at the Monterey Pop Festival in 1967 and the Woodstock Festival in 1969 served to introduce classical Indian music to general Western audiences.

Leading American percussionists in Rock n' Roll, such as the Grateful Dead's Mickey Hart, admired him and studied his technique, benefiting greatly even from single meetings. Hart, a published authority on percussion in world music, is said to have referred to Alla Rakha as "the Einstein of Rhythm." His son, Zakir Hussain is also an accomplished tabla virtuoso.

Allahabad : It is a city in the Indian state of Uttar Pradesh. The name, meaning "City of Allah", was given to the city by the Mughal Emperor Akbar in 1583. In Indian alphabets it is spelt "Ilahabad": "ilah" is Arabic for "god", and "-abad" is Persian for "place of". The modern city is on the site of the ancient holy city of Prayaga. It is one of four sites of the Kumbha Mela, the others being Haridwar, Ujjain and Nasik. It has a position of importance in the Hindu religion and mythology since it is situated at the confluence of the rivers Ganga, Yamuna, and the mythical Saraswati. Because solar events in Allahabad occur exactly 5 hours and 30 minutes ahead of Greenwich, the city is the reference point for Indian Standard Time, maintained by the city's observatory.

Allahabad Address : Allahabad Address was the Presidential Address by Allama Iqbal to the 25th Session of the All-India Muslim League on 29 December 1930, at Allahabad. Here he presented the idea of a separate homeland for Indian Muslims which was ultimately realised in the form of Pakistan

Allai : Allai is a valley bounded by Kohistan on the north and east, by the Bhogarmang valley, Nandhiar and Deshi of Deshiwals on the south, and by the Indus on the West. The valley of Allai is divided from Kohistan on the north by a range of maountains rising to over 15000 feet, and from Nandhiar and Deshi by another range running from the then British boundary to the Indus above Thakot. The average breadth of the Allai Valley is about fifteen miles, and the total area 200 square miles. Wheat, barley, Indian corn and rice are grown, and the mountain slopes at the eastern end covered with forest. Cis-Indus Swatis are the dominating tribes of the Allai range.

Allama Badruddin: Allama Badruddin(14th century) Sufi preacher, variously known as Shah Badar, Badar Awlia and Badar Pir. Almost every account of Hazrat shah jalal (R) and the 360 Awlias contains some reference to Badar Shah and his shrine in chittagong. Following the instructions of Hazrat Shah Jalal (R), Badar Shah and the twelve Awlias defeated King Achak Narayan of Taraf and established Muslim rule there. Badar Shah then started to spread the message of islam in Chittagong. Several places in Chittagong are associated with him: Badartila, Badarkhali, Badarkua and Badar Mokam. In 1340 Badar Shah helped kadal khan gazi, the general of fakruddin mubarak shah, to capture Chittagong.

The original name of Chittagong, Chattagram, is believed to have derived from the word chati or lamp. According to the legend, in the fourteenth century Chittagong was overrun by jinns and fairies who made the lives of ordinary people miserable. Badar Shah drove off these supernatural creatures by lighting a chati. Several medieval poets, such as daulat uazir bahram khan, Mohammad Khan and muhammad mukim, have mentioned Badar Shah in their poems. Shihabuddin Talish, the seventeenth-century historian, mentions Badar Shah's shrine in Chittagong in Fatiya-i-Ibriza. Badar Shah's Urs is celebrated annually at his shrine in Badarpatti on 29 ramadan.

Allama Iqbal International Airport : Allama Iqbal International Airport (IATA) is located in Lahore, Punjab, Pakistan. It was formerly called Lahore International Airport. It is named after Allama Iqbal who was a major proponent for the foundation of Pakistan. The Airport has 3 terminals, the Allama Iqbal terminal, the Hajj terminal, and a cargo terminal.

Allama Iqbal Medical College : The Government's initiative in the mid seventies to establish new seats of learning to spur medical education and research in Pakistan helped to materialize the aspirations of the teachers to open new vistas for community oriented medical education. Consequently this institution was established on May 2, 1975 as Lahore Medical College. Two years later, the College was renamed Allama Iqbal Medical College to commemorate the centenary celebrations of the great philosopher.

Allama Iqbal Open University : Allama Iqbal Open University is located at Islamabad, Pakistan. Allama Iqbal Open University started as a language institute in 1974. During the last 30 years, the university has matured into a national university offering various programmes through non-formal education system throughout the country. The main objectives of the university as communicated in the act are to provide facilities to people who cannot leave jobs and home for their educational uplift. It offers a wide range of undergraduate, graduate, masters, MPhil and doctoral programmes in the area of teacher education, science, business management, languages, and computer science. The university has also developed a number of short term educational programmes. At present AIOU relies heavily on various types of available media to teach the students in an effective manner.

Allama Muhammad Iqbal : Allama Muhammad Iqbal (November 9, 1877–April 21, 1938), was a Muslim philosopher, poet, Islamic scholar, politician, lawyer, and reformer who worked for the unity of Muslims, and was the spiritual father of Pakistan. His philosophical works are in Urdu, Persian, and English, and have also been translated into many other languages. Along with his other works his book, The Reconstruction of Religious Thought in Islam which is a compilation of his lectures in English, have been an important contribution to Islamic philosophy in the twentieth century.

As a forerunner of Pakistan movement, he headed the All-India Muslim League in early 1930s and called upon Muhammad Ali Jinnah to lead Indian Muslims towards an independent Muslim state. He never saw Pakistan and died nine years before its creation. He is commonly called Allama Iqbal, and is also known as Muffakir-e-Pakistan ("The Thinker of Pakistan"), Hakeem-ul-Ummat ("The Sage of Ummah"), and Shair-i-Mashriq ("The Poet of the East"). His birthday on November 9th is each year commemorated in Pakistan as Iqbal Day, and is a national holiday.

Allan Fakir : Allan Fakir, a Pakistani folk singer is a legendary and one of the foremost exponents of sufi music in Pakistan. He is particularly known for his ecstatic style of performance marked with extreme devotional rhetoric and sufi dance singing. His peculiarly funny body language and distinctively pleasing facial expressions marked with a broad smile, were always amusing for his audience at live performances.

Allan Octavian Hume : Allan Octavian Hume son of Joseph Hume was a Scottish civil servant and political reformer. He was the founder of the Indian National Congress. He was described by Dr. Salim Ali as the father of Indian Ornithology.

A O Hume was an administrator with a deep insight and understanding of the problems of rural India. He was a friend of Indian peasantry, the champion of the aspirations of the Indian people for self- government and the foremost advocate of India's unity and nationhood. Hume has carved out for himself a place of affection in the hearts of the Indian people. Joining the Bengal Civil Service at 20 in the year 1849, Hume spent 45 years of his life serving the Indian people.

In 1883 he initiated moves for the creation of a political organisation of the Indian people through which they could approach the British Government for constitutional reform and better treatment. It was at the initiative of Mr. Hume that the Indian National Congress was founded in 1885. Having launched the first constitutional battle, Hume worked for the promotion of India's cause abroad. He helped to start a journal called "India" in 1890, which became a weekly by 1898. As a government officer, he utilized every opportunity to do something constructive in social and economic terms. As a free man, he threw in his lot even more passionately with the Indian people. In 1894, he left India but continued his mission for the next 18 years in England. When he died at the age of 84, on July 31, 1912 the people of India mourned his death as he was one of them.

Alla-uddin Khan : Ustad Alla-Uddin Khan of Tripura holds an important place among the Hindustani classical Maestros of Indian music. From his childhood he had great devotion towards music, his unquenchable urge for music forced him to leave his home when he was eight. He mastered his great talents under the guidance of Nanu Gopal, Nandlal and Vazir Khan. The musician in him was so great that, he was awarded 'Padma Bushan' in 1958 and in 1971 'Padma Vibhushan'. He dedicated his life to music and he joined with Udaya Shankar the famous dancer in stage shows which brought him fame. His contribution to music is remembered every year during the All India Music Festival. The effort taken by him from his childhood in spite of facing many hardships made him attain mastery in the field. His life is a symbol of the fact that one can reach the peak if one works with unabated efforts.

Alley Yate : It is basically the dance of shepherds of Zanskar area of Ladakh region in Kashmir. It is a combination of poetry and dance. This dance is peculiar to the time when people go out of their homes with flocks.

Alliance for Restoration of Democracy (ARD) : The Alliance for Restoration of Democracy (ARD) is an opposition group in Pakistan. It campaigns for a return to civilian rule after the 1999 military coup. The two main political parties involved are PML-N (Pakistan Muslim League (N)) and PPPP (Pakistan People's Party Parliamentarians). Both are remnants of the political parties that ruled Pakistan from 1988-1999 and are severely hampered by their corrupt and abusive time in power. Their resistance to the Musharraf government is limited to severe criticism in the press and attempts to disrupt parliament. Anti-government cmapaigns run by the ARD have been total failures.

Almora : Almora is the cultural and geographic centre the Kumaun region, approximately 80km north of the railhead at Kathgodam. Founded in in 1560 by Kalyan Chand, the town still retains a medieval flavour best seen along the flagstone paved market that runs along the ridge that bisects the town. Walking along the market it's easy to see the influences of the many cultures that have contributed to the towns development. The buildings with elaborately carved wooden facades date back to the Chand dynasty. The small, simple wooden buildings near the military base are from the Nepali occupation of the town (1760-1817). The buildings with elaborately carved wooden facades that incorporate coloured glass and pressed metal were built during the British occupation for "natives". Many fine Raj era buildings are to be found, most prominently "Ramsey School". Some very unfortunate Indian buildings do intrude onto the market.

Almora sits at an altitude of 1645m on a ridge that projects off from the much larger Almora Massif. The views onto the main Himalaya are limited from the town itself but a short stroll up to Simtola Top (3.8km)or Kesar Devi (6.7km) rewards you with a fantastic 400km view of the mountains all the way from Api in Nepal to Bandarpunch on the Himanchal border. Most foreigners choose to stay up on the ridge above town colloquially known as Crank's Ridge. Named for the many gentle lunatics who have made it their home over the years.

Aloo Gobi : Aloo gobi (or alu gobi) is usually a "dry" Indian curry, i.e. it often does not have a liquid sauce. It is a popular combination of aloo (potato) and gobi (cauliflower) with spices. It is yellowish in color, due to the use of spices such as turmeric, and may contain onion seeds and curry leaves. A number of variations and similar dishes exist. It is a common staple of Indian buffets in North America.

Alpha Leporis : Alpha Leporis is the brightest star in the constellation Lepus. It also has the traditional name Arneb.Alpha Leporis is an older, dying star that may have already passed through a supergiant phase and is now contracting and heating up in the latter phases of stellar evolution, or perhaps is still expanding into the supergiant phase. With a mass of likely less than 10 times that of the Sun, it will likely end its life as a hot white dwarf, although if it is at the heavier end of its estimated mass it may end in a spectacular stellar explostion known as a supernova.

Alqadeer : Alqadeer is the official magazine of KRL Model College Kahuta Pakistan. It is published in English and Urdu Languages. It was pioneered in 1996. Its first editors were Prof Khalid Mahmood and Prof Waliastaan. Principal Mehr Ali Siddiki was the chief editor. In every edition 1000 copies are published. It represents the college : its creative, sports and other activities. Students show their talent here. In 2004 its last and 6th edition was published. The editors for the last magazine were Prof Ayesha, Prof Khalid Mahmood and Hina Tarar.'

Altaf Husain : Altaf Husain was an eminent journalist from Pakistan.

He was the founding Editor of Dawn Newspaper and played an important part in Pakistan movement.

Altaf Shakoor : An engineer by education and trader by profession, Altaf Shakoor is the leader of Pasban (The Defenders), a Pakistani socio-political organization which has its famous slogan "Pasban.... Voice against injustice". Born in Karachi in 1959, he closely studied the aimless political system and deep rooted exploitation in Pakistani society. He was elected as the president of students union in N.E.D. University of engineering and technology Karachi (1981-82) and was a very popular student leader of that time. He has unique cadre of workers in Pasban, mainly educated youth who want to uproot the remote control political system of Pakistan, governed by feudal s, army generals and establishment. He stresses upon the basic political education and to organize the masses at grassroots level before any movement of struggle to change the system is started.

Aluva : Aluva is a town north of Kochi in Ernakulam district of Kerala state in South India. It is one of the more industrialised town in Kerala. It is famous for the Aluva Sivarathri festival at Manal Puram (land with sand) on the banks of Periyar River.It has lost its importance nowadays because of the Bye Pass which was opened a couple of decades back. Now the vehichles on the National Highway do not need to pass through Aluva. It is located 12 km from the Cochin International Airport. Aluva also is the home for several Advaitha Ashramas. It is also the headquarters of the Federal Bank, a large Private Bank in India.

Alwar : Alwar is a city in the Rajasthan state of western India. It is the administrative headquarters of Alwar District, and was formerly the capital of the princely state of Alwar or Ulwar in British India. The princely state of Alwar was founded by Pratap Singh, a Rajput of ancient lineage, in the second half of the 18th century. His adopted son, Bakhtawar Singh, aided the British against the Marathas, and after the battle of Laswari (1803), signed a treaty of alliance with the British East India Company. A few years later, he ventured an armed incursion into neighbouring Jaipur, another similar vassal of the British, and was defeated; a fresh engagement was made, prohibiting him from political intercourse with other states without British consent. In 1857 Raoraja Bane Singh sent a force of Muslims and Rajputs to relieve the British garrison in Agra. The Muslims however deserted; the rest were defeated by the rebels.

Following the independence of India in 1947, Alwar acceded into India, and later merged with three other princely states of eastern Rajputana to form the Matsya Union on March 18, 1948. The union merged with certain other princely states and the federal territory of Ajmer to form the present-day Indian state of Rajasthan on May 15, 1949. Alwar is famous for its Sariska National Sanctuary, which until they were lost to poachers in 2005, was home to wild tigers. Alwar is an industrial centre for the region, and has a military cantonment named Itarana.

Al-Zulfiqar : Al-Zulfiqar was a leftist insurgency and terrorist organization of Pakistan. It was formed in the late seventies by the sons of former Pakistani Prime Minister, Zulfiqar Ali Bhutto, who was also the Chairman of Pakistan's biggest political party, Pakistan Peoples Party. Al-Zulfiqar was formed to avenge the killing of Bhutto by the right-wing military regime of General Mohammad Zia-ul-Haq in 1976. Zia had deposed the populist Bhutto regime in a Military coup in July 1976.

Bhutto was hanged by the Zia regime after a one-sided and controversial trial, Bhutto's two sons, Murtaza Bhutto and Shahnawaz Bhutto went into exile in Afghanistan which was then being ruled by a Soviet-backed communist government. There the two sons formed the Al-Zulfiqar along with hundreds of Pakistan Peoples Party militants who had escaped Zia's persecution.

The Al-Zulfiqar which was being funded by the Soviet-backed government in Kabul, staged a string of political assassinations, bank robberies and bombings before pulling off its most daring act when in 1981 it hijacked a Pakistan International Airlines flight from Peshawar to Kabul. The Al-Zulfiqar also attempted to assassinate Zia on a number of occasions and it made an attempt to bomb a rally in Karachi held in honour of the Pope who was visiting Pakistan in 1980.

Murtaza folded the organization's operations in Kabul when his younger brother, Shahnawaz Bhutto, died suddenly in Paris in 1985, allegedly from poisoning. Both Benazir and Murtaza insisted that he was poisoned by his young Afghan wife who had become an agent of Pakistan's notorious intelligence agency, the ISI. Murtaza eventually moved to Syria and continued low-key Al-Zulfiqar operations from there. He returned to Pakistan in 1993 after his sister became the Prime Minister of the country for the second time. However, he returned not to join Banazir, but to oppose her and form his own faction of the Pakistan People's Party. He accused Banazir and her husband, Asif Ali Zardari, of corruption and moving away from the party's original Socialist agenda. In 1997, Murtaza was assassinated by a group of police guards when they fired on his convoy of cars in Karachi. The police said that Murtaza's armed guards had fired upon them first. Murtaza supporters believe Asif Ali Zardari ordered his assassination.

Aman Setu : A key bridge on the Line of Control near Uri. The literal meaning of Aman Setu is "a bridge of peace" and it is derived from the Urdu word, aman, meaning 'peace' and a Hindi word setu, which means a 'bridge'. A part of the Aman Setu on the Srinagar-Muzaffarabad road has sunk due to the massive earthquake that hit the region.

Amar Nath : On the South of the Valley, the peaks of Amar Nath and Kolahoi springing from the same massif are found prominent in Kashmir. Amar Nath stands 17, 321 feet high and Kolahoi 17,800 feet. Kolahoi is also known as Gwash Brari. At dawn the radiant rays of the sun fall on this cone-like peak and the lurid glare of the dazzling snows is a sight. Here and there on this range, one is attracted by wild graceful flowers, wild roses, poppies, anemones and hosts of other unknown floral varieties. Shri Amar Nath is a famous ancient shrine.

It is interesting to observe the colors these ranges richly display at certain hours of the day. For its fresh-water lakes and tarns, Kashmir is known all the world over. Those lying in the valley against the charming mountain background are : the Wular Lake, the Dal Lake and the Manasbal lake. The Wular is the largest fresh-water lake in India and according to some, perhaps in Asia too. It lies to the north-cast of the valley with mountains overlooking it.

Amar Shonar Bangla : Amar Shonar Bangla (My Golden Bengal) is a song written and composed by esteemed poet Rabindranath Tagore,. Even though the word Shonar means golden, the expression Shonar Bangla means precious Bengal. The first 10 lines of the song constitute the national anthem of Bangladesh. It was adopted in 1972. The song was written in 1906. The English translation was done by Syed Ali Ahsan. The song was written during the period of Bangabhanga (Bengali—

1905 Partition of Bengal)—when Bengal was divided in two halves by the British government based on religion. This song, along with a host of others, was written to rekindle the unified spirit of Bengal. It is said that the music of the song ws inspired by the Baul singer Gagan Harkara.

Amararama : Amararama is one of the Pancharama Kshetras which is located at Amaravati town near Guntur city in Andhra Pradesh in South India. Lord Shiva is known as Amareswara Swamy or Amaralingeswara Swamy here. The temple is situated on the southern bank of Krishna River. The consort of Lord Amareswara Swamy is Bala Chamundika. The Sivalinga at this place is installed and established by Lord Indra. Maha Shivaratri is the main festival celebrated at this temple.

Amaravathi Reservoir : Amaravathi Reservoir is created by a dam in the district of Coimbatore, India. The steep Amaravathi dam across the river Amaravathi about 25 km from Thirumoorthy Dam. There is a well laid-out park and on climbing the steep dam on steps, one can have a picturesque view. There is a crocodile farm nearby and many crocodiles of all sizes can be seen basking in the sun and suddenly making a stride or piled up on one another.

Amaravati : Amaravati is an important tourist centre in Andhra Pradesh at a distance of 32 km north-west of Guntur owing to its world famous Buddhist stupa and antiquities of the 2nd century B.C. The Stupa here is the biggest with its dome measuring 49 metres and it rises to a height of 29 metres. Amaravati is a byword for sculpture among the plastic arts of the world as the Buddhist sculptures found here are perfect specimens of what is called the Andhra or Amaravati style of sculptures.

Amaravati and its neighbouring village Dharanikota were the seats of the rule of the Satavahanas and these places are full of antiquities of great archaeological values depicting scenes from the life of Buddha, embodying various Buddhist emblems and symbols, and also inscriptions in Pali character. The lofty temple of Amareswara stands on the southern bank of the river Krishna, and is considered sacred and holy. It attracts a large number of pilgrims, especially on the Sivaratri day.

Amaravati River : The Amaravati River is a tributary of Kaveri River in southern India. The Amaravati river begins in the Anjanda valley of Kerala State in India, between the Annamalai Hills and the Palni Hills. It descends in a northerly direction and widens at Kallapuram, the mouth of the Ajanda valley in Udumalpet. It joins with the Kaveri in Karur.

Amarkantak : Amarkantak is a unique natural heritage area in eastern Madhya Pradesh, India. It is located in Anuppur District. This is the meeting point of the Vindhyas and the Satpuras, with the Maikal Hills being the fulcrum. This is the place from where the Narmada River emerges. It is not only the Narmada which arises from Amarkantak, because the Son River, initially referred to as Jwalawanti of Johila, the Mahanadi and the Amadoh, which is a major early tributary of the Godavari, all rise from within the Amarkantak plateau.

As the source of the Narmada, which is more than 150 million years older than the Ganga and is considered by many Hindus to be the most sacred for all the rivers of India, Amarkantak itself is sacred to the Hindus and is deemed to be a door-way to 'nirwana'. In these hills dwell some of the most primitive of the Madhya Pradesh tribals, the Hill Korwas and Pandavas. Even today the Pandavas run away if they see any strangers approaching their village.

Geologically the Amarkantak Hills have underlying basalt (Deccan Traps). The overburden consists of bauxite and laterite, making the soil ferruginous and clayey, with an acidic or neutral reaction. There is schist and gneiss, which is why sal is to be found here despite underlying trap. Climatically Amarkantak is temperate.

Amarnath Cave : Shri Amarnath Cave situated at a height of 6000 metres above sea level is 49 Kms. from Pahalgam in Kashmir. There is a bridle path from Pahalgam to Shri Amarnath Cave. The cave is 9 metres deep and is 14 metres high in the middle. The cave is made of gypsum. Thousands of pilgrims visit the holy Shivling every year on the festival of Rakshabandan. In the cave there are idols of Shiva, Parvati and Ganesh.

Amarnathyatra : It is celebrated in the month of Shravan (July -August) each year and lasts for approximately 40 days. Thousands of pilgrims make an arduous trek up to the Amarnath cave, located at a height of 3,888 m in the Kashmir Himalayas through rocky terrains, snowy mountains under unpredictable weather conditions. They come to worship the sacred ice 'lingam' —a phallic symbol of Lord Shiva, which is a natural phenomenon and considered a miracle.

Amarnath yatra started in the year 1850 AD. Devotees believe that one can get salvation by witnessing 'Shiv lingam'. There are several legends behind its origin. It was a Muslim shephered, Buta Malik who discovered the cave and the naturally formed shiv lingam. According to popular belief, Buta malik was given a sack of coal by a sadhu. But when he open the sack at home, he found that it was full of gold. Overjoyed he went back to thank the sadhu but found the cave on the spot where they met. From then on the cave was venerated as a pilgrimas centre and a representative from the Malik family would be present at the holy shrine along with the Hindu priest during the time of the pilgrimage. It is said that Lord Shiva recounted the secret of creation to *Parvati* in this cave which was overheard by a pair of doves who became immortal an`d made this cave their eternal abode. Pilgrims still report seeing these doves at the cave.

Amartya Sen : Amartya Kumar Sen, son of Amita Sen and Ashutosh Sen, was born on 3rd November 1933 at Shantiniketan, West Bengal. He received his initial education at Shantiniketan and then Presidency College, Calcutta. He was exposed early on to the plight of the poor. As a 10-year old child, during the Bengal famine, he was shocked to see people dying of hunger on the streets of Calcutta yards away from shops stocked with food. Three years later in Dhaka a Muslim labourer was killed in communal riots outside his house. The traumatic incidents directed Sen to a relentless study of the economic mechanism underlying famines and poverty.

Amartya Sen joined Trinity College, Cambridge in 1953. He became the youngest chairman of the Department of Economics, Jadavpur University, at the age of 23. Between 1956-1998 he was Professor of Economics at various Universities in India and abroad.

Sen's contributions on welfare economics and definition of poverty in relation to development have offered a new philosophy and an alternative way to solid economic development. He was of the opinion that the World Bank system of ranking countries according to the GNP and saving rates was not enough and he helped to create the United Nations Human Development Index which has now become the most authoritative international source of welfare comparisons between countries. Some of his works include ' Choice of Techniques', ' Collective Choice and Social Welfare', ' Poverty and Famines', ' Development as Freedom' etc.

Sen is the sixth Indian to get the Nobel and the first Asian winner of the Economics Prize. Some of the honours to his credit are 'Indira Gandhi Gold Medal Award' of the Asiatic Society (1994), 'Nobel prize for Economics' (1998) for his work on ' The poorest people in Society', 'Eisenhower Medal' from USA (2000), 'Honorary Companion of Honour' from UK (2000). He also received 'Bharat Ratna', the highest civilian award in India. He has been honored with Honorary D.Litt degrees and fellowships of a large number of Indian and Foreign Universities and Institutes of repute. Now living in Cambride, Massachusetts with his third wife, an economic historian Emma Rothschild, this genius has spent a lifetime fighting poverty with analysis rather than activism.

Amb : Amb was a small princely state in what is today the North-West Frontier Province of Pakistan. The state ceased to exist in 1969, when it was merged with the province of West Pakistan. Amb was originally known as Tanawal and was the tribal homeland of the Tanoli people. The Nawabs of the Tanolis were best known for fighting against the Sikhs under Ranjit Singh.

Ambala : Ambala is a city located on the border of the states of Haryana and Punjab in India. Politically and geographically Ambala has two sub-areas: Ambala Cantt (cantonment) and Ambala City, a few kilometers apart from each other. It has a large army and air-force base within the confines of its cantonment area. Due to its geographical location, the Ambala District plays an important role in local tourism. It is the main entry to Haryana for the tourists of Punjab, Himachal, Jammu Kashmir and the union territory Chandigarh; and vice-versa. Though Ambala falls in the Haryana state, much of the population is Punjabi. It is this example that is most often feted by true Punjabis, and by Sikhs in particular, of the injustices committed by the Indian Government in the States Reorganisation Act of 1962. The overwhelming majority of Ambala's population are Punjabi speaking, with there being a very significant population of Sikhs, comprising anywhere between 35-40% of the population.

But, with the course of time, Ambala has been successful in building an identity of its own, and securing a place in some of the fast developing cities of Haryana. As per ancient Indian history, Aryan people had resided at Ambala at some point in time and during the middle century, there was a very popular place called Sarudhna near Ambala, which was the country's capital at that time. Ambala was given the status of a district during British rule, in the year 1847.

Ambalappuzha Sri Krishna Temple : Ambalappuzha Sri Krishna Temple is a Hindu temple in Ambalappuzha, Alapuzha district of kerala, south India. The Ambalappuzha Sri Krishna Temple is believed to have been built in the in the year 790 M.E by the local ruler Chembakasserry Pooradam Thirunal-Devanarayanan Thampuran. This temple is directly associated to the Guruvayoor Sri Krishna Temple. During the raids Tipu Sultan in 1789, the idol of Sri Krishna from the Guruvayoor Temple was brought to the Ambalappuzha Temple for safe keeping. The payasam served in the Ambalappuzha Temple is famous among Hindu devotees. This sweet pudding made of rice and milk has an interesting mythological legend behind it.

Ambapali : Ambapali (about 500 BC), also called Amrapali, was a royal courtesan of the republic state of Vaishali, ancient India. She finds mention in the old Pali texts and Buddhist traditions. Etymologically, Ambapali or Amrapali is derived from two Sanskrit words, "amra" meaning mango and "pali", which means leaves – thus, the literally meaning of her name is "(a child) of the mango grove". She was so named, as she was of unknown parentage, and was found at the foot of a mango tree, at one of the royal gardens of the republic state of Vaishali.

Ambapali grew to be a lady of unsurpassed beauty, charm and grace and many young nobles of the republic wished for her company. Ultimately, to avoid confrontation, she was accorded the status of the state courtesan of the then metropolis of Vaishali, the capital city of the republic of Vaishali. Stories of her beauty traveled to the Magadha empire, a hostile neighbour of the republic state of Vaishali, and Bimbisara, the Magadha emperor became infatuated with her and she also bore a son to him, named Vimala Kondanna. Before meeting her, to combat her raving beauty, king Bimbisara was constrained to appoint a parallel courtesan for his capital city of Rajgir. Bimbisara is said to have married her during an incognito visit during his invasion of Vaishali.

Ambapali once desired to have the privilege to serve food to the Buddha. The Buddhist traditions state that the invitation was accepted by the Buddha, much against the wishes of the ruling aristocracy of Vaishali state. Ambapali received Buddha with her retinue, which was comparable to royal paraphernalia. The Buddha accepted the meals. Soon thereafter, Ambapali renounced her position of courtesan and accepted Buddhist faith, and remained an active supporter of the Buddhist order. Her son by Bimbisra too became a monk.

Amber Fort and Palace : It is one of the most magnificent destinations in Jaipur located on the hills just 11km out of Jaipur. It was built by Raja Man Singh in 1600 AD, continued by Raja Jai Singh and then completed to its present form by Sawai Jai Singh in the eighteenth century. The fort is an example of a fascinating blend of Hindu and Muslim architecture built in red sandstone and white marble.

Ambikapur : Ambikapur is a small town in the state of Chhattisgarh in India. It is the capital town of Surguja district, the largest district of Chhattisgarh. The district of

Surguja is spread over an area of 22,237 km2, and is rich in forests. Most of the terrain of the district is forested and hilly. Major tourist areas near Ambikapur are Ramgarh, Kudargarh, Dipadih, Rakasganda, Sitabengara, Tattapani and Semarsot. Ambikapur is inhabited by people from all over the country. Moderate weather and a serene environment make it an ideal place for settlement. Unlike the capital town, major district population comprises of aboriginal population. Among these indigenous tribes are the Pandos and Korwas, who are still living in rural areas.

Ambukuthi Mala : Ambukuthi mala is the tallest mountain in the Wayanad district of Kerala, India. It is 12 km from Sulthan Bathery and near Ambalavayal. Three pre-historic caves (Edakkal Caves) are located at a height of 1000 mts on Ambukuthi mala. You have to get down at Edakkal and do a 1 km trekking to reach these caves. One can see the new stone age pictorial writings on the walls of these natural caves.

Amin Gulgee : Amin Gulgee (born 1966) is a Pakistani artist and sculptor. He is the son of the famous Pakistani artist Ismail Gulgee. He was actively discouraged from pursuing fine art by his father, and he earned a degrees in Economics and Art History from Yale University. Nonetheless, Gulgee ended up as an artist, creating works as an expression of spirituality. Gulgee works primarily with metal, creating scuptures and jewelry. His work has been inspired by Hindu and Buddhist mythology as well as Arabic calligraphy.

Amini : Amini is an island atoll in the Union Territory of Lakshadweep, India. Its total size is: 7.0 square miles. It was one of the first islands in the archipelago to be inhabited. The artistans on this island are known for making walking sticks out of coconut shells and tortoise shells as well as carved stone and coral motifs.

Amir Abdullah Khan Niazi : Amir Abdullah Khan Niazi (1915 - February 2, 2004) was a Pakistani military commander who was notable for surrendering to Indian forces in the 1971 Indo-Pakistani War. Born to a Pathan family in the Punjab, Niazi enlisted in the British Indian Army as a junior officer, and fought well during World War II. He would join the newly-formed Pakistani Army after independence in 1947 and quickly rose through the ranks, earning various awards including the Hilal-e-Jurat twice. By 1971 he had reached the rank of Lieutenant-General. He was sent in that year to East Pakistan in April following a Pakistani military crack down on Bengali intellectuals.

The crack-down against the Bengalis had gone too far, and the result saw Pakistani forces involved in a guerrilla war with Bengali Mukti Bahini who were aided by India. This would lead to later Indian involvement in the conflict, and a full-scale invasion of the Eastern wing of Pakistan by India, resulting in isolation for Niazi's forces, and with the absence of external aid, eventual surrender.

On December 16, 1971, General Niazi surrendered all Pakistani forces in East Pakistan to Indian General Jagjit Singh Aurora. Niazi along with a sizeable number of Pakistani soldiers were taken prisoner (upwards of 90,000). This was the largest number of POWs since WWII and included some government officials. Many would not be freed until two years later, with Niazi symbolically being the last prisoner of war to cross back to Pakistan. Such actions symbolized his reputation as a "soldier's general" but did not shield him from the scorn he faced upon his return to Pakistan, where he was made a scapegoat for the humiliating defeat to arch rivals India.

Amir Hamza : Amir Hamza was a popular medieval narrative poem describing the victories of the legendary warrior hero Amir Hamza. Abdul Nabi of chittagong was the first to compose Amir Hamza (1684) in Bangla based on the Persian text, Dastan-i-Amir Hamza. He was followed by Fakir Garibullah and syed hamza who jointly composed a poem on the same subject. The first part of their monumental work consisting of 70 episodes was composed by Garibullah towards the middle of the 18th century. The remaining part was completed by his disciple Syed Hamza in 1794. This version, written in Dobasi Bangla cheaply printed, became more popular than Abdul Nabi's poem, which was in manuscript.

Amir Khusro : Abul Hasan Yaminuddin Khusro (1253-1325 CE), better known as Amir Khusro Dehlavi, is one of the iconic figures in the cultural history of the Indian subcontinent. He was born in Patiali, Etah (Uttar Pradesh). In 1272 he got his first job as court poet with King Balban's nephew Malik Chhajju. In 1276 he started working as a poet with Bughra Khan (Balban's son). In 1287, Khusro want to Awadh with Ameer Ali Hatim. In 1288 his first historical Mathnavi Qiranus-Sa'dain was completed. In 1310, Khusro came close to Nizamuddin Aulia. In 1325, Sultan Muhammad bin Tughluq came to power. Nizamuddin Aulia expired; and so did Khusro after six months.

A Sufi mystic and a spiritual disciple of Nizamuddin Auliya of Delhi, Amir Khusro was not only one of India's greatest poets, he is also credited with being the founder of both Hindustani classical music and Qawwali. His tomb is located next to that of his master in the Nizamuddin Dargah of Delhi. He was a prolific classical poet associated with royal courts of more than seven rulers of the Delhi Sultanate. He is also popular in much of North India and Pakistan, because of many playful riddles, songs and legends attributed to him. Through his enormous literary output and the legendary folk personality, Khusrau represents one of the first Indian personages with a true multi-cultural or pluralistic identity. He wrote in both Persian and Hindustani. His poetry is still sung today at Sufi shrines throughout Pakistan and India. His work was considered to be one of the great classics of Persian poetry during the Timurid period in Transoxiana.

Amirul Islam : Amirul Islam (1918-2001) wasscientist and educationist of Bangladesh. Born in Noakhali on 1 September 1918, Amirul Islam passed Matriculation examination in 1936 and Intermediate examination in 1938. He obtained first division in both examinations. Amirul Islam secured first class in BSc (Honours) and MSc respectively in 1941 and 1942 in Chemistry from Dhaka University. He was the first Muslim student to obtain first class in honours in Chemistry from Dhaka University. He obtained PhD in Soil Science from the University of California, USA, in 1949. He served as Director of bangladesh rice research institute (BRRI) from 1973 to 1977 and developed the institute as a centre of excellence. In recognition of his commendable service to BRRI, the Board of Governors of BRRI named its laboratory as 'Amirul Islam Laboratory'.

Amitabh Bachchan : Amitabh Bachchan retired from the film industry to briefly enter politics by winning a seat in parliament from Allahabad constituency in 1984, but within a short span of time, he resigned from the Parliament. After a pause for some time he is back to silver screen to perform some selective roles. He has established his own company. Amitabh Bachchan corporation Ltd (ABCL) concerning Various facets of entertainment including film distribution, culture and music. In the same year, Amitabh Bachchan once again re-entered Indian popular culture by anchoring the hugely popular quiz program Kaun Banega Crorepati, the Indian version of Who Wants to Be a Millionaire?He is also active in television with the popular Hindi show 'karorepathi'.

Amitabh married Jaya Bhaduri, a well known actress. It was on the sets of Ek Nazar (1972) that Amitabh and Jaya Bhaduri fell in love. The couple has two children Swetha and Abishek and Abhishek has already followed his father's footsteps having starred in such movies as Refugee, L.O.C, Kuch Na Kaho etc. Bachchan has received the Padma Shri (1983) and Padma Bhushan (2005), civilian honours from the Indian government. In 1990, he won the National Award for his portrayal of a mafia don in Agneepath. In 1999, he was named BBC Superstar of the Millennium. He has also won 12 Filmfare Awards in various categories.

Amitav Ghosh : Amitav Ghosh (born 1956 in Calcutta), is an Indian author, known for his work in the English language. He was educated at The Doon School, where he was a younger contemporary of Vikram Seth, St. Stephen's College, Delhi, Delhi University and Oxford University, where he was awarded a Ph.D. in social anthropology. Ghosh lives in New York with his wife, Deborah Baker.

Amjad Ali Khan : Sarod 'samrat', Amjad Ali Khan is one of the most distinguished maestro in the world of Indian classical music. Amjad Ali Khan, born on October 9th, 1945 at Gwalior, Madhya Pradesh, is the sixth-generation sarod player in his illustrious family.

Amjad is the youngest son of Ustad Hafiz Ali Khan a musician to the royal family of Gwalior who has received musical tuition from descendants or followers of Miyan Tansen (c1520-1590), one of India's most celebrated singers and court musician to the great Mughal emperor Akbar. Taught by his father, Amjad started playing the sarod at a very young age. He made an early debut giving his first solo recital at the age of 12 in 1958. From then on there was no looking back for the master.

Ustad has achieved immense popularity in India as well as abroad. He has the distinction of being the first north Indian artist to have performed in honour of Thyagaraja at the saint musician's Thiruvaiyur shrine. He has traveled widely and performed in several international music festival. Amjad Ali Khan has won several titles and honours - the 'Padmashree' in 1975, the Sangeet Natak Academy award in1989, the Tansen Award in 1989, Sarod Samrat, UNESCO Award in 1970, Unicef's National Ambassadorship, the Padma Bhushan in 1991, the International Music Forum Award etc. In 1977, he founded the Ustad Hafiz Ali Khan Memorial Society which organises music festivals in different parts of India. He has contributed in propagating and creating music for children. Ustad lives with his wife Subbalakshmi and two sons, Amaan Ali Bangash and Ayaan Ali Bangash.

Amongmong : In Nagaland, amongmong is one of the most important festivals of the Sangtams. The predominant theme of the festival is the worship of God of the house and the three cooking stones in the fire place. The festival is observed in the first week of September every year. Amongmong festival means togetherness and stretches for six days. The object is to have a good harvest.

Amri : Amri is the site of a Pre-Harappa fortified town which flourished from 3600 to 3300 BC. The site is located south of Mohenjo Daro on [[Hyderabad, P Pakistan|Hyderabad]]-Dadu Road about 110 kilometres north of Hyderabad in Sind province of Pakistan. Situated near foothills of Kirthar Range of mountains, this was an important earlier urban center in Lower Sind. Amri is close to Baluchistan where development of earlier farming communities from 6000BC to 4000BC ultimately led to urbanization. On timeline, Amri dated after Rehman Dheri.

Amri Culture : Amri culture is attributed to Amri archaeological sites in Sindh and Balochistan provinces of

Pakistan. At least 160 settlements attributed to the Amri Culture, have been discovered, mainly in Balochistan, but also in lower Sindh. They are often distributed along the terraces of old and active river courses and consist of sites of different size and shape, which are sometimes stratified below settlements of later periods. Among these, that of the Tharro Hills, near the town of Gujo, is one of the most famous of lower Sindh

Amrita Lal Basu: Amrita Lal Basu (1853-1929) is a dramatist and actor, born in Kolkata. He was one of the pioneers of the nineteenth-century public theatre in Bengal. After passing the Entrance examination from Calcutta General Assembly's Institution, he was admitted to Medical College, but, after two years of study, dropped out to study homeopathy. For a short time he practised homeopathy in Kolkata, but soon turned to acting and writing plays.

In 1872, in co-operation with ardhendu shekhar mustafi, Amrita Lal staged Nil Darpan, the first show to be staged at the Great National Theatre. He also acted in the play, as Sairindhri. Amrita Lal was appointed manager of the Great National in 1875. His acting in Gajadanagada O Yuvaraj, a play written on the occasion of the visit of the Prince of Wales to Kolkata, satirising flatterers, incurred the wrath of the authorities. He was arrested along with the playwright-cum-director, Upendra Nath, who had also acted in the play.

Amrita Pritam : Amrita Pritam (August 31, 1919 – October 31, 2005) was a Punjabi poet and writer who migrated to India 1947, when the former British India was partitioned into India and Pakistan. She was born in 1919 into a Sikh family in Gujranwala, presently in Pakistan, the only child of a school teacher and a poet. Her mother died when she was eleven and she was saddled with adult responsibilities early on.

Amrita began to write at an early age, and her first collection was published when she was only sixteen years old, the year she married an editor to whom she was engaged in early childhood. She was very sad when some one million Muslims, Hindus and Sikhs were brutally killed in communal violence that followed the partition in 1947. She wrote extensively about that human dilemma.

A number of her works have been translated into English, including her autobiographical works Black Rose and Revenue Stamp (Raseedi Tikkat in Punjabi). She was a recipient of Padmabhushana and Jnanapeetha awards.

Amritsar : Amritsar, meaning "Pool of the Nectar of Immortality", is the administrative headquarter of Amritsar District in Punjab, India. It has a population of over 1,000,000 in Amritsar city and over just over 3,096,077 in Amritsar district from the 2001 Indian census. It is located in the northwest part of India in the State of Punjab, 32 miles east of Lahore. Its name came from Sanskrit Amrta-sarovar = "Nectar Lake"; in Hindu belief Amrta (nectar) is a liquid that Hindu devas drank to keep them immortal. It is home to the Harmandir Sahib, also known as the Golden Temple, and is the spiritual and cultural centre of the Sikh Religion. In Maharaja Ranjit Singh's time, Amritsar had superseded Lahore as the pre-eminent city of Punjab. It is also the location of the Amritsar Massacre and Operation Blue Star.

Amritsar Massacre : The Amritsar massacre, also known as the Jallianwala Bagh massacre, was named after the place (Jallianwala Bagh, in Amritsar), where, on April 13, 1919, British Indian Army (Pathan, Baluch and Gurkha) soldiers opened fire on an unarmed innocent gathering, killing at least 397 men, women and children according to official records. However, according to private sources, the numbers of dead was over 1000 and wounded more than 1200. According to Civil Surgeon Dr Smith, the figures were over 1800. The Casualty figures were never fully ascertained for political reasons.

Amrtanandamayi Devi : Amrtanandamayi Devi also known as 'Amma', 'Ammachi' or 'Mother' (born September 27, 1953), was born Sudhamani in the small village of Parayakadavu, near Kollam, Kerala. She is widely respected as a loving humanitarian and revered by some as a mahatma (great soul) and a living saint.

Sudhamani was born to a family of fisher folks. Her schooling ended when she was nine and began to take care of her younger siblings and the family domestic work full-time. From these humble beginnings started the journey of a young woman on the path to 'universal motherhood', which took her to the United Nations General Assembly, where she addressed the world. Her devotees claim that she had many mystical experiences as a child. Since 1981, she has been teaching spiritual aspirants all over the world. She founded a worldwide organization, the Mata Amritanandamayi Mission Trust, which is engaged in many spiritual and charitable activities.

Anai Mudi: The Anai Mudi is the highest peak in the Cardamom Hills in Kerala, India, in the southern region of Eravikulam National Park. It is located 10°10'N 77°4'E. At a height of 2,695 meters, it is the highest elevation in South India. Anai Mudi peak is situated in Idukki District of Kerala State.The peak belongs to Munnar Panchayat. Anaimudi peak is also a part of the Western Ghats.

Anand : Anand is a city in Gujarat state of western India. It is the administrative centre of Anand District. Anand is known as the Milk Capital of India. It became famous for Amul dairy and its Milk revolution. This City hosts the National Dairy Development Board (NDDB) of India and (Anand Agricultural University) Anand lies between Ahmedabad and Vadodara and is a major railway stop on this line. Anand's Mukhi's are part of the Patel family living in Jeevandeep Society. Late Jashbahi Somabhai Patel "Mukhi" (Nana Adadh) Late Mahendra Jashbhai Patel "Mukhi" Nana Adadh is part of Anand and is home to the Swaminarayan Mandir along with Revandas ni Khadki and Darvajavari khadki

Ananda Bazar Patrika : Ananda Bazar Patrika is one of the premier Bengali language daily newspapers in India. It is published from Kolkata, and simultaneously from Siliguri, and has a national circulation. The paper was founded in 1922.

Ananda Marga : Ananda Marga (the Path of Bliss) an ideology propounded by Anandamurtiji (Prabhat Ranjan Sarkar) in 1955 in Bihar, India, that all living creatures possess a limitless thirst for infinity and that Brahma alone is that infinite entity. It believes that all human beings, irrespective of caste, community, creed and colour are equal and that they are ordained to pursue a universal dharma (to love the Universal Father). Ananda Marga is opposed to all sorts of exploitation and hypocrisy in the name of religion.

Ananda Vikatan : Ananda Vikatan is a leading Tamil language weekly magazine published from Chennai, India. It is part of the Vikatan group. Started as a weekly, Vikatan has now evolved as Vikatan group and became an icon in the Taminadu magazine industry. They have always been in sync with time wheather it's detail, content or the language. They have had a fair success in all the other magazines that have come out with. They have been established targeting women, kids, crime report lovers, religious minded as "Aval Viaktan", "Sutti Vikatan", "Junior Vikatan" and "Sakthi Vikatan" respectively.

Anandamatha : Anandamatha is a famous Bengali novel, written by Bankim Chandra Chattopadhyay and published in 1882. It is one of the most important novels in the history of Bengali and Indian literature. Its importance is heightened by the fact that it became synonymous with the struggle for Indian independence from the British Empire. The word Anandamatha can be roughly translated as The temple of joy.

Anandpur Sahib : Anandpur Sahib is a holy Sikh city and one of the five most holy places in Sikhism. It was created by Guru Tegh Bahadur.

Anandpur Sahib Resolution : The Anandpur Resolution or Anandpur Sahib Resolution was a political statement made by a Sikh political party, the Shiromani Akali Dal in 1973. It effectively demands that the central Indian government should cede control to a Sikh, Punjabi government. It also states that it aims to reclaim some territory given over to other Indian states and territories, it is silent on the issue of Pakistan Punjab but deals with the concept of an Indian federal government.

The demands in the resolution became a central tenet of the Sikh separatist calls for an independent state, called Khalistan. The strongest proponent of whom was Sant Jarnail Singh Bhindranwale. The resolution itself is split into several constituent parts including a political cause and an economic policy.

Anantapur : Anantapur is the headquarters of the Anantapur District. It occupies the southwest corner of the southern Indian state of Andhra Pradesh. The border district has Karnataka to the west, Chitoor District to the South, Kadapa district to the east and Kurnool district to the North. The district was constituted in 1882 from the erstwhile district of Bellary. The economy is principally agrarian with very few industries. With very little rainfall the district is one of the most backward provinces in the state. Prominent crops include rice, cotton, maize, chillies, sesame, and sugar cane. Silk trade, limestone quarrying, iron and diamond mining constitute the few industries that are there.

Ananthagiri Hills : Anantagiri is a breathtakingly beautiful resort sheltered in the lush undulating ranges of the Eastern Ghats in Andhra Pradesh. It is considered to be a perfect head off to get away from the blistering summer months.

Anarkali : Anarkali is a bazaar (market) located on Mall Road in Lahore, Punjab, Pakistan. It is one of the oldest markets on the South Asia. According to legend, Mughal Prince Salim, later to become Emperor Jahangir, fell in love with a girl named Anarkali as a young prince. As she was a dancing girl, not of noble birth, the romance was forbidden by the prince's father, Emperor Akbar. Anarkali, whose title means "pomegranate bud" (bestowed for her beauty), was buried alive in a wall said to be located within the bazaar, by the order of the Mughal Emperor Akbar. Whether or not Anrkali existed is a totally controversial, there is not the slightest of the evidence that Prince Salim ever fell in love with a courteson, even the earliest Indian film made on the subject, declares Anarkali to be a fictional character. Furthermore, she is nowhere to be mentioned in Salim's autobiography.

Ancestral Goa : A centre for Art, Culture & Environment. Located at Loutolim, 9 kms from Margao, it is an aesthetically developed open air site designed to illustrate Goa's traditional past. Set in eco-friendly surroundings, this mock-up village traces 100 years of Goa's lifestyles and heritage alongwith a depiction of daily village activity and folk culture. Local artefacts and handicrafts are available at the handicraft centre and art gallery. The legend of the Big Foot is narrated there- With a pure heart, place your foot on the rock enbedded footprint and you will be blessed with luck. The Big Foot Eat-out offers exotic goan cuisine with spices, vegetables and fruits handpicked from the spice garden and fruit orchard, watered by an ancient system of irrigation. Flanking this is a bird habitat and a rubber plantation from which rubber is extracted and processed. A giant size footprint, 'Big Foot'-the only designer dance floor in Goa is used as a venue for the promotion of art, dance, music and traditional culture.

Another major attraction here is 'Natural Harmony'-the longest laterite monolythic sculpture in India measuring 14 x 5 metres which makes this a must see place for every visitor Sculpted in grecoroman style, in a record time, this horizontally ethced, Sant Mirabai playing the ektara found its way into the Limca Book of Records.

Andaman and Nicobar Islands (A & N Islands, or ANI) : The Andaman and Nicobar Islands is a union territory of India. It is located in the Indian Ocean, in the southern reaches of the Bay of Bengal. It is comprised of two island groups—the Andaman Islands and the Nicobar Islands—which separate the Andaman Sea to the east from the Indian Ocean. These two groups are separated by the 10°N parallel, the Andamans lying to the north of this latitude, and the Nicobars to the south. The capital of this territory is the Andamanese town of Port Blair.

Andaman District : Andaman district is a district of India, one of two districts in the Indian Union Territory (UT) of Andaman and Nicobar Islands. The district's administrative territory encompasses all of the Andaman Islands, which are located in the Indian Ocean (Bay of Bengal, bordering with the Andaman Sea). The district government is headed by a Deputy Commissioner, who in turn reports into the Lt. Governor of the Andaman and Nicobar Islands.

Andaman Islands : The Andaman Islands are a group of islands in the Bay of Bengal, and are part of the Andaman and Nicobar Islands Union Territory of India. Port Blair is the chief community on the islands, and the administrative center of the Union Territory. The Andaman Islands form a single administrative district within the Union Territory, the Andaman district (the Nicobar district was separated and established as a new district in 1974). The population of the Andamans was 314,084 in 2001.

Andaman Sea : The Andaman Sea is a body of water to the southeast of the Bay of Bengal, south of Myanmar and west of Thailand; it is part of the Indian Ocean. It is roughly 1200 kilometers long (north-south) and 650 kilometers wide (east-west), with an area of 797,700 km^2. Its average depth is 870 meters, and the maximum depth is 3,777 meters. At its southeastern reaches, the Andaman Sea narrows to form the Straits of Malacca, which separate the Malay Peninsula from the island of Sumatra.

Andamanese : The Andamanese is a collective term to describe the peoples who are the aboriginal inhabitants of the Andaman Islands and Nicobar Islands, located in the Bay of Bengal. Anthropologically they are often classified as Negritos, represented also by the Semang of Malaysia and the Pygmies of the Philippines. They have lived on the Andaman Islands for at least 14 000 years and had very little contact with external societies for nearly all this period. This comparatively long-lasting isolation and separation from external influences is perhaps unequalled.

However, this changed in the mid-1800s after the British established penal colonies. Increasing numbers of Indian and Karen (Burmese) settlers arrived, encroaching on former territories of the Andamanese. Today only the Sentinelese, who live exclusively on North Sentinel Island, have been able to completely maintain their independent state, resisting attempts to contact them. The Jarawa have also managed to remain substantially apart from the later colonisers and settlers; other Andamanese groups have had more extensive contacts, resulting in drastic reductions in territory and numbers, with several peoples becoming extinct altogether.

Until the 19th century, their habit of killing all shipwrecked foreigners and the remoteness of their islands prevented modification of their culture or language. Cultivation was unknown to them, and they lived off of hunting indigenous pigs, fishing, and gathering. Their only weapons were the bow, fishing nets and harpoons. The Andamanese were the only people who in the 19th century knew no method of making fire, carefully preserving embers in hollowed-out trees from fires caused by lightning strikes.

Andar Qila Mosque : Andar Qila Mosque built on the top of a high hill called 'Andar Qila' (the inner fort) is the first Mughal building in Chittagong city. The Persian inscriptions in the mosque reveal that Subahdar shaista khan built it in 1667. The real builder of the mosque was possibly Buzurg Umed Khan, the eldest son of the Subahdar and the conqueror of Chittagong, but his name has not been cited in the inscription. The mosque is now completely devoid of its original ornamentation save the traces of the merloned-frieze in the parapet in the rear. The four inner walls are now covered with costly modern cut-tiles from Japan. The exterior face of the walls is plastered and white-washed.

The cross-vaulted roof over the flanking rectangular bays calls for special comment. This particular feature of the mosque, hitherto not noticed in Bengal architecture, appears to have been directly derived from north Indian Mughal architecture, such as can be seen in the Turkish Sultana's Bath at Fathpur-sikri. Such cross-vaults abound in Iranian architecture from the 12th century onwards. Two earlier examples of this feature in Muslim architecture are to be seen in the Qusyr Amra (c 714) and in the Baghdad Gate of the City of Raqqa.

Andhra Pradesh : Andhra Pradesh is a state in south-eastern India and is part of the linguistic-cultural region of South India. It lies between 12°41' and 22°N latitude and 77° and 84°40'E longitude, and is bounded by Maharashtra, Chhattisgarh and Orissa in the north, the Bay of Bengal in the east, Tamil Nadu to the south and Karnataka to the west. Andhra Pradesh is the fifth largest state in India and it forms the major link between the north and the south of India. It is the biggest and most populous state in the south of India. It is considered the rice bowl of India. The state is crisscrossed by two major rivers, the Godavari and Krishna.

Andhranatyam : This dance is a 2000-year old temple dance performed by devadasis as a form of worship. Agama Nartanam, Carnatakam and Darbari Aatam are different forms of Andhranatyam. During the period of Hinayana Buddhism, this art form was practised as Nruthyam—a form of worship to God. Dr Nataraja Ramakrishna and Nagalakshmi are dedicated to this art form.

Andrott : Andrott is an island in the Union Territory of Lakshadweep, India. It is a protected territory and not a tourist destination. Most of its inhabitants are conservative Muslims.

Anegondi : Anegondi is a small village located on the north side of the Tungabhadra and opposite to the Vittala Temple. Anegondi was famous for being the supposed original capitol city of the Vijayanagara Empire. This began when Mohammad Tughlaq, Sultan of Delhi, defeated the King of Anegondi and appointed Malik Nayab, his representative, to rule over the city. During this time, the brothers Hakka and Bukka organised a group following Vidyaranya's advice that successfully recaptured Anegondi without bloodshed through sneaking into the Anegondi fort and taking Malik Nayab prisoner while he was drunk. Later on, Hakka and Bukka would found the Vijayanagara Empire with Anegondi as its capital, though it was moved to Vijayanagara in northern Karnataka as the empire continued to expand.

Angela Gomes : Angelà Gomes is a Social worker from Bangladesh. She won the prestigious Magsaysay Award in 1999 for community leadership. She leads the organisation Bachte Shekha (Learning to Live) in the Jessore region of the country. It teaches rural women a vast range of income-generating skills, including handicrafts, raising crops, poultry and livestock, fish farming, beekeeping and silk making. Her organisation benefits some 20,000 women in atleast 400 villages.

Angika : Angika is a language of the Ang or Anga region of India, a 58,000 km^2 area of Bihar, Jharkhand and West Bengal states. It is spoken by more than 30 million of the Indian population, and around 50 million worldwide. Angika is also spoken in Mumbai, Delhi, Kolkata, Durgapur, Punjab, Vadodara, Surat, Patna, Ranchi, Jamshedpur, Bokaro and other parts of the country. Angika is also spoken in Cambodia, Vietnam, Malaysia and other Southeast Asian countries. Besides this, a sizeable Angika speaking population exists in countries such as the United States and the United Kingdom.

Angika is closely related to Gujarati, Bengali, Oriya, and Assamese. It is grouped in with the Bihari languages. Angika is highly intelligible with other Bihari languages. The first poet of Hindi literature, Saraha, was also the first poet of the Angika language and literature. Saraha belongs to the 8th century, and is the first poet whose poetry is availabe in written form

Angling : Jia Bhoroli, the sparkling snow fed river that flows north of Sonitpur district in Assam is the tourist's ultimate destination. The fishing spots on the Bhoroli are an anglers paradise. It is the natural habitat of the Golden Fish.

Angrabadi : Angrabadi is actually, a temple complex which accommodates the temples of Lords Ganpati, Ram-Sita and Hanuman and Shiva in Jharghand. The Shankracharya Swami Swarupanand Saraswati, having been captivated by serene, placid and celestial beauty of Angrabadi rechristened it as Amreshwar Dham.

Anil Kumble : Anil Radhakrishna Kumble (born 17 October 1970 in Bangalore, Karnataka) is an Indian cricketer and has been a member of the Indian cricket team since 1990. Kumble is currently the highest wicket-taker for India in one-day internationals and Test matches.

Kumble is a right arm leg spinner. He has an unorthodox style of bowling and is most famous for his googly. He is one of only two bowlers ever (the other being Jim Laker) to have taken all 10 wickets in a Test innings. On 6 October 2004, Anil Kumble became only the third spinner in the history of Test cricket (after Shane Warne and Muttiah Muralitharan) and second Indian bowler (after Kapil Dev) to have captured 400 Test wickets.. In 2005, he was awarded the Padma Shri, a civilian award from the Government of India.

Anita Ratnam : Anita Ratnam, one of the India's most gifted artists is an accomplished classical dancer and choreographer.

With a career spanning three decades and over 1000 performances in 15 countries, this multifaceted personality has made significant contributions in other fields as Choreographer, Scholar, Television Personality and Cultural Activist.

Anjali Ved Pathak Bhagwat : Anjali Ved Pathak Bhagwat (maiden name Anjali Ved Pathak) is a rifle shooter from India. In 2002 Commonwealth Games at Manchester, she won four golds in the individual and pairs events of Air rifle and Smallbore Rifle (Three positions).

She was awarded the Arjuna award in 2000 and the Rajiv Gandhi Khel Ratna jointly with Beenamol for 2002–2003.

Anju Boby George : Anju Bobby George, made history when she won the bronze medal in Long Jump at the World Athletics Championships 2003 in Paris. With this achievement, she became the first Indian athlete ever to win a medal in a World Athletics Championship clearing 6.70 m.

Anju was born on April 19th, 1977 in in Changanasseri, Kerala . In the School Athletic meet in 1991-92, she came first in 100 m hurdles and relay and second in long jump and high jump events and became the women's champion. Anju's talent was noticed in the national schools games where she won third place in 100 m hurdles and 4x100 m relay. She was the Calicut University Champion during her college days.

Although she started with Heptathlon, she later began to concentrate on her jump events and went on to win long jump medal in the 1996 Delhi junior Asian championship. In 1999 Anju set the national record for triple jump in the Bangalore Federation Cup and Silver medal at the South Asian Federation Games in Nepal. In 2001 Anju bettered her own record in long jump to 6.74 m, her best till date in the National Circuit Meet at Thiruvananthapuram. In the same year she also won gold for triple jump and long jump in the Ludhiana National games. Anju reigned supreme in her events in the Hyderabad National games also. Anju became the first

Indian woman to win a bronze medal clearing 6.49 m at the Commonwealth Games at Manchester 2002. She also won the gold medal at the Busan Asian Games. She received the prestigious Arjuna ward (2003) for eminent sports persons from the government of India after her success in the World Athletic meet.

Anju now ranks 6th in the world. Anju's journey to success from rank 61 in 2001 to rank 6 in 2003 within a short span of two years, was one of sheer hard work and intensive planning. The credit for her success goes to her husband and coach Bobby George who according to her was the biggest influence who helped her in realising her potential and achieving the goal. Both Anju and Bobby George work in the customs department and are settled in Chennai.

Anjuman-i-Mufidul Islam : Anjuman-i-Mufidul Islam was founded in Calcutta in 1905 under the auspices of Ibrahim Mohamad Duplay of Surat to undertake humanitarian activities consistent with the religious beliefs and practices of Muslims. Its main aim was to revive social consciousness among Muslims through education and culture. Eminent persons such as Justice Sharfuddin, Prince Golam Mohamad Shah, Nawab khwaja salimullah, Nawab syed nawab ali chowdhury, khwaja nazimuddin, ak fuzlul huq, mohammad azizul haque, Khan Bahadur SK Fazi Elabi, huseyn shaheed suhrawardy; and KB Manzur Murshed served the organisation as its president at different times between 1905 and 1947. The Anjuman organised a movement for the education of poor Muslims, and established public libraries and arranged debates. In addition to these activities, its important work was to bury unclaimed Muslim dead bodies.

Anjuman-i-Ulama-i-Bangala : Anjuman-i-Ulama-i-Bangala an association established in Calcutta (1913), aimed at (a) preaching Islam and spreading Islamic education; (b) writing books and pamphlets countering the hostile views propagated by Christian Missionaries and other religionists; (c) reforming Muslim society in the light of the Holy Quran and Sunnah. Among the founding members of the Anjuman were maulana abul kalam azad, Maulana maniruzzaman islamabadi, Maulana mohammad akram khan, Maulana m abdullahil baqi and Dr muhammad sahidullah. For publicity and information dissemination, the organisation published a paper entitled Al-Eslam (1915-1921).

Anjuman-i-Wazin-i-Bangla : Anjuman-i-Wazin-i-Bangla a socio-religio-political organisation founded in Calcutta in 1911 by Maulana Abu Bakr Siddique (1859-1939), the Pir Sahib of Furfura (Hughli), Moulavi Wahed Hossain, and Munshi Sk Abdur Rahim, editor of the Mihir-o-Sudhakar. Maulana Abu Bakr Siddique was the chief patron of the Anjuman and its life president. After his death (1939), his son Maulana Abdul Hai became its president. Moslem Hitaisi, Islam-Darshan, Hanafi, Shariate Islam, and Chhunnat-al-Jamait were mouthpieces of the Anjuman.

Anjuna : Anjuna is a village in Goa, one of the twelve Brahmin comunidades of Bardez. It was a famous destination for hippies during the sixties and seventies. It currently faces the problems that all of Goa faces: garbage disposal, unauthorized land conversion, usurpation of comunidade land, and a disregard for the rule of law. Its church, founded in 1595, is dedicated to S. Miguel, and celebrates the feasts of S. Miguel (September 29) and Nossa Senhora Advogada (second week of January). There are three large chapels in the parish: the one to S. Antonio (Praias), to Nossa Senhora de Saude (Mazalvaddo), and to Nossa Senhora de Piedade (Grande Chinvar). The chapel at Vagator became the church of the new parish of Vagator, dedicated to S. Antonio, sometime last century.

Ankamma Festival : Ankamma festival is celebrated for five days in the month of Ashadha. It is the festival of Andhra Pradesh. The deity is placed in a Palanquin and taken in a procession early in the morning. The floor is decorated with rangavali. A heap of cooked rice is offered and a ram is sacrificed on the evening of the following day. Ankamma on a tiger—shaped vehicle and her sister Mahalakshmamma on a jackal—shaped vehicle are taken to a four- shelled cart, along with a basket. The villagers drop neem leaves and cooked rice into the basket. A lizard, a pig, a goat, a fowl and a human form made of flour are impaled on the spikes of the cart. The procession goes to the temple accompanied by the music and dance. On the fourth day devotees observe a fast and fulfil their vows.

Balls of rice flour and jaggery are offered to Ankamma, Mahalakshmamma, poleramma and poturaj carts with vessels of cooked rice and Bengal gram are taken around the temple and offered to the deity. A ram and a goat are sacrificed to Ankamma, Mahalakshmamma respectively. On the fifty day, Ankamma and Mahalakshmamma go hunting towards the north of the village on the respective vehicles. There a ram's ear is cut and the ram is driven to the temple. All things necessary for a feast to Ankamma and her relatives are provided in the temple and its doors are closed for three days. It is believed that if anyone opens the door within these three days, his head would break into pieces.

Ankleshwar : Ankleshwar or Anklesvar is a town in Gujarat state of India. The city is located approximately ten kilometers from Bharuch (Broach) in Bharuch District. Ankleshwar has an industrial township called G.I.D.C. (Gujarat Industrial Development Corporation), which is the biggest industrial township in Asia. Ankleshwar also has a regional ofice for ONGC (oil and natural gas commission). Today, Ankleshwar has over 100 big and small chemical plants. These chemical plants produce insecticides, speciality chemicals, and paint. The pharmaceutical company Zydus Cadila has a plant to make active pharmaceutical ingredient in Ankleshwar. Ankleshwar is well connected by Indian National Highway 8 (Mumbai to New Delhi) and by the Western Railway Division of Indian Railways.

Annada Prasad Bagchi: Annada Prasad Bagchi (1849-1905) was a portrait painter and a master of oil paintings of late 19th and early 20th century Bengal. Born in village Shikharbali under the district of 24-Parganas, Annada Prasad Bagchi received his early education at the Assembly's Institution at Calcutta. He got his early training in art at a copperplate-engraving workshop at Jorasanko where he received instructions from Nilmoni Mukherjee.

Annada Prasad's reputation as a portrait painter and as a master of oil paintings prompted lord northbrook to commission from him several portraits including that of Dr Rajendralal Mitra and keshab chandra sen. Bagchi's paintings were exhibited in several art exhibitions in Calcutta and Madras. Bagchi's paintings exhibited in the government-sponsored exhibition in New Imperial Museum in December 1874 were highly acclaimed. The portraits he displayed at the exhibition of 1879 were among the most priced paintings. It was around this time that Bagchi was acclaimed as the Sir Joshua Reynolds of Bengal by george campbell, Lt Governor of Bengal.

Bagchi was also instrumental in founding the Artist's Press and the publication of the first art journal in Bangla Shilpa Puspanjali (1885-86). Though only a few issues of the journal were published, it aimed at inculcating artistic awareness among people. He was associated with several art organisations including Bangiya Kala Sangsad of which he was the president. Annada Prasad Bagchi died in1905 at the age of 56

Annakoot : Annakoot is celebrated in Uttar Pradesh, which is devoted to feasting and Govardhan puja in the evening and rounded up next day by Bhaiya Dooj when sisters apply vermilion tika (auspicious mark) on the forehead of their brothers who reward them with money. On Dooj weapons, pen and inkpot are also worshipped.

Annamacharya : Sri Tallapaka Annamacharya (1424-1503) is an Indian poet and musician widely regarded as the Telugu pada kavita pitaamaha (Grand old man of simple poetry). An ardent devotee of Lord Venkateswara of Tirupati, AP, Annamacharya(also known as Annamayya) successfully composed more than 30,000 krithis (a Carnatic composition) in the carnatic music tradition, a feat which is near impossible to replicate! They were found engraved on copper plates which were hidden for centuries inside the Sri Venkateswara temple at Tirumala. Annamacharya's considered his compositions as floral offerings to God. In the poems, he praises Venkateswara, describes his love for him, argues and quarrels with the Lord, confesses the devotee's failures and apprehensions, and surrenders himself to Venkateshwara. His songs are classified into Adhyaatama and Sringaara samkirtanaas.

Annamalai Hills : Annamalai (Anamalai or Anamalah) Mountains are a mountain range and wildlife sanctuary in the Western Ghats range of southern India, straddling the border between Kerala and Tamil Nadu states. The park is part of the South Western Ghats montane rain forests ecoregion, and preserves montane rain forest, montane grassland, and stunted Shola forests. It is home to a number of endangered species, including the Asian Elephant, Tiger, and Nilgiri Tahr.

Annie Besant : Annie Besant was born in London to Irish parents. In 1893, she left for India having been influenced by the Indian culture and civilization. She was famous as a social worker, educationalist and journalist.

She became a staunch supporter of Indian Independence Movement and her contribution to India's freedom struggle was remarkable. She founded the Home-Rule League. She revived the Theosophical Society. In 1915, she chaired the Calcutta session of the Indian National Congress. She also edited 'New India'. She established Indian Boy Scouts Association. She received a prestigious award for her work for scouts. She also studied Hinduism. India is indebted to Annie Besant for her immeasurable work for freedom struggle, educational advancements and social reforms. She died at the age of 86.

Ansar Burney Trust : The Ansar Burney Trust is a human rights organization in Pakistan. Established in 1980 by Ansar Burney, advocate in the Pakistani port city of Karachi, the Ansar Burney Trust was the first organization to introduce true human rights in Pakistan. With a mission to work as a non-political, non-governmental and non-profitable organization, the Trust started working against all forms of injustices, cruel inhuman and degrading treatment, child abuse, cruelty to women and other more subtle forms of human and civil rights violations without any discrimination or affiliation. The Ansar Burney Trust headed by Mr. Ansar Burney is a network of human rights organizations working for the deliverance of justice, better treatment of human beings and for the rights and freedoms of civil liberties.

Anshi National Park : The Anshi National Park is an evergreen tropical rainforest situated in the North Kannada district in Karnataka. The park covering an area of 340 sq km is considered as India's most endangered wildlife park. Anshi lies on the Karwar- Londa highway and is part of the Dandeli wildlife sanctuary. Anshi got the designation as National Park in1987. Dandeli is a small town located on the banks of the Kali river in Karnataka. The forests around this town was established as Dandeli wildlife sanctuary in 1975 with an area of around 500 sq kms. The Anshi National Park and the adjoining Dandeli wildlife sanctuary together make up the Dandeli Wildlife Division of the Karnataka Forest Department.

Anshuman Gaekwad : Anshuman Gaekwad (born September 23, 1952) is an Indian cricketer who represented the nation in 40 Test matches and 15 one-day internationals. He later coached the Indian cricket team. Anshuman is known as the great wall against pace bowlers. Some say he made it to the team only because of this virtue however, when West Indian pace bowlers were a nightmare for batsmen worldwide, Anshuman's stonewalling became essential. He made his Test debut against the West Indies at Kolkata on December 27, 1974 and his last appearance in a Test match was against England at Kolkata itself on the last day of 1984.

Being a right-handed batsman, Gaekwad scored 1985 runs from 40 Tests at an average of 30.07 with 2 centuries and 10 half centuries to his credit. He scored his highest(201)in Test matches against Pakistan at Jalandhar in 1982-93. This innings, where he spent 671 minutes, is the best example for his patience and concentration as a batsman.

Antara Gange : Antara Gange is a mountain situated in the Shathashrunga mountain range in southeastern Karnataka. Antara Gange literally means "Ganges from deep" in Kannada. It is about two miles from the town of Kolar. Antara Gange is famous for the temple situated on mountain. There in the temple is a pond which gets continuous flow of underground water which comes out of the mouth of a basava (stone bull). There is a steep narrow path to the very top of the mountain. There are seven villages on this mountain. Therhalli is one such village.

Anti-Sikh Riots, 1984 : The 1984 Anti-Sikh Riots took place in India after the assassination of Indira Gandhi on October 31, 1984. India's Prime Minister Indira Gandhi was assassinated by two of her Sikh guards acting in the aftermath of Operation Bluestar. Over the next four days nearly 3000 Sikhs were massacred in systematic riots planned and led by Congress activists and sympathizers. The then Congress government was widely criticized for doing very little at the time, if not acting as a conspirator, especially since voting lists were used to identify Sikh families. The then Prime Minister Rajiv Gandhi, son of Indira Gandhi allegedly made a statement "When a big tree falls, the earth is bound to shake" on the Sikh carnage. His widow, Sonia Gandhi and current President of the Congress Party, officially apologized in 1998 for the events of November, 1984. The most affected regions were neighborhoods in Delhi. The riots were a key antagonist in the subsequent Punjab insurgency.

As an indication of the complexity of politics involved since the riots, Dr. Manmohan Singh a Sikh became the Prime Minister of India on a Congress mandate May 22, 2004 acting on Sonia Gandhi's request. It is also important to note that many ordinary Indians of different religious dispositions made significant efforts to hide and help Sikh families as outlined in affidavits of Sikh victims and have been active in seeking appropriate justice.

Anuppur District : Anuppur District has an area of 3701 km^2, and a population of 667,155 (2001 Census). 309,624 people are from scheduled tribes and 48,376 are scheduled castes. The District is bounded by Koriya District of Chattisgarh state on the east, Bilaspur District of Chattisgarh on the southeast, Dindori District of Madhya Pradesh on the southwest, Umaria District of Madhya Pradesh on the west, and Shahdol District on the northwest and north. The District was created on 15

August 2003 out of Shahdol District. It is part of Rewa Division. Anuppur District is mostly hilly and forested. The Narmada River originates from the hill of Amarkantak in the Maikal Hills, and the Son River originates nearby.

Anwar Pasha : Anwar Pasha (1928-1971), a martyred intellectual and litterateur, was born on 15 April 1928 at Dabkai village in Murshidabad. He started his teaching career as superintendent of Manikchak High Madrasah and later on taught at Bhabta Azizia High Madrasah (1954) and Sadikhan Diar Bohumukhi Higher Secondary School (1957). In 1958 he joined Pabna Edward College and then, in 1966, the Department of Bangla, Dhaka University.

Anwar Pasha was a staunch supporter of the liberation war and he dreamt of an independent Bangladesh. Unfortunately, he could not see his dream realised, because, shortly before 16 December, he was picked up from his university flat, taken to Mirpur and killed brutally along with other intellectuals. His dead body was recovered and buried in the compound of the Dhaka University mosque. In 1972, Anwar Pasha was posthumously honoured with the Bangla Academy Award for his literary achievements.

Anwarul Karim Chowdhury : Anwarul Karim Chowdhury was a diplomat from Bangladesh who was appointed in 2002 as United Nations Under-Secretary-General and High Representative for the Least Developed Countries, Landlocked Developing Countries and Small Island Developing States. Before this, he was the Bangladeshi ambassador to the United Nations in New York; he was replaced by Iftekhar Ahmed Chowdhury.

A P J Abdul Kalam : Dr. Avul Pakir Jainulabdeen Abdul Kalam, born October 15, 1931, Tamil Nadu, India, usually referred to as Dr. A.P.J. Abdul Kalam, is the President of India. He is also a notable scientist and an engineer. Dr. Kalam has the unique distinction of having received honorary doctorates from at least thirty universities, as also India's three highest civilian honours—the Padma Bhushan in 1981; the Padma Vibhushan in 1990; and the Bharat Ratna in 1997.

Apa Tani : The Apa Tani, also spelled as Tani or Apatani, is a tribal group of about 25,000 in the Apatani plateau Jiro in the Lower Subansiri district of Arunachal Pradesh, India. As they are of Tibetan origin, their language belongs to the Tibeto-Burman family Most of the Apatanis are loyal followers of the Donyi Polo faith, who pray to an array of spirits and souls for blessing. Abo-Tani, the primal man, analogous to Adam in the Christian faith, is considered to be the sole ancestor of all Apatani and other Animist tribes in the surrounding regions. The Apatanis have a culture that contains remanants of the archaic Tibetan culture. Prior to a marriage, the liver of a chicken plays a significant role in fortune telling. Festivals such as Myoko and Dree are based on agricultural cycles, and Murung is celebrated for general prosperity and peace in the village. Though simple, the dress of the Apatanis elaborate colorful, yet simple styles. Tattoing and the stuffing of large nose plugs were once popular among the women, although this practice has gradually been falling into decline in the recent years.

Aparajeyo Bangla : Aparajeyo Bangla is one of the most well known sculptures dedicated to the Bangladesh Liberation War in 1971.

It is located in the campus of Dhaka University, just infront to the Arts Building. In Bangla, the phrase means "Unvanquished Bengal".

Aparna Popat : India's top woman shuttler Aparna Popat is one of the finest badminton players in the world. Her graceful movements on the court, her deft half volleys and her immense concentration make her stand apart from the rest. She took up the sport of Badminton at the age of 8 and by the time she was 13, winning National level and State level tournaments became a habit.

She captured her first senior national title, defeating Manjusha Pagwankar at Pune in 1998. Aparna has been winning the senior national title since 1998, and there seems to be no rival to match up to her shuttle skills at the national level. She created history when she lifted the women's singles title for the eighth year on trot in the 69th Senior National Badminton Championship at Jamshedpur in February 2005.She is currently ranked 23rd in the world.

Aparna Sen : Actress, Director, Screenwriter and Editor, Aparna Sen has been one of the most celebrated member of Indian film industry for the last four decades. Born in 25th October, 1945 in Kolkata, West Bengal, Aparna Sen is the daughter of veteran critic and filmmaker Chidananda Dasgupta.

In her early youth, charismatic and beautiful Aparna Sen was impressed by European cinema that strongly affected her art life. She started her film career as an actress at the age of 16. She is is a perfect example of a rare combination of beauty and brains. She has been honored with India's most prestigious Padmashree Award in 1986 for her contribution to cinema, the Satyajit Ray Memorial Millennium Award by the Rotary Club for Profound Contribution to Indian Cinema and the Satyajit Ray Lifetime Achievement Award by the Cine Central Film Society. Three times National Award winning director, she has also served on juries at many international/national film festivals, such as International Film Festival of India, Moscow International Film Festival, and the Hawaii International Film Festival.

Aparna Sen, who was listed among the 100 best looking Indian women of the century is currently the Editor of a famous Bengali Monthly women's Magazine 'Sananda' published by Ananda Bazar Patrika group, where her editorials tackle social issues. Independent in her life, Aparna didn't have the sweetest married life. She married thrice and has three daughters. Presently married to a professor Kalyan Ray residing in the US, she has tried to make long distance relationship work. Konkona Sen Sharma, daughter of Aparna Sen and well known writer Mukul Sharma is a national award winning actress for the film Mr. and Mrs. Iyer. Aparna on a personal front loves cooking, talking to her grand daughter and indulging in the occasional poetry. This multitalented woman is now busy working on her latest film 'Gulel' in Hindi.

Apollo Hospitals : Apollo Hospitals is a major Hospital chain based in Chennai, India. It was founded by Dr.Prathap C. Reddy in 1983. Today, Apollo is the largest private healthcare provider in Asia with branches in India, Sri Lanka, Bangladesh, Ghana, Nigeria, Qatar, and Kuwait.

Appam : Appam, a fermented rice pancake, is a speciality of the South Indian coastal state of Kerala. It has a soft spongy middle, laced with crispy edges. Rice powder is mixed with water and yeast, and the batter is left to ferment for 6 hours. The batter is poured into a vessel called appachatti and tossed with oil to make a circular appam. It is usually eaten with a side dish made of coconut called chutney, or with sweetened coconut milk. It can also be served with stew, or typically with kadala—a spicy dish made with Bengal Gram.

Appam also refers to another South Indian sweet dish, which owes its origins to Tamil Nadu. This is made with flour, jaggery, clarified butter—ghee—and bananas. A batter made out of flour, jaggery and banana is poured into a vessel called appakarai, which has ghee heated to a high temperature. The appams take the shape of small cups, and are fried until deep brown. Appams are a festive sweet, made on Gokulashtami—the birthday of Hindu deity, Krishna.

Applied Economics Research Centre (AERC) : Applied Economics Research Centre (AERC) is a distinguished research institute of University of Karachi. It was established in 1973 by government of Sindh and financially assisted by Ford foundation. Initially it offered M.A.S course but now it offers M.A.S, M.Phil, and Ph.D courses. It also has largest economics research library in Pakistan. During last three decades it earned a respectable name as top research centre of economics and related sciences.

Appu Ghar : Appu Gharis a kiddie amusement park i New Delhi for anyone of any age. This theme park includes haunted houses and some roller coaster. Appu, was both the cartoon mascot, and a live elephant mascot that became the beloved star of the 1982 Asian Games in New Delhi, India. This amusement park got the name from that Mascot's name. "Appu" is the name of the elephant and "Ghar" means "house".

April Fools' Day : April Fools'Day (April 1) sees poets from all over the country gather at Chandigarh to recite verses in a jocular vein. Even those who do not ordinarily enjoy poetry look forward to the Maha Moorkh Sammelan, or Conclave of Colossal Fools. No other city in India hosts such a gathering.

A Q M Badruddoza Chowdhury : AQM Badruddoza Chowdhury was sworn in as President of the People's Republic of Bangladesh on 14 November 2001 and held office till 21 June, when he resigned.

Born on 1 November 1932 in Munsif Bari, Comilla (in maternal grandfather's house) Prof Chowdhury hails from a respectable Muslim family of Majidpur Dayhata, Srinagar (in the historic Vikramapura), Munshiganj district.

Second son of late Kafil Uddin Chowdhury (Minister in East Pakistan and an architect of the United front in 1954) and Mrs Sufia Khatun, he was educated at St Gregory's High School, Dhaka College, Dhaka Medical College and University of Wales, UK. He started his career in the medical profession. He came to be regarded as one of the topmost Specialist Internist in the country. He joined politics in 1979 when President Ziaur Rahman founded the Bangladesh Nationalist Party; he was its founding Secretary General. Badruddoza Chowdhury was appointed Deputy Prime Minister (Senior) in President Ziaur Rahman's Presidential Cabinet, 1979 in charge of the Ministry of Health and Population; senior most Minister in Begum Khaleda zia's cabinet, 1991 in charge of the Ministry of Education and Science and Technology & Culture.

A R Cornelius : A. R. Cornelius, a Catholic, was the Chief Justice of the Supreme Court of Pakistan from May 13, 1960 to February 29, 1968. He was a Justice of the Supreme Court for about 17 years.In 1954, the National Assembly of Pakistan tried to change the constitution to establish checks on the Governor-General's powers, in order to prevent a repeat of what had happened to Nazimuddin's government. In response, Ghulam Muhammad dismissed the Assembly, an action that was challenged in the Supreme Court. Ghulam Muhammad emerged victorious when the CJ Muhammad Munir upheld the dismissal in a split decision, despite the dissenting opinion written by the renowned Justice A. R. Cornelius, and despite protests from the members of the Assembly.

A R Mallick : Dr. AR Mallick was (1918-1998) historian, education advisor and administrator. Born 31 December 1918 in Rajapur village of Dhaka district, Azizur

Rahman Mallick completed BA Honours (1939) and Masters (1940) in History from the University of Dhaka, where he joined as lecturer in 1941. In 1943, he joined Chittagong College and later, worked in Rajshahi College for a short period. He obtained PhD degree from the University of London in 1953 and after coming back home he joined the Department of History, University of Rajshahi. During the period of work at the university he served as dean of the faculty of Arts and also as the provost of a residential hall.

Dr AR Mallick was appointed vice-chancellor of the University of Chittagong in 1965. He was an ardent activist in the War of Liberation. After the independence, he became the education advisor to the government of Bangladesh. He also served as High Commissioner of Bangladesh in India. In 1975, Dr Mallick was appointed Minister of Finance, a position which he held for a short period and later he joined as a professor in the Department History, Jahangirnagar University. Dr Mallick was associated with many professional and social organisations and institutions. He was President, asiatic society of Bangladesh and Bangladesh Itihas Samity. He was also Chairman, Bangla Academy. Dr AR Mallick died in 1998.

A R Rahman : A.R.Rahman, the musical maestro of Indian Cinema was born on 6th January,1966 in Madras, to a musically affluent family. This genius with his exceptional talent, has reached heights of success that people his age can only dream of. Even then this small man remains humble and credits all his inspiration and success to Allah.

Born as Dileep Kumar to parents R.K.Sekhar, a music composer and mother Kasturi (alias Kareema Begum), he came to be known as A.R Rahman later when the family converted to Islam. Dileep started learning piano at the tender age of four. As his father passed away early, the pressure of supporting the family fell on young Dileep Kumar.

Dileep joined Illaiyaraja's troupe as a keyboard player at the age of 11 and had to drop out of school. He also played on the orchestra of M.S.Vishwanathan and Ramesh Naidu and accompanied Zakir Hussain and Kunnakudi Vaidyanathan on world tours. All this experience enabled him to earn a scholarship to the famed Trinity College of Music at Oxford University from where he obtained a degree in Western Classical Music. After he returned he continued to be a part of various music troupes. He was also a part of local rock bands like Roots, Magic and Nemesis Avenue where he performed with his future colleagues like Ranjit Barot and Sivamani. In 1987, he got a chance to compose a jingle to promote Allwyn's new Trendy range of watches. His work was appreciated and he got many more offers. He has done jingles for popular ads like Parry's, Leo Coffee, Boost, Titan, Premier Pressure Cooker, Asian Paints etc. Rahman went on to compose more than 300 jingles and received awards and recognition for his work, in the five years he continued in advertising.

In 1989, he started a small studio of his own, called Panchathan Record Inn, attached to his house. It was here that he began experimenting in sound engineering, design and production. The turning point in his life was when he met the famous director Mani Ratnam and was signed on to compose music for his super hit film 'Roja'. Rahman got the national award for the best music director that year. From then on there was no looking back for him. He got offers from a lot of directors from the south and the Hindi film 'Rangeela' and later 'Bombay' established his popularity in the north too. Rahman music wave arrived with a big bang in the tinsel world with sales of more than 40 million albums over a period of 3 years. He has also dabbled in playback singing with songs like 'Hamma Hamma' in Bombay, 'Dil Se Re' in Dil Se etc.

Apart from making music for films, Rahman has also done compositions for patriotic albums like ' Vande Mataram' a tribute to the motherland released simultaneously in 28 countries across the world and 'Jana Gana Mana' which brought together many of the countries classical and contemporary musical maestros, both released under the prestigious Label of Sony Music. He has also worked and performed with internationally reputed artists such as Apache Indian, David Byrne, Michael Jackson and with Andrew Webber Lloyd for his album 'Bombay Dreams'. He has received numerous awards in recognition of his talent. Padmasree from the government of India in 2000 being one of them.

Arabian Sea : The Arabian Sea is the part of the Indian Ocean bounded on the east by India, on the north by Baluchistan and Sind provinces of Pakistan and part of the southern Persian littoral, on the west by Arabian Peninsula, on the south, approximately, by a line between Cape Guardafui, the north-east point of Somalia, and Kanyakumari (Cape Comorin) in India. It was known as the Sindhu Sagar to Indians in the Vedic period of their history.

It has two important branches — the Gulf of Aden in the southwest, connecting with the Red Sea through the strait of Bab-el-Mandeb; and the Gulf of Oman to the northwest, connecting with the Persian Gulf. Besides these larger ramifications, there are the gulfs of Cambay and Kutch on the Indian coast. Its islands are few, the chief being Socotra, off the African, and the Laccadives, off the Indian coast.

Ocean trade routes have crossed the Arabian Sea since ancient times, linking the Near East with East Africa, India, Southeast Asia, and China. Historically, sailors in a type of ship called a dhow used the seasonal Monsoon winds to cross the sea. The sea forms part of the chief shipping route between Europe and India via the Suez Canal, which links the Red Sea with the Mediterranean Sea.

The maximum width of the Arabian Sea is approximately 2,400 km, and its maximum depth is 4,652 metres, in the Arabian Basin approximately at the same latitude as the southernmost tip of India. The Indus River, also known as the Sindhu river, is the largest river flowing directly into this sea; others include the Narmada, Tapti, Mahi, and the numerous rivers of Kerala in India. The Arabian Sea coast of central India is known as the Konkan Coast, and that of southern India is known as the Malabar Coast. The countries with coastlines on the Arabian Sea are India, Iran, Oman, Pakistan, Yemen, Somalia and the Maldives.

Arain : Arain is a Muslim tribe settled mainly in the Punjab and Sindh provinces of Pakistan. Arain are mainly involved in agriculture and form a significant percentage in the Pakistan Army. The population of Arains exceed over 10 millions. Arain originally were one of the Semitic tribes that came and settled in South Asia from Middle East. Most of them were the members of Muhammad bin Qasim army which conquered Pakistan in 714-715 and many settled here.

Araku Valley : Araku Valley is a famous hill station located in the state of Andhra Pradesh in India. It is located 115 km from the Vishakhapatnam district, close to the Orissa state border. This place lures people with pleasant weather, hills and valleys. The natural beauty of this valley comes alive with its rich landscape. The area of the valley is roughly 36 km and the altitude is between 600 and 900 m above the sea level.

The journey to this place on the Ghat road with thick forests on either side is in itself interesting and pleasant. One can have a wonderful trekking trip. 46 tunnels and bridges will greet you on the way. The Ananthagiri hills on the way to Araku Valley are famous for coffee plantations. The Borra caves, located 29 km from Araku Valley, are a nearby tourist attraction. Located on the Eastern Ghats of India, the valley is inhabited by tribal people. One of the other attractions of this valley is a tribal museum. The valley is connected through both rail and road to the city of Vishakapatnam.

Arang : The city of temples, Arang is situated on the Raipur- Sambalpur highways. One of the place is the 11th century Bhandewal Jain temple. Apart from this, some of the other temples are Baaghdewal, Mahmaya, Danteshwari & Jain temples.

Aranmula Kannadi : Aranmula kannadi or Aranmula metal mirror is a special type of mirror produced at Aranmula, a village in the state of Kerala in India. These unique metal mirrors are the result of Kerala's rich cultural and metallurgical traditions. The British Museum in London has a 45 centimeter tall Aranmula metal mirror in its collection. The origins of the Aranmula metal mirrors are linked with the Aranmula Parthasarathy Temple. Legend has it that eight families of experts in temple arts and crafts were brought by the royal chief to Aranmula from Tirunelveli district to work in the Parthasarathy temple centuries ago. Some undisclosed metals are alloyed with copper and tin to cast the mirrors. The procedure and metallurgy is now only known to a single family in Aranmula. To achieve their highly reflective surface, the finished mirrors need to be polished for one or two days.

Arasavalli : Arasavalli is the ancient Hindu temple situated near Srikakulam town of Andhra Pradesh in South India. It has Suryanarayana Swamy as the presiding deity. Ratha Saptami is the most important festival which is celebrated in this temple. People suffering with eye and skin diseases are believed to be cured by the god at this temple.

Arati Gupta : Arati Gupta (Saha) (24 September 1940 - 23 August 1994) was born in Calcutta, West Bengal, India. Arati was initiated in swimming at the early age of four, and her talent was spotted by Sachin Nag. From 1945 to 1951 she won 22 State competitions including an all-India record in 1949. She took part in the Helsinki Olympics in 1952 along with Dolly Nazir. On 29 September 1959 she was the first woman from Asia to swim the English Channel, from Cape Gris Nez, France to Sandgate, England. She swam the 42 miles in 16 hours 20 minutes, and hoisted the flag of India at Sandgate. She was awarded Padmashri in the year 1960. She died on 23 August 1994 of jaundice. In 1998, a set of Indian stamps was issued to commemorate the contribution of Indian women in various fields, including Arati Gupta.

Aravalli Range : The Aravalli Range is a range of mountains in western India running approximately 300 miles northeast-southwest across Rajasthan state. The northern end of the range continues as isolated hills and rocky ridges into Haryana state, ending near Delhi. The highest peak is Guru Shikhar in Mount Abu. Rising to 5653 feet, it lies near the southwestern extremity of the range, close to the border with Gujarat. The city of Ajmer with its lake lies on the south slope of the range in Rajasthan. The Aravalli Range is the eroded stub of a range of ancient folded mountains. The range rose in a Precambrian event called the Aravalli-Delhi orogen. The range joins two of the ancient segments that make up the Indian craton, the Marwar segment to the northwest of the range, and the Bundelkhand segment to the southeast.

Archaeological Survey of India : Archaeological Survey of India is an Indian government agency in the Department of Culture that is responsible for archaeological studies and preservation of cultural monuments. According to its website, ASI's function is to "explore, excavate, conserve, preserve and protect the monuments and sites of National & International Importance."

Archaeological Survey of India (ASI) is the successor of the Asiatic Society of British archaeologist Sir William Jones, founded January 15, 1784. In 1788 it begun to publish journal The Asiatic Researches and 1814 built its first museum in Bengal. ASI in its current form was founded in 1861 under British colonial administration by Sir Alexander Cunningham with the help of the then Viceroy Canning. At the time, its domain also included Afghanistan. After the independence, it came under Ancient Monuments and Archaeological Sites And Remains Act of 1958.

Archer Kent Blood : Archer Kent Blood (1923-2004) was an American diplomat in Bangladesh. He served as the last American Consul General to Dacca, East Pakistan. He is famous for sending the strongly-worded Blood telegram protesting against the atrocities committed in the Bangladesh Liberation War.

Archha : Orchha 75 miles from Gwalior, was founded in the 16th century by the Bundela Rajput chieftain Rudra Pratap, on the banks of Betwa river. Orchha's fort complex, approached by a multiarched bridge has three palaces, set in an open quadrangle. The most spectacular of these are:

Ardeshir Cowasjee : Ardeshir Cowasjee is a renowned Zoroastrian newspaper columnist from Pakistan. His hard-hitting column (published in Pakistan's oldest newspaper Dawn) has exposed corruption, nepotism and government incompetence for the last twenty years.

No Pakistani journalist has ever had access to so many inside sources in the Pakistani bureaucracy and military as has Mr. Cowasjee. This has allowed him to expose some of the biggest scandals of the Pakistan government.

Arghun Dynasty : Arghun Dynasty was established in Sindh by Shah Beg a descendent of Genghiz Khan. Arghun dynasty ruled between 1521-1554 and replaced by Tarkhan dynasty.

Arial Khan River : Arial Khan river is one of the main south-eastward outlets of the river Padma. Bifurcating from the Padma at 51.5-km southeast of Goalandaghat in Rajbari district, the river flows through Faridpur and Madaripur districts before falling into the Tentulia at the northeastern corner of Barisal. Madaripur town stands on the rightbank of the Arial Khan. The river is navigable throughout the year and is under tidal influence. The normal range of tides at Madaripur is 0.32m. Total length of the river is 160 km.

On its way, the Arial Khan maintains its link with the Padma through a number of streams and canals or khals such as the Naria, Palang, Moynakata, Bhubaneshwar, Kumar Kailar and Nayabhangi. The river maintains a meander channel through its course and is erosional in nature. A number of settlements has already been destroyed due to severe riverbank erosion and the process is continuing. Madaripur town now faces the threat of erosion. bangladesh water development board has taken measures to save the town and a groyne has already been constructed. Piajkhali, Chowdhurirhat, Utrail, Dattapara, Kabirajpur, Latikhola, Chhabipur and Madaripur are some of the important places on the banks of this river. To improve irrigation and agriculture in the region served by it the Bangladesh Water Development Board has taken up the Arial Khan Rejuvenation Project.

Arikamedu : Arikamedu is an archaeological site near Pondicherry, southern India, where Mortimer Wheeler conducted its best-known excavation in the 1940s. According to Wheeler, Arikamedu was an Indian fishing village which had been built up by Roman traders into a major port. It flourished for centuries until the Romans left. Various Roman artifacts, such as a large number of amphorae bearing the mark of Roman potter schools VIBII, CAMURI and ITTA, have been found at the site, supporting the view on an ancient trade between Rome and south India.

Arjan Singh (Marshal of the Air Force) : Arjan Singh DFC was born on April 15, 1919 in Lyalpur, and educated at Montogmery (then a part of undivided India, and, now in Pakistan). He entered RAF Cranwell in 1938 and was commissioned as a Pilot Officer in December 1939. He was awarded the Distinguished Flying Cross (DFC) in 1944, and commanded the Indian Air Force Exhibition Flight in 1945. He was Chief of the Air Staff or CAS, from August 1, 1964 to July 15, 1969, and was awarded the Padma Vibhushan in 1965. He was Lt. Governor of Delhi and was made Marshal of the Air Force in January, 2002.

Arjun Munda : Arjun Munda (born January 5, 1968) is the Chief Minister of Jharkhand, a state of India. He first took that position on March 18, 2003 and held it until his resignation on March 2, 2005 which occurred after inconclusive state elections and the intervention of the state's governor, Syed Sibtey Razi. Ten days later, on March 12, 2005, however, Munda was reappointed chief minister, and won a vote of confidence in the state assembly on March 15, 2005, by a vote of 40 to 37.

With only 35 years behind him upon his appointment as Chief Minister, Arjun Munda was the youngest ever Indian to hold that post. His political career began in the 1980's as part of the Jharkhand movement, spearheaded by the Jharkhand Mukti Morcha. This movement sought to create a tribally-dominated state from the southern area of India's northern Bihar state. Munda's political clout grew due to his focus on helping tribals and other backwards. In 1995, he was elected to the Bihar state assembly, representing Kharswan. He retained that seat in 2000 and 2005 elections, but as of 2000, he was a member of the Bharatiya Janata Party.

Jharkhand was formed in 2000, with the BJP forming the first government under Babulal Marandi. Arjun Munda served as the Social Welfare Minister in his cabinet. In 2003, as the non-BJP Legislators supporting the government called for Marandi's replacement, it was Munda, viewed as a strong tribal leader, who was considered the best alternative. His second term, which began in March of 2005, has been likewise marked by the need of support for several independent Legislators.

Arjun Singh : Arjun Singh (born November 5, 1930, Madhya Pradesh) is a veteran Congress (I) politician. He is the Human Resources and Development (HRD) minister in the current Indian government headed by Manmohan Singh. He held the same post in the Narasimha Rao government also.

He has served as a minister in the Rajiv Gandhi government, and has held the post of Chief Minister of Madhya Pradesh and Governor of Punjab. He was conferred the Outstanding Parliamentarian Award for the year 2000.

Arjuna Award : The Arjuna awards were instituted in 1961 by the government of India to recognize outstanding achievement in National sports. The award carries a cash prize of Rs 300,000, a bronze statuette of Arjuna and a scroll. Over the years the scope of the award has been expanded and a large number of sportspersons who belonged to the pre-Arjuna Award era, were also included in the list. Not only that the number of disciplines for which the award was to be given was also increased to include indigenous games and also in the physically handicapped category.

The Government has recently revised the Scheme for Arjuna Award for outstanding performance in sports and games. As per the revised schematic guidelines, to be eligible for the Award, a sportsperson should have had not only good performance consistently for the previous three years at the international level with excellence for the year for which the Award is recommended, but also have shown qualities of leadership, sportsmanship and a sense of discipline.

Armed Forces Day in Bangladesh : Observed on November 21. In 1971, the Liberation Armed Forces launched a combined offensive against the Pakistani Occupation Armies. On December 16, 1971, the Pakistan Army surrendered with 93,000 troops to the combined forces ending the Liberation War of Bangladesh and the Indo-Pakistani War of 1971 simultaneously.

Aroon Purie : Aroon Purie is an Indian journalist. He is the current (2005) editor of the India Today, an news magazine of India; and has held this position for the last three decades since the inception of the magazine in 1975.

Arpangachhia River : Arpangachhia river is the river Betna flowing southward through the district of Satkhira enters the Sundarbans and takes the name of Arpangachhia. The river is navigable near the mouth and debouches into the Bay of Bengal as Malancha. The Arpangachhia-Malancha is navigable and is subject to tidal influence throughout the year. The Patri Island has risen at the mouth of the river.

Artcell : Artcell (or ArtCell) is a progressive metal band of Bangladesh. The band is arguably the first progressive metal band of the country and usually experiments with tunes from other metal genres such as grunge and thrash. The current band members were school friends in Dhaka. Ershad used to be the guitarist of a band named Tantrik back in 1999. Current vocalist, Lincoln, joined Tantrik just before the group disbanded. They were looking for a bassist and a drummer, when through friends, they met Cezanne and Shaju. The members later renamed their band to Artcell in August 1999 and the band was officially formed in November 1999.

Arthashastra : Arthashastra (also spelt Arthasastra) is an ancient Indian treatise on economics and politics written sometime between the 4th century BC and 150 AD by the 'kingmaker' Chanakya (also known as Kautilya or Vishnugupta) during the early years of the Mauryan Empire. Arthashastra is sometimes translated simply as Economics. The literal Sanskrit may also be interpreted as Science of Wealth, Science of Material Gain, Science of Polity (i.e. of civil government or state) or Handbook of Profit. It explores the demands of statecraft in the prosperous but unsettled Mauryan Empire under Chandragupta Maurya. As such, it can be considered a precursor to Machiavelli's The Prince Centrally, Arthashastra argues for a benevolent autocracy managing an efficient and solid economy. It discusses the ethics of economics and the duties and obligations of a king. Many of the topics discussed are still prevalent in political philosophy and economics.

The scope of Arthashastra is, however, far wider than statecraft, and it offers an outline of the entire legal and bureaucratic framework for administering a kingdom, with a wealth of descriptive cultural detail on topics such as mineralogy, mining and metals, agriculture, animal husbandry and medicine. Although he wrote in a period of absolute rule by emperors, Chanakya also focuses on issues of welfare (for instance, redistribution of wealth during a famine) and the collective ethics that hold a society together. The authorship of Arthashastra has been disputed. While there is no direct evidence against

Chanakya being the sole author, some analysts have argued that internal stylistic variations suggest collective authorship.

Arun Jaitley : Arun Jaitley (born December 28, 1952) is an Indian politician and a former minister for commerce, industry, law and justice of the Union Government of India. He was born in New Delhi. He did his schooling from St. Xavier School, New Delhi, finishing school in 1969-70. He graduated in Commerce from Shri Ram College of Commerce, New Delhi (1973). He graduated in Law from the Faculty of Law, University of Delhi in 1977. He has been practicing law before the Supreme Court of India and several High Courts in the country since 1977. He is a designated Senior Advocate. He was the Additional Solicitor General of India for the Government of India in the year 1990. He has authored several publications on legal and current affairs.

Arun Jaitley became the spokesman of the Bharatiya Janata Party during the period preceding the 1999 general election. He has since been accused by several in the party of giving off the record briefings to spread rumours. Subsequently, he joined the council of ministers as the Minister of State with independent charge of the newly created Department of Disinvestment on October 13, 1999. He took over as Minister of State for Information and Broadcasting (independent charge) in 1999 and got additional charge of the Ministry of Law, Justice and Company Affairs. On November 7, 2000 he was elevated as a Cabinet Minister with the charge of Law, Justice and Company Affairs and the additional charge of the Ministry of Shipping. He demitted office as Union Minister of Law, Justice and Company Affairs on July 1, 2002 to join as General Secretary of the Bharatiya Janata Party(BJP) and functioned as its national spokesman till January, 2003. He joined the Union Cabinet again as the Minister of

Commerce & Industry and Law &Justice on 29th January, 2003.

Aruna Asaf Ali : Aruna Asaf Ali (16 July 1909—29 July 1996), was an Indian freedom fighter. Veteran of the Quit India Movement of 1942 Aruna Asaf Ali nee Ganguli, was an ardent socialist. She went underground in the 40s.

After Gandhiji and other Congress leaders were arrested, she unfuried the national flag at the August Kranti Maidan. She was imprisoned in 1930, 1932 and 1941. She was elected the first Mayor of Delhi. She was posthumously given the Bharata Ratna Award in 1997.

Aruna Roy : Aruna Roy is an Indian politician and social activist. Aruna Roy was born in Chennai, and served as an officer in the Indian Administrative Service from 1968-1975. She resigned in order to devote her time to social work and social reform. She joined the Social Work and Research Center in Tilonia, Rajasthan, which had been set up by her husband Sanjit 'Bunker' Roy.

She worked at the SWRC until 1983, then moved to Devdoondri in 1990 and set up the Mazdoor Kisan Shakti Sangathana, a group which is a working example of a transparent organization. The MKSS built a grassroots movement that has triggered broad debate and a nationwide demand for the public's right to scrutinize official records—a crucial check against arbitrary governance.

Aruna Roy is a strong supporter of the movement for Right to Information, which succeeded in getting the Rajasthan Right to Information Bill passed. Her contribution to the cause has been widely appreciated. In 2000, she was awarded the Ramon Magsaysay award for Community Leadership and International Understanding, along with J Arputham, the President of the National Slumdwellers'

Federation. Aruna Roy requested that the award be given to the Mazdoor Kisan Shakti Sangathana, but was informed that it was only given to individuals. She put the award money into a trust to support the process of democratic struggles. She is currently one of the members of National Advisory Council.

Arunachal Dragon Force : The Arunachal Dragon Force (ADF), also known as the East India Liberation Front, is a violent secessionist movement in the eastern Indian state of Arunachal Pradesh. The ADF seeks to create an independent state resembling the pre-British Teola Country consisting of area currently in Arunachal Pradesh as well as neighboring Assam.

Arunachal Pradesh : Arunachal Pradesh is a region administered by India as a state. It is part of what are called the Seven Sister States of the Northeast of India. Arunachal Pradesh borders the state of Assam to the south and Nagaland to the south east. Myanmar lies to the east of the state, Bhutan to the west, while the McMahon Line separates it from the zone of control of the People's Republic of China to the north. Itanagar is the capital of the state.

Arunachal Pradesh is one of two main disputed regions between India and China, the other being Aksai Chin: the People's Republic of China does not recognize the state of Arunachal Pradesh, nor the McMahon Line, which it regards as an illegal line of occupation. Instead, China calls the area South Tibet, and splits the area nominally among six border counties of Tibet Autonomous Region: (from west to east) Cona, Lhünzê, Nang, Mainling, Mêdog, and Zayü. At the same time, both the PRC and India have defined a Line of Actual Control, and it is widely believed that this dispute is not likely to result in actual hostilities.

Arunachaleshwara Temple : Arunachaleshwara Temple in Tiruvannamalai the home of Annamalayaar or Arunachaleswarar (Lord Shiva worshipped as a Shiva Lingam) and Unnamulaiyaal (Apitakuchambaal - Parvati), is one of the largest temples in India. It occupies a special place in the Saivite realm and is regarded as one of the Pancha Bhoota Stalams (one of the five grand temples associated with the five basic elements) – associated with the element Fire, the other four being Tiruvanaikkaval (Water), Chidambaram] (Space), Kanchipuram (Earth) and Sri Kalahasti (Wind) respectively. Shiva is said to have manifested himself in the form of a massive column of fire, whose crown and feet, Bhramma and Vishnu attempted in vain to reach. A celebration of this manifestation is seen today in the age old traditions observed in the Shivaratri and the Karthigai Deepam Utsavams held here.

Arundhati Roy : Susanna Arundhati Roy the first Indian woman to have won Britain's prestigious Booker Prize, was born on 24th November 1961 in Bengal and grew up in Aymanam village, Kottayam, Kerala. When she was just 16, she left her home and settled in Delhi. There she did her degree in Architecture at the Delhi School of Architecture.

In 1990s she became known for her work as screenwriter. Her debut novel 'The God of Small Things' which shot her into prominence in 1997, by winning the prestigious British Booker prize in London and becoming an international best seller. The book, which took almost five years to complete, gives an insight to the social and political life in a village in South India through the eyes of seven year old twins and how it effects/disrupts their small lives.

In the years following her success, she has turned to social activism. She has been an active participant in public demonstrations against the construction of the Sardar

Sarovar Dam on the Narmada river in Western India and has donated a substantial amount around 1.5million rupees, equivalent to her Booker Prize money, for the cause. She was even arrested along with other protestors for campaigning for the cause.

With her latest publications, Arundhati is carving a niche for herself as a political journalist. This unusual women who has been on several lists of 'the 50 most beautiful women in the world' is not intimated by her success and fame but is an inspiration to all those who seek to speak up against the powers in support of the poor and the oppressed. She now lives in Delhi with her husband Pradip Krishen and his two daughters Pia and Mithva from a previous marriage.

Arvalem Caves : The celebrated caves of Arvalem, belonging to a remote era of Goa, are in a westerly direction not far away from the temple of Rudreshwar and are of archaeological interest. A mythical background is attached to these caves. Some are of the opinion that these caves have been carved by the travelling Buddhist monks. An inscription is noticed on a Shivalinga with a circular top in cave No.2 Its is in Sanskrit and in Brahmi characters of the 7th century A.D. It reads as Sambalura-vasi Ravih.

ARY Group : The ARY Group is a Middle East based company owned by a Pakistani businessman, Haji Abdul Rahman Yaqoob (ARY). The ARY Group is into various sectors, which include retail, residential and TV channels.

Arya Samaj : Arya Samaj (Aryan Society or Society of Nobles) is a Hindu reform movement in India that was founded by Swami Dayananda in 1875. He was a sannyasin (renouncer) who believed in the infallible authority of the Vedas. Dayananda advocated the doctrine of karma and reincarnation, and emphasised the ideals of brahmacharya (chastity) and sanyasa (renunciation).

Arya Samaj unequivocally condemned iconolatry, animal sacrifices, ancestor worship, pilgrimages, priestcraft, offerings made in temples, the caste system, untouchability and child marriages, on the grounds that all these lacked Vedic sanction. It aimed to be a universal church based on the authority of the Vedas. Dayananda stated that he wanted 'to make the whole world Aryan'. That is, he wanted to develop a missionary Hinduism based on the universality of the Vedas. To this end the Arya Samaj set up schools and missionary organisations, extending its activities outside India. It now has branches around the world. It has a disproportional amount of adherents among people of Indian ancestry in Suriname and the Netherlands, in comparison with India.

Arya Samaj is a global organisation having about 8000 and odd Arya Samaj units popularly known as Arya Samaj Temples but not in the orthodoxical appearance. They are rather the conrtolling offices of the philanthropic activities undertaken by the team in the society. The apex body of Arya Samaj ie. SARVADESHIK ARYA PRATINIDHI SABHA is based at Delhi.CaptDev Ratan Arya is the President and Shri Vimal Wadhawan Arya is the Secretary of the SAPS.

Aryabhata : Aryabhata (476 – 550) is the first of the great mathematician-astronomers of the classical age of India. He lived in Kusumapura, which his commentator Bhaskara I (629 AD) identifies with Pataliputra (modern Patna). Aryabhata's Magnum Opus, the Aryabhatiya, is a concise text of 123 stanzas in Sanskrit that provide insight into his discoveries. It presents astronomical and mathematical theories in which the Earth was taken to be spinning on its axis and the periods of the planets were given with respect to the sun (in other words, it was heliocentric).

Aryabhata gave close approximation for Pi. He also propounded the Heliocentric theory of the universe, thus predating Copernicus by almost one thousand years. The 8th century Arabic translation of the Aryabhatiya was translated into Latin in the 13th century, before the time of Copernicus. Through this translation, European mathematicians may have learned methods for calculating square and cube roots, and it is also possible that Aryabhata's work had an influence on European astronomy. Aryabhata was the first astronomer to make an attempt at measuring the Earth's circumference since Erastosthenes. Aryabhata accurately calculated the Earth's circumference as 24,835 miles, which was only 0.2% smaller than the actual value of 24,902 miles. This approximation remained the most accurate for over a thousand years.

Aryan Invasion Theory : The "Aryan Invasion Theory", abbreviated AIT, is a complex polemical construct used in the context of discussions of South Asian prehistory of the period 3000BC to 1000BC. Max Muller, a German Indologist appointed by British during colonial rule in India, has coined the term. The point at dispute is whether the original speakers of Indic languages were autochthonous to the Indian subcontinent, or entered the region from outside.

The case of the supporters of the AIT may be set down as follows. Unlike in the case of Mesopotamia where there are readable written inscriptions dating as far back as the "Sumerian period in 3100 BC, there are no written records from the Indian subcontinent before the third century BC except the Indus Valley seals which remain by general academic consensus unreadable despite occasional claims to the contrary. Yet, one must bear in mind that the earliest Hindu scriptures, the Vedas, were orally transmitted and hence cannot be dated. One set of written records from northern Syria dated to the early second millennium BC does contain several names and words that bear very close relationship to Vedic Sanskrit. Vedic

Sanskrit is an Indo-European language like classical Latin and Greek. This means that, analogous to the process by which the English language has spread from an island off the coast of continental Europe to cover all of North America and Australia, the languages that developed into English, German, French, Italian, Greek, Russian, Farsi, Pashto, Punjabi, Gujarati, Bengali and Sinhala are all directly derived from a common ancestor which was spoken in a single relatively small area at a point in the distant past. There is no general agreement on either the exact date or place of this proto-Indo-European language even with the benefit of several complex arguments based on the linguistic, archaeological and philological evidence. Current mainstream opinion regards the Indian subcontinent as almost certainly an area into which an Indo-European branch diffused rather than from which the Indo-European branch could have spread over its subsequent range.

Aryan Race : The term Aryan race refers to a model of racial identity that was prevalent in Europe from around the 1880s through to 1945, most notably in Nazi Germany. It has become associated with the theory that the Indo-European peoples constitute a master race. The word "Aryan" derives from cultures of Iran and India. It was originally used in various Indo-Iranian languages. Possibly it originally referred to clan-identity, but it certainly later had a meaning roughly similar to "noble" or "honorable". It was sometimes used by the speakers of these languages to refer to those who were ennobled by spirtual knowledge. Support for the superiority of the Aryan race is sometimes referred to as Aryanism. This should not be confused with the unrelated religious belief known as Arianism.

Aryavarta : Aryavarta is the ancient name for northern and central India. It is erroneous to give this name to the whole of India, since the borders of Aryavarta have been described differently in sources from different times. The Manu Smriti gives the name to "the tract between the Himalaya and the Vindhya ranges, from the eastern to the western sea". The Vasistha Dharma Sutra I.8-9 and 12-13 locates Aryavarta to the east of the disappearance of the Sarasvati in the desert, to the west of Kalakavana, to the north of the mountains of Pariyatra and Vindhya and to the south of the Himalaya. Baudhayana Dharmasutra gives similar definitions and declares that Aryavarta is the land that lies west of Kalakavana, east of Adarsana, south of the Himalayas and north of the Vindhyas. Patanjali's Mahabhaya defines Aryavarta like the Vasistha Dharma Sutra.

Another sutra confines Aryavarta to the Ganga—Yamuna doab, and considers people from beyond this area as of mixed origin, and hence not worthy of emulation by the Aryans. Some sutras recommend expiatory acts for those who have crossed the boundaries of Aryavarta. Baudhayana Srautasutra recommends this for those who have crossed the boundaries of Aryavarta and ventured into Afghanistan and other far away places. Aryavarta may thus have different definitions. In some later texts, Northwest-India is even seen as "impure", probably due to invasions. The Karnaparva 43.5-8 states that those who live on the Sindhu and the five rivers of the Punjab are impure and dharmabahya.

Arzi Hukumat-e-Azad Hind : Arzi Hukumat-e-Azad Hind, was a puppet state established by Indian nationalists-in-exile in areas of British India and Southeast Asian British colonial territory occupied by Imperial Japan during the Second World War. It was founded and led by Netaji Subhas Chandra Bose on October 21, 1943 in Singapore with the fiscal and political assistance of the Axis Powers, namely Japan. While it possessed all the nominal requisites of a legitimate government, it lacked both universal political recognition and large and definite areas of sovereign territory until the government assumed control of the Andaman and Nicobar Islands from Japan in 1943. It had the backing of the "Azad Hind Fauj", known in English as the Indian National Army (INA), who were in collaboration with, and were resourcefully dependent on, the Imperial Japanese Army. The government of Azad Hind had its own currency, court and civil code, but in practical application the government was for a Japanese anti-Western, anti-imperialist ideological initiative against the British in India.

It survived in a limited legal form until the collapse of the Japanese Empire in 1945. The existence of Azad Hind was essentially coterminous with the existence of the Indian National Army. While the government itself continued until the civil administration of the Andaman Islands was returned to the jurisdiction of the British towards the end of the war, the limited power of Azad Hind was effectively ended with the surrender of the last major contingent of INA troops in Rangoon and the death of Subhas Chandra Bose in a plane crash in 1945.

A S Bokhari : Prof. Syed Ahmed Shah Patras Bokhari (1898–1958) was a Pakistani educationist, broadcaster, diplomat and essayist. Before independence of Pakistan in 1947, he was director general of the All India Radio. Basically he was a professor of English literature and thus served as principal of the Government College Lahore. The famous Urdu poet Faiz Ahmed Faiz and the leader of free verse in Urdu, Noon Meem Rashid etc were among his famous students. After the independence of Pakistan, he served as the permanent representative of the country in the United Nations from 1949–52. He died during his service and is buried in New York, USA. A. S. Bokhari was born in Peshawar, NWFP, and educated in Government College Lahore. His thin volume of essays,

Patras Kay Mazameen (Essays of Pitras), is considered the asset of Urdu humor. Due to his global vision he was known as 'a citizen of the world.'

Asansol : Asansol is an important industrial city in the state of West Bengal, India and the third largest city in West Bengal, after Kolkata and Howrah. It is a sub-division located in Burdwan District, in the western periphery of the state, adjoining the state of Bihar. The city's economy is based on primarily the coal and steel industries. Situated in the Damodar River valley, the city has evolved and expanded over time to a current population of one million, ranking it 29th in India.

Asansol was built on the sides of the Grand Trunk Road and is essentially a linear city stretching approximately forty kilometeres along this ancient highway. The city has very good road and railway connectivity with Kolkata, and is a divisional headquarters of the Eastern Railways, a subsidiary of Indian Railways. The railway station is an important junction for the Eastern Railways, transporting people as well as minerals, grain and finished goods. It has a direct route to Jamshedpur and its industries that passes via Adra and Puruliya to the south of Asansol. There are also direct trains from here to New Jalpaiguri that connects the city to Darjeeling, a famous hill station in north West Bengal.

Asfandyar Wali Khan : Asfandyar Wali Khan is the Leader of the Awami National Party in Pakistan. His father, Khan Wali Khan, was the party's first President. He is the grandson of Khan Abdul Ghaffar Khan. Asfandyar Wali Khan is the son of Khan Abdul Wali Khan and grandson of Khan Abdul Ghaffar Khan. He is the present President of the Awami National Party and has served as Member of Provincial Assembly, Member of National Assembly and presently Senator in Pakistan's Parliament.

Asha Bhonsle : The famous playback singer, Asha Bhonsle has sung over 20,000 songs in practically every Indian language and also in English. She has a unique style of singing.

Asha was born on 8th September, 1933 in Goar, Maharastra to a family of musicians, the Mangeshkar's. Asha started her career in her elder sister Lata Mangeshkar's shadow. Her first song was from the movie 'Chunaria' (1948) and her first solo was for the movie 'Raat Ki Raani' (1949). In the beginning her talents were not known much and it was music directors like O.P. Nayyar and R.D. Burman who gave her a chance and helped Asha to get out of the image of her sister. She has a unique voice- a sexy, cheerful style of singing of her own. Famous hits like 'Piya tu', 'Dum Maro Dum' are a proof of her unique style.

Asha has also sung for private albums; Hindi pop and ghazals. She is at ease with both ghazals as well as fast numbers. She was the first Indian Singer to be nominated for the Grammy Award in 1997 and in 2001 she won the Dada Phalke Award and Dayawati Modi Award.

Asha Posley : Asha Posleywas first actress in Pakistani films. Asha Posley was the daughter of music director Inayat Ali Nath and was heroine in the first ever released film in Pakistan which was Teri Yaad (1948). She did not succeed as a heroine and appeared in many of B Grade films in the 1950s.

Later in her career she was stereotyped in mostly vamp roles. Her last film was Insaaf (1986). She died in Pakistan in 1998 after 12 years retirement.

Ashfaq Ahmed : Ashfaq Ahmed (22 Aug 1925 - 7 Sep 2004), was a distinguished writer, playwright, broadcaster, intellectual and spiritualist from Pakistan. His prime qualities of heart and hand earned appreciations across the borders. He was regarded by many as the best Urdu short-story writer after Saadat Hasan Manto, Ismat Chughtai and Krishan Chandar following the publication of his famous short-story "Gaddarya" [The Shepherd] in 1955.

Ashoka Chakra : The Ashoka Chakra is an ancient Indian depiction of the Dharma wheel, the Wheel of Life and Cosmic Order (Chakra means wheel; Dharma means cosmic order). The wheel has 24 spokes, each of which signifies a spiritual principle.

The Ashoka Chakra has been widely inscribed on many relics of the Mauryan Emperor Ashoka The Great (Reigned 273-232 BCE), most prominent among which is the Lion Capital of Sarnath and The Ashoka Pillar. The most visible use of the Ashoka Chakra today is at the center of the National flag of Republic of India (adopted on 22 July 1947), where it is rendered in a Navy-blue color on a White background, by replacing the symbol of Charkha (Spinning wheel) of the pre-independence versions of the flag.

Ashoka Pillar : It is at Saranath, 10km north of Varanasi. Sarnath, the place where Buddha gave his first sermon is a popular Buddhist pilgrimage centre. The Ashoka pillar stands in front of the main stupa where Ashoka sat and meditated. The Sarnath Archaeological Museum at Ashoka Marg, houses a copy of Ashoka's lion pillar and some sculptures.

Ashoka the Great : Ashoka the Great was the emperor of the Mauryan Empire from 273 BCE to 232 BCE. After a number of military conquests, Ashoka reigned over most of South Asia and beyond, from present-day Afghanistan to Bengal and as far south as Mysore. An early supporter of Buddhism, Ashoka established monuments marking several significant sites in the life of Shakyamuni Buddha, and according to Buddhist tradition was closely involved in the preservation and transmission of Buddhism. In his edicts he is reffered to as "Devaanaampriya" or "The Beloved Of The Gods".

One of the greatest emperors known to Indian history, Ashoka, was the grandson of Chandragupta Maurya and the son of Bindusar. Born in 294 BC as second son to Bindusar, the King of Patliputra, Ashoka was not heir apparent. After his father died, his elder brother Suman was to take over the reins of the Kingdom. But as most of the ministers found Ashoka more efficient, they helped him attain power.

Ashoka was a good administrator and at first set about restoring peace in his kingdom. Ashoka was initiated into Buddhism, after which his life was completely transformed. He religiously followed the principles of Buddhism—that of truth, charity, kindness, purity and goodness. He did his bit towards the propagation of this religion by engraving it's principles on pillars throughout his kingdom. The Ashoka pillars, as they are now called, were over 40 feet high and extremely heavy. He also attempted to spread this religion to Syria, Egypt and Macedonia, and sent his son Mahendra and daughter Sangamitra to Sri Lanka for this purpose.

Ashoka opened charitable hospitals and dispensaries for the welfare of the poor. He planted trees to provide shade and opened inns for the shelter of travelers and laid out green parks and gardens to beautify his kingdom. Wells and tanks were also constructed for the benefit of his people. He believed in non-violence and so he banned the sacrifice of animals. Besides this he opened clinics for birds and animals too. In his edicts he is reffered to as "Devaanaampriya" or "The Beloved Of The Gods". He died in 232 BC. After doing a great deal of good for his kingdom and the world at large. His fame has spread far and wide. To commemorate his rule and its implications the Government of India has adopted the Ashoka Chakra as its national symbol, which can be seen till today on the national flag.

Ashokastami Fair : At Unakotitirtha in Kailashahar sub-division is held the *Ashokastami fair* in March-April every year. Thousands of pilgrims from different parts of the state assemble here to offer Puja to the numerous rock-cut images of gods and goddesses found on the walls of the Unakoti hill.

Ashoknagar District : Ashoknagar District is a district of Madhya Pradesh state in central India. The city of Ashoknagar is the administrative headquarters of the district. The district has an area of 4673.94 km^2. It is bounded on the east by the Betwa River, which separates it from Lalitpur District of Uttar Pradesh and Sagar District of Madhya Pradesh. Vidisha District lies to the south. The Kali Sindh River forms the western border of the district, which separates it from Guna District. Shivpuri District lies to the north. The district has a population of 688,920 (2001 census). It is divided into four tehsils, Ashoknagar, Chanderi, Issagarh, and Mungaoli. The district was created on August 15, 2003 when it was split from Guna District.

Ashraf Jehangir Qazi : Ashraf Jehangir Qazi (b. 1942) is the Special Representative of the UN Secretary-General for Iraq, and a former senior Pakistani diplomat. He was appointed by UN Secretary-General, Kofi Annan, on 14th of July, 2004. His predecessor, Sérgio Vieira de Mello, was killed in the Canal Hotel bombing on August 19, 2003.

Prior to this current assignment, he was Pakistan's ambassador to the United States since September 2002. Before that he was Pakistan's High Commissioner to India (since 1997), ambassador to China (1994-97), to Russia (1991-94), to then-East Germany (1990-91) and Syria (1986-88). He also had diplomatic assignments in Copenhagen, Tokyo, Cairo, Tripoli and London.

Ashtamudi Lake : Ashtamudi Lake (Ashtamudi Kayal) is in Kollam district of Kerala state in south India. Ashtamudi Lake is designated a wetland of international importance under the Ramsar Convention.

Ashvamedha: The Ashvamedha, or the horse-sacrifice is one of the most important royal rituals of Vedic religion (1st millennium BC, the last recorded performance dates to the 4th century AD), described in detail in the Yajurveda (books 22–25) and the pertaining commentaries.

Asia Pacific Institute of Information Technology : APIIT, short for Asia Pacific Institute of Information Technology, is an educational institution specializing in providing Information Technology (IT)-related education and training programmes, consulting services and research and development activities. More over, APIIT also provide you Business Courses. Formed and based originally in Malaysia, APIIT now has established may other centres throughout the Asia Pacific region, including Pakistan, India and Sri Lanka and, Australia. APIIT was initiated by the Malaysian government and is funded by the Sapura Group.

Asian Elephant : The Asian Elephant, sometimes known as the Indian Elephant (Elephas maximus) is one of the two or three living species of elephant, and the only living species of the genus Elephas. It is smaller than its African relatives, and the easiest way to distinguish the two is the smaller ears of the Asian Elephant. Asian elephants tend to grow to around two to four meters (7-12 feet) in height and 3,000-5,000 kilograms (6,500-11,000 pounds) in weight.

This animal is widely domesticated, and has been used in forestry in Southeast Asia for centuries and also for use in ceremonial purposes. Historical sources point out they were sometimes used during the harvest season primarily for milling. Wild elephants attract tourist money to the areas where they can most readily be seen, but damage crops and may enter villages to raid gardens.

Asianet : Asianet is a premier Indian company that provides services in satellite telivision, cable TV, broadband internet connections, web hosting and VoIP services.The comapany is owned by Asianet Communications Limited, headed by Dr.Raji Menon, with its head offices at Studio Complex, Puliyarakonam, Thiruvananthapuram. Aisanet operates three Malayalam televison channels, including the Asianet channel, which was the first private television channel in Kerala.

Asianet began its operations by telecasting for two hours daily in 1993 which was increased to round the clock. The Global channel came into being first as a segment catering to the Gulf viewers and grew into a 24-hour channel in 2001. The channel was relaunched as Asianet News on May 1, 2003 signifying an increased stress on news and current affairs in deference to viewers' demands. On July 23, 2005 Asianet launched its third channel—Asianet Plus, a complete entertainment channel for the youth. The signals of Asianet cover the entire Indian sub-continent, Sri Lanka, China, the South East Asia, the entire Persian Gulf, the UK, Europe, USA and the lower half of the former Soviet Union. This is virtually half the Globe, reaching sixty-odd countries.

Asiatic Lion : The Asiatic Lion (Panthera leo persica) is a subspecies of lion. The last remnant of the Asiatic Lion, which in historical times ranged from Greece to India through Iran (Persia), lives in the Gir Forest National Park of western India. About 300 lions live in a 1,412 km^2 (558 square miles) sanctuary in the state of Gujarat. In 1907 there were only 13 lions left in the Gir, when the Nawab of Junagadh gave complete protection to them.

Unlike the tiger, which prefers dense forests with adequate cover, the lion inhabits the scrub-type deciduous forests. Compared to its African counterpart, the Indian lion has a scantier mane. The lion seldom comes into contact with the tiger which also lives in India, but not in the Gir region as this forest is hotter and more arid than the habitat preferred by the tiger.

Asiatic Society : The Asiatic Society was founded by Sir William Jones (1746-1794) on 15 January 1784 in Calcutta, the capital of British India, to enhance and further the cause of Oriental research. It was formerly known as "The Royal Asiatic Society of Bengal."

Asif Nawaz : Asif Nawaz (Asif Nawaz Janjua) was Chief of Army Staff, Pakistan (1991–1993) Asif Nawaz's tenure as Chief of Army Staff was ended abruptly by his death on 8 January 1993, apparently from a heart attack. He is widely remembered as having died under mysterious circumstances.

Askari Aviation : Askari Aviation is based in Rawalpindi, Punjab, Pakistan. Askari Aviation was established in 1995, to maintain, operate and market aircraft / helicopter compatible to international standards. Askari Aviation also offers to co-ordinate and generate necessary financial resources or enter into joint venture satisfying specific requirements of its client. The flying and maintenance crew is based on highly qualified, experienced professionals from the Armed Forces of Pakistan. This offers highest quality of service and safety standards, ensuring commitment to professional excellence.

Asma Jahangir : Asma Jilani Jahangir (born 1952 Lahore) is a Pakistani lawyer and human rights activist.

She has been the United Nations Special Rapporteur on Freedom of Religion or Belief of the Commission on Human Rights since 2004. She took over this position from being UN Special Rapporteur on Extrajudicial, Arbitrary and Summary Executions.

Born into a family with a long history of human rights work, Jahangir herself became involved at a young age in protests against the military regime in Pakistan. She completed her law degree in 1978. She cut her teeth during agitation against the Hudud Laws put in place as part of Gen. Muhammad Zia-ul-Haq's Islamization program in Pakistan. She is a founding member of the Human Rights Commission of Pakistan, and has served as Secretary-General and later Chair of the same. Asma Jahangir is also law partner and co-founder with her sister Hina Jilani of Pakistan's first all-female law practice.

Asom Gana Parishad : Asom Gana Parishad (Assam Peoples Association), political party in Assam, India. The party recently split, with former Chief Minister,Prafulla Kumar Mahanta, forming the Asom Gana Parishad (Progressive). AGP was formed after the historic Assam Accord of 1985 when Prafulla Kumar Mahanta was elected as the youngest chief minister of the country. The AGP has formed government twice from 1985 to 1989 and from 1996 to 2001.

Assam : Assam is a northeastern state of India with its capital at Dispur. Located just below the eastern Himalayan foothills, it is surrounded by the other northeastern states: Arunachal Pradesh, Nagaland, Manipur, Mizoram, Tripura and Meghalaya. Assam and its commercial capital Guwahati form the gateway to the northeastern states, together called the seven sisters. These states are connected to the rest of India via Assam's border with West Bengal and a narrow strip called the

"Chicken's Neck." Assam shares international borders with Bhutan and Bangladesh.

Assam Agitation : The Assam Agitation (or Assam Movement) was a popular movement in Assam between 1979 and 1985 against illegal immigrants. The movement, led by All Assam Students' Union and the All Assam Gana Sangram Parishad, set an agitational program to compel the government to identify and expel the illegal immigrants. The agitational programs were largely non-violent, but there were incidents of acute violence, like the Nellie Massacre. The agitational program ended in 1985 following the Assam Accord that was signed between the agitation leaders and the Government of India. The agitation leaders formed a political party, Asom Gana Parishad, which came to power in the state of Assam in the elections of 1985.

Assam Bengal Railway : Assam Bengal Railway was conceived in the late eighties of the nineteenth century with the objective of developing communication system of the eastern region of British India, particularly, Assam and Eastern Bengal. By that time, railways had come to expand in different parts of the subcontinent. In the eastern region, the only important railway system was the eastern bengal railway extending from calcutta to kushtia near the confluence of the river garai with the ganges. In 1870, an extension was made up to Goalanda at the confluence of the brahmaputra and the Ganges. It was not before 1902 that this line was further extended up to Dhubri in Assam. The line to Goalanda was expected to absorb the traffic passing through that place in boats and newly introduced steamships along the Ganges between Calcutta and the northwest and along the Brahmaputra between Calcutta and the northeast.

Assam Forest Museum : This museum is situated at South Kamrup Division, Guwahati. It has collections of timber, cane and ivory work, tusks and horns and models of buildings and bridges. Visit : 10am—4pm weekdays. Saturdays 10am -1.30pm

Assam Macaque : The Assam Macaque (Macaca assamensis) is a macaque living in India, Nepal, Vietnam and southern China. These animals are diurnal. They are 50-73 cm long plus a tail of 19-38 cm. Males weight 10-14,5 kg., females 8-12 kg. The Assam Macaques feed on fruits, leaves, inverbrates and cereals.

Assam Rifles : The Assam Rifles are a paramilitary force. Currently there are 33 battalions of Assam Rifles under the control of the Indian Ministry of Home Affairs (MHA). The first form of what is now the Assam Rifles was Cachar Levy, a paramilitary police force of 750 men that was formed under British colonial rule in 1835. It was formed as police unit to protect settlements against tribal raids and other assaults as British rule slowly moved to northwards. In 1870 the existing elements were merged into three Assam Military Police battalions in the Lushai Hills (later 1st battalion), Lakhimpur (2nd battalion) and Naga Hills (3rd battalion). A fourth battalion was formed 1915 in Imphal. During the World War I, Assam Military Police troopers were part of the Indian forces that fought for Britain in Europe and Middle East. The name Assam Rifles was assigned in 1917 as recognition of their part in the war. After the war they served in Northern India against rebellions and riots.

During the World War II, the Assam Rifles helped manage the influx of refugees coming from Burma fleeing the Japanese advance in 1942. They also organized a resistance group called Victor Force or V-Force on the Burmese border to harass Japanese communications. Troopers also served in the battle of Kohima and earned numerous unit citations. Between the end of World War II and Indian independence, the Assam Rifles were composed of 5 battalions that were one part of the civil police under the Assam Inspector General of Police. After independence, the Indian government assigned the Assam Rifles its own Director General.

As the numbers of the force and the number of battalions gradually increased, the rank of the force commander was also upgraded until now it is that of lieutenant general. One of the tasks of the unit was to keep order in the aftermath of the 1950 Assam earthquake and assist in resettlement. In October 1962 the Assam Rifles were the frontline troops in the beginning of the Chinese-Indian War. The Assam Rifles also maintained their peacekeeping roles in the Northern India in the face of tribal unrest and insurgency. The Assam Rifles also handle medical assistance, aid in basic education, assist in reconstruction and agriculture and handles communications in remote areas.

Assam State Museum : The Assam State Museum has collections of archaeology, sculpture, paintings, metal, ivory and woodwork, costumes and ethnology. There are exhibits of reconstructed huts of Assamese tribes. You can walk right through these village huts. There are also displays of weavings and musical instruments. It is open from 1000 to 1630 from Tuesday to Saturday and 0800 - 1200 on Sundays. Closed on Mondays and second Saturdays.

Assam State Zoo and Botanical Gardens : The Zoo and the landscaped Botanical gardens are located about 5km east of the railway station. The zoo mostly has open enclosures with swamp tapirs, tigers, leopards, Assam's famous one horned rhinos and a rich bird life among other species. Open daily except Fridays.

Astor Wildlife Sanctuary : Astor Wildlife Sanctuary is located in Kaghan Valley, Northern Areas, Pakistan.

Astor Wildlife Sanctuary covers 416 sq km on the north side of the Astor Valley from the junction with the Indus River to the confluence with the Parashing Gah.

Asvaghosa : Asvaghosa was an Indian philosopher-poet, born in Saketa in Central India. He is believed to have been the first Sanskrit dramatist, and is considered the greatest Indian poet before Kalidasa. He was first a student of non-Buddhist teaching, but upon losing an argument with Parshva converted to Buddhism. He became a religious adviser to the Kushan king Kanishka.

Atal Bihari Vajpayee : Shri. Atal Bihari Vajpayee, the ex Prime Minister of India, is a multi faceted political personality. He was born on 25th December 1924, at Gwalior, Madhya Pradesh to parents Krishna Bihari Vajpayee, a school teacher and Krishna Devi. He was educated at Victoria alias Laxmibai College, Gwalior and D.A.V. College, Kanpur and holds a Postgraduate degree in Political Science.

Shri Vajpayee's first brush with nationalist politics was in his student days, when he joined the Quit India Movement of 1942 which hastened the end of British colonial rule. A student of political science and law, it was in college that he developed a keen interest in foreign affairs, an interest he has nourished over the years and put to skilful use while representing India at various multilateral and bilateral foray. For a while he studied law, but midstream he chose to become a journalist. This choice was largely influenced by the fact that as a student he had been an activist in India's struggle for freedom. Shri Vajpayee had embarked upon a journalist's career, which was cut short in 1951 when he joined Bharatiya Jana Sangh.

As a founder-member of the Jana Sangh, 1951-1977 (now known as Bharatiya Janatha Party) he served as the party's president and took it to new heights. He served as the BJP's president for the first five years of its existence, laying the foundation for the party's awesome growth in the last one decade. As a parliamentarian, he has been elected to the Lok Sabha nine times and to the Rajya Sabha twice.

Apart from politics, Shri Vajpayee has participated in various social and cultural activities. The Krishna Bihari Vajpayee Trust set up by him in the name of his late father promotes a number of constructive activities for the uplift of the deprived and poor as well as children. He has been a Member of the National Integration Council since 1961. Some of his other associations include being President of All India Station Masters and Assistant Station Masters Association (1965-70); Pandit Deendayal Upadhyay Smarak Samiti (1968-84); Deen Dayal Dham, Farah, Mathura, U.P; and Janmabhomi Smarak Samiti, 1969 onwards.

Vajpayee has many literary and artistic accomplishments to his credit. India's second highest civilian honour, the Padma Vibhushan, was conferred upon him in 1992 in recognition of his selfless dedication to his first and only love, India, and his more than half-a-century of service to society and the nation. In 1994, he was named India's 'Best Parliamentarian'. Over the decades, he has emerged as a national leader who has mass appeal and commands respect for his liberal worldview and commitment to democratic ideals.

Ataur Khan Rahman : Ataur Khan Rahman (1928-1997) was actor, singer, music composer and film director. He was born on 11 December 1928 in Ramkantapur village of manikganj district in Bangladesh.

Khan Ataur Rahman received nine awards in recognition of his contribution to film industry. These included Pakistan Film Festival Award, Nigar Award, international film festival awards at Moscow and Tashkent, and the National Film Award of Bangladesh. Khan Ataur Rahman died on 1 January 1997.

Atharvaveda : The Atharvaveda is a sacred text of Hinduism, part of the four books of the Vedas: the 4th Veda. According to tradition, the Atharvaveda was mainly composed by two groups of rishis known as the Bhrigus and the Angirasas. The Atharvaveda, while undoubtedly belonging to the core Vedic corpus, in some ways represents an independent parallel tradition to that of the Rigveda and Yajurveda. The Jaina and Buddha texts are considerably more hostile to the AV (they call it Aggvana or Ahavana Veda) than they are to the other Hindu texts. They even call it a non-Aryan Veda concocted by paippalada for human sacrifices. The Hindu texts too have taken a less than charitable view and have on occasions omitted the reference to the "Atharvan" text in the context of Vedic literature, though some attribute this to the fact that the Atharvaveda was a later addition chronologically. The Atharvan Parisishthas themselves state that specific priests of the Mauda and Jalada schools should be avoided. It is even stated that women associated with Atharvan may suffer from abortions

Athirapally Waterfall : Athirapally is a waterfall on the banks of Chalakkudy River. It is 800ft high and is situated in Thrissur district of Kerala, India

Atif Aslam : Atif Aslam is a Pakistani musician. He was born in Wazirabad, Gujranwala and educated in Lahore and Rawalpindi. Atif has won several awards for his performace both in India and Pakistan. Atif Aslam has already reached at a great place at this young age and he surely looks like he is going to provide more quality stuff to his listeners.

Atisa Dipamkara Shrijnana : Atisa Dipamkara Shrijnana (982 - 1054 CE) was a Buddhist teacher who reintroduced Buddhism into Tibet after King Langdharma had nearly destroyed it. He studied and mastered all of the traditions of Buddhism in India. After different trials to invite him to Tibet, he finally accepted the invitation and came to Tibet for the rest of his life. Some Tibetan sources say he was also abbot of Vikramashila University at one point, one of the great centers of Buddhist learning after Nalanda University.

Atish Raj : Atish Raj was a seminal Industrial and avant-garde Pakistani rock band formed and fronted by eccentric Pakistani music journalist and writer, Nadeem F. Paracha. Even though the band only recorded two albums between 1994 and 1995 and distributed only a few thousand copies, the demand for these albums has grown among new fans of experimental music in Pakistan. Paracha's legacy and reputation as an iconoclastic and eccentric journalist and writer and the country's frontline music critic has further heightened curiosity and interest in the band's albums.

A T N Bangla : ATN Bangla is a Bengali language digital cable television channel. It transmits from its studio in Dhaka, Bangladesh The channel is transmitted in South Asia, the Middle-east, Eurpope, and North America. The channel offers a wide variety of programming including news, movies, dramas, talk shows, and more. The channel started broadcast in South Asia from 15 July 1997. Broadcasts to Europe began in 2001. One of its programmes, Amrao pari (We, too, Can), won an Emmy award at the 32nd Academy of Television Arts and Science Awards in 2002. The documentary was shot and directed by 18 teenagers from Bangladesh, and was focused on the true story of Abul Khaer, a 9 year old boy, who stopped a passanger train from approaching a disjointed railtrack, and prevented a train disaster.

Atrai River : Atrai river is one of the sacred rivers mentioned in the Mahabharata. Its ancient name was Atrei.

It originates about 10 km northeast of Shiliguri town of West Bengal (India). Then it flows west of the Jamuna. It is the westernmost distributary of the Brahmaputra. It changes its name from Karatoya to Atrai near Khansama upazila of Dinajpur district. It again enters Bangladesh through naogaon district. The channel bifurcates northwest of Chirirbandar and unites again southwest of it. The western part is called the Gabura and the eastern part the Kankra. It flows through the eastern part of Dinajpur town and enters West Dinajpur of West Bengal after passing through Bhusir Bandar and Samjia Ghat.

The river then flows due south to Manda upazila dividing the east-central and west-central parts of the Barind Tract. It flows south and turns southeast, then flows through Chalan Beel and meets the Hurasagar river. It meets Jamuna near Baghabari through Hurasagar. The Atrai has several tributaries of which the Punarbhaba is the best known. Fakirni and Baral on the rightbank and the Karatoya on the leftbank also deserve mention. In the greater Rajshahi-Pabna region its tributaries are the Tulsiganga, Nandakua, Baranai and Baral. The length of the river is about 380 km.

Attock : Attock is a District located in the northwest of the Punjab province of Pakistan. The district was created in 1904 by the merger of Talagang tehsil from the Jhelum District and the Pindigheb, Fatehjang and Attock tehsils from Rawalpindi District of British Raj. The original name was Campbellpore district after Sir Campbell who founded the city of Campbellpore to the southeast of Attock Town. The name of the district was changed to Attock in 1978.

Aurangabad Caves : Lies 3 km north of Aurangabad, Maharashtra. They were excavated out of a south facing hill side overlooking the town. These caves fall into two groups about 1.5km apart. These are 10 caves belong to the Buddhist era and were excavated between 3rd and

11th century. Caves 3, 6 and 7 are specially worth visiting. The Western group of caves comprises caves 1 to 5 and the eastern group has caves 6 to 10. Cave 2 has a shrine and columned hallways, with a large Buddha as Teacher in a seated position on a panel. In cave 3, there are superb carvings on the 12 pillars of the hall way, which illustrate the jataka stories. Cave 4, a chaitya is the oldest of the lot. Cave 6 has a large Buddha and a supporting figure of Ganesh. Cave 7 is regarded as the most interesting with its images of women like Hariti and the six goddesses, including Padmini. In the rear of the hall is a large Buddha in a preaching position.

Aurangzeb : Aurangzeb also known as Alamgir I, was the ruler of the Mughal Empire from 1658 until 1707. He was and is a very controversial figure in Indian history. Unlike his predecessors, Aurangzeb led a remarkably austere and pious life. Strict adherence to Islam and Sharia (Islamic law)—as he interpreted them—were the foundations of his reign. He backed up his faith with action, abandoning the religious tolerance of his predecessors. During his reign many Hindu temples were defaced and destroyed, and many Indians converted to Islam.

Aurangzeb used vast military might to expand and consolidate the Mughal empire, at high cost. His rule inspired revolt which he constrained during his life, but which exploded and completely changed India after his death. His policies polarized India in ways that continue to this day.

Austagram Mosque : Austagram Mosque a five-domed structure, widely known as Qutb Shah's Mosque, is located in the Bhati region of present Kishoreganj district. Restored and repaired by the Department of Archaeology, Bangladesh, the mosque has now been given a better look.

The mosque is not dated by inscription. Local legends ascribe the building to the saint Qutb Shah, whose tomb is nearby. But at what time the saint flourished here and constructed the mosque is not known. However, the constructional and decorative aspects of the building, such as the curved cornice, the semi-circular mihrab niches, the two centred pointed arches, the corner towers rising up to the roof level, terracotta ornamentation and the panel decorative designs on the outer surface of the walls, suggest that it is a product of the Sultanate period and may be dated approximately in the second half of the 16th century.

Avani Moolam : The Avani Moolam festival celebrated in Madurai on the Moolam constellation day in the month of Avani, depicts of the legendary sports of Lord Shiva at Madurai. It is a picturesque festival with distinctive local colour, the eating of pittu, is a part of the day's engagement for the devotees.

Avu Devata Festival : It is the festival of Andhra Pradesh. The Avu Devata festival is celebrated for three days in the month of Jyeshtha. On the first day the devotees go to the cave and worship the deity whose idol is brought in a carriage decorated with flowers and installed at a certain place. On the second day several other idols are brought there. On the third day these deities are offered Puja and the people who should follow them back to their places are fed. In the evening, these deities are given a send—off and the Avu Devata is also taken back after the cave in the hill is decorated and worshipped. Ordinary umbrellas, silk umbrellas, embroidered umbrellas and peacock feathers are offered to the deity in fulfillment of vows. A fair is held in connection with this festival.

Dappepallc in Rayachoti taluk of Cuddapah district has Brahmagiri, a cave with the images of Erreddaiah and

Paseddaiah and the form of a cow. It was believed that, in the distant past, two bulls born in the village exhibited super natural powers. To perpetuate their memory the villagers deified them and the images of the bulls and their cow were kept in a cave. Even now when the rains fail, the priest takes bath and goes to the cave in his wet clothes to worships 'Avu Devata'. They will offer coconuts, milk, sugar, incense and eatables. It is believed that it generally rains within a week.

Awadh : Awadh (also known in various British historical texts as Oudh, Oundh or Oude) is a region in the center of the modern Indian state of Uttar Pradesh. The modern definition of Awadh geographically includes the districts of Ambedkar Nagar, Bahraich, Balrampur, Barabanki, Faizabad, Gonda, Hardoi, Lakhimpur Kheri, Lucknow, Allahabad, Kaushambi, Pratapgarh, Rai Bareilly, Shravasti, Sitapur, Sultanpur, and Unnao. The traditional capital of Awadh has been Lucknow. The region is home to a distinct dialect, Awadhi. Awadh figures in early Indian history as the Aryan kingdom of Kosala, with Ayodhya as its capital. Modern Awadh is finds historical mention only in the time of Akbar, in the late fifteenth century.

Awami National Party : The Awami National Party (ANP, Awami meaning People) is a nationalist political party (leftist) in Pakistan. The Party is mostly famous among the Pashtuns of Pakistan in NWFP, Balochistan, Federally Administered Tribal Areas, Western Punjab, Northern Areas. The Party's current president is Asfandyar Wali Khan. At the last legislative elections, 20 October 2002, the party won 1.0 % of the popular vote but no seats.

Awan : Awan is an Arabic word, which means helpers. Awans claim that they are the descendents of Hazrat Abbas, the uncle of Prophet Mohammad and one of the sons of the fourth Caliph, Hazrat Ali. Awans are among the earliest Islamic forces to enter the South Asia with the army of Muhammad bin Qasim. Awan tribe has martial tradition as they formed fighting force of many armies over the centuries. Awans joined the armies of Slave Dynasty and Khilji dynasty during the Delhi Sultanate. Amir Taimur during his invasion of South Asia met a great resistance by the Governor of Meerut Qilladar Ilyaas Awan Alvi. Amir Taimur defeated Ilyaas Awan after one and a half month of fighting. Amir Taimur was impressed with the courage and bravery of Ilyaas Awan he wrote about him in his memoirs. Awans held prominent military positions during most of the Mughul Era, likewise, they previously held during the Sultanate Period.

Awaran : Awaran district is in the center of Balochistan province of Pakistan. The district consists of three tehsils, i.e., Mashkai, Awaran, Jhal Jhao; eight patwar circles – Jairi, Gajar, Parwar, Peelar Jah, Awaran, Gashkore, Peelar Jhao and Camp Jhao; and 216 mauzas (villages). Over 98% of the people of the area are Muslims. There is a small Zikri minority. The population of Awaran is estimated to be over 200,000 in 2005. Awaran has witnessed a steady rise in population. The whole population has always been rural. The tribes in Awaran are divided into several clans. The Baloch tribes in the district are Bizenjo, Mohammed Hasni, Sajdi, Mirwani, Rakhshani, Musiani, Sumalani and Mengal

Ayak or Bhimana : This festival is celebrated by Kolam tribal inhabiting Laindiguda, Utmur Taluq Adilabad district in Andhra Pradesh. This falls in the Kolam month of Satti. Ayak also known as Bhimana or Bhimdev, is the principal deity of the Kolams. He is represented by a carved wooden mace usually crowned with a bunch of peacock feathers, a pot containing pher or a belt of bells, marwar or anklets and small dolls made of mud. All these are kept in a thatched shed. On a Thursday, the relies of Bhimama are brought and kept in the heart of the village in a small green lead enclosure. On the first day a fowl or a goat is sacrificed. On the following day the relics of the dirty are taken to Mohamloddi, a hill stream about eighteen kilometers from the village for bathing the deity. After bringing back the deity to bath in the evening, a buffalo purchased collectively is sacrificed. Fowl and goats are sacrificed by individuals to fulfil their vows. The meat of the scarified animal is cooked and eaten by all the people of the tribe. Before meal is served to all the priest carrying cooked jowar mixed with the food of the sacrificed animals, goes around the village and places small quantities of it on all the cornerstones and comes back. The deity is taken to its original abode the following day. This festival last for three days.

Ayaz Amir : Ayaz Amir, an intellect of independence, is a renowned Pakistani journalist, most famous for his columns in the newspaper Dawn and as a bold politician as well.

His columns are critical of the Pakistani army's role in politics throughout the history of the country.

Ayodhya : Ayodhya is an ancient city of India, the old capital of Awadh, in the Faizabad district of Uttar Pradesh. Under the British Raj the city and the administrative area around it was called Oudh. It is on the right bank of the river Gogra, 555 km east of New Delhi. The word ayodhya is Sanskrit for "not to be warred against". Some Puranas like the Brahmanda Purana (4/40/91) consider Ayodhya as one of the six holiest cities.

In the first few centuries of the Common Era it was caled Saketa. Saketa, or Shaqi was conquered by the great Kushan / Yuezhi Emperor Kanishka c. 137 CE, who made it the administrative centre of his eastern territories. The name occurs again in Faxian as Shazhi in the early fifth century. It is not clear when the name changed, but by the time of the visit of the Chinese pilgrim monk, Xuanzang, c. 636 CE, it was known as Ayodyha (Ayoude). Ayodhya is also the centre of the Ayodhya Debate concerning the Ram Janmabhoomi temple and the Babri Mosque. The mosque was destroyed in 1992 by rioters due to the belief that the Ram Janmabhoomi existed prior to the mosque's construction and that the temple was the birthplace of Rama.

Ayub Ali : Ayub Ali (1887-1995) was a Bangladeshi educationist and Islamic thinker. Born at Telikhali under Bhandaria upazila of Pirozpur district, Abul Khair Muhammad Ayub Ali was the son of Maulavi Abdul Wahed and Mrs Abida Khatun. He had Madrasa education at first and then he took western education. He passed BA Honours and MA Examinations in Islamic Studies from Dhaka University in 1943 and 1944 respectively. He also obtained a second MA degree in Persian from Dhaka University in 1950.

Ali got "Alamiah Diploma" in 1953 and PhD in 1955 from the Al-Azhar University, Cairo. He entered Government education service as a Lecturer at Dhaka College in 1944. He was Principal of Rajshahi Madrasa (1958-1969), Sylhet Government Aliya Madrasa (1970-1973) and Dhaka Aliya Madrasa. His History of Traditional Islamic Education in Bangladesh is a commendable work. In appreciation of his long services as an educationist Ali was awarded the Ekushe Padak in 1976.

Ayub Bachchu : Ayub Bachchu is a famous Bangladeshi pop musician and one of the leading guitarists in the country. Born in Chittagong, he was initially a member of the band Souls. Later he founded his own band titled LRB (the acronym originally came from Little River Band, but since another band already had that name,

Bachchu changed it to Love Runs Blind). He is well-known for his distinctive headgear.

Ayub National Park : Ayub National Park is located beyond the old Presidency on Jhelum Road. It covers an area of about 2,300 acres and has a play-land, lake with boating facility, an aquarium and a garden-restaurant. Rawalpindi Public Park is located on Murree Road near Shamsabad. The Park was opened for public in 1991. It has a playland for children, grassy lawns, fountains and flower beds. A cricket stadium was built in 1992 just opposite the Public Park. The stadium is equipped with all modern facilities. Another attraction located near Rawalpindi is the mosque known as Faisal Masjid.

Ayubia : Ayubia is a park located amongst the grand Murree hills in the Rawalpindi District of Pakistan. It is a small natural park located 26 km from the Murree hill station. The park has a moist temperature and is surrounded by villages and small towns ie: Nathiagali, Dungagali, Khairagali, Changlagali, Ghora Dhaka, and Khanspur. Ayubia was named after President Ayub Khan. It has been developed as a resort complex from a combination of four mini resorts known as Khairagali, Changlagali, Khanspur and Ghora Dhaka, spread over an area of 26 Km.

Ayubia National Park : Ayubia National Park is located in the Murree hills, near Islamabad, Pakistan. The initial area of the park was 1684 ha, expanded through a northern extension in 1998 to make a total of 3312 ha. The park supports one of the best remaining examples of moist Himalayan temperate forest in Pakistan and is surrounded by seven major villages and three small towns. The national park consists entirely of reserve forests, which spill out of the park area on the west and south sides. The scenery is superb with huge pine forests covering the hills and providing shelter to the larger and smaller mammals. Ayubia National Park is a major recreation area visited by large numbers of local tourists, mostly from Islamabad and Abottabad.

Ayurveda : Ayurveda or ayurvedic medicine is a comprehensive system of medicine, first described by Charaka around the beginning of the Common Era, Presently the central document of Ayurveda is considered to be Charaka Samhita which is a treatise of 500 drugs compiled by Charaka under the patronage of Buddhist Emperor Kanishka who belonged to the Kushan dynasty and ruled the kingdom of Bamiyan. Charaka was the court physician Kanishka. Bamiyan is a part of Afghanistan. The gigantic statues of Buddha destroyed by Taliban were excavated during the regime of Kanishka.

Medicine made rapid strides under the highly rationalist environment fostered by Buddhism in India. One of the most notable discoveries of Charaka is of the miraculous effects of a plant called Snake-root on hypertension nearly 2000 years ago. A drug called reserpine is extracted from Snakeroot to treat hypertension. Most traditionalists acknowledge Ayurveda as a part of basic Vedic Knowledge, in which it is considered as an Upa-veda (subsidiary or auxiliary Veda). Others, the modern scholars consider that though the word 'Ayurveda' though contains 'Veda', has nothing to do with the four Vedas. Ayurveda also had a tradition of surgery. Two early texts of Ayurveda are the Charaka Samhita and the Sushruta Samhita.

Ayyankali : Ayyankali (1863 - 1914) was a leader of the Indian lower caste Dalits ("Untouchables"). Ayyankali was born in 1863 at Perunkattuvila in Venganoor, Thiruvananthapuram, Kerala. During his times, Dalits were not allowed to walk along public roads. The Dalit women were not allowed to cover their breasts in public places.

Ayyankali organized Dalits and fought against these discriminations. By 1900 Dalits got freedom to walk the public roads, and later, by 1914, Dalit children were allowed to join schools. Also, Dalit women got freedom to cover their nakedness by the efforts of Ayyankali. He founded the Sadhujana Paripalana Sangham in 1905. He was also nominated to the Sri Moolam Legislative Assembly of Travancore in 1910.

Azad Jammu and Kashmir : Azad Jammu and Kashmir, is part of the Pakistani-administered part of the former princely state of Jammu and Kashmir, along with the Northern Areas. The name Azad Kashmir means "Free Kashmir" in Urdu. India does not recognize Azad Kashmir as a part of Pakistan and refers to the region encompassing Azad Kashmir and the Northern Areas as Pakistan Occupied Kashmir(POK). It covers an area of 13,300 km^2 (5,135 mi^2), with its capital at Muzaffarabad, and has an estimated population of over three million people.

Azam Khan : Azam Khan (Mahbubul Haque Khan) (born February 28, 1950) is a famous Bangladeshi pop singer. He was the pioneer in Bengali pop music creation and started a group called "Uchcharon" with a literal meaning of "Enunciation" in the early 1970s. He was a freedom fighter who fought against the Pakistani army in the Liberation war of Bangladesh in 1971. After the war, he introduced an energetic brand of music. His first concert in television was broadcast in 1972 in Bangladesh Television. His famous tunes include "Ore Salekha, Ore Maleka", "Ami Jare Chaire", "Ashi Ashi bole tumi", "Rail liner bostite..". Now in his 50s, Azam Khan still has a cult following among people in their 20s as well as earlier generations who are in their 30s and 40s.

Azamgarh : Azamgarh is a town in the Uttar Pradesh state in India. The town serves as the headquarters of a district, similar to a county in the United States, with the same name. Like most towns in northern parts of India, Azamgarh is situated on the banks of a river—in this case on the Tons River. Azamgarh was founded around 1665, by a powerful landlord named Azam Khan.

Azamgarh became a center of learning with the founding of Shibli National College, by the Muslim theoligan Shibli Nomani. Around 1913, Mr. Nomani, inspired by the works of Sir Syed Ahmed Khan of Aligarh Muslim University, established a college drawing scholars from all parts of Uttar Pradesh (then United Province) and northern India. Azamgarh is well connected to other parts of the state, and the recent launch of direct train connections with Bombay and Delhi (Mumbai and Delhi) has made this town more accessible.

Azim Hasham Premji : Azim Hasham Premji, founder of Wipro Limited, India's biggest and most competitive IT company based in Bangalore, was born on July 24th 1945 in Bombay. Premji was forced to leave his studies in computer science from Stanford University, California, USA at the age of 21 to take over the family business of vegetable oils when his father M.H. Premji, suddenly passed away in 1966. He has since after a gap of over thirty years completed his degree in Electrical Engineering.

The Amalner-based vanaspathi manufacturing company, the Western India Vegetable Product later became Wipro Products Ltd, Wipro Technologies and Wipro Corporation. Under Premji's leadership Wipro embarked on an ambitious phase of expansion and diversification. The company's IT division became the world's first to win SEI CMM level 5 and PCMM Level 5 (People Capability Maturity Model) certification, the latest in quality standards.

Premji's story of success and prominence clearly shows how determination and perseverance, when coupled with knowledge, clear vision and proper planning, enable one to reach the peak of success and leadership. A straight forward person, he doesn't believe in resorting to bribery or corruption to get things done and associates quality with integrity. In the year 2001, Premji established Azim Premji Foundation, a not-for-profit organization with a vision of influencing the lives of millions of children in India by facilitating the universalisation of elementary education. The foundation works closely with the state governments of Karnataka, Andhra Pradesh, Madhya Pradesh etc and the programs cover over 5000 rural schools. Premji contributes the financial resources for the foundation.

Azimpur Girls High School : Azimpur Girls High School is a secondary school in Azimpur, Dhaka, Bangladesh. It was established in 1857 by the Welfare Association of Government Employees. In 1999 the school had an enrollment of some 2,700 students and a faculty of 82.

Azimpur Mosque : Azimpur Mosque located beside the Azimpur public graveyard in the city of Dhaka, the mosque has been so extensively repaired and altered that it now seems from outside to be a modern building. A Persian inscription still fixed over the central doorway of the mosque records that it was built by one Faizullah in 1746 AD. It is a two-storied structure, the lower one being a vaulted platform. The upper storey consisted of the main mosque building and a spacious structure to the north of the mosque, but the latter is no longer extant. A stairway on the northeastern corner leads up to the top of the platform.

Aziz Bhatti : Aziz Bhatti was born in Hong Kong in 1928. He moved to Pakistan before the independence of 1947. There he enlisted with the newly formed Pakistani

Army and was commissioned to the Punjab Regiment in 1950.

On 6 September 1965, the Indo-Pakistani War of 1965 broke out between India and Pakistan. Major Bhatti was posted in the Burki area of Lahore sector, as the company command Major Bhatti chose to move his forward platoon under constant fire from Indian tanks and artillery. He resisted for five days and nights defending a Pakistani outpost on the strategic BRB canal. He led his men from the front under constant attack from Indian batteries. Although he countered every Indian offensive in his area, on the fifth day he was hit by an enemy tank shell. He died instananeously.

Each year, Major Bhatti is honoured in Pakistan on the 6 September, also known as Defense Day. Bhatti was awarded the Nishan-e-Haider, the nation's highest award for gallantry for the exemplery courage he displayed till his death.

Aziz Mian : Aziz Mian is one of Pakistan's most famous singers of qawwali. Aziz Mian was one of the more traditional Pakistani Qawwals. His voice was high pitched and powerful, but this was not the reason for his success. Aziz Mian was not only a great singer but also a great philosopher, he often wrote his own poems.

B

Baati : Baati is a hard, unleavened bread cooked in desert areas of Rajasthan, Malwa and Gujarat in North India. It is prized there for its exceptionally long life and high energy content, as well as the minimal quantity of water required in its preparation. It is always eaten with dal.

They are prepared with dough of wheat flour that is a bit thick and crusted (unlike chapati). You make hard balls of them. Now for bafla, you have to boil them into the water for half an hour or so...and then you bake them on the cakes made of cow-dung or in the oven.

Baba Adam Shahid : Baba Adam Shahid a saint who lies buried in the courtyard of an old mosque at Abdullapur, a village in vikramapura, not far from Rampal (Munshiganj district). An Arabic inscription attached to the mosque refers to its construction by one Malik Kafur, an officer of Sultan jalaluddin fath shah (1481-1486). In the inscription there is no reference to Baba Adam Shahid, nor there is any authentic information about the saint in any other source. Formerly scholars thought that Baba Adam Shahid was one of those sufis who are believed to have come to Bengal before the Turkish conquest. Whether any sufi came to Bengal before the Turkish conquest is yet to be proved; it is also doubtful whether Baba Adam Shahid came to Bengal before the conquest of Bakhtiyar Khalji. Baba Adam's date may be fixed towards the end of the 14th century.

Baba Amte : Murlidhar Devidas Amte (born December 24, 1914), or Baba Amte, as he is fondly known, was born in Hinganghat located in Wardha District of Maharashtra state of India. He was from a family of jagirdars. Trained in law, Baba Amte started a lucrative practice at Wardha, but, moved by the poverty he saw around him, he decided to dedicate himself to social justice.

One of India's most revered social and moral leaders, Baba Amte has devoted his life to the care and rehabilitation of leprosy patients, even allowing his body to be used for experiments to grow leprosy germs. His ashram at Anandwan, recognised and respected around the world, has done much to dispel prejudice against leprosy victims.

Baba Amte also launched the Bharat Jodo (Unite India) movements from Kashmir to Kanyakumari in 1985 and Assam and Gujarat in 1988, with the mission of establishing peace and raising environmental consciousness. He has used his various honours and award, amounting to INR 15 million, to the running of his Anandavan Ashram. In 1990, Baba Amte left Anandavan to live along the Narmada to fight against social injustice.

Baba Ramdev : Baba Ramdev, also known as Swami Ramdev, is an Indian Hindu swami (saint). He was born in a very humble family of Narnaul. A few months after he was born half of his body was paralysed but he recovered. He studied in a local school till 8th standard and then decided to study under the "Guru-Shishya" tradition of ancient India. Soon he became a wandering ascetic and starting practicing yoga-sadhana at Gangotri.

In 1995, Swami joined the order of ancient-monks. Swami Ramdev was initiated into the ascetic order by Swami Shankerdevji Maharaj. In the course of pursuing his ascetic endeavors, Swamiji spent many years undertaking a thorough study of ancient Indian scriptures. At the same time, he also practiced intense self-discipline and meditation.

He teaches that God resides in every human being and that the body is God's temple. He is a firm believer in the concept of Vashudhav Kutambkam (the whole World is one family) and decries practices that discriminate on the basis of caste, creed or gender. His fundamental belief is that expressions of love, affection and compassion towards all living things are the true worship of the Creator.

Swamiji has taught several aspects of traditional Indian scriptures such as Ashtadhyayee, Mahabhashya and Upanishads along with six systems of Indian Philosophy in various Gurukuls (traditional Indian systems of education). He has helped establish Gurukuls in Kishangarh, Ghashera, and Mahendragarh in India. Swamiji has also founded the Patanjali Yogpeeth Trust which has built several institutions. In addition to helping people learn about Yoga and spirituality, these institutions also provide a comprehensive facility that promotes the practice of Ayurveda – the traditional system of holistic medicine developed in India.

Swamiji's unique contribution has been in helping ordinary people lead a healthy life through the practice of Pranayama. In very simple terms, Pranayama can be thought of as a series of techniques for breath control that were developed as a part of the ancient Indian system of Yoga. Heretofore, these techniques were often thought of as being esoteric and complex and portrayed as being unsuitable for lay people. Consequently, their use was often limited to advanced practitioners of Yoga and undertaken only under the strict supervision of an experienced teacher. Swamiji has worked diligently to break these barriers and help make the practice of Pranayama achievable by the ordinary layperson.

Viewers of the TV show and attendees at the camp have reported significant improvements in their health - citing relief from many illnesses such as Diabetes, Heart Disease, Arthritis, Thyroid Problems, Hypertension and Stomach ailments.

Babbar Akali Movement : A radical outgrowth of the Akali movement for the reform of Sikh places of worship during the early 1920's. The latter, aiming to have the shrines released from the control of priests who had become lax and effete over the generations, was peaceful in its character and strategy. In the course of the prolonged campaign, Akalis true to their vows patiently suffered physical injury and violence at the hands of the priests as well as of government authority.

Babra Sharif : Babra Sharif was the foremost figure in the Pakistani film industry during the 1980s and late 1970s. She worked with many famous names fo her time, namely Shahid, Nadeem, Waheed Murad, and even Muhammad Ali. She had great success in Urdu films in Pakistan.

She did a variety of roles which proved her versatality as an actress. Some critics have also considered her as the best actress of her time in Pakistan, she was the first actress in the region who blended action and romance. She worked in more than 100 movies.

Babra Sharif Massacre : To protest against the arrests

of Bacha Khan, Dr. Khan Sahib, Qazi Attah-ullah, Arbab Abdul Ghafoor Khan and other notables, it was decided that the Khudai Khidmatgars would in a peaceful procession march from Charsadda to Babra. In July 1948 the provincial governor of NWFP promulgated an ordinance which authorized the government of detaining any one indefinitely and confiscating their properties without disclosing any reason to the detainee. On 12th August 1948, The march was announced ahead of time in the major newspapers, all participants were told to congregate at Charsadda empty handed and to peacefully march to the Babra grounds. There seemed to be no objection from the government, but on the 12th, they surrounded the Babra grounds with militia units, police forces, armored vehicles and tanks.

Total casulaties in the massacre were estimated to be 150 killed and 400 wounded some eyewitness put the death toll at 1300. Some have said that over two hundred and fifty bodies were thrown into the river, many never recovered. The wounded were not allowed admission in hospitals and Doctors threatened with punishment if they did provide treatment.

Babri Mosque : The Babri Mosque was a mosque constructed by order of the first Mugal emperor of India, Babur, in Ayodhya in the 16th century. Before the 1940s, the Mosque was called Masjid-i Janmasthan ("mosque of the birthplace"). The mosque stood on the Ramkot ("Rama's fort") hill (also called Janamsthan ("birthplace"). It was destroyed by hostile Hindu activists in a riot on December 6, 1992.

It was alleged that Babur's commander-in-chief Mir Baki destroyed an existing temple at the site, which many Hindus believe was the temple built to commemorate the birthplace of Rama, an incarnation of Vishnu and ruler of Ayodhya. The Babri Mosque was one of the largest

Mosques in Uttar Pradesh, a province of India with some thirteen million Muslims. Although there were several older Mosques in the city of Ayodhya, with a substantial Muslim population, including the Hazrat Bal Mosque constructed by the Shariqi kings, the Babri Mosque became the largest.

Babur : Zahir-ud-din Mohammad Babur *(February 14, 1483 – December 26, 1530)*, popularly known as "Babur", meaning lion, was the founder of Mughal Empire in India. He was born in Farghana, now in Uzbekistan, on February 14, 1483. The Mughal Empire founded by him lasted for 331 years.

Babur was a descendant of Timur on his father's side and of Chengez Khan on his mother's side. When Babur's father Umar Sheikh Mirza died in 1494, he inherited the ancestral kingdom of Farghana. He was only 14 years old at that time. Babur faced many hardships during this period of his life. He was driven out of his father's state and for two years became a wanderer. In 1504, he came to Afghanistan and occupied Kabul. Here he assumed the title of Padshah.

On account of his precarious position in Central Asia, after crossing the Indus, he invaded India five times. The fifth expedition resulted in the death of Ibrahim Lodhi in the first battle of Panipat, in April 1526. Panipat was merely the beginning of the Mughal rule; Akbar laid its real foundation in 1556. At the time of the battle of Panipat, the political power in India was shared by the Afghans and the Rajputs. In the battle of Kanwaha, Babur defeated the Rajput leader Rana Sanga of Mewar. In 1528, he captured Chanderi from the Rajput chief, Medini Rao and a year later he defeated the Afghan chiefs under Mahmud Lodhi in the battle of Ghagra in Bihar. These conquests made Babur the "Master of Hindustan", and the founder of Mughal Empire in the Sub-continent.

Babur did not live long to rule his Kingdom. Towards the end of Babur's life, his eldest son Humayun fell seriously ill. It is said that in a religious ceremony, he transferred his son's illness to himself and sacrificed himself in order to save Humayun. As Humayun recovered, the former became worse and after two or three months Babur died at Agra on December 26, 1530. Babur was buried at Kabul, in accordance with his own wishes.

Babur's personality can be judged by his own memoirs Tuzk-i-Baburi, also known as Babur Namah, written in Turkish, personally transcribed by his son Humayun, and afterwards translated into Persian during the reign of Akbar. It is considered among the most enthralling and romantic literary works of all times. Babur possessed in him the qualities of a born leader. He was not only a brilliant general but also a great swordsman who had the quality of correctly gauging the strength and the weakness of the commanders and armies opposed to him. Babur was a man of extraordinary energy and strength. He had been known to take up a man under each arm and run with them round the battlements of a fortress. He swam and crossed all the rivers of the Indian Sub-continent. He was perpetually in saddle, riding 80 miles a day. Babur was pre-eminently a man of faith. "Nothing happens" he used to say, "but by the will of God".

During his brief period of absolute rule over India, Babur did not have the time, or indeed the opportunity, to set the affairs of state in permanent manner. Babur on his death left an empire barely held by force of arms, and lacking any consolidated civil administration. After him his 23 years old son Humayun came to power to rule an empire set up by his father.

Badal Roy : Badal Roy (born Amerendra Roy Choudhury in Bangladesh, 1945) is a tabla player and percussionist known for his work in jazz, cross-cultural music, and experimental music. Roy emigrated to New York City in 1968, working as a busboy and waiter in various Indian restaurants. Soon, however, he began performing with Steve Gorn at a restaurant called Raga, eventually attracting the attention of Miles Davis. Davis invited Roy to join his group, and Roy's playing is documented on Davis's On the Corner album. Roy subsequently performed and recorded with many leading jazz musicians, including Davis, Dave Liebman, and Ornette Coleman. In the 1990s Roy began performing with the Brazilian guitar duo Duofel.

Roy is essentially self-taught, and consequently his playing is freer than that of many other tabla players, who adhere more strictly to the tala system of Indian rhythm. He often plays a set of up to five tabla (tuned to different pitches) at a time, which he plays melodically as well as rhythmically.

Badan Singh : Badan Singh (1722 – 1756) was the formal founder of the princely state of Bharatpur. He was nephew of Churaman. After the death of Churaman on 22 September 1721 there were family disputes between Badan Singh and Mohkam, son of Churaman. Badan Singh aligned with Jai Singh of Jaipur to avoid the anger of Mohkam Singh. In this family feud Jai Singh supported Badan Singh.

Bade Fateh Ali Khan : Bade Fateh Ali Khan (born: 1935) is amongst the foremost Khayal vocalists alive today in Pakistan, and the last significant exponent of the Patiala gharana (stylistic lineage). He is the younger of the singing duo "Amanat Ali-Fateh Ali", who enjoyed immense prestige and success in Pakistan as well as India, until the demise of Amanat Ali Khan (1932-1974).

Amanat Ali-Fateh Ali became celebrities while still in their childhood in undivided India, and achieved their highest official recognition in 1969, when the President of

Pakistan conferred on them the Pride of Performance Medal. The "Bade" (elder) prefix got attached to Fateh Ali's name after younger Pakistani musicians with similar names started making waves with an entirely different genre of music.

Fateh Ali and his late brother were trained by their father, Akhtar Hussain, a distinguished vocalist in the patronage of the princely state of Patiala in colonial, undivided India. Their grandfather, Ali Baksh, also served the same court, and was a cofounder of the Patiala gharana. The prodigious talent of Amanat Ali- Fateh Ali received early encouragement at the Patiala court. They had a glorious debut in 1945 at Lahore, sponsored by the influential connoisseur, Pandit Jeevanlal Mattoo Their breakthrough came at the All-Bengal Music Conference in Calcutta in 1949, when Amanat Ali was 17, and Fateh Ali was 14, after which they never looked back. Life changed dramatically for the budding stars when India was partitioned in 1947, and the family opted to migrate to Pakistan.

Overcoming destitution in their new home, the duo swung back, while still in their teens, to earn their rightful place amongst the foremost vocalists of the subcontinent. Fateh Ali was dealt a devastating blow with the demise of his brother Amanat Ali in 1974. Fateh Ali is reported to have suffered a deep depression for over a year and a half, following which he joined Radio Pakistan as a supervisor.

The two brothers as a duo had neatly dividing their singing by specialisation. Amanat Ali Khan had a gifted voice and he embellished his singing in broad sweeps by lagao, and blossoming out in the upper register while Fateh Ali engaged in intricacies of the countless behlawas and complex taans, in a much lower and gravelly voice, respectively drawing inspiration from two elders of their gharana, Ustad Bade Ghulam Ali Khan and Ustad Ashiq Ali Khan.

Fateh Ali was urged to restart his performing career, but would break into tears when first beginning to sing. Fateh Ali Khan eventually overcame this emtional block, and started singing as a duo with his younger brother Hamid Ali Khan, as well his nephews, Asad Amanat Ali Khan or Amjad Amanat Ali Khan who are both sons of his late brother Amanat Ali Khan. The absence of Amanat Ali made Fateh Ali redevelop and re-align his singing style. He had to fill the void left by Amanat Ali in the middle of his career, which in any case is not an easy thing to do. The void was only partly filled by Hamid, Amjad Amanat and Asad Amanat Ali Khan, as these three have occupied a relatively junior role in comparison with the almost equal footing that Amanat Ali and Fateh Ali fulfilled as a duo.

Though trained also in the mediaeval Dhrupad genre, the uncle-nephew duo restricts its repertoire to the modern mainstream genre, Khayal, and the romanticist genres, Thumrees, Dadra, and Ghazal. The pair has, since their alliance, performed widely in Europe, North America, the Middle East, and South Asia, and released several recordings. One highly unsual CD released in 1995 is entitled "Ragas and Sagas", which is a collaboration with Norwegian Saxaphonist Jan Garbarek. Fateh Ali has performed all over the world and has many students internationally.

In the latter half of the 20th century, the Patiala style of Khayal vocalism has been represented by two streams of the gharana. One stream, gave the music world the Amanat Ali and Fateh Ali duo. The other stream, through its training of Kasur gharana vocalists, produced Bade Ghulam Ali Khan (1903-1968), his brother Barkat Ali Khan (1907-1963), and the former's son, Munawwar Ali Khan

(1933-1989). With the stylistic distinctiveness and continuity of Khayal gharanas having fallen prey to socio-cultural changes on both sides of the India-Pakistan border, Fateh Ali Khan is the last of the thoroughbred Patiala vocalists.

Badhya Bhumi Smriti Soudha : Badhya Bhumi Smriti Soudha (Slaughter-place Memorial) was built to commemorate the death of some of the nation's finest intellectuals and others, who were killed at the very end of the war of liberation (1971) by the Pakistani army with the help of their collaborators at Rayer Bazar brick field of Dhaka. The memorial edifice was constructed at the place where the mass killing took place. Among the people killed indiscriminately were educationists, physicians, journalists, writers, film directors and other professionals.

In 1993 Government of Bangladesh decided to erect a memorial at the site of this barbarous act. The Ministry of Housing & Works Department and the Institute of Architects Bangladesh jointly organised a national level architectural competition for the design of the memorial. Out of 22 entries the jurors selected the design proposal of Architect Farid Uddin Ahmed and Architect Md Jami-al-Shafi. Public Works Department was responsible for the implementation of the project and its completion took about three years, 1996 to 1999. The whole site of 3.51 acre has been divided by a square grid of 15.24m by 15.24m. The main platform is raised 2.44m above the street level.

The main entry to the memorial is at the southeast corner of the site that places the visitor in front of a Banyan tree. This tree represents the original Banyan tree at the nearby Physical Education College where the martyrs were tortured first and then brought to this brickfield to be killed. Apart from the Banyan tree, which is evergreen, all the other trees used in the landscaping are deciduous. They remain leafless during the month of December that adds to the sense of grief during the

Intellectuals Martyr Day (14 December), observed every year.

Badr Auliya : Badr Auliya is said to have come to Chittagong with eleven other saints, who lie buried in different tombs scattered throughout the region. He is respected as the foremost of the twelve saints who preached Islam in Chittagong. As such Chittagong is popularly known as Bara Auliyar Desh (land of twelve saints). Tradition associates Badr with human settlement in this district. The inhabitants of Chittagong venerate him as their guardian saint.

The Buddhists, the Hindus and the Chinese respect him as an inferior god or a spirit, the Muslim pay homage to him as an Aulia or saint. His name is invoked by the boatman of eastern Bengal along with other five saints called Panch Pir. The tomb of Badr Auliya is situated in a locality known as Badarpatti or Badarpati, near modern Bakshir Hat, a part of the old fort area, Anderkilia (Inner Fort), of Chittagong. The enclosed tomb complex had a gateway on the east. The square tomb building was constructed with heavy walls. The roof is gently curved and crowned with a big dome. There is a sandstone inscription tablet on the left side of the west facade of the monument. The tablet has five lines of Arabic inscriptions in Naskh written horizontally within sections.

Badrinath : Badrinath, a citadel to Lord Vishnu, situated at a height of 3,155 m is the place where Vishnu, Ganga, Saraswathi and Alaknanda confluence. Build in early ninth century AD, Badrinath is one of the most revered Hindu shrines of India dedicated to Lord Vishnu. It is also one of the four Dhams restored by Adi Shankaracharya in an effort to unify the country, along with Kancheepuram in Tamil Nadu in the south, Dwarkapuri in the west and Jagannath Puri in the east (Sringeri mutt in Karnataka state is also claimed to be the fourth peetha). Lakshmi, the consort of Vishnu loved Badri trees that were found in plenty in the area, hence the name Badrinath. It is also known as 'Tapobhumi', the land of meditation and penance and 'Bhubaikunth' (heaven on earth).

Sri Badrinath Ji temple is located between the two mountain ranges of Nar and Narayan, with the Neelkanth peak(6977m) in the background. In the 8th century AD Adi Sankaracharya came to Badri and restored the ancient Badrinath idol from the Narad Kund and established in the Ganyr cave near Tapt kund. Tapt Kund, the hot water spring with natural curative properties believed to be the abode of Lord Agni faces the shrine. The pilgrims take a holy dip in the Taptakund before entering the temple. The temple remains closed from October to April due to the winter snow, when temperatures fall to sub-zero degrees.

The pilgrims generally pay homage to the departed souls of their near ones in the Brahma Kapal, a flat platform on the banks of the river Alakananda. A rock boulder Sheshnetra, with the impression of Sheshnag, a mythological serpent and Charanpaduka, a boulder with foot prints of Lord Vishnu are of religious significance to the devotees. The other places of worship in Badrivishal complex are Gupt kashi (Arddh -Narisvara and Viswanath temples), Panch Kedar (Mad Maheswaray, Tungnath, Rudra nath, Kalpanath and Kedarnath) Vyas Gulfa and Ganesh Gulfa (where saint Vyas dictated the Mahabharata to Ganesha), Bhim pul (where Bhim and Hanuman met), Hemkund Sahib are other places where pilgrims offer prayers and oblations.

Badshahi Masjid : The Badshahi Masjid, literally the 'King's Mosque', was built in 1673 by Aurangzeb in Lahore, Pakistan. It is one of the city's best known landmarks, and a major tourist attraction epitomising the beauty and grandeur of the Mughal era.

Capable of accommodating up to 60,000 worshippers, it is the second largest mosque in Pakistan, after the Faisal Mosque in Islamabad. The architecture and design of the Badshahi Masjid is closely related to the Jamia Masjid in Delhi, India, which was built in 1648 by Aurangzeb's father and predecessor, emperor Shah Jahan.

Bagakain Lake : Bagakain Lake popularly known as Baga Lake is a natural lake in the hill district of bandarban. It is located on one of the peaks of the Politai Mountain Range in Naitong mauza of ruma upazila, about 29 km east of the banks of the river Shankha. The lake is rectangular. It is bounded on three sides by mountain peaks covered with thick bamboo bushes. The lake is a plateau of height between 457 and 610m above the sea level and 38m deep. It is a closed lake and there is a small spring named Bagachhara, which is 153m deep. There is no outlet for draining out water from the lake. The lake is composed of the soft rocks of the bhuban formation. The main source of water is the spring. However, there are also other sources such as rainfall, surface drainage and spring seepage. The water of the lake is used by the local tribal people as drinking water but sometimes it changes colour and looks turbid. It is suspected that there is a hot spring at the bottom of the lake and the colour of the lake's water changes due to the discharges of that hot spring. Geologists believe that the lake is either the crater of an inactive mud volcano or it was originated due to falling of meteorites from the outer space. Some also argue in favour of a big landslide.

Bagelkhand : Bagelkhand (or Baghelkhand) is a region in central India, in northeastern Madhya Pradesh state. It includes the Madhya Pradesh districts of Anuppur, Rewa, Satna, Shadol, Sidhi, and Umaria, and the adjacent Uttar Pradesh district of Sonbhadra. The Baghels, who give their name to the region, are a branch of the Solanki

Rajputs who once ruled in Gujarat and migrated eastward in the 13th century. Vyaghra Dev was the first Solanki ruler who came to this area from Gujarat and established his rule. Vyaghra is Sanskrit word which means Bagh in Hindi. The descendants of Vyaghra Dev are known as Baghels.

Bagelkhand Agency was a collection of princely states in British India. The agency was established in March 1871. Until that date Bagelkhand was under the Bundelkhand agency, with which it is geographically and historically connected. From 1871 to 1933 Bagelkhand agency was under the political superintendence of the Governor-General of India's agent for Central India, and under the direct jurisdiction of a political agent who was also superintendent of the Rewa state, residing ordinarily at Satna or Rewa. The agency consisted of Rewa state and eleven minor states and estates, of which the more important were Maihar, Nagod and Sohawal. The other states were Jaso, Kothi, Baraunda, Paldeo, Kamta-Rajaula, Taraon, Pahra, and Bhaisaunda.

The total area was 14,323 square miles, and the population in 1901 was 1,555,024, a decrease of 11% over the previous decade, due to the results of famine. The rainfall was very deficient in 1895-1897, causing famine in 1897; and in 1899-1900 there was drought in some sections. In 1931, the eleven smaller states were transferred to Bundelkhand Agency, and in 1933 the agency was dissolved, and Rewa state was placed under the authority of the Resident of Indore. After Indian independence in 1947, the princely states that made up the Bagelkhand Agency were merged with Rewa to form Vindhya Pradesh state, which was in turn merged into Madhya Pradesh on November 1, 1956.

Bagelkhand Agency : Bagelkhand Agency was a collection of princely states in British India. The agency was established in March 1871. Until that date Bagelkhand was under the Bundelkhand agency, with which it is geographically and historically connected. From 1871 to 1933 Bagelkhand agency was under the political superintendence of the Governor-General of India's agent for Central India, and under the direct jurisdiction of a political agent who was also superintendent of the Rewa state, residing ordinarily at Satna or Rewa.

The agency consisted of Rewa state and eleven minor states and estates, of which the more important were Maihar, Nagod and Sohawal. The other states were Jaso, Kothi, Baraunda, Paldeo, Kamta-Rajaula, Taraon, Pahra, and Bhaisaunda. The total area was 14,323 square miles, and the population in 1901 was 1,555,024, a decrease of 11% over the previous decade, due to the results of famine. The rainfall was very deficient in 1895-1897, causing famine in 1897; and in 1899-1900 there was drought in some sections. In 1931, the eleven smaller states were transferred to Bundelkhand Agency, and in 1933 the agency was dissolved, and Rewa state was placed under the authority of the Resident of Indore.

After Indian independence in 1947, the princely states that made up the Bagelkhand Agency were merged with Rewa to form Vindhya Pradesh state, which was in turn merged into Madhya Pradesh on November 1, 1956.

Bagerhat : Bagerhat is a district in South-western Bangladesh. It is a part of the Khulna Division. Bagerhat district has a total area of 3959.11 square kilometers. It is bounded by Gopalganj District and Narail District on the north, The Bay of Bengal on the south, Gopalganj District, Pirojpur District and Barguna District on the east and Khulna District on the west. Main rivers of the district are Panguchi, Daratana, Madhumati River, Pasur River, Haringhata, Mongla River, Baleswar, Bangra and Goshairkhali. Bagerhat is divided into 9 upazilas, 77 union parishads, 1031 villages, 687 mouzas, 3 municipalities, 27 wards and 56 mahallas. The upazilas are Bagerhat sadar, Chitalmari, Fakirhat, Kachua, Mollahat, Mongla, Morrelganj, Rampal and Sarankhola.

Bagh : Bagh District was carved out of Poonch District in 1988. The district shares its borders with Muzaffarabad District in the north, with Poonch district in the south, with Baramulla District of the Indian state of J&K in the east and is bounded to Pakistan in the west. Total area of the district is 1368 square kilometers. Total population of the district according to 1998 census stands at 395000, which is estimated to be 404,000 according to 1999 projections. The district is divided into 3 tehsils. Bagh district is linked to Muzaffarabad by two roads, one via Sudhan Gali (80Km) and the other through Kohala (97Km). It is situated 46Km from Rawalakot. The district is well known for its confectionery and bakery products.

Bagha Jatin : Bagha Jatin, born Jatindranath Mukherjee (7 December 1879–10 September 1915) was an Indian revolutionary activist against British rule. He was one of the leaders of the Yugantar party that was the main association of revolutionaries in Bengal, and was instrumental in the planned Indo-German Conspiracy during World War I.

Jatin, a man with a strong sense of self-respect and national pride, came in contact with aurobindo ghosh, and took part in climbing, swimming and shooting in the body building Akhda. While working for the Yugantar, he met Naren (Manabendra Nath Roy) and the two soon gained the confidence of one another. In 1908 Jatin, with some revolutionaries, was implicated in the Alipore Conspiracy Case. In the judgement Barin Ghosh was deported for life, many others were sentenced to various terms and the Anushilan Samiti was declared illegal and banned. Jatin and Naren, acquitted for want of evidence, went in hiding to Hawra-Shibpur area and continued underground works with other revolutionaries.

Jatin was once again arrested in the Hawra-Shibpur Conspiracy Case, and those who were arrested with him were given the common name 'Jatin's gang'. They were so ruthlessly tortured that some of them died and some went insane. Jatin, though acquitted in this case also for want of evidence, was dismissed from service. When in jail, Jatin and Naren made a long term programme to capture power through armed insurrection. They planned to unite different groups of patriots and with this intention Naren travelled extensively all over India as a Sanyasi and organised the revolutionaries in Bengal and elsewhere. The leaders of various groups gathered together on the occasion of relief works during the floods in Hughli and Midnapore. They chose Jatin Mukherjee and Rashbehari Bose as leaders for Bengal and northern India respectively.

Attempts were made to organise the Indian revolutionaries outside India also. A Yugantar Ashram was formed at San Francisco and the Shikh community took active part in the struggle for freedom. With the outbreak of the First World War, the Indian revolutionaries of Europe gathered together in Berlin to form the Indian Independence Party and sought German assistance, to which the German government agreed. The Indian Independence Party sent an emissary to Jatin Mukherjee to negotiate with the German Consul General in Calcutta. In the meantime Jatin was made the Commander-in-Chief of the entire revolutionary forces. Naren, leaving Jatin in hiding in Baleswar (Orissa), went to Batavia to negotiate a deal with German authorities there for the shipment of arms and financial help.

Police, however, discovered the hideout of Jatin in a paddy field. On 9 September 1915, after heavy exchange of fire, two revolutionaries surrendered. Police found Jatin dead with two others injured. Of the two injured one died later and was identified as Chitta Priya Roy Choudhury of Madaripur

Bagha Mosque : Bagha Mosque situated at Bagha, about 25 miles southeast of Rajshahi town, survives in a fairly good state of preservation. The mosque was built on the western bank of a fairly large tank within a brick-walled compound, 48.77m square. The mosque compound could be entered by two old arched gateways—one on the north and the main one on the south comprising a simple oblong curved structure with a turret on either side.

Baghel : Baghel or Vaghela is the name of a rajput clan. They are a branch of the Solanki clan, which in turn belongs to the Agnivanshi lineage. The Baghelkhand region in India, part of the present-day state of Madhya Pradesh, takes its name from that of this clan. The region was ruled in past centuries by dynasties belonging to the clan. Rewa was the premier princely state ruled by the Baghel clan.

Bagh-i-Hamza Mosque : Bagh-i-Hamza Mosque situated in the locality of 'Bagh-i-Hamza' in the northern quarter of the city of Chittagong, the mosque has been thoroughly restored and enlarged on the northern and eastern sides, and now wears a modern look. Built entirely of brick the original mosque is oblong in plan. The four exterior angles are strengthened by octagonal towers, which rise above the parapets and terminate in solid kiosks and cupolas. These cupolas, being encircled at their bases by a row of curved petals, are crowned with kalasa finials. There are three arched doorways in the east and one each on the north and south sides; all have now been remodelled. Corresponding to the three eastern doorways there are three renovated semi-octagonal mihrabs inside the qibla wall. The central mihrab and the central doorway have traditional outward projections with bordering ornamental turrets. These turrets are also extended beyond the roof and topped over with small cupolas and kalasa finials.

Baghsar : Baghsar is situated at 975m above sea-level in the Samahni valley. The Sar, local name for a lake, is nearly half kilometre long sheet of clear water that soothes the senses of the visitor. On top of a hill is the famous Moghul Fort over-looking the lake that adds grandeur to the area. This four storey massive structure of granite is a feat of Mughal engineering that has stood the ravages of time. It has also played important roles in history during the times of Ahmed Shah Abdali, Ranjit Singh and Gulab Singh. It is said that the Mughal Emperor Janghir, on his way back from the Kashmir Valley, fell ill and ultimately died in this fort. Baghsar looks like a giant amphitheatre with the beautiful lilly flowers covered lake at the floor and lush green hills surrounding it. The hills are covered with Cheerh(pine) trees.

Bahadur Shah I : Muazzam Bahadur Shah (October 14, 1643 – February 1712), also known as Shah Alam I was a Mughal emperor of India from 1707 to 1712.

Born in Burhanpur, he was the eldest son of the emperor Aurangzeb. Aurangzeb had succesfully imposed Sharia law within his kingdom through harsh enforcement of strict edicts. This led to increased militancy by many constituencies including the Marathas, the Sikhs, and Rajputs, who along with other territories broke from the empire after his death.

Prior to Bahadur Shah's ascension to the throne he had been installed by his father as governor of the northwest territories, including Sikh-controlled parts of Punjab. The new governor relaxed enforcement of Aurangzeb's severe edicts, and an uneasy peace ensued between the Sikhs and the Mughal empire for a short time.

After Aurangzeb's death, Bahadur Shah took the throne, and the Mughal Empire, due both to Aurangzeb's overextension and cruelty, and to Bahadur's weak military and leadership qualities, entered a long decline. For example, a war of succession began immediately after Aurangzeb died. One younger brother, Prince Azam Shah, proclaimed to be emperor and marched towards Delhi, where he fought Bahadur Shah unsuccessfully and lost. Another, brother, Muhammad Kam Baksh, was killed in 1709.

A more moderate man than his father, Bahadur Shah sought to improve relations with the militant constituencies of the rapidly crumbling kingdom. However, Bahadur Shah could do little to mitigate the damage already done by his father. He died in 1712 at Lahore while making alterations to the Shalimar Gardens, and was followed by his surviving son Jahandar Shah on the Mughal throne.

Bahadur Shah Zafar : Bahadur Shah Zafar, was the last of the Mughal emperors in India. He was born on October 24, 1775, and was the son of Akbar Shah II. He became the Mughal Emperor upon his father's death on September 28, 1838.

Emperor Bahadur Shah II presided over a Mughal empire that stretched barely beyond the modern city of Delhi. The Sikh Empire in the Punjab and Kashmir, the Maratha Empire and the British Empire were the most dominating political and military forces in the India of the 19th century. Hundreds of minor kings fragmented the land. The emperor was paid some respect and allowed a pension and authority to collect some taxes, and maintain a token force in Delhi by the British, but he posed no threat to any power in India. Bahadur Shah II himself did not excel in statecraft or possess any imperial ambitions.

As the Indian rebellion of 1857 spread, Indian regiments seized Delhi. Seeking a uniting figure for all

Indians, Hindu and Muslim alike, most rebelling Indian kings and the Indian regiments accepted Zafar as their Emperor of India, under whom the smaller Indian kingdoms would unite until the British were defeated. Zafar was the least threatening and least ambitious of monarchs, and the legacy of the Mughal Empire was more acceptable a uniting force to most allied kings than the domination of any other Indian kingdom.

When the rebellion was crushed, he fled to Humayun's Tomb and hid there. However, he was captured and his sons Mirza Mughal and Khizar Sultan and his grandson Abu Bakr were executed in his presence and, famously, their severed heads presented to him.

He was exiled to Rangoon, Burma (now Yangon, Myanmar) in 1858 along with his wife Zinat Mahal, and the remaining members of the family. A formal end was declared to the Mughal Dynasty that began with Babur in 1526. The title of Emperor of India was eventually (in 1877) taken over by the British monarch, in the person of Queen Victoria, and held until 1948, with retroactive effect to August 15, 1947.

Bahadur Shah died in exile on November 7, 1862 and is buried near Shwe Degon Pagoda, Yangôn, and the place of his burial is currently known as Bahadur Shah Zafar Dargah. His wife Zinat Mahal died in 1886.

Baharampur : Baharampur is a city in the West Bengal state of India. Baharampur is the administrative capital of the Murshidabad district. The 1991 population of the city was 126,400. The city is located approximately 200 km north of Calcutta at 24°4'N 88°9'E and is situated on the east side of the Bhagirathi River, a major distributary of the Ganges. The city's industries include silk weaving, ivory carving, rice and oil-seed milling, and precious-metal working. It is also a rail and road hub of the West Bengal state and is an important agricultural center. Baharampur was founded and fortified in 1757 by the British East India Company and continued as a cantonment until 1870. The cantonment was constituted as a municipality in 1876. In 1857 the first major armed battle of the Indian Mutiny of 1857 took place in Baharampur.

Bahawalnagar District : Bahawalnagar District is a of Pakistan. The town of Bahawalnagar lies in that district. The boundaries of Bahawalnagar District in the East and South touches the Indian territory while Bahawalpur district lies on its West and river Sutlej flows on its Northern side across which are situated Okara, Pakpattan and Vehari districts.

Bahawalpur : The State of Bahawalpur was a princely state of the Punjab in what is now Pakistan, stretching along the southern bank of the Sutlej and Indus Rivers, with its capital city at Bahawalpur. The state was counted amongst the Punjab states rather than the neighbouring Rajputana states (now Rajasthan) to the southeast. After two centuries of varying degrees of independence, the state became part of Pakistan in 1947. In 1941, the state had a population of 1,341,209 living in an area of 45,911 km^2 (17,494 sq mi). It was divided into three districts : Bahawalpur, Rahimyar Khan and Bahawalnagar.

Bahmani Sultanate : The Bahmani Sultanate (Also called the Bahmanid Empire) was a Muslim state of the Deccan in southern India. The sultanate was founded in 1347 by the Turkish governor Ala-ud-Din Bahman Shah, who revolted against the Sultan of Delhi, Muhammad bin Tughluq. His revolt was successful, and he established an independent state on Deccan out of the Delhi Sultanate's southern provinces. The Bahmani capital was Ahsanabad (Gulbarga) between 1347 and about 1425, when it was moved to Muhammadabad (Bidar). The Bahmani contested for control of the Deccan with the Hindu Vijayanagara empire to the south. The sultanate reached the peak of its power during the vizierate (1466–1481) of Mahmud Gawan. After 1518 the sultanate broke up into five states, Ahmednagar, Berar, Bidar, Bijapur, and Golconda, known collectively as the Deccan sultanates.

Bahraich : Bahraich is a small town in the state of Uttar Pradesh in India. Located on the Saryu River, a tributary of river Ghaghra, Bahraich is 125 km north-east of Lucknow, the state capital. The towns of Barabanki, Gonda, Lakheempur and Sitapur share local boundaries with Bahraich. A factor which makes this town important is the international border shared with the neighboring country, Nepal.

Bahraich got its name from the arabic word bahr which means a large body of water. Situated on the bank of river Ghaghra, it was named Bahraich. Although a small town, Bahraich happens to be a very old town of India. It was inhabited around the 10th century. Bahraich is very famous because of the mausoleum (Dargah) of Ghazi Saiyyad Salar Masud, a famous eleventh century Islamic saint and soldier. His Dargah is a place for reverence for Muslims and Hindus alike. It was built by Firoz Shah Tughlaq. It is believed that people taking bath in the water of this Dargah become free of all skin diseases.

Bahram Saqqa Tomb : Bahram Saqqa Tomb a monument of archaeological interest, is situated in Burdwan (West Bengal), and the place where the saint is buried is called after him Pir-Bahram. The saint is variously called Pir, Darvish and Haji. But at Burdwan, he is known as Pir Bahram or Bahram Saqqa. The mortal remains of the saint are interred inside a single domed mausoleum. The entrance with a portico in front is from the south. The tomb of Pir Bahram conforms to the square single-domed tomb style of Bengal architecture, maintaining links with similar earlier monuments. The dome seems to be of bulbous type with a Kalasa finial though it appears to be very squat. The height of the dome seems to be disproportionate to the main structure. The cornice is curved in the Bengali fashion in vogue in the Pre-Mughal period.

Bahria University : Bahria University is a multi-campus university, with its headquarter in Islamabad, Pakistan. It was established by the Pakistan Navy. It is a development of the Bahria Colleges, established in the late 1980s by the Pakistan Navy for the education of children of naval personnel. In 1995, this was extended to the Bahria Institute of Management and Computer Sciences (BIM&CS), established in affiliation with the University of Peshawar and offering BBA and BSc (Computer Science) programmes, followed in 1997 by MBA and MSc (Computer Science). In 2000, Bahria University was established, offering a variety of programmes up to PhD, with specialties in Earth Science and branches of Psychology. Its units comprise the BIM&CS at Karachi and Islamabad, the Institute of Professional Psychology at the P.N.S. Shifa Karachi, the Pakistan Naval Academy Karachi, and the Pakistan Navy War College, Lahore.

Bahuda JatraSimlipal National Park : In Orissa, the National Park nature has epitomized the beauties of a pulsating tropical forest – its hypnotic rhythm of rolling hills and rich valleys, its sylvan glory on red and saffron soil, its playful brooks and amid rocky glens, its perennial rivers with crystal pools, cascading rapids and gorgeous falls, and its azure blue sky are unmistakably picturesque and awe-inspiring. The perennial water regime owes itself to the unique geological and geomorphological qualities, unique in the country. The return 'car festival' is celebrated in the beginning of the month of Shravana (July-August)

Bahujan Samaj Party : The Bahujan Samaj Party is a political party in India. It is a party formed to represent both low caste and Dalit (untouchable) persons, those at the bottom of India's caste system. The BSP has two high-profile, charismatic leaders, Kanshi Ram and Mayawati. In the 13th Lok Sabha (1999-2004) it had 14 (out of 545) members. Though avowedly a national party, the BSP has yet to exert much influence outside of the large state of Uttar Pradesh, whose government the party has led several times. The deep and mutual hostility between the BSP and the Samajwadi Party – the other leading state party in Uttar Pradesh, whose support is mainly OBC or kshatriya – has led the BSP into government with its erstwhile ideological enemies, the Bharatiya Janata Party (whose leadership doesn't discriminate on basis of caste]). The party's political symbol is an elephant.

Baichung Bhutia : Baichung Bhutia (born December 15, 1976 in Tinkitam) is one of the most famous football player from India. He is known by his fans as the torchbearer of Indian Football in the international arena. Baichung born in a sleepy hamlet in South Sikkim district.

He won an SAI Scholarship at age of nine to attend the Tashi Namgyal Academy in Gangtok. He went on to play for several school and local clubs in his home state of Sikkim. A stellar performance at the 1992 Subroto Cup brought him to the notice of the football establishment. In 1993, at the age of sixteen, he left school to join the professional East Bengal Club in Calcutta. In 1995, he moved to JCT Mills, Phagwara, which went on to win the India National Football League that year. Bhutia was a top scorer in the league, and was chosen to play in the Nehru Cup. He was named "1996 Indian Player of the Year", and has won numerous other awards.

In 1997 he returned to East Bengal, and became team captain in the 1998-99 season. In 1999 he travelled overseas to play for the Bury Football Club in Manchester, England, improving his conditioning and strategy. In 2002 he returned to India and played for the Mohun Bagan AC for a year before returning again to the East Bengal Club, and helping them to win the Asean Cup Club Championship. He also signed up to play for Perak FC, the Malaysian championship club, from August to October of 2003. He signed an endorsement deal with Adidas India Marketing Pvt. Ltd in November of 2003.

Baichung Stadium : Baichung Stadium is a football stadium in Namchi, the district headquarters of South Sikkim district in the state of Sikkim, India. The stadium was built in honour of Baichung Bhutia, India's most well known contemporary footballer. The state plans to actively promote the sport made popular after Bhutia became the first Indian to play in an European league and captain the national team.

Baiga : Baiga is a tribe found in Madhya Pradesh and Jharkhand states of India. The largest number of Baigas is found in Baiga-chuk in Mandla district of Madhya Pradesh. Till fairly recently the Baigas practiced 'dahiya' cultivation, that is, slash and burn. Thousands of squire miles of sal forests have been clean destroyed by them in the progress of their dahiya cultivation, the ground being afterwards occupied by dense scrub of low sal species springing from the stumps. The Baigas are courageous woodsman and hunter.

Baigunbari Hunting Park : Baigunbari Hunting Park was a hunting and pleasure park of the Nawabs of Dhaka. Baigunbari is located at Sadullahpur mauja, Biralia Union, savar. Although the work of setting up the park was started by khwaja alimullah, it was completed during the time of Nawab abdul ghani. The natural setting of this high-low hilly forest area was very conducive for breeding animals and birds for hunting. The Nawab of Dhaka proclaimed the forest land of Sadullapur as a wildlife sanctuary. Because of wide grounds on either side of a lake the area had an appropriate ambience for animals and birds as well as for hunting. The Nawab of Dhaka used to bring various species of indigenous and exotic deer, peacocks, wild-cocks, francoline partridges, hares etc and set them free in the forest for breeding. In addition, there used to be plenty of huntable hogs and various types of birds on the banks of the lakes of the forest. No one except persons close to the Nawabs could hunt there. In 1895 the Nawab gave warnings to unauthorised hunters in his forest area by putting notices in newspapers. He announced that those who would be found hunting without permission would be prosecuted and would have to pay compensation.

Bairagir Bhita : Bairagir Bhita is a temple site within the citadel of mahasthan (pundranagar), about 76m south of the northern rampart. Excavated in 1928-29, the site proved to be the remains of two fragmentary temples of the early and late Pala periods (8th-9th century and 11th century) along with some subsidiary structures in the open courtyard to the north enclosed within a perimeter wall.

Baisakhi : Baisakhi celebrated with joyous music and dancing, is New Year's Day for Panjabis. It falls on April 13, though once in 36 years it occurs on 14th April. It was on this day that the tenth Sikh Guru, Guru Gobind Singh, founded the Khalsa in 1699. Sikhs visits *Gurdwaras* and listen to kirtans. After the prayer, *kada prasad* (sweetened semolina) is served to the congregation. The function ends with *langar,* the community lunch. Processions are taken out, at the head of which are the *panj piaras*. Mock duels and bands playing religious tunes are part of the processions. School children also enthusiastically take part in them. For people in villages this festival is a last opportunity for relaxing before they start harvesting of corn. Processions and feasting follow readings of the holy scripture of the Sikhs, *Guru Granth Sahib.*

Baisipali Wildlife Sanctuary : Officially created on November 7, 1981, Baisipali Wildlife Sanctuary is located in Nayagrh, Orissa, India, adjacent to the Satkosia Gorge Sanctuary. It is 168.35 square kilometers of sanctuary land, home to bears, elephants, leopards, Sambar Deer, and spotted deer.

Baisipalli Wildlife Sanctuary : In Orissa, Baisipalli Wildlife Sanctuary was established in 1981 in the Eastern Ghats and rises from almost sea level to about 900 metres. The sanctuary extends over 166 square kilometres. Apart from elephants and tigers there are also sambar, mouse deer and a fascinating variety of fauna including migratory and resident avifauna.

Baitul Mukarram Mosque : Baitul Mukarram Mosque is the National Mosque of Bangladesh. Its construction began on 27 January 1960, and has been going on in phases. In the late 1950s Dhaka grew very rapidly. Abdul Latif Ibrahim Bawani first came up with the idea of building a grand mosque with a large capacity.

The 'Baitul Mukarram Mosque Society' was formed in 1959 to facilitate the project. Land was allocated for the mosque complex at the meeting point of Old and New Dhaka. The site was also in close proximity to the central business district of the city. Architect T Abdul Hussain Thariani was commissioned to design the mosque complex. The plan included shops, offices, libraries and parking areas within the complex.

The design of the mosque reflects the architecture of the period as can be seen from the use of a white and almost cube-form for the main building. A Mosque without a dome over the roof of its main prayer hall must have been a unique experiment. The main building is eight storied and 99 feet high from the ground level. According to the original plan, the main entrance of the mosque was to be on the eastern side. The shahan on the east is 29,000 square feet with ablution space on its south and north sides. The absence of a dome on the main building is compensated by the two shallow domed entrance porticoes, one on the south, and the other on the north. The elevation of these porticoes consists of three horseshoe shaped arches, the middle of which is bigger than the rest. Two patios ensure that enough light and air enter the prayer hall.

The Baitul Mokarram mosque is modern in its architectural style. But it has not discarded traditional principles of mosque architecture. It has found its place in the hearts of the Muslims because of the resemblance of its form to the famous Kaba *at Mecca*.

Bajaj Auto : Bajaj Auto is a major Indian automobile manufacturer. It is based in the western Indian state of Maharashtra, with plants in Akurdi and Chakan, near Mumbai. Bajaj Auto makes motorscooters, motorcycles and the auto rickshaw. Bajaj Auto does not manufacture cars as of 2004.

Baji Rao : Shrimant Baji Rao Vishwanath Bhatt (August 18, 1699- April 25, 1740), also known as Baji Rao I, was a powerful 18th century Brahmin who served as Peshwa (Prime Minister) to the fourth Maratha Chhatrapati (King) Shahu between 1719 until Baji Rao's death. He is also known as Thorala (Marathi for Elder) Baji Rao.

Like his father, despite being a Brahmin, he took up leading his troops. He is credited with expanding the Maratha Empire created by its founder, Shivaji, to help reach its zenith during his son's reign twenty years after his death. Baji Rao is thus acknowledged as the most famous of the nine Peshwas.

Baji Rao was the son of the first Bhatt family Peshwa, Balaji Vishwanath. He was appointed by Shahu as Peshwa upon the death of his father, thus making the position of Peshwa hereditary in the Bhatt family.

Standing tall, poised and confident before Shahu and his court the young new Peshwa Baji Rao is said to have thundered, "Let us transcend the barren Deccan and conquer central India. The Mughals have become weak indolent womanizers and opium-addicts. The accumulated wealth of centuries in the vaults of the north, can be ours. It is time to drive from the holy land of Bharatvarsha the outcaste and the barbarian. Let us throw them back over the Himalayas, back to where they came from. The Maratha flag must fly from the Krishna to the Indus. Hindustan is ours".

He fixed his piercing gaze on Shahu and said, "Strike, strike at the trunk and the branches will fall off themselves. Listen but to my counsel, and I shall plant the Maratha banner on the walls of Attock". Shahu was deeply impressed and is said to have cried with blazing eyes,"By heaven, you shall plant it on the throne of the Almighty".

Baji Rao is famous for rapid tactical movements in battle using his cavalry, hence he is often called a cavalry general. Two examples are the Battle of Palkhed in 1728 when he out-manouvered the Mughal Governor of the Deccan province, and again in the battle against the Mughal Emperor, Muhammad Shah at Delhi during 1737.

Bajirao died on April 25, 1740 still in his prime. He died of a sudden fever while inspecting his jagirs at the village of Khargon, near the city of Indore. His mortal remains were consigned to flames on April 28, 1740, at Raverkhed on the river, Narmada.

Baji Rao I : Baji Rao I, was a powerful 18th century Brahmin who served as Peshwa (Prime Minister) to the fourth Maratha Chhatrapati (King) Shahu between 1719 until Baji Rao's death. He is also known as Thorala (Marathi for Elder) Baji Rao. Like his father, despite being a Brahmin, he took up leading his troops. He is credited with expanding the Maratha Empire created by its founder, Shivaji, to help reach its zenith during his son's reign twenty years after his death. Baji Rao is thus acknowledged as the most famous of the nine Peshwas.

Bajji : Bajji is a snack item that is popular all over India. Japan's tempura and the USA's onion fries or fritters, which use a batter of flour and eggs, are close cousins of the bajji. It is basically cut vegetable dipped in gram flour batter and deep fried in oil. While potato slices, egg plant, onions and chili peppers are the most common there are really no rules. Zucchinis, mushrooms, green or red bell pepper, among others, work quite well. It is typically served as an appetizer or a tea time snack and finds its perfect match in beer or wine. Great on a rainy day.

Bakayang : T he Kinnauri men and women perform this dance as a prelude to the Dakyang. In this dance men and women enter in a single file and then form a circle.

Bakkhali River : Bakkhali river is the only important river in Cox's Bazar district of Bangladesh. It rises from the ranges that divide Chittagong from Arakan and flows north, then turning to the west flows past Ramu and Cox's Bazar towns and falls into the Maheshkhali channel.

Bakr-Id : Iduzzoha (Idul-Korbab) or Bakr-Id is the other compulsory celebration of Muslims, when animal sacrifice is made. The mythological basis of the observance, older than Islam is related to Prophet Abraham of the old testament.

Bakr-Id : Iduzzoha (Idul-Korbab) or Bakr-Id is the other compulsory celebration of Muslims, when animal sacrifice is made. The mythological basis of the observance, older than Islam is related to Prophet Abraham of the old testament.

Bal Gangadhar Tilak : Bal Gangadhar Tilak, was an Indian nationalist, social reformer and freedom fighter who was the first popular leader of the Indian Independence Movement. Tilak sparked the fire for complete independence in Indian consciousness, and is considered the father of Hindu nationalism as well. 'Swaraj is my birthright, and I shall have it!' This famous quote of his is very popular and well-remembered in India even today. Reverently addressed as Lokmanya (meaning "Beloved of the people" or "Revered by the world"), Tilak was a scholar of Indian history, Sanskrit, Hinduism, mathematics and astronomy.

After graduation, Tilak began teaching mathematics in a private school in Pune and later became a journalist. He organized the Deccan Education Society to improve the quality of education for India's youth. Tilak founded the Marathi daily Kesari (The Lion) which fast became a popular reading for the common people of India. He demanded the British immediately give the right to self-government to India's people.

Tilak joined the Indian National Congress in the 1890s, but soon fell into opposition of its liberal-moderate attitude towards the fight for self-government. Tilak opposed the moderate views of Gopal Krishna Gokhale, and was supported by fellow Indian nationalists Bipin Chandra Pal in Bengal and Lala Lajpat Rai in Punjab. In 1907, the Congress Party split into the Garam Dal (literally, "Hot Faction"), led by Tilak, Pal and Lajpat Rai, and the Naram Dal (literally, "Soft Faction") led by Gokhale during its convention at Surat in Gujarat.

Tilak proposed various social reforms, such as a minimum age for marriage, and was especially keen to see a prohibition placed on the sale of alcohol. His thoughts on education and Indian political life have remained highly influential — he was the first Congress leader to suggest that Hindi, written in the devanagari script, should be accepted as the sole national language of India, a policy that was later strongly endorsed by Mahatma Gandhi. However, English, which Tilak wished to remove completely from the Indian mind, remains an important means of communication in India. But the usage of Hindi (and other Indian languages) has been reinforced and widely encouraged since the days of the British Raj, and Tilak's legacy is often credited with this resurgence. Another of the major contributions relates to the propagation of Sarvajanik (public) Ganesh festival, over 10-11 days from Bhadrapada Shukla (Ganesh) Chaturthi to (Anant) Chaturdashi (in Aug/Sept span), which contributed for people to get together and celebrate the festival and provided a good platform for leaders to inspire masses. His call for boycott of foreign goods also served to inspire patriotism among Indian masses.

Tilak was a critic of Mahatma Gandhi's strategy of non-violent, civil disobedience. Tilak was considered the political and spiritual leader of India by many, and Gandhi is considered his successor. Tilak is also today considered the father of Hindu Nationalism. He was the idol of Indian revolutionary Vinayak Damodar Savarkar, who penned the political doctrine of Hindutva.

Balagokulam : Balagokulam is a children's movement founded during the middle of 1970 in Kerala, India. It aims at enriching moral and social values in children and achieves their objective through the teachings of Lord Krishna. The Organization was registered in 1981 as a Nationwide cultural movement and it now has mission all over India. The slogan of Balagokulam is "Sa+nization is backed by Rashtriya Swayamsevak Sangh and it has missions in US and UK.

Balaji Vishwanath Bhatt : Balaji Vishwanath Bhatt (1660 - April 2, 1719 AD), also known as Peshwa Balaji Vishwanath or Diwan Balaji Vishwanath, was a Chittpawan Brahmin, who eventually became the first Peshwa (Marathi for Prime Minister) under the reign of the fourth Maratha Chattrapati Shahuji.

He is famous for assisting a young Shahuji in consolidating his grip on a Maratha Empire that was fragmented as a result of persistent attacks by the Mughal Emperor Aurangzeb between 1685 and 1707.

Balakat Dance : The Dodavas tribes perform this dance during the harvest time.

Balakot : Balakot, located about thirty kilometres from the city of Mansehra, is a town in the North-West Frontier Province of Pakistan. It is a famous tourist destination of the region is one of the first stops for tourists who wish to visit the secluded but beautiful Kaghan valley of the North-West Frontier Province of Pakistan. The river Kunhar runs through the city and is one of the main reasons for the beauty of this area. Balakot is also the main city in this area, and is surrounded by many smaller towns and villages.

Balakram National Park : This park has been established in the west Garo Hill district in an area of 220sq km. The nearest town is William Nagar about15km. The railhead Guwahati is about160km from the park. The nearest airport is Guwahati which is 170km from the park.

The vegetation consist of tropical moist deciduous type. The predominant species is moist hill sal. Mammals found in the park are binturong, clouded leopard, leopard cat, wolf, sloth bear, elephant, loris, serow, Reptile found is python. The birds are hornbill, hoolock etc.

Balasore : Balasore was an early trading port for British, French and Dutch ships in the early age of Enlightenment and became a colonial part of first Danish India, later British India. In 1763 Balasore became a Danish possession, governed from Tranquebar, as part of Danish India. Due to the shallowness of its bay, the trading post was abandoned, leaving behind only a small settlement in the area. On 7 November 1845, all Danish India was sold to the British, who made it part of British India.

Balawaristan : Balawaristan is another name for the Northern Areas, Pakistan. The Northern Areas include Gilgit and Chitral. The regions of Baltistan, and Ladakh are also considered to be a part of Balawaristan by the nationalist parties of Gilgit. However, the majority of people in Baltistan, Ladakh and Kargil maintain that historically Baltistan, Ladakh and Kargil are not part of Balawaristan.

The name Balawaristan is used mainly by nationalists of Gilgit region, such as the Balawaristan National Front, who are seeking to define a separate identity for Gilgit, Baltistan and Ladakh regions from that of the Kashmir Valley and Jammu. This movement has little or no support in Baltistan or Ladakh regions.

Balbir Singh Sr. : Balbir Singh Sr. (born on October 10, 1924) is a hockey player from India, who has been a member of three Olympic gold medal winning teams: 1948 Summer Olympics (London) ; 1952 Summer Olympics (Helsinki) ; 956 Summer Olympics (Melbourne) He was the flagbearer of the Indian Olympic Contingent at the 1952 Helsinki Olympics and 1956 Melbourne Olympics.

In 1957, he became the first hockey player to be awarded the Padma Shri. He was also a member of the Indian hockey team that won the silver medal at the Asian Games 1958 as well as the Asian Games 1962. He lit the

Sacred Flame at the Asian Games 1962 which were held in New Delhi. He coached the Indian team for the 1971 World Cup in which India won the silver medal. He was the manager of the Indian team for the 1975 World Cup which India won.

Baldah Garden : Baldah Garden is a a botanical garden located at Wari in the old part of the city of Dhaka. It is one of the oldest botanical gardens established in this part of Bengal by a private individual. The naturalist, philanthropist and poet Narendra Narayan Roy Chaudhury, landlord of the Estate of Baldah, established the garden on his own property in 1909. It is divided into two units. The larger unit is named Cybele after the Greek nature goddess of fertility. It is roughly rectangular, with the northern side slightly cutting a corner, and measures about 136 metres in length and 76 metres in width. The smaller unit, Psyche meaning 'soul', is approximately 100 metres long and 45 metre wide.

Chaudhury passionately enriched the garden with rare plant species collected from different parts of the world until his death in 1943, when further expansion of the garden came to a halt. This situation continued until 1962, when the garden was handed over to the government of East Pakistan and the Forestry Department took charge of managing the garden. After the creation of Bangladesh in 1971, the Department of Forestry of the new government began to work with renewed vigour for its improvement, with the result that most of its past glory has now been restored with the addition of two new greenhouses and modernisation of civil amenities inside the garden. The Baldah Garden is now managed as a satellite unit of the National Botanical Garden by the Department of Forestry.

Baldah Museum : Baldah Museum is situated at Wari, Dhaka near the Christian cemetery. It was established in 1925 as a 'house museum' by Narendra Narayan Roy

Chaudhury, zamindar of Baldah, an estate of Dhaka district. Before his death in 1943, he executed a will according to which the whole of the expenditure for the museum and garden should be met from the estate. The ground floor of the residence had been utilised to display antiquities. In the porch were placed two cauldrons. One long rectangular hall contained a mixed collection of coins, beads and books on art. A second room showed models of village and town life, and ivory and silver filigree works. In the third room was a rich collection of arms and weapons. In the fourth room were coral and other treasures from the sea. These collections were later transferred to the Dhaka Museum (now the National Museum of Bangladesh). The garden, popularly known as baldah garden was developed simultaneously. Although relatively small in size, it still possesses a unique collection of native and exotic plants, and is maintained as a special place of interest.

Baleshwar Temple : Amidst the main city of Champawat is the historical "Baleshwar Temple". Built by the rulers of Chand dynasty, Baleshwar Temple is a marvelous symbol of stone carving. There isn't any historical manuscript that dates the Baleshwar temple, however it is believed to be built between 10–12 century A.D. The main Baleshwar temple is dedicated to Lord Shiva (who is also know as Baleshwar). There are two other temples in the compound of Baleshwar, one dedicated to Ratneshwar and other to Champawati Durga. The temple is built on South Indian Architecture with magnificent Stone Carving works. Close to the Baleshwar Temple is a "Naula" (freshwater resource) which has now dried up. On the day of Mahashivratri, a very crowded fair is held in the Baleshwar Temple compound.

The exteriors of Ratneshwar and Champawati Durga temples are carved with the different posters of the local deities. The stone carving work is magnificent. Baleshwar temples at Champawat has been declared as an Indian National Heritage Monument and is looked after by Archaeological Survey of India (ASI) since 1952.

Bali Khela : Bali Khela (literally, game of strength) folk wrestling, popular in chittagong. The exact origin of this sport is not known but it is traditionally believed to have started during the Mughal period. Many Hindu and Muslim families still bear the titles of 'malla' or 'bali'. Affluent zamindars used to keep in their employment well-known wrestlers for security and status. Their physical prowess was judged through bali khela. The winners used to be hailed as 'bali' (powerful).

Balimela Reservoir : The Balimela Reservoir is located in Orissa, India. Water to the Balimela Power Station is taken from Balimela Reservoir through a 4 K.Ms. long Pressure Tunnel.

Balka Khalji : Balka Khalji (1230-1231) governor of Bengal under Delhi Sultan iltutmish, was a partisan of Ghiyasuddin iwaz khalji. He issued coins in 627 AH (1230 AD) in the joint names of himself and Sultan Iltutmish. Possibly, by inscribing the name of Sultan Iltutmish, Balka Khalji tried to placate the Delhi Sultan.

Balka ruled Bengal as an independent sovereign for about eighteen months. It is astonishing that during this period, Iltutmish took no notice of the affairs of Bengal. He, however, led an expedition against Balka Khalji in the year 1231. Balka fought against the Delhi army bravely and for a time eluded capture. Eventually he was made a captive and killed. With the fall of Malik Ikhtiyaruddin Balka Khalji, the rule of the Khaljis in Bengal came to an end and there began the rule of the Turks of non-Khalji origin

Ball River : Ball river is one the offshoots of the river Shibsa in Khulna district of Bangladesh. It flows southwest through the Sundarbans and meets the Arpangachhia. The joint flow of both the rivers debouches into the Bay of Bengal as the Malancha. True to the meaning of its name ('ball' means strength) the river is deep and violent.

Baloch : The Baloch are an Iranian people inhabiting the province of Balochistan in Iran and Pakistan as well as neighboring areas of Afghanistan and the southeast corner of the Iranian plateau in Southwest Asia. The Baloch speak Baluchi, which is considered a north-western Iranian language and the Baloch are generally considered an Iranian people accordingly. The Baloch are predominantly Muslim, with most belonging to the Hanafi school of thought of Sunni Islam, but there are also a significant number of Zikri Muslims in Balochistan. Some 70 percent of the total Balochi population live in Pakistan. About 20 percent inhabit the coterminous region of southeastern Iran. Balochi population is estimated at about 4,800,000. In Pakistan the Balochi people are divided into two groups, the Sulaimani and the Makrani, separated from each other by a compact block of Brahui tribes.

Balochi : Balochi (also Baluchi, Baloci or Baluci) is a north-western Iranian language and the principal language of Balochistan. There are several other minor languages which are spoken at the ethnic borders of Pakistani and Iranian Balochistan (Sistan and Baluchistan). The speakers of minority languages (Brahui, Saraiki, Sindhi, and Persian (Dehwari dialect)) are bilingual. Persian and English were used as official languages in western Balochistan (Iran-Afghanistan), the Khanate of Balochistan, and British Balochistan. In 1947, the independent Khanate of Balochistan announced Balochi as an official and national language, a policy which was continued until March, 1948.

In 1948, with the incorporation of Balochistan into Pakistan, Balochi was replaced as the official language and Urdu as the national language. The official language in the areas of Gwadar (occupied by Sultanate of Oman until 1958) was Arabic. Balochi has several dialects. Linguists agree on the following two major dialects: Eastern Balochi and Western Balochi.

Balochistan : The province of Balochistan (or Baluchistan) in Pakistan contains most of historical Balochistan and is named after the Baloch. Neighbouring regions are Iranian Balochistan to the west, Afghanistan and Federally Administered Tribal Areas, Pakistan to the north and Punjab and Sindh to the east. To the south is the Arabian Sea. The principal languages in the province are Baluchi, Pashto, Brahui, and Persian. The capital and largest city is Quetta.

Balochistan has a population of around 7 million inhabitants. The Baloch numerically dominate the south of the province, while the Pashtuns are the majority in and around Quetta and the north. Near the Kalat region and other parts of the region the Brahui are a significant presence, while along the coast various Makrani peoples of mixed origins can be found such as the Meds and small groups of descendents of African slaves known as the Hubshi can also be found. Persian-speaking Dehwars also live in the Kalat region and further west towards the border with Iran. In addition, hundreds of thousands of Afghan refugees can be found in the province including Pashtuns, Tajiks, and Hazaras. Sindhi farmers have also moved to the more arable lands in the east.

Balochistan (Baluchistan): The province of Balochistan in Pakistan contains most of historical Balochistan and is named after the Baloch. Neighbouring regions are Iranian Balochistan to the west, Afghanistan and Federally Administered Tribal Areas, Pakistan to the north and Punjab and Sindh to the east. To the south is the Arabian Sea. The principal languages in the province are Baluchi, Pashto, Brahui, and Persian (Farsi). The capital and largest city is Quetta.

Balochistan is located at the eastern edge of the Iranian plateau and in the difficult to define border region between Southwest, Central, and South Asia. It is geographically the largest of the four provinces at 347,190 $km^2$and composes 42% of the total land area of Pakistan. The population density is very low due to the mountainous terrain and scarcity of water. The southern region is known as Makran. A region in the centre of the province is known as Kalat.

Balochistan has a population of around 7 million inhabitants. The Baloch numerically dominate the south of the province, while the Pashtuns are the majority in and around Quetta and the north. Near the Kalat region and other parts of the region the Brahui are a significant presence, while along the coast various Makrani peoples of mixed origins can be found such as the Meds and small groups of descendents of African slaves known as the Hubshi can also be found. Persian-speaking Dehwars also live in the Kalat region and further west towards the border with Iran. In addition, hundreds of thousands of Afghan refugees can be found in the province including Pashtuns, Tajiks, and Hazaras. Sindhi farmers have also moved to the more arable lands in the east.

Balochistan National Party : The Balochistan National Party is a regional political party in Balochistan, Pakistan. At the last legislative elections, 20 october 2002, the party won 0.2 % of the popular vote and 1 out of 272 elected members.

Balochistan University of Engineering and Technology : Balochistan University of Engineering and Technology is located in Khuzdar, Balochistan, Pakistan. Balochistan Engineering College was established at Khuzdar in 1973-74. In 1994, the Balochistan Engineering College was renamed to Balochistan University of Information Technology and Management Sciences. It offers degree programs in Civil Engineering, Mechanical Engineering, Electrical Engineering and Computer System Engineering.

Balochistan University of Information Technology and Management Sciences : Balochistan University of Information Technology and Management Sciences is located in Quetta, Balochistan, Pakistan. It offers degree programs in Engineering, Computers, Business and Sciences. Balochistan University of Information Technology and Management Sciences (BUITMS) has been planned and is being developed as a premier seat of learning and is expected to attract the students from all over Pakistan and neighboring countries in the region. Balochistan University of Information Technology and Management Sciences is an institution that is provincial in implementation but national, regional and global in its outlook.

Balpakram : A National Wildlife Park, located in South Garo Hills and 167 Kms from Tura in Meghalaya. The literal meaning of Balpakram is the "land of perpetual winds". There is a great precipice or deep gorge in Balpakram and is popularly compared to the Grand Canyon of U.S.A. It is believed that here, the spirits of the dead dwell temporarily before embarking on the final journey. It is home to the rare Lesser Panda, the Indian bison and the Stag like Serow. A variety of medicinal herbs locally called "dikges" grow abundantly in Balpakram.

Balti : Balti is a language spoken in Baltistan, in the Northern Areas of Pakistan. Baltistan—prior to 1947 division of Indian Subcontinent—was part of Ladakh province. The language is a sub-dialect of Ladakhi and an archaic dialect of the Tibetan language. Many of the consonants that are silent in most modern Tibetan dialects are pronounced in Balti. Balti is also the name of the Tibetan Balti script, which was replaced by the Persian script in the 17th Century. Recently a number of Balti scholars and social activists are trying to repromote the use of the Balti script [Yige] which will also help to preserve indigenous Ladakhi and Balti form of culture and racial identity.

Balti : The Balti are a people of Ladakhi/Tibetan descent with some Dardic admixture whose population of 400,000 is found in Pakistani-controlled Baltistan (a former district of Ladakh); and in Kargil and Leh districts of Ladakh, a region in Indian-controlled Jammu & Kashmir. The Balti language belongs to the Tibeto-Burman family and is a sub-dialect of Ladakhi.

Baltistan : Baltistan is a region to the north of Kashmir, bordering the Chinese region of Xinjiang. It is situated in the Karakoram mountains just to the south of K2, the world's second highest mountain. It is an extremely mountainous region, with an average altitude of over 3,350 m (11,000 ft). It is inhabited principally by Balti Muslims of Tibetan descent.

The region is divided between India and Pakistan. Pakistani Baltistan (the districts of Skardu (Skardo) and Ganche) lies within the Northern Areas of Pakistan, a de facto federal dependency of Pakistan administered directly from Islamabad; its main town is Skardu. It contains the highest peaks of the Karakoram, including K2. Indian Baltistan (the district of Kargil) is located in the north of the Indian state of Jammu and Kashmir.

Baltistan Wildlife Sanctuary : Baltistan Wildlife Sanctuary is located in Baltistan, Northern Areas, Pakistan. Baltistan Wildlife Sanctuary covers 415 sq km in Baltistan, contiguous with the Astor Wildlife Sanctuary to its south and east. It lies south of the Indus River, between Rondu and Shengus villages. Important wildlife includes Snow Leopard, Brown Bear, Lynx, Tibetan wolf, Tibetan fox, Markhor, Blue sheep and Asiatic ibex.

Baltit Fort : In former times survival of the feudal regimes of Hunza was ensured by the impressive Baltit fort, just above Karimabad. The foundations of the fort are said to date back around 700 years, but there have been rebuilds and alterations over the centuries. In the 16th century the Thum married a princess from Baltistan who brought master Balti craftsmen to renovate the building as part of her dowry. The architectural style is a clear indication of Tibetan influence in Baltistan at the time. The Mirs of Hunza abandoned the fort in 1945, and moved to a new palace down the hill. The fort started to decay and there was concern that it might possibly fall into ruin. Following a survey by the Royal Geographic Society of London, a restoration programme was initiated. The programme was completed in 1996 and the fort is now a museum run by the Baltit Heritage Trust.

Baltoro Glacier : The Baltoro Glacier, at over 70 kilometers long, is the longest glacier outside of the polar regions. It is situated in northeast Pakistan and runs through the center of the second tallest mountain range on Earth — the Karakoram. At 8,611 m (28,251 ft) K2 is the tallest mountain in the region, and three others within 20 km top 8,000 m.

The glacier is situated in a large arena hemmed by high peaks on the southern slopes of the central Karakoram Range, in the Baltistan area of Jammu and Kashmir.

The glacier gives rise to the Shigar River, which is a tributary of the Indus River. Large tributary glaciers feed the main Baltoro glacier. These include a glacier from the southwestern slopes of the Gasherbrum peak and a tributary glacier from the northwestern slope of the Masherbrum peak, both in the Karakoram mountain range.

The trough of this glacier is very wide and its central part is a vast snowfield. Small valley glaciers form icefalls where they meet the trunk glacier. The sidewalls vary from very steep to precipitous. The glacier has carved striations on the surrounding country rocks. Moving ice has formed depressions, which serve as basins for numerous glacial lakes.

Baltoro Glacier : The Baltoro Glacier, at over 70 kilometers long, is the longest glacier outside of the polar regions. It is situated in northeast Pakistan and runs through the center of the second tallest mountain range on Earth — the Karakoram. At 8,611 m (28,251 ft) K2 is the tallest mountain in the region, and three others within 20 km top 8,000 m. The glacier is situated in a large arena hemmed by high peaks on the southern slopes of the central Karakoram Range, in the Baltistan area of Jammu and Kashmir. The glacier gives rise to the Shigar River, which is a tributary of the Indus River. Large tributary glaciers feed the main Baltoro glacier. These include a glacier from the southwestern slopes of the Gasherbrum peak and a tributary glacier from the northwestern slope of the Masherbrum peak, both in the Karakoram mountain range.The trough of this glacier is very wide and its central part is a vast snowfield. Small valley glaciers form icefalls where they meet the trunk glacier. The sidewalls vary from very steep to precipitous. The glacier has carved striations on the surrounding country rocks. Moving ice has formed depressions, which serve as basins for numerous glacial lakes.

Balu River : Balu river runs mainly through the extensive Swamps of Beel Belai and those east of Dhaka, joining the Shitalakshya near Demra. It has a narrow connection through the Suti Nadi near Kapasia with the Shitalakshya, and also by way of the Tongi Khal with the Turag; there is also a link with the Shitalakshya near Kaliganj. Although it carries floodwater from the Shitalakshya and the Turag during the flood season, the

Balu is of importance mainly for local drainage and access by small boats.

Balukhand Sanctuary : Covering an area of 72 square kilometres, this sanctuary was established in 1984 to protect the shoreline nesting sites of olive ridley and green sea turtles in Orissa. There are various groups of black buck existing on land.

Bamabodhini Patrika : Bamabodhini Patrika was amonthly journal edited by Umeshchandra Dutta (1840-1907) from 1863. He together with some other young Brahmo leaders established Bamabodhini Sabha in 1863, aiming to educate Bengali housewives and to publish books and journals for their mental upliftment. Bethune School was founded in 1849, and the total number of Girls' Schools in Bengal in 1863 was 35 with students numbering only 1183. Umeshchandra and others tried to penetrate Bengali families through the medium of a journal to spread women's education. Bamabodhini Patrika was the result of this pioneering effort.

Bamba Dhura : Bamba Dhura is the Himalayan mountain peak situated in the Pithoragarh district of Uttaranchal, India.The altitude of the summit is 6,334 M.It is situated on the north west ridge over the end of Kalabaland Glacier in eastern part of the district, left to the Milam Glacier.Kalabaland Dhura 6,105 M is situated on the west of this peak and Chiring We 6,559 M, are on the same massif.Bamba Dhura massif is the part of divide between Kalabaland and Lassar valley.This peak was first of all climbed to summit in 1977 from south by col between Bamba Dhura and Chiring We.The peak has been ascent through south east and west ridge between the two peaks

Bamboo Work : Bihar is greatly noted for its bamboo work. Bamboo sends itself to multifarious uses. The use of cut bamboo as a containers to drink water is an ancient practsice; as also simple scoops for kitchen use. Large containers far storing grain are a common sight. In fact the rural people in remote, bamboo graving are as still keep their precious possessions in bamboo basket with side. Against this tradition, commendable experiments work has been done in Patna to adopt these very object to modern use, In fact a whole house can very neatly be filled up through bamboo articles. Finely shaped lamps and lanterns, elegant furniture, complete tableware, travel kit, almost anything seems possible to get from the bamboo.

Banana Chips : Banana chips are dehydrated slices of banana, covered with sugar. The chips are crispy and have a sweet taste. Variants of banana chips may be covered with chocolate. Usually, the chips are produced of underripe bananas, of which slices are boiled in oil, which are then dried, and to which preservatives may be added. The chips are often part of muesli and nut mixes.

Banar River : Banar river is one of the main rivers of the Madhupur Tract in Bangladesh. Several streams originating from the highland of the Tract north of Madhupur and Phulbari upazilas join at the southeast of Trishal to form the Banar. Flowing south the river bifurcates into two, the eastern arm flows into the Old Brahmaputra and the southeastern arm falls into the Shitalakshya. The eastern arm which meets the Old Brahmaputra flows further ahead and ultimately joins with the Shitalakshya. Finally the Banar becomes a tributary of Shitalakshya

Banarasidas : Banarasidas (1586-1643) was the first poet in India to write an autobiography—Ardha Kathanaka (The Half Story). He wrote it when he was 55. He lived during the reign of Akbar, Jahangir and Shahjahan. Banarasidas was a friend of the nawab of Jaunpur Chini Kilechkhan. He was also an occasional chess partner of

Padishah Shahjahan. When Akbar died suddenly, there was terror because no one was in charge.

Banas : The Banas is a river of Rajasthan state in western India. It is a tributary of the Chambal River, which in turn flows into the Yamuna, a tributary of the Ganges. The Banas is approximately 512 kilometres in length. It originates in the Khamnor Hills of the Aravalli Range, about 5 km from Kumbhalgarh in Rajsamand District. It flows northeast through Mewar region of Rajasthan, meets the Chambal near the village of Rameshwar in Sawai Madhopur District. The cities of Nathdwara, Jahanpur, and Tonk lie on the river. Major tributaries include the Berach and Menali on the right, and the Kothari, Khari, Dai, Dheel River, Sohadara, Morel and Kalisil on the left. The Banas drains a basin of 45,833 km^2, which lies entirely within Rajasthan. It drains the east slope of the central portion of the Aravalli Range, and the basin includes all or part of Ajmer, Bhilwara, Bundi, Chittorgarh, Dausa, Jaipur, Pali, Rajsamand, Sawai Madhopur, Tonk, and Udaipur districts.

Bandbaja : Bandbaja is Pakistan's first online music magazine. Formed in 2003 by several college students, the magazine received immediate recognition because of its relentless critique of the Pakistani music scene. The popularity of Bandbaja gave rise to several similar online music websites and portals through out Pakistan.

Bandha : Bandha is considered as "the forgotten forerunner of the lyrical Odissi". Practised by Gotipua dancers and characterised by acrobatic poses, bandha is now flourishing in places like Raghurajpur, Konark, and Pithapur in Puri district and some akahdas (gymnasiums) in the heart of Orissa. Bandha is characterised by intricate postures of the body. Aloka Kanungo, the renowned Odissi danseuse, is trying the fusion of the traditional bandha with modern Odissi.

Bandhani : The tied and dyed fabrics, known as Bandhej or Bandhani, of Saurashtra and Kutch are perhaps the finest produced in India. Amongst these, the most intricate and refined styles are to be found in Jamnagar, Bhuj and Mandavi. Jamnagar Bandhej is produced on superfine cotton Mulmul and Muslim, sometimes combined with gold checks and motifs worked in Jamdani technique. The Mandavi and Bhuj work is on silk with a woven gold border, had motifs embroidered in gold wire known as Badla. Since the designs w.ere circular and on a blue black background, they were known as Chandrakhani or moonshaped.

Bandhavgarh National Park : Bandhavgarh National Park is located in Umaria district of Madhya Pradesh state in India. Bandhavgarh was declared a national park in 1968 with an area of 105 km^2. The buffer is spread over the forest divisions of Umaria and Katni and totals 437 km^2. The park derives its name from the most prominent hillock of the area, which is said to be given by Lord Rama to his brother Laxman to keep a watch on Lanka. Hence the name Bandhavgarh (Bandhav=Brother, Garh=Fort). This is a Small National Park, Compact, yet full of game. The density of the tiger population at Bandhavgarh is the highest known in India. This is also white tiger country. These have been found in the old state of Rewa for many years. Maharaja Martand Singh captured the last known in 1951. This white tiger, Mohan, is now stuffed and on display in the palace of the Maharajas of Rewa.

Bandipur National Park : The Bandipur National Park is one of the most fascinating wild-life centers, established in 1930's by the Mysore Maharajahs. It was once the Mysore Maharaja's private hunting park. Later in 1941, it was expanded to adjoin the Rajiv Gandhi National Park (Nagarhole)in the northwest and Kerala's Wayanad Wildlife Sanctuary in the southwest and Tamil Nadu's

Mudumalai Wildlife Sanctuary in the south which now together constitute the Niligiri Biosphere Reserve.

Bandipur lies in the southern state of Karnataka. It stretches along the Kerala-Tamil Nadu border and lies on the Mysore—Ooty highway and covers a forest area of 874.2 square kilometers and 780-1455 m above sea level. The temperature in Bandipur ranges between 10 degrees and 35 degrees centigrade. The park has an average annual rainfall of 1200mm.

Bandna : Perhaps the most popular festivals is Bandana Parab during the black moon of Kartik month (Kartik Aamavashya) in Jharghand. This festival is mainly for the benefit of animals and symbol of animal worship. The songs of this festival are called Ohira. Farmers clean their animals, feed them well, give them complete rest, decorate and ornate them.

They sing songs of admiration as an acknowledgement for their contribution. The primitive people believe that animals also have spirits which might harm or benefit them. So as to pacify these spirits as well as for better performance they worship their animals. The alluring of the week long festival takes place on the last day. Bulls and buffalos are chained to a strong pole and they are attacked with a dry animal hyde. The angry and excited animals hit the dry skin with its horns and the crowd enjoy looking at its vigorousness, anger and excitement. A unique aspect of Bandna is the wall embellishment with the folk painting.

Baneshwar Fair : Held in the Dungarpur district of Rajasthan, the fair derives its name from the revered Shiva Linga of that area. Predominantly a tribal affair with more than half the congregation being Bhils, thousands gather near the confluence of the Mahi and Som rivers to worship, sing and dance. A silver image of Mavji, a reincarnation of Kalki, an avatar of Lord Vishnu is brought on horse back. Magic shows, acrobatic displays and merry-go-rounds add fun and frolic to the religious celebrations.

Banga Samsriti Sammelan : Another cultural mela on an ambitious scale is the Banga Samsriti Sammelan held annually in Calcutta. Usually a 15-day festival it represents all the different features of Bengali performing arts, traditional and modern, rural and urban. The Sammelan has came to acquire a highly representative character.

Banga Sena : Banga Sena are a group demanding the creation of a separate Hindu Republic, called Bangabhumi, in southwestern Bangladesh. The are headed by Kalidas Baidya and are an outlawed group in Bangladesh.

Bangabandhu Jamuna Multipurpose Bridge : Bangabandhu Jamuna Multipurpose Bridge opened in June 1998, is the longest bridge in Bangladesh as well as in South Asia, and the 11th longest bridge in the world. It was constructed over the river jamuna, mightiest of the three major rivers of Bangladesh, and fifth largest in the world in terms of volumetric discharge. The bridge established a strategic link between the eastern and western parts of Bangladesh. It generates multifarious benefits for the people and especially, promotes inter-regional trade in the country. Apart from quick movement of goods and passenger traffic by road and rail, it facilitated transmission of electricity and natural gas, and integration of telecommunication links. The bridge, stretching from tangail to sirajganj is located on the Asian Highway and the Trans-Asian Railway which, when fully developed, will provide uninterrupted international road and railway links from South-east Asia to North-west Europe.

Bangabandhu National Stadium : Bangabandhu National Stadium is the national stadium and main sports arena in Dhaka, Bangladesh. It is located at Motijheel at the heart of the capital city, Dhaka. The stadium is variously known as Number 1 National Stadium, Dhaka Stadium etc. It's current name was given to honour Sheikh Mujibur Rahman, the father of the nation, also known as "Banga bandhu" or "friend of Bengal". Currently, the stadium is used for football. Total seating capacity is 36000. It was also home to the Bangladeshi cricket team until March 1, 2005.

Bangabandhu Sheikh Mujib Medical University : Bangabandhu Sheikh Mujib Medical University country's only university of medical education and research established in Dhaka in 1998. During the days of Pakistan, in East Pakistan, which is Bangladesh today, there were several medical colleges that offered the MBBS degree. There was no scope for advanced post-graduate studies in medicine. In order to create facilities for post-graduate medical education, the Institute of Post-graduate Medicine and Research (IPGMR) was established in Dhaka in 1965.

The IPGMR was entrusted with postgraduate teaching and research, but was not itself a degree-awarding institution. The country's oldest university (established in 1921), the university of dhaka, awarded degrees of the IPGMR study programmes together with the MBBS degree of the medical colleges. During the late 1990s the government of Bangladesh adopted a plan to establish several new universities in sectors such as science and technology, medicine and agriculture. This resulted in the conversion of IPGMR into a full-fledged medical university through an ordinance enacted by parliament on 30 April 1998. The new university was given the name Bangabandhu Sheikh Mujib Medical University (BSMMU), after the name of Bangabandhu Sheikh Mujibur Rahman.

Bangabandhu Sheikh Mujibur Rahman Agricultural University : Bangabandhu Sheikh Mujibur Rahman Agricultural University the second agricultural university of Bangladesh, located at Salna in the district of Gazipur. As per the law enacted by the National Assembly, through an Ordinance (Presidential Order No. 16 of 1998), the President of the country established the university in November, 1998 redesignating the former Institute of Postgraduate Studies in Agriculture (IPSA). The university started functioning from 1998 with a view to providing higher education, research facilities, technology innovation and transfer in different branches of agricultural science. The university has been named in memory of Bangabandhu Sheikh Mujibur Rahman.

Bangabazar : Bangabazar is a popular market for selling of economy garments at Fulbaria in dhaka. People from all over the country as well as foreigners flock here to buy garments for personal use and gifts. Many retail traders also come here to make wholesale purchases. Bangabazar, however, did not begin as a garments market. It started in 1965 as a trading spot where vendors and hawkers brought headload of goods everyday. The location was close to the main railway station of the time and was an ideal place for sale of snacks, drinks, items of day-to-day use, and souvenirs.

Bangabda : Bangabda Bangla calendar, also known as 'Bangla Sal', was promulgated by the Mughal emperor akbar in 1584 AD. The new calendar was initially known as Tarikh-e-Elahi and was introduced on 10 or 11 March 1584. Though the new calendar was promulgated in the twenty-ninth year of Akbar's reign, it dates from his ascension to the throne on 5 November 1556.

The length of a year in the Bangla calendar, as in the Gregorian calendar, is counted as 365 days. However, the actual time taken by the earth in its revolution around the sun is 365 days 5 hours 48 minutes and 47 seconds. To make up this discrepancy, the Gregorian calendar adds an extra day to the month of February every fourth year (except in century years not divisible by 400). The Bangla year did not take into account these extra hours. Bangla months too were of different lengths. In order to counter this discrepancy and make the Bangla calendar more precise, a committee to reform the Bangla calendar was set up on 17 February 1966 under the auspices of the bangla academy and under the guidance of muhammad shahidullah. Under the recommendations of the committee, the months from Baisakh to Bhadra were to be counted as of 31 days each, while the months from Asvin to Chaitra were to be considered as of 30 days, with Chaitra having 31 days every four years.

Bangabhaban : Bangabhaban official residence of the President of Bangladesh. It was originally the temporary official residence of the British Viceroy of India, and later, of the Governor of East Bengal, and was known as Governor House. The present site of Bangabhaban has a long history. During the sultanate period a saint called Hazrat Shahjalal Dakhini used to reside in the area. He along with his disciples were mercilessly killed by the men of the ruling Sultan (881 AH). He along with his disciples were buried here. With the passage of time, the place became famous as a mazar, and later was abandoned. During the Mughal rule, Mirza Mukim was the official in charge of Nawara Mahal under subadar Mir Jumla. His residence was on the southern side of Purana Paltan Maidan.

There were two big hillocks inside and outside of his residence. One of them still lies within the boundary of Bangabhaban. The large tank inside came to be known as Motijheel (lake of pearls) because of the legend that Mirza Mukim's daughter used to throw her ornaments there. The area was probably abandoned towards the end of Mughal period. There is still a building called Manuk House within the Bangabhaban compound. It is conjectured that it belonged to an Armenian zamindar named Manuk during British rule. Nawab Khwaja Abdul Ghani of Dhaka bought the place from Manuk. He also built a bungalow there, which he named as Dilkusha Garden.

Bangabhaban : Bangabhaban official residence of the President of Bangladesh. It was originally the temporary official residence of the British Viceroy of India, and later, of the Governor of East Bengal, and was known as Governor House.

On the partition of bengal in 1905, the government of East Bengal and Assam bought a portion of the place, and a building was constructed for the Viceroy of India. The Viceroy used to stay here during his visits in East Bengal up to 1911. Until 1947, the place was known as Governor House. The building was damaged by a storm in 1961 and was rebuilt. Construction of the new building was completed in 1964. The then Governor of East Pakistan abdul monem khan used to reside in the building.

The Governor House was renamed as Bangabhaban on 12 January 1972 when Justice abu sayeed choudhury became the first constitutional President of the country. It is still the official residence of the President of Bangladesh. Bangabhaban has high boundary walls on all four sides. The main building is a three-storeyed palatial complex. All around this building are greenery strewn with trees. The floor-space of the ground floor is 6,700 sq metre. The President's residence is on the north-east corner, comprising two storeys. The President has two suites along with five well-furnished spacious bedrooms. The President's office, the office of the civil and military secretaries to the President, offices of other officials, and separate rooms for audience with local and foreign visitors are also located in the ground floor. In addition, there is a cabinet room, banquet hall, darbar hall, state dining hall, mini auditorium and a lounge for local visitors. In addition to the

President's residence, there are five rooms for officials, a control room and a studio in the first floor. In the second floor, there are four suites for foreign heads of state and government.

Bangabhumi : Bangabhumi also known as Bir Bango, is a proposed Hindu republic in southwestern Bangladesh envisioned by many groups, such as the Swadhin Bangabhumi Andolan and the Banga Sena. The movement was founded in 1973 in India soon after Bangladeshi independence to support the Hindu refugees from Bangladesh, who were targetted by the Pakistani army in 1971. However, this movement did not receive much support at that time. The leader of the Banga Sena, Kalidas Baidya claims numerous recruits are ready for armed conflict. The movement openly became active again on 2003 when it declared the independence of Hindu Republic of Bangabhumi.

Bangadarshan : Bangadarshan is a monthly literary journal, founded in 1872 by bankimchandra chattopadhyay (1838-1894), who also served as its editor up to April 1876 and was its main contributor. Though his editorship lasted for only four years, its contribution to bangla language and literature, especially in the formation of Bangla prose, is immense. The language employed by Bangadarshan was sadhu bhasa, chaste Bangla, of a high standard. It published essays on literature, society, science, politics, religion and philosophy as well as novels.

Bangali River : Bangali river is a continuation of the Ghaghat river of Rangpur. It maintains connection with the Jamuna in the east, and with the Karatoya (through the Katakhali) in the west. Flowing south, it receives the Baulai, an offshoot of the Jamuna and further south bifurcates into two courses - the western course known as the Halhalia and the eastern one retains the original name. The Bangali arm receives the Manash-Madhukhali, a distributary of the Jamuna north of Dhunat, and within a few kilometres again bifurcates to send an arm due south, known as the Ichamati (Sirajganj). The Bangali flows southwest from this point and receives the Halhalia west of Dhunat and the Bogra-Karatoya further south near Khanpur. The united Bangali- Karatoya is the Phuljhor, which joins the Atrai-Baral flowing from the Hurasagar. The Sirajganj-Ichamati is joined by the Kazipur distributary of the Jamuna in Kazipur upazila. The combined stream falls into the Phuljhor at Nalka.

Bangalore : Bangalore is the capital of the Indian state of Karnataka. Bangalore is located in Southwestern Karnataka on the Mysore Plateau and has an average elevation of 920 meters. With an estimated metropolitan population of 6.5 million in 2006, it is India's third largest city and fifth largest metropolitan area. Though historical referencences to the city predate 1000 AD, a modern written history of continious settlement exists only after 1537, when Kempe Gowda I, who many regard as the architect of modern Bangalore, built a mud fort in the vicinity of the city and established it as a provice of the imperial Vijayanagara Empire.

Banganga : Banganga is a place in the Malabar Hill area of Mumbai City. It is believed that in mythical times the great Lord Rama, an incarnation of God Vishnu, shot an arrow in the ground to provide for fresh water for drinking. The place where the arrow hit the ground there issued out a stream of fresh and sweet water gushed forth from a tributary of the Ganga, over a thousand miles away. Hence the place is known as Banganga.

Bangaram : Bangaram is 2006 Telugu film directed by Dharani(Dhool fame), produced by A.M Rathnam, and has Pawan Kalyan, Reema Sen, and Meera Chopra. Earlier in 2001, A.M Rathnam teamed up with Pawan Kalyan for Khushi, which is one of the biggest blockbusters in

Tollywood. Music by VIdyasagar has released into the market on March 17, 2006 and the audio is making good money.

Bangiya Mussalman Sahitya Patrika : Bangiya Mussalman Sahitya Patrika is a Bangla literary quarterly was the mouthpiece of the Bangiya Mussalman Sahitya Samiti, established on 4 September 1911 in calcutta.

Bangiya Mussalman Sahitya Samiti : Bangiya Mussalman Sahitya Samiti a literary organisation of Bengali Muslims, founded in 1911 by a number of young Muslim writers including Mohammad maniruzzaman islamabadi, muhammad shahidullah, mohammad yakub ali chowdhury, mohammad mozammel huq. They were ostensibly inspired by the bangiya sahitya parishat (1893). Muhammad Shahidullah was elected secretary of the organisation.

The organisation was influenced by the rising Muslim separatist trends. Its objectives included cultivation and preservation of bangla literature, writing biographies of pirs and dervishes, encouraging Muslim writers, establishing harmony between Hindus and Muslims. It arranged monthly meetings and annual conferences. Of the seven literary conferences arranged by it, five were held in Calcutta, while one was held in Chittagong and another in Bashirhat.

Bangla Academy : Bangla Academy founded on 3 December 1955 at Burdwan House, Dhaka, was the outcome of the language movement of 1952, and, as such, a symbol of the movement and of Bengali nationalism.

Since its inception, it has been playing a significant role in the development and modernisation of Bangla. Though 1952 is a milepost in the language movement, the struggle to give Bangla due recognition may be traced back to the second decade of the 20th century. At a meeting of the vangiya sahitya parishad in 1925, chaired by haraprasad shastri, Dr muhammad shahidullah proposed the use of Bangla for academic and literary purposes. At the All-India Muslim Education Conference chaired by ak fazlul huq, he called upon the Government of Bengal to set up a translation department. On 31 December 1948, in his presidential address at the East Pakistan Literary Conference held in Dhaka, he proposed the establishment of a language academy.

The Academy publishes six journals: the bangla academy patrika (quarterly), Uttaradhikar (quarterly), the Bangla Academy Bijnan Patrika (half-yearly), the Bangla Academy Journal (half-yearly in English), Dhanshaliker Desh (juvenile quarterly) and Lekha (monthly). Apart from publications, the Bangla Academy also holds seminars and discussions on different subjects, cultural functions, etc.

Bangla Academy Award : This award is offered to the writers in recognition of their creative genius in consideration of their overall contribution in the field of Bangla language and literature. The award was introduced in 1960 AD. From its very inception till 1984 the awards were scheduled to be offered on six subjects like poetry, novel, short stories, essays, juvenile literature and translation. In 1985 a changed schedule was introduced to offer awards to two writers for their overall contributions in the field of Bangla language and literature. At present awards are given in three distinctive fields: (a) poetry/novel/short story; (b) research/essay/science; (c) translation/drama/juvenile literature.

The award is normally given every year in the above areas of intellectual activities. In the absence of competent awardee in any of the fields in a particular year, no award is given in that year. The award is scheduled to be given to individuals only, and no institution or group is entitled to it. Every award is valued one lakh taka in cash. The awardee is entitled to the cash money, a certificate and a raplica of honour. Besides, the awardee is offered the fellowship of Bangla Academy.

Bangla Calendar : The Bangla calendar also known as Bônggabdo in the Bengali language, is the traditional calendar used in Bangladesh and Bangla-speaking regions of India. The calendar is based on the solar year. New Year's Day falls between 13 April and 15 April. Under the Mughals, agricultural taxes were collected according to the Hijri calendar. However, as the Hijri calendar is a Lunar Calendar, the agricultural year did not coincide with the fiscal year. Therefore, farmers were hard-pressed to pay taxes out of season. In order to streamline tax collection, the Mughal Emperor Akbar ordered a reform of the calendar. Accordingly, Fatehullah Shirazi, a renowned scholar and astronomer, formulated the Bangla year on the basis of the lunar Hijri and Bangla solar calendars. The new Fasli San (agricultural year) was introduced on 10/11 March 1584, but was dated from Akbar's accession to the throne in 1556. The new year subsequently became known as Bônggabdo, or Bengali year.

Bangladesh : The People's Republic of Bangladesh is a South Asian country bordering India, Myanmar and the Bay of Bengal. Together with the West Bengal State of India, it comprises the ethno-linguistic region of Bengal. It means "Country of Bengal", but the word Bangla (Bengal) has obscure origins.

The borders of Bangladesh were set by the partition of India in 1947, when it became the eastern wing of Pakistan, separated from the western wing by 1,600 km (1,000 miles). Despite their common religion, the ethnic and linguistic gulf between the two wings was compounded by the Government's, often from West Pakistan, neglect and persecution. This resulted in the independence of Bangladesh in 1971, after a bloody war supported by India.

The years following independence have been marked by political turmoil, with 13 different heads of government (of which two were assassinated), and at least four coups. The last two political transitions were lawful.

The population of Bangladesh ranks 8th in the world, but its area is ranked 93rd, which is approximately 144,000 sq km. It is 3rd among Muslim-majority nations, though it has a slightly smaller Muslim population than the Muslim minority in India. It is the most densely populated country larger than 700 km^2 in the world. Geographically dominated by the fertile Ganges-Brahmaputra Delta, the country has annual monsoon floods, and cyclones are also common. Bangladesh is one of the founding members of South Asian Association for Regional Cooperation (SAARC), BIMSTEC, and a member of the OIC and the D-8.

Bangladesh Agricultural University (BAU) : Bangladesh Agricultural University (BAU) was established as the only university of its kind in Bangladesh in 1961. The scheme for the establishment of BAU was finalized on 8 June 1961 and its ordinance was promulgated on 18 August 1961. With the appointment of its first Vice-Chancellor, the university formally came into existence on 2 September 1961 and started functioning with the College of Animal Husbandry and Veterinary Science at Mymensingh as its nucleus. Currently the university has 6 faculties and 43 departments covering all aspects of agricultural education and research.

Bangladesh Air Force : The Bangladesh Air Force, is the branch of the Bangladesh Armed Forces. The Bangladesh Air Force was formed at Dimapur, Assam on 28 September 1971. At that time, the embryo of Bangladesh Air Force (BAF) was formed as 'Kilo Flight' to assist the Mukti Bahini (Freedom Fighters). Initially, 'Kilo Flight' consisted of three aircraft (given by Indian Air Force), 09 officers and 47 airmen. Squadron Leader Sultan

Mahmud (retired as Air Vice Marshal and Chief of the Air Staff of BAF) was appointed as the commander of the 'Kilo Flight'. After having some basic training on air to ground weapon delivery, 'Kilo Flight' successfully bombed Fuel storage in Chittagong and Narayangonj area and thus the journey of BAF had commenced.

After liberation in 1971, the Bangladesh Air Force was initially equipped with left-over Pakistan Air Force equipment, mostly F-86 Sabres, and even these were few. Other equipment was donated from India and included: C-47 Dakotas, DHC-3s and Alouette Helicopters. Despite the lack of aircraft, the Pakistan Air Force prior to 1971 had a large number of Bengali pilots, many of them distinguishing themselves, this provided the Bangladesh Air Force with a good number of trained pilots.

Currently the Bangladesh Air Force is armed mostly with Chinese jets, A-5s and F-7s. Recently it also procured Russian MiG-29s, although this has caused a controversy in political circles due to the cost, and the lack of an immediate threat to Bangladesh. The controversy has led to talk of withdrawing the aircraft due to the costs involved in maintaining them. C-130 Hercules have also been ordered by the Bangladesh Air Force, and should enter service soon. Bangladesh Air Force also bought Jian F-7MG's in the mid '90s and recently bought 16 F-7G's from China which are modern updated version of MiG-21'Fishbeds' but with revised wing design and more modern Avionics and weaponry recently developed by China.F-7MG is fitted with Western-made radar and equipment. The F-7G is a further improved version introduced in 2002.

Bangladesh Army : Bangladesh Army, or Bangladesh Shena Bahini in Bangla, is a branch of Bangladesh Armed Forces. The 110,000-member, seven-division army is modeled and organized along British lines, similar to other armies on the Indian subcontinent. However, it has adopted U.S. Army tactical planning procedures, training management techniques, and noncommissioned officer educational systems. It is supported by artillery, armored, and combat units. It is also eager to improve its peacekeeping operations capabilities and is working with the U.S. military in that area.

Bangladesh Army was formed during the Bangladesh Liberation War of 1971. Initially, it consisted of Bengali soldiers and officers from the East Bengal Regiment and other groups of the Pakistan Army who joined the independence war. The newly formed army was organized into several brigades. Z force, under Major Ziaur Rahman, consisted of 1, 3 and 8 East Bengal Regiment. S Force, under Major shafiullah, was created in October 1971 and consisted of 2 and 11 East Bengal. The K Force, commanded by Khaled Mosharraf was created with 4, 9 and 10 East Bengal.

Bangladesh Atrocities : During the Bangladesh War of 1971, widespread atrocities were committed against the Bengali population of East Pakistan (now Bangladesh), at a level that within Bangladesh, 'genocide' is the term that is used to describe the event in almost every major publication and newspaper. A smaller number of non-Bengali citizens were also killed in clashes with the Mukti Bahini. The actual extent of the atrocities committed is not clearly known, and opinions vary, as the next section discusses. However, there is little doubt that numerous civilians were tortured and killed during the war. A large section of the intellectual community of Bangladesh were murdered mostly by the Al-Shams and Al-Badr forces, at the instruction of the defeated Pakistani Army. There are many mass graves in Bangladesh, and newer ones are always being discovered, such as one in an old well near a mosque in Dhaka located in the non-Bengali region of the city which was discovered in August 1999. The first night of war on Bengalis, which is documented in telegrams from the American Consulate in Dhaka to the United States State Department, saw indiscriminate killings of students of Dhaka University and other civilians.

Bangladesh Awami League : The Bangladesh Awami League or the Bangladesh People's League is the main opposition party in Bangladesh and the political catalyst for Bengali discontent and rebellion in 1971. In the 2001 general election it got 40% of the vote and 62 of 300 seats, making it the second-largest party behind the Bangladesh Nationalist Party.

Bangladesh Awami League is the oldest and biggest political party of Bangladesh. It originated in the soil of the country and evolved with the evolving hopes and aspirations of the people living on the Padma- Meghna-Jamuna delta. It is the party that gave leadership in the glorious Liveration Was. Awami league is one of those political parties in the world under whose leadership struggles were led and won, tearing apart the chains of domination and servitude. Awami League represents the mainstream of the progressive, non-communal, democratic and nationalist politics of Bangladesh.

This half-a-century- old party has a glorious of relentless and uncompromising struggle against autocracy and communalism, against political and economic domination. Its greatest achievement is the emancipation of the Bangalee people from the colonial rule of Pakistan. This was the party that both germinated and helped blossom the Bangalee nationalism: the independence won in 1971 is the undying monument of that grand success of Awami League as a political party. Bangabandhu Sheikh Mujibur Rahman, our Father of the Nation, gave the leadership to the people and the party that took us through the glorious War of Liberation. Since then, the party has worked tirelessly to combat autocracy and communatlism, to nourish the non communal political tradition and to institutionalize democracy through establishing a constitutionally elected government. The party is now headed by Sheikh Hasina, the daughter of the late Sheikh Mujibur Rahman

Bangladesh Bank : Bangladesh Bank is the central bank of Bangladesh. It is owned completely by the Government of Bangladesh. After the liberation war, and the eventual independence of Bangladesh, the Government of Bangladesh reorganized the Dhaka branch of the State Bank of Pakistan as the Central Bank of the country, and named it Bangladesh Bank. This reorganization was done persuant to Bangladesh Bank Order, 1972, and the Bangladesh Bank came into existence with retrospective effect from 16th December, 1971.

Bangladesh Bank performs all the functions which a central bank of any country is expected to perform, and such functions include maintaining the price stability, supporting the economic and monetary policies of the central government, managing the country's foreign exchange and the gold reserve. Like all other central bank across the globe, Bangladesh Bank is both the Government's banker and the banker's bank, a "Lender of the Last Resort". Bangladesh Bank, like most of the central banks of different countries, exercises monopoly over the issue of currency and the banknotes. Except for the 1 and 2 taka notes, it issues all other denominations of Bangladeshi Taka.

Bangladesh Betar : Bangladesh Betar is the state-owned radio broadcasting organisation of Bangladesh. It was also known as Radio Bangladesh between 1975 and 1996. Radio transmission in the region now forming Bangladesh started in Dhaka on December 16, 1939. Initially, the station was located in old Dhaka. Later, the station was relocated to Shahbag. It played an important role during the Bangladesh Liberation War of 1971. During the war, it was known as Shwadhin Bangla Betar Kendro (Independent Bengal Radio Station).

Bangladesh Bombings : On 17 August 2005, around 500 bomb explosions occurred at 300 locations in 63 out of the 64 districts of Bangladesh. The bombs were exploded within a half hour period starting from 11:30 am. A terrorist organization, Jama'at-ul-Mujahideen Bangladesh (JMB) claimed responsibility for the bombings. The group, led by Shaykh Abdur Rahman and the elusive Siddiqur Rahman (a.k.a. Bangla Bhai), is alleged to be affiliated with Al Qaeda and other Islamist terrorist organizations. Another terrorist group, titled Harkat-Ul Jihad al Islami was also associated with JMB in executing the co-ordinated attack. Following the blast, both groups were banned by the Government of Bangladesh. The explosion killed 2 people (a child in Savar, near Dhaka, and a Rickshaw-puller in Chapai Nawabganj District).

Bangladesh Communist Party (Leninist) : Bangladesh Communist Party (Leninist), a communist party in Bangladesh. BCP(L) was founded in Calcutta in the fall of 1971, by several small communist splinter fractions. The core of founders of BCP(L) consisted of Kazi Jafar Ahmad, Rashid Khan Menon and Ranu from the Communist Samanay Kendra, Amul Sen and Nazrul Islam from Communist Sanghati Kendra and Nasim Ali from the Hatiar group. Communist Samanay Kendra originated from the students movement and Communist Sanghati Kendra was a splinter group of East Pakistan Communist Party (Marxist-Leninist) that had revolted against the annihiliation line.

Bangladesh Export Import Company (BEXIMCO) : Bangladesh Export Import Company (BEXIMCO) is a Bangladeshi industrial conglomerate. The industries under this group include Textiles, Basic Chemicals and Pharmaceuticals, Jute, Marine Foods, Real Estate and Development. Beximco services include Engineering, Media, Information Technology, Trade and Financial Services.

Bangladesh Famine of 1974 : Possibly over a million people died in the Bangladesh famine of 1974, from July 1974 to January 1975, although the Bangladesh government claimed only 26,000 people died.

The causes are generally thought to be a combination of natural disasters (cyclones, droughts and floods) in the early 1970's, combined with various local and internationally influenced socio-political factors which followed the Bangladesh Liberation War in 1971.

Bangladesh Freedom Foundation : The Bangladesh Freedom Foundation is a non-partisan, independent, non-government, and non-profit national philanthropic institution committed to promote fundamental freedoms of the citizens of Bangladesh by providing support to programmes that promotes and strengthens civic initiative and citizen's participation.

The Bangladesh Freedom Foundation supports innovative ideas and actions in confronting challenges of fundamental freedoms of the citizens of Bangladesh. It provides grants to programmes that promote freedom from poverty, freedom from igno- rance, freedom from oppression. Established in May 1999, Freedom Foundation also aims at promoting and strengthening indigenous philanthropy and local resource mobilisation for development and social change.

The Foundation is committed to bringing communities and citizens in need together with those who have the capacity and will to share and care. Foundation's grant programme is a catalyst to local resource mobilisation and capacity building. It also works towards creation of conducive environment for strengthening of the non-profit sector and volunteerism in Bangladesh with specific emphasis on supportive institutional, legal and policy environment.

Bangladesh Gano Azadi League : Bangladesh Gano Azadi League (Bangladesh People's Freedom League) is a political party in Bangladesh. The party president is Alhaj Abdus Samad. The party is a member of the centre-left 11-Party Alliance. In the 2001 parliamentary elections the party ran three candidates, in the 3 Nowabganj constituencies. Samad stood in the constituency Nowabganj-3, and got 468 votes (2.15%). In Nowabganj-1, party candidate Mohammed Nazrul Islam got 108 votes (0.04%) and in Nowabganj-2 Mohammed Bazlur Rahman got 204 votes (0.09%).

Bangladesh Gazette: The Bangladesh Gazette is a regular government publication in which public service appointments, postings, and administrative orders are announced. In addition, this gazette often contains service rules and important government decisions issued by various ministries/divisions. It is published every Thursday under the title of The Bangladesh Gazette. The government also publishes occasional supplementary issues known as The Bangladesh Gazette, Extraordinary. Historical antecedents of The Bangladesh Gazette can be traced back to similar documents published during British rule in India. One of the earliest available references goes back to 29 March 1787 which relates to the removal and appointments of the district collectors in the Bengal Presidency, published in the Calcutta Gazette.

No authority below the status of an assistant secretary in a ministry/division or an officer of equivalent rank in an attached department is authorised to sign and issue a notification for publication in The Bangladesh Gazette, whereas only an authority not below the status of a deputy secretary of a ministry/division is authorised to sign and issue a notification for inclusion in an issue of The Bangladesh Gazette, Extraordinary. The issues of The Bangladesh Gazette as well as those of the Extraordinary Gazette are considered most valuable public documents, and are available to the general public on payment.

Bangladesh Infantry Regiment : The Bangladesh Infantry Regiment is an infantry regiment of the Bangladesh Army. It was formed in 2001 as the second regiment of Bangladesh's infantry, behind the East Bengal Regiment.

Bangladesh Islami Chhatra Shibir (BICS) : Bangladesh Islami Chhatra Shibir (BICS) (Bengali for 'Bangladesh Islamic Students Camp') is the student wing of the Islamist party Jamaat-e-Islami in Bangladesh.

It gained control over student union councils in several public university campuses, including Chittagong University, Rajshahi University and Shahjalal University of Science and Technology. It has raised controversy regarding its use of violence to gain influence over many educational institutions.

Bangladesh Khilafat Andolan : Bangladesh Khilafat Andolan (Bangladesh Caliphate Movement) is a hardline Islamist political party in Bangladesh, founded by Hafezzi Huzur after the 1981 presidential elections. Hafezzi Huzur had been a presidential candidate in 1981. He came third, scoring 387 215 votes (1.79%). His candidacy was supported by the Islamic Republican Party and Bangladesh Justice Party.

The programme of Bangladesh Khilafat Andolan includes introduction of the principles of the Qur'an and Sunnah in the construction of the state, reorientation of the judicial system towards Sharia law, Islamisation of the educational system, reorganisation of Zakat and Wakfs, etc.. The party is staunchly opposed to U.S. occupations of Iraq and Afghanistan, and has participated in many rallies and protests on the issue. In June 2004, ahead of a visit to Bangladesh by Donald Rumsfeld the party issued a statement calling him a "perpetrator of genocide in Iraq and Afghanistan, a war criminal, enemy of mankind and Allah".

Bangladesh Lekhika Sangha : Bangladesh Lekhika Sangha is an organisation promoting the interest of the women writers of Bangladesh. Established in December 1973 in Dhaka, its founding members were poet begum sufia kamal, Begum khodeja khatun, Begum Shams Rashid, Syeda Lutfunnessa and Begum Majeda Khatun. Begum Khodeja Khatun was the founder President of Bangladesh Lekhika Sangha.

Since 1985, a literary award entitled Bangladesh Lekhika Sangha Shahitya Padak is given every year to two renowned writers of the country, irrespective of gender, on the anniversary of the organisation Bangladesh Lekhika Sangha has expanded its activities in Chittagong, Rajshahi, Khulna and Kushtia and about 300 writers are its members.

Bangladesh Liberation War : The Bangladesh Liberation War (two other names are also used occasionally) refers to an armed conflict between West Pakistan (now Pakistan) and East Pakistan (now Bangladesh) that lasted for roughly nine months, from 26 March until 16 December 1971. The war resulted in Bangladesh's independence from Pakistan. During the Partition of India, Pakistan, as a country, gained independence on 14 August 1947 following the end of British rule over South Asian countries. The division was made based on religion. Pakistan was created out of Muslim majority territories in the West and East, and India was created out of the vast Hindu majority regions in the centre. The Western zone was popularly (and for a period of time, also officially) called West Pakistan and the Eastern zone (modern-day Bangladesh) was called East Bengal and later, East Pakistan. The capital of Pakistan was established in Karachi in West Pakistan and then moved to Islamabad in 1958.

West Pakistan (consisting of four provinces: Punjab, Sindh, Balochistan and North-West Frontier Province) dominated the divided country politically and received more money from the common budget than the more populous East. Although East Pakistan was the majority province in terms of population, political power remained firmly in the hands of West Pakistanis, specifically the Punjabis. After the assassination of Liaquat Ali Khan, political power began to be concentrated in the President of Pakistan, and eventually, the military. The nominal elected chief executive, the Prime Minister, was frequently sacked by the establishment, acting through the President.

The situation reached a climax when in 1970 the Awami League, the largest East Pakistani political party, led by Sheikh Mujibur Rahman, won a landslide victory in the national elections winning 160 of the 162 seats allotted for East Pakistan, and a majority of the 300 total seats in the National Assembly. This gave the Awami League the right to form a government. However, the leader of Pakistan People's Party, Zulfikar Ali Bhutto, refused to allow Rahman to become the Prime Minister of Pakistan. Instead, he proposed a notion of two Prime Ministers. Bhutto also refused to accept Rahman's Six Points. On 3 March 1971, the two leaders of the two wings along with the President General Yahya Khan met in Dhaka to decide the fate of the country. Talks failed. Sheikh Mujibur Rahman called for a nation-wide strike.

Sheikh Mujibur Rahman declared at a historic public meeting held at Ramna Race Course (renamed Suhrawardy Uddyan) on 7 March, 1971, attended by around 2 million people, The struggle this tune is the struggle for freedom, the struggle this tune is the struggle for independence. It was a defacto declaration of independence. In 25th March 1971, in a preplanned manner, the Pakistan army embarked on what may be termed as history's worst genocide. A military crackdown was ordered, and Bangabandhu Sheikh Mujib was arrested and taken away to West Pakistan. But just before he was arrested he sent out a call for the liberation war to begin. After nine months of war, the Pakistani occupation forces surrendered in Dhaka on 16th December 1971 after killing an estimated three million people. Due to the heroic resistance and supreme sacrifices of the valiant freedom fighters Bangladesh finally became an independent sovereign state.

Bangladesh Military Academy (BMA) : Bangladesh Military Academy (BMA) is the training institute for the officer-cadets of Bangladesh Army, Bangladesh Navy, and Bangladesh Air Force. It is located in Bhatiari near Chittagong city, in the Chittagong District of south-east Bangladesh. Following the independence of Bangladesh from Pakistan in the Bangladesh Liberation War of 1971, Bangladesh Military Academy was established in Comilla on 11 January 1974, for training of officers of the Army. The Academy chose a verse by national poet Kazi Nazrul Islam, Chiro Unnata Momo Sheer as its motto. The Academy was moved to its current location in Bhatiari in 1976. Regular training courses commenced from 1978. The first batch of officers of Bangladesh Army graduated from the academy in 1979. Beginning from 1983, it also started providing training for Bangladesh Navy and Air Force.

Bangladesh National Herbarium : Bangladesh National Herbarium a scientific organisation where plant specimens collected from different parts of the country are documented and preserved as reference material. The issue of establishing a herbarium at Dhaka was raised by the Department of Botany, University of Dhaka during the UNESCO symposium on Scientific Problems of Humid Tropical Deltas held in Dhaka in March 1964. FR Fosberg, the chairman of the visiting committee for tropical herbaria, held a discussion with the head of the Department of Botany, University of Dhaka on the issue and submitted a report to the government of East Pakistan emphasizing the immediate need for establishing a herbarium.

Bangladesh National Museum : The Bangladesh National Museum, originally established on 20 March 1913, albeit under onother name, and formally inaugurated on 7 August 1913, was accorded the status of the national museum of Bangladesh on 17 November 1983. It is located Shahbag, Dhaka. The museum is well organized and displays have been housed in several departments like department of ethnography and decorative art, department of history and classical art, department of natural history, and department of contemporary and world civilization. The museum also has a conservation laboratory.

Bangladesh Nationalist Party : Bangladesh Nationalist Party (BNP) is currently the ruling political party in Bangladesh. It was founded on September 1, 1978, by former president Ziaur Rahman. The party ruled the country five times. The party's chair is Begum Khaleda Zia, the Prime Minister of Bangladesh. Currently, it is in power with a two-thirds majority in the national parliament. In the 2001 elections the BNP and its allies got 47% of the vote and 215 of the 300 seats in Parliament.

The BNP promotes a right-of-center policies, and is often accused by its detractors of being too soft on the right-wing segments of the political establishment. The party has often found itself governing the country during times of great challenge to the state. President Ziaur Rahman, during his tenure, reestablished multi-party democracy in Bangladesh. He also gave the country an independent foreign and defense policy, and moved away from the pro-Indian positions that the previous administration had espoused.

Bangladesh Navy : The Bangladesh Navy has a strength of 10,900 (940 officers) (1997 estimate). It is mostly limited to coastal patrolling, but it is paying to have an ULSAN class frigate built in South Korea. The Bangladesh Navy was forged in times of war. In 1971, with West Pakistan imposing a military rule in East Pakistan, the Bangladesh Liberation War was truly underway. Many Pakistani Naval sailors and officers defected to form the Bangladesh Navy. Initially, there were two ships and 45 navy personnel. These ships carried out many successful raids on the Pakistani fleet. But both of these ships were mistakenly hit and destroyed by Indian fighter planes on December 10 1971, when they were about to launch a major attack on Mongla seaport. According to official figures from Bangladesh, a total of 334 naval freedom fighters were involved with the fledgling navy with 22 becoming martyrs. These sailors aided the Indian troops immensely as well as carrying out their own daring raids on Pakistani troops, mainly Operation Jackpot.

Bangladesh Railway : Bangladesh Railway is the state-owned Railway company of Bangladesh. It came into being following the independence of Bangladesh in 1971. It is a descendent of the East Pakistan Railway which itself was spun off from the Assam-Bengal Railway. Bangladesh Railway headquarter is located in the southern port city of Chittagong, which had historically been the south-eastern terminus of the Assam-Bengal Railway. As of 2005, Bangladesh Railway has a total of 2,706.1 kilometres of railroads. Out of that, 923 km are broad gauge (1.676

meter) tracks (mostly in the western region), while the remaining 1,822 km are meter gauge tracks (mostly in the central and eastern regions).

Bangladesh Rifles : Bangladesh Rifles is a paramilitary force in Bangladesh. It is mainly associated with guarding the borders of the country. Its origin can be traced to the Eastern Frontier Rifles which was established in 1920. This became the East Pakistan Rifles after the Partition of India in 1947. Following the Bangladesh Liberation War of 1971, and the independence of Bangladesh from Pakistan, it became Bangladesh Rifles in 1972.

Bangladesh Road Transport Corporation (BRTC) : Bangladesh Road Transport Corporation (BRTC) is the state-owned transport corporation of Bangladesh. It was established under the Government Ordinance No.7 of 1961 dated 4 February 1961. Following the independence of Bangladesh in 1971, it assumed its current name. BRTC is a semi-autonomous corporation under the Ministry of Communication. The governing body includes the Communication Minister, the Communication Secretary, the Director of the corporation, and other officials.

BRTC provides both passenger and cargo transport services. Currently, BRTC operates three international bus lines (Dhaka to Kolkata, Agartala, and Siliguri in India). Inside Bangladesh, it operates inter-district bus services through its bus depots in Chittagong, Bogra, Comilla, Pabna, Rangpur, Barisal, and Sylhet. It also operates intra-city bus services in many major cities of the country.

Bangladesh Scouts : The Bangladesh Scouts are the national Scouting organisation of Bangladesh. Scouting was founded in Bangladesh as part of the British Indian branch of The Scout Association, and continued as part of the Pakistan Boy Scouts Association until the country's divided sections split in 1971 during the Bangladesh Liberation

War. Following its independence, Bangladesh became an independent member of the World Organisation of the Scout Movement in 1974. The organisation has 721,635 members as of 2004. During the Bangladesh Liberation War, in April 1971, members of the Bangladesh Boy Scout Association volunteered to carry the mail from the Bangladesh Army field post offices to the nearest Post Office in India.

Bangladesh Shilpakala Academy : Bangladesh Shilpakala Academy (National Academy of Fine and Performing Arts) is the principal state-sponsored national cultural center of Bangladesh. It is a successor to the former Pakistan Arts Council. Shilpakala Academy was established at Segunbagicha, Dhaka in 1974 by the Ministry of Cultural Affairs, Govt. of Bangladesh. The academy consists of five administrative divisions: (1) Research and Publication Division, (2) Finance, Accounts and Planning Division, (3) Fine Arts Division, (4) Drama Division and (5) Music and Dance Division. These divisions are run by five directors. The Director General, who is appointed by the Government of Bangladesh, is the chief executive of the academy.

The principal objectives of this institution are presenting the Culture of Bangladesh and fostering the arts including fine arts, music, dance and drama. The activities of the Academy include patronizing and helping artists, sanctioning grants to Government-approved cultural institutions and organisations, conducting research on traditional heritage and culture, arranging art exhibitions and organising festivals of music and drama at national and international levels. It also holds cultural functions, arranges conferences, seminars, symposiums, workshops, debates, etc.

Bangladesh Shishu Academy Award for Literature : The Academy adorns one Bangladeshi litterateur with the award for his/her overall contribution in the field of juvenile literature. The award was introduced in 1396 BS. A poet or a litterateur is entitled to this award once during his life time. No provision is made for giving the award posthumously. The awardee is entitled to an amount of taka twenty five thousand in cash, one crest and a certificate of honour.

Bangladesh Sports Control Board : The Bangladesh Sports Control Board is the national overseer of the control authorities of 29 different sports in Bangladesh. It is responsible to the Ministry of Sports in the national government, based in Dhaka.

Bangladesh Television : Bangladesh Television, also known by its acronym BTV, is the state-owned Television network in Bangladesh. It started broadcasting Black-and-White transmission on 25 December 1964. It was known as Pakistan Television at that time, and was renamed Bangladesh Television after the independence of Bangladesh. Broadcasts in full colour started from 1980.

BTV has a national channel which is broadcast from Dhaka. This transmission is relayed to the whole country via local relay stations in major cities of the country. There is also a regional station located in Chittagong which broadcasts local programs in the evening. In 2004, BTV started worldwide broadcasts through its satellite based branch, BTV world. BTV is primarily financed through the television license fees. Although it has produced many award-winning programs, it has often been criticized for being the mouth-piece of the ruling government

Bangladesh University of Engineering and Technology (BUET): Bangladesh University of Engineering and Technology is regarded by some as the foremost Engineering University in Bangladesh. About five thousand students are enrolled in undergraduate and postgraduate studies engineering, architecture, planning and science in this institution. The total number of teachers is over 400. The University has continued to expand over the last three decades with the construction of new academic buildings, auditorium complex, halls of residence etc.

The BUET campus is in the heart of the capital city of Dhaka. It has a compact campus with halls of residence within walking distances of the academic buildings. At present the campus occupies 76.85 acres (311,000 m^2) of land. The academic area is confined in and around the old campus occupying 30.24 acres (122,000 m^2) of land defined by Shahid Sharani, Bakshi Bazar road and the Asian Highway. This area accommodates five faculties, two institutes, the administrative building, the central library, main sports facilities, the auditorium complex, the BUET Club and eighty two units of residential accommodation of teachers, staff and employees and the Vice-Chancellor's bunglow.

BUET was established in the late 19th century as a survey school for training surveyors. Dhaka Survey School was established at Nalgola, in Old Dhaka in 1876 to train surveyors for the then Government of Bengal of British India. Later, generous grants from Nawab Ahsanullah, a renowned Muslim patron of Education and member of the Nawab family of Dhaka enabled it to expand as a full fledged engineering school. Ahsanullah School of Engineering offered three-year diploma courses in Civil Engineering, Electrical Engineering and Mechanical Engineering. In recognition of the generous financial contribution from the then Nawab of Dhaka, it was named after his father Khawja Ahsanullah. It moved to its present premises in 1912.

After the partition of India in 1947, it was upgraded to Ahsanullah Engineering College, as a Faculty of Engineering under the University of Dhaka, offering four-year bachelor's courses in Civil, Electrical, Mechanical,

Chemical and Metallurgical Engineering. In 1962, it was renamed as East Pakistan University of Engineering and Technology (EPUET). A partnership with the Agricultural and Mechanical College of Texas (renamed Texas A&M University in 1963) was forged, and professors from A&M came to teach and to formulate the curriculum. After the liberation war of 1971, Bangladesh became independent, and EPUET was renamed to BUET.

Bangladeshi Independence Day : March 26 is celebrated as the Independence Day in Bangladesh. This commemorates the declaration of independence, and the start of Bangladesh Liberation War in 1971. The day is a national holiday in Bangladesh, and is celebrated with parades, and paying of respect at Jatiyo Smriti Soudho, the national memorial at Savar near Dhaka.

Bangshi River : Bangshi river is familiar as Banshi or Bangshi, an important tributary of the Dhaleshwari river. It originates from the foot of the Madhupur Tract. The river flows through the eastern part of Mymensingh district and travels southwards to fall into the Dhaleshwari after entering Dhaka district near the junction of Savar and Kaliakair upazilas. In its northern reaches the river joins with the Old Brahmaputra and ultimately turns into an offshoot of the Old Brahmaputra. Length of the river is 238 km. Its peak flow is 1,000 cumec and the minimum flow is only 5 cumec at Mirzapur. It is navigable only in the monsoon season.

Banihal Pass : Banihal pass, at an altitude of 2832 metres above the sea level, lies in the Pirpanjal range. The Pripanjal range separates the Kashmir valley of the Indian state of Jammu and Kashmir from the outer Himalaya. Banihal pass remains snow covered during the winter, and Jawahar tunnel, named after the first Prime Minister of India, was constructed for round the year surface transport. The Jawahar tunnel is operational since 22nd December 1956.

Banjara Embroidery : Think of nomad, caravaners, gypsies and you think of them as "free people". Free from the binds of urban life, they evoke dreams of the life spirit roaming without fetters. And it is from this that the Banjaras in Andhra Pradesh seem to have captured their exuberant clothes. Nomads in the past, the Banjaras today aggregate in groups called 'tandas'. Staying in communes, they still strive to preserve the fascinating and unpredictable traditions of their ancestors. Tattooed women with hands weighed down by ivory bangles create the memorable mirror work which the Banjaras are famous for.

Banjara Needle Crafts (Embroidary) : Banjara Needle work is a local tribal craft practised by the 'Banjaras' (tribals) of Telangana Region. It differs from the embroidery of Gujarati and Kutch Banjara. It has a style of its own, the originality and brightness are accentuated by its matchless quality. Needlework is an integral part of this craft and patterns are basic geometric combinations, squares, triangles and diamonds. The Banjaras produce exuberant embroideries using colourful threads. All they need is a piece of cloth and a needle and their imagination gets going. Intricate stitches in vibrant colours and the use of beads, shells and mirrors conjure a magic created by nimble fingers.

The distinctive feature of their work is the extensive use of mirrors. A rich appearance is created by filling the background with simple chain stitch, herringbone, long and short stitch. Typical items include cushion covers, bags, skirts, 'kurtas', dress sets for girls and women, blouse pieces, bedspreads and other household furnishings. The Crafts Council of Andhra Pradesh with its sustained market promotion is revitalising the art by improving the quality and standard of work by assisting them in procuring better raw material.

Bank Alfalah Limited : Bank Alfalah Limited was incorporated on June 21, 1997 as a public limited company under the Companies Ordinance 1984. Its banking operations commenced from November 1, 1997. The bank is engaged in commercial banking and related services as defined in the Banking companies ordinance, 1962. The Bank is currently operating through 104 branches in 36 cities, with the registered office at B.A.Building, I.I.Chundrigar, Karachi.

Bank of India (BOI) : Bank of India (BOI) is one of India's leading banks, with about 2500 branches in India and some 20 branches and representative offices abroad. Recently (September 2005) the Bank entered its centenary year.

Bankim Chandra Chatterjee : Bankim Chandra Chatterjee was an Indian poet and author, most famous as the composer of Vande Mataram, the national song of India.

Bankim was educated at the Hooghly College and belonged to an orthodox family. He did for Bengali fiction what Michael Madhusudan Dutt had done for Bengali poetry, that is, he brought in imagination. Chatterjee, following the discipline of Isvarchandra Gupta, began his literary career as a writer of verse. Fortunately he was not slow to feel that poetry was not his metier. He then turned to fiction. His first attempt was a novel in Bengali submitted for a declared prize. The prize did not come to him and the novelette was never published. His first fiction to appear in print was Rajmohan's Wife. It was written in English and was probably a translation of the novelette submitted for the prize.

Bankim Chatterjee was superb story-teller, and a master of romance. He is also a great novelist although his outlook on life was neither deep nor critical, nor was his canvas wide. But he was something more than a great novelist. He was a path finder and a path maker. Chatterjee represented the English-educated Bengalee with a tolerably peaceful home life, sufficient wherewithal and some prestige, as the bearer of the torch of western enlightment. No Bengali writer before or since has enjoyed such spontaneous and universal popularity as Chatterjee. His, novels have been translated in almost all the major languages of India, and have helped to stimulate literary impulses in those languages.

Bankin C. Chaterjee : Bankin C. Chaterjee was the composer of the National song 'Vande Mataram'. He was considered to be a leading litterateur of Bengali literature. He was born at Kantal-para in West Bengal. In 1882, he wrote 'Anandmath'. Besides, he also wrote novels 'Krishna Charitra',' Durgesh Nandini',' Chandhrani','Visha Brikṣha', 'Kapal Kundala'.

In his famous satirical book, 'Kamala Kanter Daftar', he highlighted the social evils that prevailed in the society pertaining to injustice to the poor and he advocated remedial measures to balance the degree of equality between have and have-nots in the society. All his works bear unmistakable stamp of nationalism and Indian culture.

Bankura : Bankura is located in the western part of the Indian State of West Bengal. It is a part of Bardhaman Division of the State and included in the area known as "Rarh" in Bengal. It ranks fourth according to Population and literacy rate of 2001 Census in the State. The District Bankura is bounded by latitude 22038′ N and longitude 86036′ E to 87047′ E. River Damodar flows along the northern boundary of the district. The adjacent districts are Bardhaman in the north, Purulia in the west and Paschim Medinapure in the south. The Survey of India (SOI) toposheets covering the districts are 73I, 73J, 73M and 73N. Bankura is a town in Bankura District.

Bannerghatta National Park : Bannerghatta National Park is situated half an hour drive away from the City of Bangalore (22 km south of Bangalore), Karnataka, India. The hilly place is the home for one of the rich natural, zoological reserves. The 25,000 acre (101 km^2) zoological park makes this a major tourist attraction of Bangalore.

The Bannerghatta Tiger and Lion Reserve has a reserve of Indian tigers, lions and other mammals. A mini safari here helps to fund the reserve. The Tiger Reserve has been recognised by the Forest Department of India and has acquired a fairly nice image in terms of maintenance despite some tragic incidents and alleged careless mishaps.

Bannu : Bannu is city in NWFP province of Pakistan. It is a divisional administrative center, an important road junction and market city. The present location of the town was founded by Sir Herbert Edwardes in 1848, and was formerly called Edwardesabad. It was a leading British military base, especially in actions against Afghan border tribes. The Bani Zai tribe of Afghans lives here. Bannu is called Bana and Bani Gul in the local Pashto language.

Bansuri : The bansuri, one of the oldest musical instruments in India, is a side-blown flute made of bamboo or reed with six or seven-holes. The bansuri is associated with the Hindu God Krishna, who is often depicted playing it. Another common and similar Indian flute played in South India is the Venu. Other names by which a bansuri is known in India are bansi, and murali.

There are two varieties of bansuri: the traverse, and the fipple. The fipple variety is usually played in folk music and is held away from the lips like a whistle. Because of the flexibility and control it offers, the traverse variety is preferred in classical music.

Banswara : Banswara is a city in Banswara District in south Rajasthan in India. Banswara princely state was founded by Maharawal Jagmal Singh. It gets the name from dominance of "bans" or bamboo forests. It is also known as 'City of Hundred Islands', due to presence of numerous islands in the Mahi River, which flows through Banswara.

Banswara District : Banswara District has an area of 5,037 km^2, 1.47% of Rajasthan state, India. The city of Banswara is the district headquarters. It is bounded on the north by Udaipur District, on the northeast by Chittorgarh District, on the east and southeast by Madhya Pradesh state, on the southwest by Gujarat state, and on the west by Dungarpur District.

The District lies in the Mahi River basin. The Mahi flows north through the district from its origin in the Vindhya Range of Madhya Pradesh, entering the district from the southeast and flowing north towards the northern end of the district, where it turns southwest to form the boundary between Banswara and Dungarpur districts before entering Gujarat and emptying into the Gulf of Cambay.

Banswara is part of the Vagad region of southern Rajasthan, which includes Banswara and Dungarpur districts. The region is mainly inhabited by tribals, predominantly Bhils.

Banswara District has rich flora and fauna. The forests include mainly teak. The wildlife includes a large variety of wild animals like panther, chinkara, etc. Common birds in the region are fowl, partridge, black drongo, grey shrike, green bee-eater, bulbul, parrot etc.

Bappa Rawal : Bappa Rawal, born Prince Kalbhoj, was the 8th ruler of the Guhilot dynasty. He founded the state of Mewar (c.734) in present-day Rajasthan, India.

Bappa was also blessed by Harita, a sage of the Mewar region, with kingship. He based the capital of

Mewar in the fortress city of Chittor. In order to face of Muslim invasions across the western borders of Rajputana, Bappa united the smaller states of Ajmer and Jaisalmer to repel the invaders. During the next 800 years, Chittor becomes the symbol of Hindu resistance in western India.

Muslims started attacking India within a few decades of the birth of islam. For a few hundred years they had no success. Bin Qasim was able to defeat Dahir in Sindh but was routed by Bappa Rawal. Qasim attacked Chittore, which was ruled by Mori Rajputs, via Mathura. Bappa, of guhilote dynasty, was a commander in Mori army and so was Dahir's son. Bappa defeated and pursued Bin Qasim through Saurashtra and back to Sindh. After this resounding defeat of the caliphate at the hands of Bappa, for next few hundred years there were no more Islamic incursions into India.

Bappi Lahiri : Bappi Lahiri is one of the leading and famous music directors on Bollywood, India. He introduced Disco in India through his work on the 1982 film Disco Dancer.

BAPS : Bochasanwasi Shri Akshar Purushottam Swaminarayan Sanstha or BAPS is a branch of the Hindu Swaminarayan sect with more than 1,000,000 followers worldwide and a greater presence outside South Asia than any other Hindu group. Formally established as BSS (Bochasanwasi Shri Swaminarayan Sanstha, later becoming BAPS) on June 5, 1907 CE by Swami Yagnapurushdas (Shastriji Maharaj), BAPS describes itself as "a socio-spiritual organization with its roots in the Vedas, revealed by Bhagwan Swaminarayan in the late 18th century."

Barak River : Barak river is an upstream part of the Surma and Kushiyara located in Assam (India). Near Badarpur (Assam) the Barak separates into two branches, the Surma and the Kushiyara, which rejoin in Sylhet Basin after entering into Bangladesh. The Barak river at places is also known as the Kalni, Bheramohona, Baleshwar and Meghna.

Baral River : Baral river is one of the offshoots of the Ganges. Originating at Charghat upazila of Rajshahi district, the Baral flows through Natore and Pabna and finally meets with the Hurasagar after joining with the Karatoya south of Shahjadpur. The total length of the river is 147 km, average width is 125m and average depth is about 6m. The river receives water from the Ganges only in the monsoon season. But it maintains its flow throughout the year with local runoff water and water from Chalan Beel. Its drainage area is about 230 sq km. Some important places located on the banks of the Baral are: Charghat; Baraigram, Bagatipara, Gurudaspur, Chatmohor and Bera

Baran District : Baran District is a district of the state of Rajasthan in western India. The town of Baran is the district headquarters. It is bounded on the north and east by Madhya Pradesh state, on the south and southwest by Jhalawar District of Rajasthan, and on the west and northwest by Kota District of Rajasthan. The district has eight tehsils, Anta, Atru, Baran, Chhabra, Chhipa Barod, Kishanganj, Mangrol, and Shahabad.

Before Indian independence in 1947, most of present-day Baran District was part of the princely state of Kota, although Shahabad tehsil was a discontinuous portion of Jhalawar princely state, and Chhabra tehsil was a discontinuous portion of Tonk princely state. After Indian independence, The rulers of the princely states acceded to the Government of India, and the present-day Baran District was made part of Kota District. Baran District was carved out of Kota District on April 10, 1991.

Barasat : Barasat is a city in the outskirts of Calcutta (Kolkata), West Bengal, India.The city is an important railway and roadway junction. It is located in the Ganges Brahmaputra delta region in the district of North 24 parganas,West Bengal state in the eastern India. The Bangladesh border - at Petrapole is situated about 100 km from the city.

Some important roads that pass through this town are National Highway 34 (Krishnanagar Road leading towards North Bengal);Jessore road (road leading to Jessore in Bangladesh via Bongaon ; Road leading to Basirhat etc.

Baratang : Baratang (coordinates: 12° N 93° E) is an island in the Andaman Islands, India, with an area of approximately 238 km². It is one of the main islands of the Great Andaman group, a closely-set archipelago in the Bay of Bengal, adjoining the Andaman Sea. Middle Andaman is to its north, and South Andaman to the south. The islands of Ritchie's Archipelago lie some 20 km to the east. Port Blair, the capital of the Indian Union Territory of Andaman and Nicobar Islands, is located approximately 100 km to the south.

Also known as Baratang Island, but it is more commonly referred to as simply "Baratang". Baratang contains the only known examples of mud volcanoes in India. These mud volcanoes have erupted sporadically, with recent eruptions in 2005 believed to have been associated with the 2004 Indian Ocean earthquake. The previous major eruption recorded was on 18th February 2003. There are other volcanoes in the area, the Barren Island volcano which is the only active volcano in South Asia and the Narcondum volcano which is considered to be a dormant volcano.

Barbarikon : Barbarikon was the name of a sea port near the modern-day city of Karachi, Pakistan, important in the Hellenistic era in Indian Ocean trade. It is mentioned briefly in the Periplus of the Erythraean Sea.

It is also a Greek version of the term Barbaricum, designating areas outside civilization and/or the Roman Empire.

Bardhaman : Bardhaman is a district in West Bengal. The main town is Bardhaman. Bardhaman District has an area of 7024 km^2, and a population of 6,895,514 (2001 census). It is bounded on the north by Birbhum and Murshidabad districts, on the east by Nadia District, on the southeast by Hooghly District, on the southwest by Bankura and Purulia districts, and on the northwest by Jharkhand state. The district has six sub-divisions, Asansol Sadar (North), Sadar (South), Durgapur, Kalna, and Katwa. It was amongst the first districts to have a 100% literacy rate.

Bardhaman is the most resourceful district in West Bengal both industrially and agriculturally. The eastern part is enriched by the alluvial soil of river Bhaghirathi (minor stream of river Ganga), and is one of most productive agricultural regions in West Bengal. The western part of the district, chiefly Asansol, is rich in coal and other mineral resources. This part is highly industrialised and contains various factories based on iron and steel processing, as well as many cement factories. Durgapur, Burnpur, and Kulti are in the western part of the district. It also contains power plants at Durgapur and Dishergarh.

Bardoli : Bardoli Satyagraha Ashram in Surat district was the place which Sardar Vallabhbhai Patel launched his Satyagraha in 1928 which installed a new hope about the efficiency of the non-violent method of struggle.

Bardoli Satyagraha : The Bardoli Satyagraha of 1925 in the state of Gujarat, India during the British Raj was a major episode of civil disobedience and revolt in the Indian Independence Movement. It's success gave rise to Vallabhbhai Patel as one of the greatest Indian freedom fighters. The momentum from the Bardoli victory aided in the resurrection of the freedom struggle nationwide. In 1930, the Congress would declare Indian independence, and the Salt Satyagraha would be launched by Gandhi.

Baredi Dance : It is performed by male members of the Ahir (cowherd) community of the Bundhelkhand region on the occasion of Diwali. This dance is known as Raut dance in the Chattisgarh region.

Bareilly : Bareilly is a city in Uttar Pradesh State in northern India on the Ramganga River. It is the capital of Rohilkhand Division and is a center for the manufacture of furniture and for trade in cotton, grain, and sugar. The city's population in 2001 was 6,17,350. This fast-growing city is also known as 'Bans-Bareilly', due to its big Bamboo market. Bareilly is also famous for 'Surma'. It is famous as being the home-town of former Miss World Priyanka Chopra. Bareilly is also known as the counter-magnet city because it is equidistant from New Delhi and Lucknow and has a lot of potential for setting up industries to attract people to settle. Historically it was the part of the ancient Kingdom Panchal. In the Medieval period it was under Rohillas. India's premier veterinary research institute-IVRI is located here. The city was built by Mukrand Rai in 1657. The geographical location of Bareilly is between latitude 28°22'N and longitude 79°27'E

Barendra Museum : Barendra Museum was the first museum to be established in Bangladesh in 1910. The museum started out as the collection for Barendra Anushandhan Samiti or Barendra Investigation Society and got its current name in 1919. The Zamindars of Rajshahi and Natore, notably Kumar Sharat Kumar Ray, donated their personal collections to Barendra Museum. Excavation at Sompur Bihara was started by the society along with Calcutta University in 1923. In 1964, the museum became a part of Rajshahi University.

Barfi : Barfi or burfi is an Indian /Pakistani sweet made from condensed milk, cooked until it solidifies. Barfi is often flavoured with mango, pistachio and spices, and is sometimes served with a chocolate topping. Visually, barfi sometimes resembles cheese, and may have a hint of cheese to it. For this reason, barfi is sometimes called "Indian cheese cake". Barfi is popular all over India and is often a part of Indian festivals, especially Holi.

Bari Mosque : Bari Mosque an imposing structure of pre-Mughal period, stands at Chhota Pandua in the Hughli District of West Bengal. It is an oblong building measuring 70.41m by 12.5m and having no enclosed shan (courtyard) in front. Two parallel rows of basalt pillars (1.83m high) divide the mosque into three aisles, resulting in sixty-three bays. The roof of 63 domes, now lost, rested on the arcades and brick-pendentives. The domes were arranged in three rows of 21 each in conformity with the alignment of the aisles. The basalt pillars were reused from pre-Islamic structures and are not of uniform design; some bear traces of Hindu or Buddhist imagery.

The mosque had 21 arched openings. Three more were provided on either side of the building to give access to the aisles from the flanks. All these side openings except one have been sealed. As a result, the mosque has now only 22 entrances from which its local name, Bais Darwaza, *originates.* The authenticity of this legendary account has not yet been substantiated. Some elements, such as the use of red thin bricks for construction, the reportedly low hemispherical shape of the lost domes of the roof, typical stone pillars in the liwan, utilization of lithic materials quarried from demolished temples and low pointed arched doorways etc have been taken to suggest an early 14th century date for the mosque.

Barind Tract : Barind Tract largest Pleistocene physiographic unit of the bengal basin, covering an area of about 7,770 sq km. It has long been recognised as a unit of old alluvium, which differs from the surrounding floodplains. In Bangla, it is spelled and pronounced as Varendra Bhumi. Geographically this unit lies roughly between latitudes 24°20´N and 25°35´N and longitudes 88°20´E and 89°30´E. This physiographic unit is bounded by the karatoya to the east, the mahananda to the west, and the northern bank of the ganges to the South. A lower fault scarp marks the eastern edge of the Barind Tract, and the little jamuna, atrai and Lower Punarbhaba rivers occupy fault troughs. The western part of this unit has been tilted up; parts of the western edge are more than 15m higher than the rest of the tract and the adjoining Mahananda floodplain. The southern part of the main eastern block of the Barind Tract is tilted down towards the southwest and passes under lower Atrai basin sediments in the south. The Barind Tract covers most parts of the greater dinajpur, rangpur, pabna, rajshahi, bogra, joypurhat and naogaon districts of Rajshahi division.

Baripada : Baripada is the headquarter of Mayurbhanj district, Orissa state, India. Baripada is an excellent place to stay and tour the Mayurbhanj region, a region with one of the most important wildlife parks of India (Simlipal), lush valleys, forest lands and scores of ancient temples. Rathyatra (Car Festival) is one of the main attractions of Baripada. Baripada is also the home of Mayurbhanj Chhau dance, an ancient Hindu dance form.

Barisal : Barisal is located in south-central Bangladesh. Formerly a district called Bakhraganj, it is now a division. The town lies in the Ganges (Padma) River delta on an offshoot of the Arial Khan River (Kirtonkhola). The Barisal town was under the control of the Roychoudhury family, which now has moved to Calcutta. Incorporated as a municipality in 1876 and upgraded to city corporation in 2002, it is a trans-shipment center for rice, hides, and pulses. Bakery, textile, Pharmaceutical products are output of a few industrial installation. It is linked by steamer with Dhaka (73 miles [117 km] north) and with Chittagong to the southeast. Road communication improved in last decade with building of few bridges. There is a medical college (Sher-e Bangla Medical College) affiliated with the National University. It also has a famous Cadet College—Barisal Cadet College (est. 1985) which has a number of record results on both HSC and SSC board exams.

Barisal : Barisal is located in south-central Bangladesh. Formerly a district called Bakhraganj, it is now a division. The town lies in the Ganges (Padma) River delta on an offshoot of the Arial Khan River (Kirtonkhola). The Barisal town was under the control of the Roychoudhury family, which now has moved to Calcutta. Incorporated as a municipality in 1876 and upgraded to city corporation in 2002, it is a trans-shipment center for rice, hides, and pulses. Bakery, textile, Pharmaceutical products are output of a few industrial installation. It is linked by steamer with Dhaka (73 miles [117 km] north) and with Chittagong to the southeast. Road communication improved in last decade with building of few bridges. There is a medical college (Sher-e Bangla Medical College) affiliated with the National University. It also has a famous Cadet College—Barisal Cadet College (est. 1985) which has a number of record results on both HSC and SSC board exams.

Barisal Airport : Barisal Airport (IATA: BZL, ICAO: KBZN) is located in southern city of Barisal of Bangladesh. It is a new airport of the country. Only domestic flights go from here.

Barisal City : Barisal City is divisional headquarter of Barisal Division. It consists of 30 wards and 50 mahallas. The area of the town is 16.37 km^2. Barisal municipality was established in 1957 and was turned into a City Corporation in 2000. City has one police academy. Barisal was a semi-independent area in Mughal period. In course of time it fall under Bengal Nawab and British India, later passed to Bangladesh.

Barisal Division : Barisal division is located in south-central Bangladesh. Formerly a district called Bakhraganj, it is now a division. The town lies in the Ganges (Padma) River delta on an offshoot of the Arial Khan River (Kirtonkhola). The Barisal town was under the control of the Roychoudhury family, which now has moved to Calcutta. Incorporated as a municipality in 1876 and upgraded to city corporation in 2002, it is a trans-shipment center for rice, hides, and pulses. Bakery, textile, Pharmaceutical products are output of a few industrial installation. It is linked by steamer with Dhaka (73 miles [117 km] north) and with Chittagong to the southeast. Road communication improved in last decade with building of few bridges. There is a medical college (Sher-e Bangla Medical College) affiliated with the National University. It also has a famous Cadet College - Barisal Cadet College (est. 1985) which has a number of record results on both HSC and SSC board exams.

Barkhan : Barkhan district is in the center of Balochistan province of Pakistan. Barkhan is derived from Baro Khan, the founder of the Barozai family of Pannis, who either ruled this area on behalf of the governors of Sibi or owned it himself. Barkhan, was given the status of a district on 31 December 1991. Presently, there is one sub-division, one tehsil and one sub-tehsil in the district. The district is controlled by a Deputy Commissioner and he is assisted by one Assistant Commissioner, one Tehsildar and two Naib-Tehsildars. One Deputy Superintendent of Police is also posted in the district headquarters Barkhan. Over 99% of the people of the area are Muslims. The population of Barkhan is estimated to be over 185,000 in 2005. The whole population has always been rural. The major Baloch tribe in the district is Khetran.

Barkhan : Barkhan district is in the center of Balochistan province of Pakistan. Barkhan is derived from Baro Khan, the founder of the Barozai family of Pannis, who either ruled this area on behalf of the governors of Sibi or owned it himself. Barkhan, was given the status of a district on 31 December 1991. Presently, there is one sub-division, one tehsil and one sub-tehsil in the district. The district is controlled by a Deputy Commissioner and he is assisted by one Assistant Commissioner, one Tehsildar and two Naib-Tehsildars. One Deputy Superintendent of Police is also posted in the district headquarters Barkhan. Over 99% of the people of the area are Muslims. The population of Barkhan is estimated to be over 185,000 in 2005. The whole population has always been rural. The major Baloch tribe in the district is Khetran.

Barrackpore : Barrackpore sub-division, under District of North 24 Parganas in the state of West Bengal, is an old and famous administrative territory, dotted with people from almost all provinces of India. It is a place of historical significance in many ways, and the revolt for independence of 1857 started here, by the legendary martyr, Mangal Pandey.

Barren Island : Barren Island (coordinates :12°16'N 93°51'E) is located in the Andaman Sea, one of the most easterly of the Andaman Islands. It is the only confirmed active volcano in South Asia. The island along with the rest of the Andamans is part of the Indian union territory of Andaman and Nicobar Islands, and lies some 135 km northeast of the territory's capital, Port Blair. The first recorded eruptions of the volcano dates back to 1787. Since then the volcano has erupted more than 6 times, most recently on May 28, 2005.

Barren Island : Barren Island (coordinates:12°16'N 93°51'E) is located in the Andaman Sea, one of the most easterly of the Andaman Islands. It is the only confirmed active volcano in South Asia. The island along with the rest of the Andamans is part of the Indian union territory of Andaman and Nicobar Islands, and lies some 135 km northeast of the territory's capital, Port Blair. The first recorded eruptions of the volcano dates back to 1787. Since then the volcano has erupted more than 6 times, most recently on May 28, 2005.

After the initial eruption in 1787, further eruptions were recorded in 1789, 1795 and the last confirmed one being in 1803-04 (another eruption is also believed to have occurred in 1852). After a gap of nearly 2 centuries, the island had another eruption in 1991 that lasted 6 months and caused considerable damage. There was another eruption in 1994-95 and the most recent one started in 2005. The latest eruption is considered to be linked to the 2004 Indian Ocean Tsunami. After the recent eruptions, the island which still sees the odd tremor is being promoted as a niche tourist destination as the tsunami battered territory seeks to bring in more revenues.

Bartaman Patrika : Bartaman Patrika is the only anti-Establishment Bengali language newspaper published from Kolkata, the capital of the Indian state of West Bengal. Apart from the Kolkata edition, the newspaper has four other simultaneous editions, published daily from four major towns of West Bengal — Siliguri, Burdwan, Malda and Midnapore. The newspaper was founded by Mr. Barun Sengupta, the legendary newsman based in Kolkata. He started his career with the Ananda Bazar Patrika, worked with them for quite a long time and touched the prime of his career. On retiring from that group he started his own initiative, Bartaman, which was to create history in time to come. Within the first 20 years since its inception,

Bartaman has established itself as a major broadsheet daily in West Bengal. Its strengths are its strong anti-Establishment (in Bengal, anti-Marxist, anti pseudo leftists, rather) stance, uncompromising voice and a devoted readership and wide circulation.

Basant : Basant, sometimes called Jashan-e Baharaan (Spring Festival), is a Pakistani festival celebrating the arrival of Spring. Traditionally, celebrants dress in bright yellow or green, and many people fly kites from rooftops. In the city of Lahore, the festival lasts three days. In most other cities, there is only a one-day celebration. The Basant festival heralds the end of winter and arrival of spring. It is celebrated in the entire sub-continent, and particularly in Pakistan, with flying kites - perhaps because spring generally brings a clear sky and just the right amount of wind. For its fans, kite flying is pure fun

Basant Panchami : Basant Panchami is the most famous of the seasonal fairs. It heralds the advent of spring. Fields of mustard present a unique and colourful sight all over rural Punjab which looks like a newly wedded damsel resplendent in her gorgeous golden yellow. There is a spirit of gay abandon in the air and the Punjabi is rightly infected with the spirit. His heart and soul become one with nature and he expresses his elevated spirit in song and dance. The Basant fair is held in many villages of the Punjab. People put on yellow costumes appropriate to the season. One huge mass of mustard blossom seems walking down to the fair. Kite-flying was a popular entertainment of the people on this occasion. Often on the Basant Panchami day, if there was a good breeze, one could see nothing but innumerable multi-colored kites in the sky, swishing over in all directions.

Basant Panchami : Basant Panchami is the most famous of the seasonal fairs. It heralds the advent of spring. Fields of mustard present a unique and colourful sight all over rural Punjab which looks like a newly wedded damsel resplendent in her gorgeous golden yellow. There is a spirit of gay abandon in the air and the Punjabi is rightly infected with the spirit. His heart and soul become one with nature and he expresses his elevated spirit in song and dance. The Basant fair is held in many villages of the Punjab. People put on yellow costumes appropriate to the season. One huge mass of mustard blossom seems walking down to the fair. Kite-flying was a popular entertainment of the people on this occasion. Often on the Basant Panchami day, if there was a good breeze, one could see nothing but innumerable multi-colored kites in the sky, swishing over in all directions.

Basava : Basava (also known as Basaveshwara or Basavanna) is known as the founder of the lingayat (Lingayats) religious movement in India. He brought on a social transformation, often referred as "revolution," in that he changed the lower caste people into a higher thinking of God or Shiva. He is said to have been a mystic by temperament, an idealist by choice, a statesman by profession, a man of letters by taste, a humanist by sympathy and a social reformer by conviction.

Basava was also a part of "Bhakti Pantha" of 12th century and one of the main figures with his contemporary lingayata or blessed people sect of Hinduism. He and his followers with Allama defined a new way of looking at God and life with numerous "Vachanas" (sacred hymns).

Bashundhara City : Bashundhara City is the largest business centre and shopping mall in Bangladesh. It was opened to public in 2005. It is located at Panthapath, near Karwan Bazar, in Dhaka city. The complex has a mall, several multiplex movie theatres, a theme park, and business offices. It is often claimed that Bashundhara city is the largest shopping mall in South Asia. The mall has space for 2500 retail stores and cafeterias and also possesses a large underground gymnasium and top floor food court along with an indoor theme park. The Bashundhara City building also has rooftops garden and is a brilliant symbol of the emerging city of Dhaka.

Basilica of Bom Jesus : This world heritage monument built in 1695 is a fine example of Jesuit architecture and has emerged as a landmark in the history of Christianity. It is situated in Old Goa, 9kms from the Capital Panjim. It is a world renowned church which contains the body of St. Francis Xavier; a pupil of the soldier-turned—saint, Ignatius Loyola (the founder of the Order of Jesuits), who died while on a sea voyage to China on December 2,1552. The following year, while transferring Francis Xavier's remains to Goa, in accordance with his wishes, it was found that the saint's body was as fresh as the day it was buried. This miraculous phenomenon attracts huge number of devotees from all over the world, especially during the public viewing of his body every ten years. The saint is believed to have miraculous powers of healing, and pilgrims would come from all over the country to offer prayers.

This church is one of the richest churches in Goa and is carpeted with marble flooring and inlaid with precious stones. Apart from the elaborate gilded altars, the interior of the church is simple. The church also holds paintings of St. Francis Xavier. The Tomb of St.Francis Xavier (1696) was the gift of the last of the Medicis, Cosimo III, the Grand Duke of Tuscany. It was carved by the 17th century Florentine sculptor Giovanni Batista Foggini. It took 10 years to complete. The casket containing his body is made of silver. The holy relics of the saint is displayed every 10 years during the anniversary of the Saint's death. The Feast is organised on 3rd December every year.

Basista Ashram : Basista Ashram in Assam believed to be the Hermitage of sage Basistha (Vasistha), this Ashram is situated on Sadhya Chal Hill, 12km from Guwahati. The Ashram is an important place of pilgrimage and a place of natural beauty with three mountain streams Sandhya, Lalita, and Kanta flowing nearby. Its picturesque charm makes it an ideal picnic spot.

Basmati : Basmati is a variety of long grain rice, famous for its fragrance and delicate flavour. Its name means "Queen of Fragrance" in Hindi.

Basmati rice has been cultivated in India and Pakistan for hundreds of years, and some varieties are now grown in the United States. The Himalayan foothills are said to produce the best basmati and Dehra Dun is the most prized of these varieties. Patma is a basmati rice grown in West Bengal. The best types of basmati rice are aged for several years before they are milled and sold.

The grains of basmati rice are much longer than they are wide, and they grow even longer as they cook. They stay firm and separate, not sticky, after cooking. Basmati rice is available both as a white rice and a brown rice. Both of these cook in about 20 minutes. Due to the high amount of starch clinging to the rice grains, many cooks wash this rice before cooking it. Soaking it for half an hour to two hours before cooking makes the grains less likely to break in cooking.

Bastar District : Bastar District is a district of the state of Chhattisgarh in central India. Jagdalpur is the district headquarters. The district has an area of 8755.79 km^2. Bastar District is bounded on the northwest by Rajnandgaon District, on the north by Kanker District, on the northeast by Dhamtari District, on the east by Navarangpur and Koraput districts of Orissa state, on the south and southeast by Dantewada District, and on the east by Gadchiroli District of Maharashtra state.

Administratively, the district is divided into four tehsils, Jagdalpur, Kondagaon, Keshkal, and Narainpur. The district has two municipalities, Jagdalpur and Kondgaon. Jagdalpur, the administrative headquarters, is a beautiful city having population of about 1.5 lakhs (150,000).

Bastar and Dantewada districts were formerly part of the princely state of Bastar. The state is described in Nandini Sundar, Subalterns and Sovereigns. After Indian independence in 1947, the princely states of Bastar and Kanker acceded to the Government of India, and were merged to form Bastar District of Madhya Pradesh state. The district, which had an area of 39,114 km^2, was one of the largest in India. In 1999, the district was divided into the present-day districts of Bastar, Dantewada, and Kanker, which constitute Bastar Division. In 2000, Bastar was one of the 16 Madhya Pradesh districts that formed the new state of Chhattisgarh.

Batakamma Festival : Batakamma is the most popular festival throughout Teleangana and some parts of Rayalaseema. It commences on the first day of the lunar month, Aswayuja and ends on Mahamavami one day before Dussehra. This is in worship of goddess Lakshmi born as Batakamma. Every house wife, after taking bath arranges different kinds of flowers of various colours in the shape of a stupa on a platter of reeds or bamboo or brass and on the top goddess Lakshmi in turmeric is installed. This is called Batakamma.

After puja, it is kept in a corner of a room and during evening all the house wives dressed in clothes and finely carry the Batakamma by turns either to a temple or lake or river side. All the images are placed on even ground and the women folk singing songs and clapping their hands, bending and rising move in a circle around them. Lastly they float the images of turmeric in the water with devotional singing. The festival goes on for nine days and the last day of the festival is called Chaddula Batakamma.

Batala : Batala, a town located on the Amritsar-Pathankot railway line, is a sub-divisional headquarters of Gurdaspur district of Punjab state, India. The town has a historical importance in the history of Sikhism as Guru Nanak, the founder of Sikh faith was married to Bibi Sulakhni, the daughter of Moolchand, a trader from this town. Batala is a market place for agricultural commodities. The town has several industrial and manufacturing facilities, particularly connected with cotton weaving and ginning; and production of sugar.

Bathinda : Bathinda is a city in Punjab state of northwestern India. It is the administrative headquarters of Bathinda District. The City of Bathinda is one of the largest railway junctions of northern India and has the highest fan-out (6) of any junction on the Indian Railway network. It also boasts of the largest Cantonment (military area) of Asia and is known as Sharjah of Punjab due to sand dunes. Bathinda is located in the Indo-Gangetic alluvial plains. An alluvium is a rich mixture of clay, kankar, sandy clay and sand. Bhatinda also boasts of 2 Thermal Plants- Guru Nanak Dev Thermal Plan in Bathinda City and Guru Gobind Singh Super Thermal Plant at Lehra Mohabbat, Guru Gobind Singh Oil Refinery, and a National Fertilizers Plant, a Govt. Engineering College and now an upcoming Medical College.

Bathkamma : It is a folk dance practised in the Telangana region by newly married women.

Battle of Basantar : The Battle of Basantar or the Battle of Barapind (December 4th—16th, 1971) was one of the vital battles fought as part of the Indo-Pakistani War of 1971 in the western sector of India. Despite being outnumbered, the Indian troops won a hard fought battle that secured this vital area in the Punjab/Jammu sector. The result was that more than 350 square miles of Pakistani territory was occupied by Indian forces. The name Battle of Basantar actually encompasses the entire gamut of battles and skirmishes fought in the Shakargarh sector.

Battle of Buxar : Battle of Buxar (October 1764) was a significant battle fought between the forces under the command of the British East India Company on the one side, and the combined armies of Mir Kasim, the Nawab of Bengal ; Nawab of Awadh; and Shah Alam II, the Mughal Emperor. The battle fought at Buxar, a town (currently in Bihar state, India) located on the bank of the Ganges river, was a decisive battle won by the forces of the East India Company.

The battle resulted into securing of Diwani rights to administer the collection and management of revenues of large areas which currently form parts of Indian states of West Bengal, Bihar, Jharkhand, and Uttar Pradesh, as well as of Bangladesh. The Battle of Buxar heralded the establishment of the rule of the East India Company in the eastern part of the Indian subcontinent.

Battle of Chawinda : The Battle of Chawinda was the largest tank battle since World War II, fought as part of the Sialkot Campaign in the Indo-Pakistani War of 1965. The battle saw huge casualties on both sides, though Pakistan managed to stave off the Indian thrust. The tank battles fought in the area between Charwa and Chawinda from 8th to 21 September 1965 were among the biggest battles of the 1965 War.

Battle of Diu : The naval Battle of Diu was a critical sea battle that took place on 3 February 1509 near Diu, India, between Portugal and a joint fleet of Mamlûk Burji Sultanate of Egypt, Ottoman Empire, Calicut and the Sultan of Gujarat, with technical maritime assistance from the

Republic of Venice and the Republic of Ragusa (Dubrovnik).

Battle of Hilli : Battle of Hilli or the Battle of Bogra was a major battle fought in the Indo-Pakistani War of 1971 and Bangladesh Liberation War. It is generally regarded as one of the most pitched battles that took place in East Pakistan, now Bangladesh. The attack on the north western border town Hilli even preceded the war and there was continual fighting for nineteen consecutive days from November 22, 1971 to December 13, 1971. Sporadic fighting continued until December 16 when Pakistanis surrendered formally.

The battle was a significant one as it involved great personal valour on both sides. This is highlighted by the fact that soldiers on either side won their nation's highest military honours. This battle was also unique in that it had started before the official start of the India Pakistan war but continued right until the formal surrender of Pakistan. Unlike other battles in the East where the invading army dominated, Pakistan forces gave a very good account of themselves before the combined might of the Indian military managed to occupy the area. After the war the Indians had sent a team of experts to study the battle on the ground and determine reasons why such a heavy force as described above could not break through that sector till the end.

Battle of Khanua : The Battle of Khanua (1527) was the second of the series of three major battles, victories in which gave Mughal warlord Zaheer-ud-din Babur overlordship over north India. The First Battle of Panipat was the first of the series, the battle of Ghaghra was the last. This battle was fought near the village of Khanwa, about 60 km west of Agra on March 17, 1527. Babur defeated a formidable army raised by Rana Sanga of Mewar in this battle and firmly established his rule over North India

Battle of Kulachal : The naval Battle of Kulachal took place on 10 August 1741 (31 July OS), when forces of Marthanda Varma, the Raja of the erstwhile Indian State of Travancore (also known as Tiruvitamkur) defeated forces of the Dutch East India Company (also known as VOC), and the allied Rani of Eleyadathu Swarupam at Kulachal (anglicised to Colachel or Kolachel) in India. This is considered the first example of an organised Asian power defeating a European naval power. Previous attempts on the West coast of India by native sailors like Kunjali Marakkar in the early 16th century, and by Kanhoji Angre in the early 18th century were on a smaller scale and more guerrilla in nature. The Raja's success is attributed to the tactical genius of his prime minister, Ramayyan Dalava.

This battle is important because it marked the decline of Dutch influence over India, assisting the British East India Company's rise and eventual British rule.

Battle of Longewala : The Battle of Longewala December 5—December 6, 1971 was part of the Indo-Pakistani War of 1971, fought between Indian and Pakistani forces in the Thar Desert of the Rajasthan state in India. It is generally regarded to be one of the decisive battles in the two week long war. Against insurmountable odds, the Indian 'A' company of 120 odd soldiers of the 23rd Bn, The Punjab Regiment, managed to repulse a 2000-3000 strong 51st Infantry Brigade backed by the 22nd Armoured Regiment of Pakistan. Longewala was a strategic point en route to capturing vast tracts of land and also a pivotal theatre of war in engaging India on the western front. The Indian victory in this battle ensured that Pakistan had no way of countering the Indian Army in the west and eventually succumbed to a swift defeat in the war.

Battle of Mahidpur : The Battle of Mahidpur was fought during the Third Anglo-Maratha War between the

Marathas and the British at Mahidpur, a town in the Malwa region, on December 21, 1817. This battle led to the final destruction of Maratha power. Baji Rao II, who was trying to consolidate Marathas, finally surrendered in June 1818. British abolished the position of Peshwa and Marathas were limited to the small kingdom of Satara.

Battle of Plassey : The Battle of Plassey was a battle that took place on June 23, 1757, on the banks of the Bhagirathi River, about 150 km north of Calcutta. It is near Murshidabad, then the capital of the Nawab of Bengal) in India. The word Pâlash, is an extravagant red flowering tree Flame of the forest), and gives its name to a small village near the battlefield.

The battle was between Siraj Ud Daulah, the last independent Nawab of Bengal, and the forces of the British East India Company. Siraj-ud-Daulah's army commander had defected to the British, causing his army to collapse. After this defeat, the entire province of Bengal passed to the Company, and this battle is today seen as one of the pivotal battles leading to British Empire in India. The enormous wealth gained from the Bengal treasury after its victory in the battle allowed the company to significantly strengthen its military might. The battle was waged during the period when the British and French governments were fighting the Seven Years' War in Europe (1756–1763). The La Compagnie des Indes Orientales sent a small contingent to fight against the British East India Company.

Battle of Plassey : The Battle of Plassey was a battle that took place on June 23, 1757, on the banks of the Bhagirathi River, about 150 km north of Calcutta. It is near Murshidabad, then the capital of the Nawab of Bengal) in India. The word Pâlash, is an extravagant red flowering tree Flame of the forest), and gives its name to a small village near the battlefield.

The battle was between Siraj Ud Daulah, the last independent Nawab of Bengal, and the forces of the British East India Company. Siraj-ud-Daulah's army commander had defected to the British, causing his army to collapse. After this defeat, the entire province of Bengal passed to the Company, and this battle is today seen as one of the pivotal battles leading to British Empire in India. The enormous wealth gained from the Bengal treasury after its victory in the battle allowed the company to significantly strengthen its military might. The battle was waged during the period when the British and French governments were fighting the Seven Years' War in Europe (1756–1763). The La Compagnie des Indes Orientales sent a small contingent to fight against the British East India Company.

Battle of Sindh : The Battle of Sindh (February 17, 1843) was a battle between British forces under Sir Charles Napier and the amirs of the now Pakistani region of Sindh. The British were upset about the local amirs' stance during the First Anglo-Afghan War (1839–42). After giving military control of the region to Napier, who forced a new agreement with the Sindh amirs and attacked the fortress at Imamgarh, a popular revolt broke out. The Battle of Miani was the decisive victory that led to the British annexation of Sindh (excluding the state of Khairpur).

Battle of Tukaroi : The Battle of Tukaroi was a battle in March 3, 1575 between the forces of Indian Mughal emperor Jalaluddin Muhammad Akbar led by Munim Khan and the forces of Daud Khan Karrani, the sultan of Bengal. The battle led to the Treaty of Katak. The full conquest of Bengal, independent since about 1338–1339, was finished by 1576.

Batura Sar : Batura Sar is the highest peak of the Batura Muztagh, which is the westernmost subrange of the Karakoram range. It forms the apex of the Batura Wall, which is a continuously high part of the backbone of the Batura Muztagh. Alternate forms of the name of this peak are Batura, Batura I, and Batura I East. The height is also sometimes listed as 7785m, and the Western top of Batura I is of very similar height (often given as 7794m).

Baul Dance : Baul dance forms part of the religious rites of bauls. Baul songs are spiritual in theme, and while singing these songs, bauls start dancing in ecstasy. They hold an ektara in their right hand. Some wear ghunur (a string of bells) round their ankles. Usually baul dances are performed by individuals, but at times they also perform duets or group dances at their akhda. Though while dancing, bauls shake their heads and locks of hair, or twirl around and move their arms and feet, there are no ritualised gestures. The ektara plays a prominent part in the dance, sometimes being held close to the ears, sometimes high up. This dance is mainly popular in kushtia and jessore districts of Bangladesh and Burdwan and Birbhum districts of West Bengal.

Baul Geeti : Baul geeti has been such a huge influence in Bangladeshi music that it deserves being called a genre on its own. However, although Baul geeti can be characterised by particular nature of music and presentation, in general, the genre is actually also defined by a definite cult. In order to understand Baul geeti, it is necessary to understand its creators.

Baul geeti is almost exclusively performed by Bauls (hermits) who are followers of Sufism in Bangladesh. (Note that traditionally bauls were Hindus; Sufism was started following the lifestyle of Lalon Shah.) In Bangladesh, in the early days of Bauls who claimed to be Muslims, with greater focus on love of the society and harmony with nature, baul geeti had to go through a major struggle of survival as did the Bauls themselves. Bauls were subjected to harsh teasing and isolation.

However, with time, Islamists were forced by the general population to accept the Bauls and their spiritual music as part of the society.

Current day Bauls in Bangladesh are Sufis and have given up claims to be Muslims. Most live simple lives on an absolute minimum, earned mainly from performing their music. Baul songs always incorporate simple words expressing songs with deeper meanings involving Creation, society, lifestyle and human emotions. The songs are performed with very little musical support to the main carrier, the vocal. Bauls, bohemian by nature and belief, leave on grand expeditions, writing and performing music on their entire trip to earn living and disseminate notion of love and spirituality.

Bauls : Bauls are a group of mystic minstrels from the Bengal region, now divided into Bangladesh and West Bengal. Bauls are a part of the culture of rural Bengal. They are thought to have been influenced greatly by the Hindu tantric sect of the Kartabhajas. Bauls travel in search of the internal ideal, Maner Manush (Man of the Heart). The origin of the word is debated. However, it is widely agreed that it comes either from Sanskrit Batul, meaning divinely inspired insanity or Byakul, meaning fervently eager. The music of the Bauls, bAul saMgeet refers to a particular type of folk song of sung by Bauls. It carries influences of Hindu bhakti movements as well as the Shuphi, a form of Sufi song mediated by many thousand miles of cultural intermixing, exemplified by the songs of Kabir, for instance.

Bawi : In Mizoram, in the hills social system permitted was partly a type of slavery and partly a system of social security. Amongst the Lushais this was the system of the bawi. Under this system a chief would have a number of dependants (bawis) who would remain with the chief, work for him and help him in all respects and in turn would get food and shelter from the chief. He could free himself from the obligation to the chief only under certain conditions, usually on giving a mithun or payment of certain amount. Apart from the bawis, there was another class of dependants consisting of the persons captured during raids. They were called sals. The victors in a raid would kill the adult warriors and old women of the defeated side. The marriageable women and children would be taken captives. They would be treated well in the captor's family.

Bawm : The Bawm are a tribal group living in the Bandarban district and a small fraction in the Rangamati district of the Chittagong Hill Tracts in Bangladesh. Of Burmese origin and speaking a Tibeto-Burman dialect, their tribal population stands at 6,000. Their name Bawm means ties.

Owing to the efforts of Baptist Christian missionaries funded by the British government since 1918, the majority of the Bawm have converted to Christianity, and it was said that all of them are Christians. As of today, there are relatively few Bawm who still cling to their Animist faith. Even then, the concept of such ties has developed from their culture of doing collectively all things of life, including hunting, singing and dancing, eating and drinking or offering homage to gods has developed to such an extent that elements of their Animist beliefs have largely intertwined with Christianity.

One can see Animist influences in their rituals, culture, and beliefs. A few of the Christian Bawm, however, still worship Animist gods side by side with Christian gods, although the majority have abandoned much of the Animist traditions.

Bay of Bengal : The Bay of Bengal is a bay that forms the northeastern part of the Indian Ocean. It resembles a triangle in shape, and is bordered on the east by the Malay Peninsula, and on the west by the India. On the northern tip of the "bay" lie the Indian state of West Bengal and the country of Bangladesh, thus the name. The southern extremes reach the island country of Sri Lanka, and the Indian Union Territory Andaman and Nicobar Islands.

Many major rivers of India flow west to east into the Bay of Bengal: in the north, the Ganges River (or Ganga), Meghna and Brahmaputra rivers, and in the south Mahanadi, Godavari, Krishna and Kaveri rivers. The Sundarbans mangrove forest is formed at the delta of the Ganga, Brahmaputra and Meghna rivers on the Bay of Bengal. The Irrawaddy River of Burma also flows into the bay.

Major Bangladeshi ports on the bay include Chittagong and Mongla. Major Indian ports on the bay include Chennai (formerly Madras), Vishakhapatnam, Kolkata (formerly Calcutta) and Pondicherry. Cox's Bazar, on the northeastern coast of the bay, is one of the longest unbroken natural beaches of the world.

B B Lal : B.B. Lal is a well-known Indian archaeologist. He was the Director General of the Archaeological Survey of India from 1968 to 1972, and has served as President of the World Archaeological Congress. He also worked in for UNESCO committees. He received the Padma Bhushan by the Government of India in 2000. He has done excavations in the Indus Valley Civilization with Mortimer Wheeler and other archaelogists.

Beas River : The Beas River runs through the Northwestern Indian states of Himachal Pradesh and Punjab. The river was also known as Arjiki or Vipas to the ancient Indians and the Hyphasis to the Ancient Greeks. The Beas River marks the eastern-most border of Alexander the Great's conquests in 326 BC. The river begins at the Rohtang Pass in the state of Himachal Pradesh, and merges with the Sutlej in Punjab, India. The Sutlej continues into Pakistani Punjab and joins the Chenab River to form the Panjnad; the latter joins the Indus River at Mithankot. The waters of the Beas and Sutlej rivers are allocated to India under the Indus Waters Treaty between India and Pakistan

Bebinca : Bebinca is a dessert from Goa, India. The ingredients include eggs and coconut milk. The dish is prepared and consumed during Christmas time. Traditionally this desert is baked over a slow fire and one turns the Bebinca upside down before eating.

This food is also popular in the Philippines, spelled "bibingka." In the Philippine style, salted duck eggs are added into the batter before cooking, with butter or margarine and sugar being added before being served. "Bebinca" was also adopted by the International Weather System as a typhoon name

Begavati River : Begavati river is an offshoot of the river Mathabhanga. The river originates near Chuadanga town and after flowing over Bishoykhali it falls into Bhaduri Beel, 16 km south of Jhenaidaha town. Flowing further to the east, it receives the Alamkhali coming from the Nabaganga and then meets with the Chitra near Shalikha after being renamed as the Phatki from Arpara. Part of the river from its source to Jhenaidaha has dried up. The total length of the Begavati is 72 km; 40 km from Chuadanga to Alamkhali, 12 km from Alamkhali to Arpara and 20 km from Arpara to Shalikha. The Begavati maintains a lot of meanders, but shows no erosional tendency. The average width of the river from Bhaduri Beel to Alamkhali is about 50m and from that point to Chitra it is about 90m. In the dry season the depth of the river between Alamkhali and Arpara is one metre and elsewhere it is 1.5m. The discharge is close to nil in the dry season. The river is tidal up to Arpara. Bishoykhali, Alamkhali, Arpara, Shalikha are some important places on the banks of the Begavati

Begum Hazrat Mahal : Begum Hazrat Mahal, also known as Begum of Awadh, was the wife of Nawab Wazid Ali Shah. Begum Hazrat Mahal was endowed with great physical charm and grace as well as organizational skills. After, her husband was exiled to Calcutta, she took charge of the affairs of the state of Awadh, which then comprised of a large part of the current state of Uttar Pradesh, India.

During India's First War of independence (1857-58), she led a band of her supporters against the British, and was even able to seize the control of Lucknow. She declared her son Birjis Qadr as the king of Awadh. She is believed to have worked in close association with other leaders of the India's First War of Independence, including Nana Sahib.

When the forces under the command of the British re-captured Lucknow and most part of the Awadh, she was forced to retreat. She turned down all offers of amnesty and allowances by the British rulers. Ultimately, she had to retreat to Nepal, where an asylum was granted. She died there in 1879.

Begum Ra'ana Liaquat Ali Khan : Begum Ra'ana Liaquat Ali Khan was born at Almora in the United Provinces in the year 1905 and was educated at Lucknow. She obtained a first class Masters degree with honors in economics from the University of Lucknow in 1929.

Begum Ra'ana began her practical life as a teacher in the Gokhale Memorial School after completing the Teachers Diploma Course from the Diocesan College, Calcutta. She was later appointed as Professor of Economics in the

Indraprstha Girls College, Delhi. In April 1933, she was married to Nawabzada Liaquat Ali Khan. After the reorganization of Muslim League, Begum Ra'ana devoted herself to the task of creating political consciousness amongst the Muslim women. Her struggle for emancipation continued till independence of Muslims of India in 1947.

The wife of the first Prime Minister of Pakistan, Begum Ra'ana took the lead in starting the women's voluntary service in 1948. Women were encouraged to take up responsibilities in administering first aid, organizing food distribution, dealing with health problems, epidemics and clothing, and above all, in providing moral and emotional support. Ra'ana Liaquat Ali also took the initiative of introducing defense training for women.

Begumpet Airport : The Begumpet airport at Hyderabad, is currently, the only International Airport in Andhra Pradesh. The Begumpet airport provides two Check in sections Rajiv Gandhi International and NTR National with a common arrival module. The airport handles both international and domestic traffic for Hyderabad. It is the largest hub of Air Sahara with 126 flights.

The airport will be replaced by Rajiv Gandhi International Airport in March, 2008. Once this new airport becomes operational, Begumpet, which is located in the heart of the Hyderabad metropolitan area, would be used for aviation training and for flights carrying VIPs.

Behdiengkhlam : This is the most important festival dance of the Jaintias. It is celebrated annually at Jowai in Jaintia Hills during the month of July. This dance is accompanied by the tunes of drums and flute.

Behrain: Behrain Hill Station and Ski Resort is located Sarhad, Pakistan. It is one of the popular hill station in Pakistan.

Behula : Behula is the heroine the Bangla epic of Manasamangal. Manasamangal was written between the 13th and 18th centuries. Though its religious purpose is that to glorify the hindu goddess of Manasa, it is more well known for depicting the love story of Behula and her husband Lakhindar. In short, Lakhindar's father angers Manasa, who causes Lakhindar to be bitten by a snake on his wedding night, though he and Behula are enclosed in an iron made house. Behula sails alone with her husband's deadbody on a boat. She finally appeases the goddess and brings Lakhindar back to life. Behula continues to fascinate the Bengali mind, both in Bangladesh and West Bengal. She is often seen as the archetypal Bengali woman, full of love and courage.

Bekal Fort : Bekal Fort is the largest fort in Kasargod District of Kerala, south India. The fort faces the Arabian Sea. One claim is that the fort was built by Sivappa Naik of the Ikkery dynasty of Kumbla in 17th century (between 1645 and 1660). Its also said that the fort was captured by Sivappa Nail from Kolathiri Rajas. Recent archeological exploration seems to support other claims, like the fort was an extension of the construction of the Vijayanagara empire.

Around 1763 the fort was occupied by Haider Ali of Mysore. In 1792 the region containing the fort was ceded to the British, and became the Malabar District of British India. There is an Anjaneya temple inside the fort and outside the fort one can see a grant mosque which was built by Tippu Sultan, son of Haider Ali.

Tourism promotion activities are happening in the areas surrounding the fort now, under the Bekal Resorts Development Corporation (BRDC), which is an initiative by the Government of Kerala.

Bela : Bela is the capital of Lasbela district in Balochistan province of Pakistan. Bela is an ancient town in a historic tract surrounded by hills above the Arabian Sea nearly 200 km west of Karachi. Inhabited since centuries Bela is a wonder in many ways. The town is situated in a significant plain called Lasbela in Balochistan with own distinct history. The tract derives its name from the words Las which mean a plain – surrounded by hill ranges, the greater part of the area is a flat plain, and Bela is the main town at the apex of the plan over 100 kilometres from Karachi. From the early period of history till the rise of the Jamoot tribe in the middle of the eighteenth century, only a few facts are known and recorded about the history of Lasbela.

Belgaum : Belgaum is a town located in the northwest region of the state of Karnataka in India. It is the headquarters of Belgaum district. It derives its name from Sanskrit, Venugram (village of bamboos). The town is situated nearly 2,500 ft (762 m) above sea-level. Till 1961, Belgaum was a part of the Bombay state. With creation of states based on languages, it was brought under Karnataka. The city served as a major military installation for the British Raj, primarily due to its proximity to Goa, which was then an occupied Portuguese territory. Once British left India, the India Government continued and still continues to have an Armed forces installations in Belgaum. In 1961, the Indian government, under the Prime Ministership of Nehru used Belgaum to launch a crusade to liberate Goa from Portuguese occupation. Belgaum has a scenic fortress believed to date from 1519 covering about 100 acres and surrounded by a moat. Within it are two interesting Jain temples.

Bellary : Bellary takes its name from the word Balari which refers to goddess Durugamma as this goddess had manifested herself in the town. Some of the events in the great epic Ramayana are related to this historical place. It is said that Rama while searching for Sita met Sugreeva and Hanuman at a place near Hampi, the celebrated capital of the Vijayanagara empire. The history speaks volumes about significant role it acquired during Satavahanas, Kadambas, Chalukyas of Kalyani, Kalachuryas, Sevunas, and Hoysalas' period. The Vijayanagara rulers built the "City of Victory" on the bank of Tungabhadra River at Hampi in Hospet Taluk. This area which had witnessed the prosperity to its peak fell into political turmoil after the defeat of Vijayanagara in 1565 by the Deccan sultanates.

Belur : Belur (Beluru in Kannada) was the capital of the Hoysala Empire. With Halebid, this is one of the major tourist destinations in the district of Hassan in Karnataka, India. According to inscriptions discovered, it was also referred to as Velapuri. The main attraction in Belur is the Chennakeshava temple, which is one of the finest examples of Hoysala architecture. It was built by king Vishnuvardhana in commemoration of his victory over the Cholas at Talakadu in 1117 AD. Legend has it that it took 103 years to complete with Vishnuvardhana's grandson completing the work started by his grandfather. The facade of the temple is filled with intricate sculptures and friezes with no portion left blank. The intricate workmanship includes elephants, episodes from the Indian mythological epics, and sensuous dancers (the Shilabalikas). Inside the temple are a number of filigreed pillars. This temple along with the Jaina monuments at Shravanabelagola are being proposed as UNESCO world heritage site.

Belur Math : This shrine is situates at eh Belur Road, Howrah. Belur Math is the international headquarters of Ramkrishna Mission which is 16.5km from Dakshineswar across the Ganga. It is founded in 1899 by Swami Vivekananda, the world famous yogi and disciple of Sri Ramakrishna Paramhansa. This International tourist attraction is located near Belur in Howrah district. Its sprawling prayer hall with a statue of Ramakrishna is remarkable. The Belur Math shrine represents a church, mosque and temple when viewed from different angles. Its peaceful and calm atmosphere is befitting the gravity of the place.

Benapole : Benapole is the Bangladesh side of the Petrapole-Benapole border checkpost between Bangladesh and India. It is the most important checkpost of Bangladesh as the Bangladesh Land Port Authority (BLPA) is weighing the importance of the busiest land port Benapole on India-Bangladesh border in line with other Land Customs (LC) stations that cannot be recognized as full-fledged land ports. Geographically benapole is very strategic point for border trading between India and Bangladesh. With the space of time, the land port saw a continuous increase in the volume of trading between two countries.According to Land Port Authority, 90 percent of the total imported items from India comes through Benapole land port.Primarily Benapole land port was a LC station and gradually it turned into a customs division and later customs house in terms of its importance in trading. At present 143 staff including 9 officials and 134 employees are working at the Benapole land port.In 1996-97 period income from Benapole land port was around Taka 500 crore, at present it is Taka 850 crore.

Indian Government has also decided to give priority to export in Bangladesh through Benapole-Petrapole border. Kolkata, one of the commercial hubs of India, is only 80 Kilometers away from Petrapole-Benapole border. Benapole land port is also lucrative for Indian exporters for its cheaper service and equipment charges. Besides, Indian goods receive duty exemption advantage in this land port.

Benazir Bhutto : Benazir Bhutto (b. 21 June 1953 in Karachi) was the first woman to lead a Muslim country.

She was elected Prime Minister of Pakistan in 1988, only to be deposed 20 months later by the country's president Ghulam Ishaq Khan who used the 8th Amendment to dissolve parliament and force an election. She was re-elected in 1993 but was dismissed three years later amid various corruption scandals by the then president Farooq Leghari, again using his discretionary powers under the Eighth Amendment. Some of these scandals involved contracts awarded to Swiss companies during her regime and she faces charges in Switzerland which remain unresolved. Her husband, Asif Ali Zardari, spent eight years in jail until he was released November 2004. Benazir Bhutto is the eldest child of former Pakistani premier Zulfikar Ali Bhutto, son of Sir Shahnawaz Bhutto and Begum Nusrat Bhutto.

Bhutto attended Lady Jennings Nursery School and then the Convent of Jesus and Mary in Karachi. After two years of schooling at the Rawalpindi Presentation Convent, she was sent to the Jesus and Mary Convent at Murree. She passed her O-level examination at the age of 15. In April 1969, she was admitted to Harvard University's Radcliffe College. In June 1973, Benazir graduated from Harvard with a degree in political science where she was elected to Phi Beta Kappa. She attended Oxford University in the fall of 1973 and graduating with a masters degree in Philosophy, Politics and Economics. She was elected to the standing committee of the prestigious Oxford Union.

Bengal : Bengal, known as Bôngo, Bangla, Bôngodesh, or Bangladesh in Bangla, is a region in the northeast of South Asia. Today it is mainly divided between the independent nation of Bangladesh (eastern Bengal), and the Indian federal republic's constitutive state of West Bengal, although some regions of the previous kingdom of Bengal (during local monarchial regimes and British rule) are now part of the neighbouring Indian states of Bihar, Tripura and Orissa.

Bengal Engineering & Science University : The Bengal Engineering & Science University, established at Shibpur, Howrah, just opposite the city of Kolkata, is the third oldest engineering college in existence in India. It was formally established as Civil Engineering College, Calcutta, in 1856 with the idea of introducing engineering education to the country. Every year students from this institution form a large intake of the administration, management and technocracy, both in the public sector and private companies in India and abroad.

Bengal Famine of 1943 : The Bengal famine of 1943 occurred in undivided Bengal (now independent Bangladesh and the Indian state of West Bengal) in 1943. It is estimated that over three million people died from starvation, malnutrition and related illnesses during the famine.

Bengal Fox : The Bengal Fox (Vulpes bengalensis) or Indian Fox is a fox, to be found in the southern Himalaya, in Nepal, India and Bangladesh. It is a medium sized fox, with a smooth, somewhat orange coat, pale underpants, and a black tip on its tail.

Although the Bengal fox lives in pairs, it hunts alone. It undergoes a gestation period of 53 days; after, four kits are born in a den. Mates are sometimes assisted by helpers (offspring from a previous year who stayed behind to aid their parents). Hunting for its skin and flesh as well as excessive use of pesticides in agricultural fields have greatly depleted its population. In addition, its body parts are used in traditional medicine, and in some areas it is eaten.

Bengal Monitor : Bengal monitor (Varanus bengalensis), also known as the Common Indian Monitor, is a monitor lizard found throughout India. It measures upto 75 cm in body length with the tail about 100 cm in length. It feeds on small terrestrial vertebrates, ground birds and their eggs, arthropods and fish.

Although not uncommon, Monitor lizards are killed for their meat and skins and are threatened in many places by hunting. In Maharashtra in India, where the monitor is known as a ghorpad. The lizards have strong claws and in some parts of India this has led to the myth that they can cling strongly to surfaces. A persistent myth that has little support from zoology or history is that Shivaji's general Tanaji Malusare used a monitor with ropes attached for climbing the walls of the Sinhagad fort.

Bengal Muslim Party : Bengal Muslim Party formed early in 1926 by Sir Abdur Rahim for the purpose of contesting provincial elections due at the end of the year. He had resigned from the office of Chief Justice of Madras High Court (1920) to join the Bengal Government as a member of the Governor's Executive Council (1920-25). Aims of Bengal Muslim Party included working the 1919-Reforms, achieving a constitution for India based on a Federation of autonomous provinces, with the Federal Government's control restricted to such subjects as the Federal Services, communication, currency and external and inter-provincial relations. It also pledged, to quote from its manifesto, to work towards realisation of the 'democratic ideal of a government of the people, for the people' and to lead India on to the road of progress shunning the path of obscurantism.

Although overtly it was a community-based party devoted to achieving social, political and economic development of the Muslim community, it disavowed communalism. Its declared political goal was stated to be full responsible government with Dominion Status. It also emphasised on the retention of separate electorates in all elective bodies including legislatures for effective representation of minorities without reducing the 'Muslim majority in any province to a minority or even to an equality', with the option for replacement of separate electorates by joint electorate in the future. The party was in existence till the early 1930's.

Bengal Pact : Bengal Pact an agreement aimed at resolving the question of Hindu-Muslim differences. chitta ranjan das, a man of vision who sincerely believed in the principle of sharing political power with the majority Muslim community of the province, came forward to take up the task of strengthening relations between Hindus and Muslims. Soon after its announcement, the Pact created a great outcry among Hindus and Muslims in Bengal. Its bold provisions offended middle class Bengali Hindus who opposed it stubbornly because they thought that the implementation of the Pact would diminish their power and influence in political as well as in administrative spheres.

Though the pact was discarded by the Indian Congress, CR Das tried his best to get the terms of the Pact ratified by the Bengal Provincial Congress Conference held at sirajganj in June 1924. Unfortunately his premature death in 1925 came as a blow to the cause of Hindu-Muslim unity. His death was followed by the repudiation of the Pact, even by some of his own followers. A large number of Bengali Muslim politicians became shocked at this act and began to move away from the Congress as well as the Swarajya Party.

Bengal Provincial Krishak Sabha (BPKS) : Bengal Provincial Krishak Sabha (BPKS) was established in 1936 by left Congress activists to organise the peasantry through rural reconstruction programmes and to stage an agrarian revolution. Evidently, the Bengal Provincial Krishak Sabha (peasants association) was set up to counter activities of the Krishak Praja party of Ak Fazlul Huq. From the beginning of the electoral politics carried on under the constitution of 1919, the political leadership began to concentrate on rural support. With that end in view, krishak samitis (peasant committees) were set up locally by leading political parties and communities. Peasant samitis were set up throughout Bengal to affiliate the local samitis and bring them under a central political command. BPKS is one such central organisation, the other most important central one being the Nikhil Banga Praja Samiti. The first Bengal Provincial Krishak Conference of BPKS was held on 16-17 August 1936.

The Bengal Provincial Krishak Sabha conceived of the peasant struggle in the context of the nationalist movement. There were two groups to lead the BPKS: the Communist Party and the Congress Socialist Party. As the Communist Party of India was banned then, its members operated under the banner of the Congress Socialist Party, the radical wing of the National Congress. The main activists of the BPKS were ex-convicts and detainees previously arrested for activities during the Civil Disobedience agitation and terrorist activities. BPKS was largely successful in arousing consciousness among the poor peasantry about their rights in land. Local movements such as the Nankar, Tonk, and Tebhaga, which stirred Bengal in the 1940s, were mainly initiated and led by BPKS activists.

Bengal Renaissance : The Bengal Renaissance took place throughout the nineteenth century. During this period, Bengal witnessed an intellectual awakening that is similar to Renaissance in Italy. Under the impact of British rule the Indian intellect learned to raise questions about life and beliefs. It led to the creation of great literary works and questioning of established socio-religious orthodoxy. This is a very significant portion of the History of Bengal. The major players leading this included: Raja Rammohun Roy (1774-1833), Henry Louis Vivian Derozio (1809-31) and his radical disciples called, Young Bengal, Debendranath Tagore (1817-1905) and his followers,,

Akshay Kumar Datta (1820-86), Ishwar Chandra Vidyasagar (1820-91), Michael Madhusudan Dutt (1824-73), Bankimchandra Chattopadhyay (1838-94), Swami Vivekananda (1863-1902) Institutions such as the Asiatic Society (est.1784), Fort William College (1800), Serampore College (1817), Hindu College (1817) (later rechristened Presidency College), General Assembly's Institution (now known as Scottish Church College) (1830), Calcutta School-book Society (1817), Calcutta Medical College (1835), University of Calcutta (1857), and Bethune College (1879) contributed significantly to the Renaissance.

Bengal School of Art : The Bengal School of Art was an influential style of art that flourished in India during the British Raj in the early 20th century. It was associated with Indian nationalism, but was also promoted and supported by many British arts administrators. The Bengal school arose as an avant garde and nationalist movement reacting against the academic art styles previously promoted in India, both by Indian artists such as Ravi Varma and in British art schools. Following the widespead influence of Indian spiritual ideas in the West, the British art teacher Ernest Binfield Havel attempted to reform the teaching methods at the Calcutta School of Art by encouraging students to imitate Mughal miniatures. This caused immense controversy, leading to a strike by students and complaints from the local press, including from nationalists who considered it to be a retrogressive move.

Havel was supported by the artist Abanindranath Tagore, a nephew of the poet Rabindranath Tagore. Tagore painted a number of works influenced by Mughal art, a style that he and Havel believed to be expressive of India's distinct spirutual qualities, as opposed to the "materialism" of the West. Tagore's best-known painting, Bharat Mata (Mother India), depicted a young woman, portrayed with four arms in the manner of Hindu deities, holding objects symbolic of India's national aspirations. Tagore later attempted to develop links with Japanese artists as part of an aspiration to construct a pan-Asianist model of art.

The Bengal school's influence in India declined with the spread of modernist ideas in the 1920s. However Benagl continues to produce some of the best artists of Modern India. Among them the best artists of present day Bengal are Ganesh Pyne, Bikash Bhattacharya, Devajyoti Ray, Paresh Maiti.

Bengal Tiger : The Bengal Tiger or Royal Bengal Tiger (Panthera tigris tigris) is a subspecies of tiger found primarily in India. It is also found in the rainforests and grasslands of Bangladesh, Bhutan, Burma, China and Nepal. Its fur is orange-brown with black stripes.

The Bengal Tiger is now strictly protected, and is the national animal of both Bangladesh and India. After the resounding success of a tiger conservation program in India, known as the Project Tiger, the population of wild tigers has increased dramatically. The Tiger population of India now numbers at about 3,500, up from 1,200 in the 1970s. In The Sundarbans, a 2004 census found the presence of about 280 tigers in the Bangladesh side.

Bengali : Bengali or Bangla is an Indo-Aryan language of South Asia that evolved as a successor to the Sanskrit, Pali, and Prakrit languages. Bengali is the English word for the name of the language and for its speakers; in Bengali, the language itself is called Bangla, a term that now has greater currency in English. From this point forward, Bangla will be used to refer to the language.

Bangla is native to the region of eastern South Asia known as Bengal, which comprises Bangladesh and the Indian state of West Bengal. More than 98% of the total population of Bangladesh speak Bangla as a native language. It is the official language in Bangladesh and one of the official languages in the Indian states of West Bengal and Tripura. There are significant Bangla-speaking communities in the Indian states of Assam and Tripura and in immigrant populations in the West and the Middle East. With more than 200 million native speakers, it is the fourth or fifth most widely spoken language in the world (after Mandarin, Spanish, English and Hindustani (Hindi-Urdu). It is also the fourth most spoken language in terms of native speakers. Bangla is the second most commonly spoken language in India (after Hindi). Along with Assamese, it is geographically the most eastern of the Indo-European languages. Assamese, Oriya and Maithili, three other languages belonging to the Eastern Maghadan Branch of Indo-Aryan language family, are very closely related to Bangla. Standard Assamese, Oriya, and Bangla are considered by some to be nearly mutually intelligible; some local dialects of one language bear a striking resemblance to one or more dialects of the other two languages.

As a result of the Bengal renaissance in the 19th and 20th centuries, much of India's most famous literature, poetry, and lyrics are in Bangla; the works of Rabindranath Tagore (the first Asian to be awarded a Nobel Prize), for example, are in Bangla. Many of the reformist religious, philosophical, and political movements that began in that era were led by Bengalis.

Bengali : Bengali or Bangla is an Indo-Aryan language of South Asia that evolved as a successor to the Sanskrit, Pali, and Prakrit languages. Bengali is the English word for the name of the language and for its speakers; in Bengali, the language itself is called Bangla, a term that now has greater currency in English. From this point forward, Bangla will be used to refer to the language.

Benoy Krishna Basu or Benoy Basu : Benoy Krishna Basu (1908-1930) was an Bengali Indian revolutionary and freedom fighter. Benoy Basu was born on 11 September 1908, in the village Rohitbhog in the Munshiganj District, now in Bangladesh. His father, Rebatimohan Basu was an engineer. Benoy and his peer revolutionaries joined Bengal Volunteers - a group organised by Subhas Chandra Bose in 1928, at the occasion of Calcutta session of the Indaian National Congress.Soon Benoy started a local unit of the organisation in Dhaka, named Bengal Volunteers in Dacca.Later, the Bengal Volunteers became a more active revolutionary association and prepared a plan of "Operation Freedom" against the police repression in Bengal, especially against the inhuman conduct with the political prisoners in different jails. He died on 13 December 1930, as a result of a revolutiontionary battle against British police.

Benthe : This is chorous singing tradition performed ispecific community of trible called Gujjar and Bakerwal in Himachal. Dance is performed by 5-7 members.

Berar : Berar is a former province of British India, located in central India. It is now part of Maharashtra state, and where it is forms part of Vidarbha region. The boundaries of Berar have changed historically, but the British Raj province, also known as the Hyderabad Assigned Districts, corresponds to Maharashtra's Amravati Division.

The history of Berar belongs generally to that of the Deccan, the country falling in turn under the sway of the various dynasties which successively ruled in southern India, the first authentic records showing it to have been part of the Andhra or Satavahana empire. On October 1, 1903, Berar was placed under the administration of the British commissioner general of the Central Provinces, which henceforth became known as the Central Provinces and Berar. After India's independence in 1947, the Central

Provinces and Berar became a province of India, and in 1950 became the Indian state of Madhya Pradesh. In 1956, the Indian states were reorganized along linguistic lines, and Berar and Nagpur became part of Bombay state. In 1960, Bombay state was split along linguistic lines, and the southern, Marathi-speaking portion of the state, including Berar, became the new state of Maharashtra.

Berin Gali : Berin Gali is a subdistrict of Abbottabad District, in the North-West Frontier Province, Pakistan. The area is between 2 mountains Thandyani and Erajani. Its population numbers about 20,000. Ethnically, the two main tribes are the Karlal and the Qurashi. In popular local lore, the inhabitants of this area are particularly courageous. It is well known that there is no proper road.

Bethune College : Established by John Drinkwater Bethune, the Bethune College, is the first women's college in India. It was founded in 1879. It is located at 181, Bidhan Sarani, Kolkata—700006, just opposite the current campus of Scottish Church College, Calcutta. It is affiliated to the University of Calcutta.

Betla National Park : Situated in the district of Daltonganj, Palamau Sanctuary is spread over an area of 979sq.km. The core area of 232 sq. kms of the sanctuary was declared as Betla National park in September1989. The park occupies the western parts of the Chotanagpur plateau and was constituted in the year 1960 as an extension of the Hazaribagh National park. Palamau has the distinction of being the forest where the world's first tiger census was enumerated in 1932. The park became one of the earliest 9 tiger reserves in India under 'Project Tiger' in 1974.

The forests of the park have a vast range of vegetation consisting of tropical wet evergreen forests in the lower reaches, mixed (moist & dry) deciduous forests in the middle and temperate alpine forests in the upper reaches including Sal and bamboo as the major components along with a number of medicinal plants. The river Koel and its tributaries run through the northern portion of the park. There are grasslands in the river flowing area. It has waterfalls and hot springs too. Once the seat of Chero kings, there are two historical forts, one of them belonging to the 16th century deep inside the forest. The main sentinel of the old fort is visible high up on the hill with defences in three directions and three main gates

Betna River : Betna river is originating from the northeastern part of Jessore, the river flows south near Navaron of Sharsha upazila. After flowing through Kalaroa upazila of Satkhira district it enters Khulna district. It debouches into the Kobadak after being renamed as the Kalia and branching out as the Dalua at a place named Benarpota. The Dalua is now detached from the Betna due to construction of a Barrage near Benarpota. Part of the discharge of the Betna is drained through the Marichap-Kobadak and the rest is drained through the Marichap-Kholpetua. The total length of the river is about 192 km and the average width is 125m. The Betna is under tidal influence.

Navaron, Ulshi, Shankarpur, Kalaroa, Benarpota, Chapra are some important places on the banks of the Betna. In the upstream from Navaron to Kalaroa water is being used for irrigation through pumping. The downstream is navigable throughout the year. In winter, salinity increases from Jessore to Shankarpur due to lack of flow and as a result agriculture is hindered in this season.

Betul : Betul is the administrative center of Betul District located in southern Madhya Pradesh in India. It forms the southernmost part of the Bhopal Division. The District extends between 21°-22' and 22°-24' North Latitude and between 77°-10' and 78°-33' East Longitude. Betul derives its name from the small town of Betul Bazar, about 5 km south of present Betul city which was the district Headquarters. In 1822 the District Headquarters was shifted to the present place which was a village called Badnur at that time. Literal meaning of Betul is 'without (Be) cotton (tool)'. It was the last point of cotton growing area.this district has most developed town AMLA which is a tehsil too, while others are less developed,it is a town surrounded by hills from all side and was used by britishers for exportation of coal,that's why they established a railway station in the early 1910s.presently it is serving as a connecting junction for railways i.e. only access to chhindwarra district via rail.

Betwa River : The Betwa (Vetravati) is a river in Northern India, and a tributary of the Yamuna.It is being connected to Ken river in Madhya Pradesh as the first link in the ambitious river linking project in India.

Bhabanicharan Bandyopadhyay : Bhabanicharan Bandyopadhyay (1787-1848) was a Bengali writer, journalist and satirist. He was born at Narayanpur in Ukhra Pargana near Kolkata. rammohun roy's reform movements polarised the nineteenth-century intellectuals into conservatives and liberals. Bhabanicharan Bandyopadhyay was an active member of the conservative group.

Besides Bangla, Bhabanicharan Bandyopadhyay was proficient in English, Persian and Sanskrit. His proficiency in English earned him the job of banian and diwan in several European firms. However, Bhabanicharan was more interested in journalism and, in 1821, joined the Sambad Kaumudi, of which Rammohan Roy was the founder, as editor. However, he soon fell out with Rammohan on religious issues and resigned. He then started his own journal, Samachar Chandrika. The journal was extremely conservative, and its main objective was to criticise the reforms of the company government and young bengal radicalism. He was appointed the first secretary of the conservative group's dharma sabha, of which radhakanta deb was president.

Bhabha Atomic Research Centre (BARC) : The Bhabha Atomic Research Centre (BARC) is India's primary nuclear research facility. It has a number of nuclear reactors, all of which are used for India's nuclear power and research program. It was started in 1957, as the Atomic Energy Establishment, Trombay (AEET), and became India's primary nuclear research center, taking over charge of most nuclear scientists that were at the Tata Institute of Fundamental Research. After Homi J. Bhabha's death in 1966, the centre was renamed as the Bhabha Atomic Research Centre.

The first reactors at BARC and its affiliated power generation centers were imported from the west. India's first power reactors, installed at the Tarapore Atomic Power Plant (TAPP) were from the US. The primary import of BARC is as a research centre. The BARC and the Indian government has consistently maintained that the reactors are used for this purpose only: Apsara (1956; named by the then Prime Minister of India, Jawaharlal Nehru when he likened the blue Cerenkov radiation to the beauty of the Apsaras (Indra's court dancers), CIRUS (1960; the "Canada-India Reactor" with assistance from Canada), the now-defunct ZERLINA (1961; Zero Energy Reactor for Lattice Investigations and Neutron Assay), Purnima I (1972), Purnima II (1984), Dhruva (1985), Purnima III (1990), and Kamini.

The plutonium used in India's 1974 nuclear test carried out in Pokhran in the Thar desert of Rajasthan, sometimes referred to in the liberal media as a 'Peaceful Nuclear Explosion', came from CIRUS, the primary charter of which was 'peaceful' nuclear research. The 1974 test (and the 1998 tests that followed) gave Indian scientists the technological know-how and confidence not only to develop nuclear fuel for future reactors to be used in power generation and research, but also the capacity to refine the same fuel into weapons-grade fuel to be used in the development of nuclear weapons.

Bhabhar : Bhabhar is the region south of the Lower Himalayas where the alluvial grade merges into the Indo-Gangetic Plain. The name Bhabhar is derived from a local tall growing grass, Eulialopsis binata. Bhbahar is a level surface zone at the foothills of the Himalayas 34 km wide where the Himalayan rivers and streams disappear under boulders and gravels due to the porous soil and sub-soil composition of Bhabhar. As a result, the underground water level is very deep in this region.

Being at the junction point of Himalayas and the Indo-Gangetic Plain, Bhabhar contains almost all the important trade and commerce hubs of Uttaranchal. Due to the top-soil replenishment every monsoon, is also a very fertile area with significant yields per unit area. South of Bhabhar lies the alluvial stretch called the Terai.

Bhaderwah : Bhaderwah is a small valley-town in Doda district (India /Jammu and Kashmir/ Doda). Bhaderwah valley is predominantly a mountainous torrid town situated 80 km from Batote. The festive mood in the district begins with the melting of snow in April and the sprouting of greenery all round. Kailash Yatra is another famous pilgrimage of the area which is considered an important Hindu pilgrimage. Bhaderwah offers to the tourist a variety of beautiful landscape, colourful local fairs, important festival mood and unique mosaic culture, extremely and pleasant summer temperature ranges from 18 degrees to 32 degrees.

Bhadra River : Bhadra river is a gentle river all along its course. It originates from Kobadak (Kapotaksa in

Bangla) in Jhikargachha upazila of Jessore district and flows through Khulna district dividing the land between the Pasur and Shibsa rivers. Flowing through the Sundarbans, the Bhadra joins the confluence of the Pasur and the Shibsa. Locally this part is known as Mara Bhadra (dead Bhadra). Then the river flows southeast from Sutarkhali and debouches into the Pasur after a 30-km journey through the Sundarban. But a noticeable change has occurred in the course of the river, and its main flow is now riding the course of the Sutarkhali.

At present the original Bhadra follows the course of the Jhapjhapia and then falls into the Pasur. At one point it follows the course of the Habrakhali before falling into the Shibsa. The present state of the river in Dacope upazila of Khulna suggests its extinction in the near future. The Bhadra is under regular tide with a height of.21m to 3.91m. The river is about 193 km long. Lavjami, Manirampur, Kelapur, Gharnia Dumuria, Dacope, Sutarkhali, Kalbagi are some of the important places along its course.

Bhadrak: The district of Bhadrak, named after a small town, is located in the eastern part of India, within the state of Orissa. On 1 April 1993 this district was carved out from the Balasore District and became a separate entity. The district has an area of 2,677 km^2 and a population of 13,32,249 according to the 2001 census. The Bhadrak town, the haedquarter of the district, is situated at a distance of 159 km. from the state capital, Bhubaneswar,and it is famous for Bhadrakali Temple. Aradi, Chandabali, Dhamanagar, Dhamara, Guamala Nuasasan, etc are some other places of tourist interest. The language mostly spoken by the people is Oriya, though some people speak Urdu, Santhali, Bengali, etc. Salandi river passes by this district.

Bhagalpur : Bhagalpur is a town and the administrative headquarters of Bhagalpur district, Bihar state in the eastern part of India. It is a divisional town of historical importance situated on the southern bank of the Ganga river. Situated 220km east of state capital Patna and 410 km north west of Calcutta is well connected by rail and road. Bhagalpur is famous worldwide for its' silk production. The silk industry in this city is hundreds of years old and a whole clan exists that has been producing silk for generations. There is a Silk Institute and Agricultural college here, as well as a University, and Engineering, Medical and Homeopath colleges.

References to Bhagalpur can be found in Indian epics like the Ramayana and the Mahabharata where Bhagalpur has been described as the kingdom of Anga. Mandar Hill, situated 52 km south from Bhagalpur, is believed to have been used as Churner during Samudra-Manthan by God and Danav according to Hindu mythology. Ancient cave sculptures of Emperor Ashoka's regime (274 BC-232 BC) are found in the neighbourhood and at Sultangunj, 20 km west of Bhagalpur, a temple of the Gupta period (320-500) still exists. The tomb of Suja, brother of Moghul emperor Aurangzeb, in the heart of the town is reminiscent of the city's association with the Mughal period.

Ruins of ancient Vikramshila University are located 44 km east of Bhagalpur. It was the medieval centre to the conservation and propagation of Buddhist education, established by King Dharampal of Bengal (783-820) at the end of the 8th century. The gangetic plains are very fertile and the main crops include rice, wheat, maize, barley, and oilseeds. The economy of Bhagalpur is dependent mainly on agriculure and silk.

Bhagat Singh : Bhagat Singh (September 27, 1907 – March 23, 1931) was an Indian revolutionary, considered to be one of the most famous martyrs of the Indian freedom struggle. For this reason, he is often referred to as Shaheed Bhagat Singh (the word shaheed means "martyr"). He is also believed by many to be one of the earliest Marxists in India.

Bhagat Singh was born into a Jat Sikh family to Sardar Kishan Singh and Vidyavati in KhatKar Kalan village near Banga in the Jalandhar district of Punjab. As a child, he was deeply affected by the Jalianwala Bagh Massacre that took place in Punjab in 1919. When Mahatma Gandhi started the Non-Cooperation Movement in 1920, he became an active participant at the age of 13.

Bhagat Singh studied at the National College, but ran away from home to escape early marriage, and met his fellow revolutionaries. He became a member of the organization Naujawan Bharat Sabha. In the Naujawan Bharat Sabha, Bhagat and his fellow revolutionaries grew popular amongst the youth. He wrote for and edited Urdu and Punjabi newspapers published from Amritsar. In September 1928, a meeting of various revolutionaries from across India was called at Delhi under the banner of the Kirti Kissan Party. Bhagat Singh was the Secretary of the meet. His later revolutionary activities were carried out as a leader of this association.

The British government had created a commission under Sir John Simon to report on the political events ongoing in India in 1927. The Indian political parties decided to boycott the commission. When the commission visited Lahore on October 30, 1928, Lala Lajpat Rai protested the commission in a silent march, but the police chief Scott beat Lala Lajpat Rai fatally. Bhagat Singh, who was an eyewitness to this event, vowed to take revenge on Scott. He joined with other revolutionaries, Shivaram Rajguru and Sukhdev, in a plot to kill the police chief. However, in a case of mistaken identity, Bhagat Singh accidentally killed Mr. Saunders, a Deputy Superintendent of Police. He quickly left Lahore to escape the police. He shaved his beard and cut his hair to avoid recognition, a violation of one of the sacred tenets of Sikhism.

In the face of actions by the revolutionaries, the British government enacted the Defence of India Act to give more power to the police. The purpose of the Act was to combat revolutionaries like Bhagat Singh. The Act was defeated in the council by one vote. However, the Act was then passed under the ordinance that claimed that it was in the best interest of the public. In protest, Bhagat Singh and Batukeshwar Dutt, another revolutionary, planned to explode a bomb in the assembly where the ordinance was going to be passed. On April 8, 1929, Singh and Dutt threw bombs onto the corridors and shouted "Inquilab Zindabad!" ("Long Live the Revolution!"). This was followed by a shower of leaflets stating that it takes a loud voice to make the deaf hear. The bomb neither killed nor injured anyone; Singh and Dutt claimed that this was deliberate on their part, a claim substantiated both by British forensics investigators who found that the bomb was not powerful enough to cause injury, and by the fact that the bomb was thrown away from people. Singh and Dutt gave themselves up for arrest after the bomb. He and Dutt were sentenced to 'Transportation for Life' for the bombing on June 12, 1929.

Shortly after his arrest and trial for the Assembly bombing, the British came to know of his involvement in the murder of Mr. Saunders. Bhagat Singh, Rajguru, and Sukhdev were charged with the murder. Bhagat Singh decided to use the court as a tool to publicize his cause for the independence of India. He admitted to the murder and made many anti-British statements during the trial. On March 23, 1931 Bhagat Singh was hanged with his fellow comrades Raj Guru and Sukhdev, ending their role in the fight for independence.

Bhagavata Purana : The Bhagavata Purana (sometimes rendered as Bhagavad Purana, also known as the Srimad Bhagavatam, or simply Bhagavatam) is one of the Puranas, a part of the literature of Hinduism. Its focus is on the bhakti movement in which Vishnu or Krishna is understood as Bhagavat (all-embracing God). Earlier parts of the work contain stories of some devotees and objects of their devotion, avataras of God. The last and most important part of the work (i.e., the tenth canto) is an elaboration of the traditional story of Krishna.

Bhagavatha Mela : Bhagavatha Mela, one popular throughout the Tamil Nadu, is now confined to a single village, Melatur in Thanjavur district. It is held as a part of the annual Nara-Simha Jayanthi festival in May-June. A large flat thatched canopy and a small stage are put up in the streets in front of the temple and the dramas are enacted to dedicate the dcity installed in the front hall of the temple.

Bhagavatha Mela dance-drama is subdued and graceful with, mellifluous vocal and instrumental music. Dialogue of high diction and suggestive strained abhinaya and other symbolical action are its hall-marks. Violent scenes of war and killing are not enacted but only narrated. The Bhagavatha Mela dance-drama has dramatic interest, aided by classical music and dance. Every actor is well trained in Bharatha Natya.

The performance commences with the appearance of the Konangi or buffoon. He dances for a few minutes and requests the audience to witness the play patiently. A group of musicians then sing the Todaya-mangalam or invocation song followed by the introduction to the drama that is to be enacted. Lord Ganesa then appears to bless the play. A young boy is usually made to wear the mask of Ganesa and dance to the accompaniment of background music. Each actor or character is then introduced. After this elaborate introduction, the drama begins.

Bhagirathi River : The Bhagirathi refers to two major tributaries of the Ganga:

1. A turbulent Himalayan river originating from the Gangotri glacier in Uttaranchal, which flows for about 700 km before merging with the Alaknanda at Devprayag at the holy confluence (Sangam). The river downstream is known as the Ganga proper. The controversial Tehri dam lies on the Bhagirathi, near Tehri.

2. A separate distributary of the Ganga in West Bengal. It branches off from the Ganga in Murshidabad district at Nurpur, 25 Km below Farakka, runs parallel to her for about 2 Km, winds its way to the south and leaves the district north of Palashi, known as Plassey in colonial literature. The river was an important transportation channel in the early history of Bengal, with colonial trading ports coming up at Calcutta (British) and Chandannagar (Dutch/French). The river banks hosted several battles and skirmishes towards the start of the colonial era (including the Battle of Plassey), as well as earlier wars against Maratha raiders. On eastern bank lie many historic and wealthy towns like Murshidabad, Jangipur and Ziaganj.

The word Bhagirathi literally means "caused by Bhagiratha", a mythical Sagar Dynasty prince who was instrumental in bringing the river Ganga from the heavens on to the earth, in order to release his 60,000 grand-uncles from a curse of the saint Kapila. Both these tributaries are sacred to all Hindus, and it's water is considered holy (like most of the Ganga and its tributaries).

Bhagoria Haat : This colourful festival of the Bhils and Bhilalas, particularly in the district of West Nimar and Jhabua in MP, is actually in the nature of a mass svayamvara, a marriage market, usually held on the various market days falling before the Holi festival in March. As the name of the festival indicates, (bhag, to run), after choosing their partners, the young people elope and are subsequently accepted as husband and wife by society through predetermined customs. It is not always that boys and girls intending to marry each other meet in the festival for the first time. In a large number of cases the alliance is already made between the two, the festival providing the institutionalised framework for announcing the alliance publicly. The tradition is that the boy applies gulal, red powder, on the face of the girl whom he selects as his wife. The girl, if willing, also applies gulal on the boy's face. This may not happen immediately but the boy may pursue her and succeed eventually.

Earlier, the Bhagoria haat was also the place for settling old disputes; open invitations were sent to enemies for a fight in the haat. Bloody battles used to be quite common in the past but today police and administration do not allow people to go to the haat armed. The Bhagoria haat also coincides with the completion of harvesting, adding to it the dimension of being an agricultural festival as well. If the crops have been good, the festival assumes an additional air of gaiety.

Bhagta Parab : Bhagta Parab namely the festival of the devotees, comes in the end of spring season and in the beginning of summer season in Jharghand. Among the tribal, it is popularly known as worship of Budha Baba because here it has got its own meaning and procedure of worshipping. Bhagta or devotees observe fast for the worship. In the evening they carry their village priest called Laya from bathing pond to the temple. It is a peculiar sacrificial scenario when the Laya gets out of the pond after bathing the devotees make a chain, locking their thighs with each other and come forward to offer their bare chest to Laya for walk over. After the evening worship, devotees take part in dynamic and vigorous Chhau Dance.

The next day, a primitive sports of bravery is observed. The devotees pierce hooks on the back of their skin and get tied at one end of a long horizontal wooden pole, which is hanging on the top of a vertical Shal wood pole, at a height of about 30 feet or some times 50 feet. Now the other end of the horizontal pole which is connected with a rope, pulled around the pole by the people and the tied devotee display the breath taking dance in the sky.

Bhagwan Das : Bhagwan Das (January 12, 1869—September 18, 1958) was an Indian philosopher and public figure. For a time he served in the Central Legislative Assembly of undivided India.

He became allied with the Hindustani Culture Society and was active in opposing rioting as a form of protest. As a fighter for national freedom from the British rule, he was often in danger of reprisals from the Colonial government. Born in Varanasi, India, he graduated school to became a deputy in the collections bureau, and later left to continue his academic pursuits. With Dr. Annie Besant he formed a professional collaboration which lead to the founding of the Central Hindu College, which became Benaras Hindu University. Das would later found the Kashi Vidya Peeth, a national university where he served as headmaster. Das was a scholar of Sanskrit, from which he added to the body of Hindi language. He wrote approximately 30 books, many of these in Sanskrit and Hindi. Das received the Bharat Ratna award in 1955.

He belonged to the prosperous and eccentric Shah family of Varanasi. He was excommunicated from the Agrawal Samaj for advocating that going across the sea does not cause one to lose his caste. The situation arose when his son Sri Prakasa wanted to go to Britain to study law.

Bhagwan Swaminarayan : Bhagwan Swaminarayan (April 2, 1781 - 1830) was born Ghanshyam Maharaj to a brahmin family in the village of Chhapaiya, Uttar Pradesh, India.

Bhai Gurdas Ji : Bhai Gurdas Ji is one of the most eminent personalities in the history of the Sikh religion. He was a brilliant scholar and poet. He was an able missionary and an accomplished theologian. Being well versed in Indian religious thought, he was able to elaborate profoundly in the tenants of Sikhism.

Bhai Gurdas Ji was mainly a religious poet. He wrote in Sanskrit, Brij-bhasa and Punjabi. 6 Chands of 8 verses each in Sanskrit. 672 Kabits and 3 swayyas in Brij-bhasa. Varan Gian Ratnavali, 40 Vars containing 912 pauries in Punjabi.

In many of his poems Bhai Sahib Ji throws light on the customs, habits and superstitions of his contemporaries. He comments on the prevailing evils of the time. He writes about the practices on both the Hindu and Muslim communities of his day. The poems themselves reveal a profound knowledge of Indian religious thought and of the ancient Hindu scriptures. As a record of the life and times of the Gurus his compositions are invaluable. The Vars of Bhai Gurdas Ji are accepted as canonised bani. They authentically expound the Sikh doctrine and have been called the " key to understanding the holy Scriptures." His ideas remain today, progressive, constructive, practical and above all valid

According to Bhai Gurdas Ji the aim of Sikhism is to change an ordinary man into an ideal person. Such a Sikh (learner) becomes a Gursikh or a Gurmukh. A Gurmukh Sikh is one who labours hard to earn an honest living, shares his earnings with others and gives liberally to charities and worthy causes. Sikhism lays great emphasis on selfless service, sewa in the community, of joining in the company of 'holy people' of personal honesty and humility.

Bhairab River : Bhairab river is an important river in the moribund delta area. Its name means 'the terrible' and attests to the size it had reached when the main volume of the Ganges was carried by it. At present the main stream is not navigable beyond Bagherpara Upazila (Jessore district). It has two main branches, the Ichamati (Khulna-Ichamati) and the Kobadak. Part of the Khulna-Ichamati is in India and partly in Satkhira district of Bangladesh, and so it forms the boundary between the two countries.

The river is known by several names along its course. Downstream from Kaliganj to Kaikhali it is the Kalindi and the Raymangal from where it has become a large estuarine river. It splits into two, with the western arm named Hariabhanga and the eastern arm retaining the original name. Downstream from Kaikhali, the river is referred to as the Khulna-Ichamati while in the south it is the Raymangal-Hariabhanga. The total length of the Bhairab is about 250 km. In the monsoon, the Ganges feeds it, but in the dry season it becomes dry. Its lower course remains navigable throughout the year and is influenced by tides.

Khulna and Jessore towns stand on the bank of this river. In the past, the Bhairab greatly influenced development of settlements and culture in these two towns. The Hindus regard it as sacred. meherpur, chuadanga, Barobazar, kotchandpur, chaugachha, Jessore, daulatpur, bagerhat and Khulna are some of the important places located on the banks of the Bhairab.

Bhaiyathan : Bhaiyathan is a village in Surguja district in the state of Chhattisgarh in India. It is a development block which comes under Surajpur tehsil. It is 65 km west of district headquarter Ambikapur. It is situated on the bank of Rend river. Tamor Pingla Wildlife Sanctuary is a major attraction nearby. A famous Devi temple on a hill Kudargarh is just 23 km from Bhaiyathan. A 2x600 MW thermal power project has been proposed by the Union

Power Ministry in Bhaiyathan. It will be installed by Chhattisgarh State Electricity Board (CSEB). CSEB will be the first electricity board in the country to install 600 MW super ciritical units which only National Thermal Power Corporation (NTPC) has adopted so far.

Bhajan : A bhajan or kirtan is a Hindu or Sikh devotional song, often of ancient origin. Great importance is attributed to the singing of bhajans within the Bhakti. It is also one of the paths of Sikhism and in that context refers to the singing of the Sacred Hymns from the Sri Guru Granth Sahib, or "SGGS". The Sikhs place huge value on this type of singing and a Sikh is duty bound to listen to and/or sing Guru-Kirtan as frequently as possible. In Surat Shabd Yoga, bhajan means listening to the inner sounds of the Shabd or the Shabd Master

Kirtans are deeply rooted in the Vedic tradition. Bhajans are simple songs in soulful language expressing the many-splendored emotions of love for God; a complete submission or self-surrender to Him through singing.

Traditionally, the music has been Indian classical music, which is based on ragas and tala (rhythmic beat patterns) played on the harmonium and tabla (traditional Indian instruments). The Sikh Scripture contains 31 ragas and 17 talas which form the basis for kirtan music compositions.

Bhakra Dam : Bhakra Dam is a concrete gravity-arch dam across the Sutlej River, near the border between Punjab and Himachal Pradesh in northern India. The dam was part of the larger multipurpose Bhakra Nangal Project whose aims were to prevent floods in the Sutlej-Beas river valley, to provide irrigation to adjoining states and to provide hydro-electricity. Construction began in 1948 and was completed in 1963. The dam, at 741 ft (226 m), is one of the highest gravity dams in the world (compare Hoover Dam at 732 ft). The 166 km^2 Gobindsagar Reservoir, named after Guru Gobind Singh, is created by this dam. The dam provides irrigation to 10 million acres (40,000 km^2) of fields in Delhi, Haryana, Punjab, Rajasthan and Himachal Pradesh. Two power houses with a total capacity of 1000 MW flank the dam, on either side of the river. A smaller subsidiary dam, called the Nangal Dam is located a little downriver from the Bhakra Dam.

Bhakri : Bhakri is a round flat unleavened bread often used in the cuisine of western and central India, especially in the states of Gujarat and Maharashtra.

Like breads around the world, bhakri is a staple. It is made mostly from jowar flour, bajra flour, nachni flour and even rice flour (in the Konkan region). Bhakri has traditionally been the farmer's food which would be carried to the farm at the crack of dawn and make up for both breakfast and lunch. In modern days however, bhakri has been replaced by rotis and phulka's but still enjoys its own fan-following. Typically bhakri is accompanied by various curries, chutney (thecha—a thick paste of really hot green or red chilies) and raw onion. Bhakri has its own advantages from dietary point of view. Being made from cereals, it is high in protein but at the same time very easy to digest. It is made of comparatively coarse flour and hence more nutritious than the fine flour.

Bhakti Movements : Bhakti movements are Hindu religious movements in which the main spiritual practice is the fostering of loving devotion to God, called bhakti. They are monotheistic movements generally devoted to worship of Shiva or Vishnu or Shakti. The Bhakti Movement was essentially founded in South India and later spread to the North during the late medieval period. The notion of 'Bhakti' (loosely translated as devotional love to God) is of hoary antiquity. A nascent consciousness of what 'Bhakti' constitutes is already to be found in the earliest Vedas, especially in relation to deities such as

Varuna. A clearer expression of Bhakti began to be formed during the so-called Epic Period and the Puranic periods of Hindu history. Texts such as the Bhagavad Gita and the Bhagavata Purana clearly explore Bhakti Yoga or the Path of Devotion as a means to salvation.

The Bhakti Movement itself is a historical-spiritual phenomenon that crystallized in South India during Late Antiquity. It was spearheaded by devotional mystics (later canonised as Hindu saints) who extolled devotion and love to God as the chief means of salvation (moksha). The Bhakti movement in South India was spearheaded by the sixty-three Nayanars (Shaivite devotees) and the twelve Alvars (Vaishnavaite devotees). The twelve Alvars and the sixty-three Nayanars nurtured the incipient bhakti movement in South India under the Pallavas and Pandyas in the 5-7th centuries AD. They constitute and were greatly influential in determining the expression of faith in South India. The path of devotion as expounded by these mystics would later be incorporated into Ramanuja and Madhava's philosophical systems.

The Bhakti movement began to spread to the North during the late medieval ages when North India was under Muslim domination. There was no grouping of the mystics into Shaiva and Vaishnava devotees as it was in the South. The movement was spontaneous and the various mystics had their own version of devotional expression. Unlike in the South where devotion was centred on both Shiva and Vishnu (in all his forms), the Northern devotional movement was more or less centred on Rama and Krishna, both of whom were incarnations of Vishnu. Though this did not mean that the cult of Shiva or of the Devi went into decline. In fact for all of its history the Bhakti movement co-existed peacefully with the other movements in Hinduism. It was initially considered unorthodox as it rebelled against caste distinctions and made disregarded Brahmanic rituals which according to Bhakti saints not necessary for salavation. In the course of time however, owing to its immense popularity among the masses (and even royal patronage) it became 'orthodox' and continues to be one of the most important modes of religious expression in modern India.

In the period between the 14-17th centuries, a great bhakti movement swept through Northern India initiated by a loosely associated group of teachers or 'Sants'. Caitanya, Vallabha, Meera Bai, Kabir, Tulsi Das, Tukaram and other mystics spearheaded the Bhakti movement in the North. Their teachings were that people could cast aside the heavy burdens of ritual and caste and the subtle complexities of philosophy and simply express their overwhelming love for God. This period was also characterised by a spate of devotional literature in vernacular proese and poetry in the ethnic languages of the various Indian states or provinces.

Bhand Pather : It is a traditional folk theatre style combination of play and dance in a satirical style where social traditions, evils are depicted and performed in various social and cultural functions in Kashmir. Bhand Jashan is performed by a group of 10 to 15 artists in their traditional style accompanied by light music for the entertainment of people.

Bhandap : A traditional folk dance performed by the women folk of the scheduled tribe community who were the earliest settlers of Goa, in the second half of the Hindu month Bhadrapada.

Bhandarvi Poonam : On the fullmoon day in September, there is a sea of humanity, at Ambaji to seek the blessings of Goddess Amba.

Bhang : Bhang is a derivative of the leaf and flower of a female cannabis plant. It is used for making beverages and sometimes is smoked. Bhang Ki Thandai is a drink popular in many parts of North India which is made by mixing bhang with thandai, a drink prepared with a mixture of almonds, certain spices, milk and sugar. Cultivation of cannabis is illegal in many parts of the country, but bhang is widely available, and there is only a mild social stigma attached to drinking of Bhang Ki Thandai.

Bhang Lassi is another well-known drink made with bhang. Although it is rarely printed in menus, some restaurants in India and Thailand, predominantly the tourist attracting areas such as Rajasthan, serve Bhang Lassi; lassi, which is a yogurt and iced-water beverage, laced with bhang. It is commonly dubbed "special lassi".

The traditional harvest of cannabis and preparation of bhang coincides with celebrations of Holi in March and Baisakhi in April. It is believed that the traditional dance bhangra derives its name from bhang.

Bhangra : Bhangra is both a lively dance which is from the region of Punjab, now divided between North India and Pakistan, and the musical accompaniment to the dance. A variety of popular music, also called Bhangra, has developed from these traditions and has a keen youth following around the world.

Andaman and Nicobar Islands - Andhra Pradesh – Arunachal Pradesh – Assam – Bihar – Chhattisgarh – Goa – Gujarat – Haryana – Himachal Pradesh – Jammu – Jharkhand – Karnataka – Kashmir – Kerala – Madhya Pradesh – Maharashtra – Manipur – Meghalaya – Mizoram – Nagaland – Orissa – Punjab – Rajasthan – Sikkim – Tamil Nadu – Tripura – Uttar Pradesh – Uttaranchal – West Bengal

Bhangra is a fusion of music, singing and the beat of the dhol drum, a single stringed instrument called the iktar (ektara), the tumbi and an instrument reminiscent of an enlarged pair of tongs called chimta. The accompanying songs are small couplets written in the Punjabi language called bolis. They relate to harvest celebration, love, patriotism or current social issues.

Today the word Bhangra is more associated with the style of dance pop music derived from the above mentioned musical accompaniment. The dhol's smaller cousin, the dholaki, is sometimes used instead of or in addition to the dhol. Additional percussion, including tabla, is frequently used in bhangra.

Bhangra has always been popular amongst Punjabi people all over the world, but it has enjoyed a resurgence over the last ten years or so. Its raw traditional sound is often supplemented with contemporary musical styles. In its more recent history, bhangra has been fused with disco, reggae, techno, house, rap, ragga and now jungle. In fact, these new styles have been so successful that modern bhangra is now being re-exported back to India. Most of this tends to come from the UK Desi scene, a subculture found amongst the South Asian diaspora.

Bhanumathi Ramakrishna : Dr.Bhanumathi Ramakrishna, illustrious actress, directress, music directors Songstress and writer was born in Ongole. Dr. Bhanumathi is a born artiste, inheriting music from her parents and received sound training in music and histrionics from her father. Since then she has worked in over 100 pictures in almost all the languages of South India and also in Hindi.

She proved that at a time when family girls were not inclined to act in films, by acting in films she proved that even respectable family girls can act in films. She received the National Awards as Best Actress for three times.

Bharat Heavy Electricals Limited or BHEL : BHEL is an acronym for Bharat Heavy Electricals Limited, a Gas and Steam turbine manufacturer in India. This is one of the Public Sector Undertakings. Some of its manufacturing units are located in Trichi and Ranipet in Tamil Nadu, India.

Bharat Milap : Bharat Milap which is celebrated during the month of October or November is performed at Nati Imli on the day following Vijayadashmi (Dusshera). It pertains to the episode of the return of Lord Rama to Ayodhya after 14 years of exile, and his reunion with his brother Bharat. Just as the last rays of the setting sun touch the stage, the performance takes barely three minutes to enact.

Bharat Petroleum : Bharat Petroleum, a Forbes 2000 company, is one of India's largest petroleum refining corporations and is owned by the government of India. The company is headed by Ashok Sinha. Bharat Petroleum's annual sales for the year 2004–2005 stood at $12.77 billion and had earned a profit of $470 million. The company employs more than 12,400 people and has a market value of $2.94 billion.

Bharat Ratna : Bharat Ratna is India's highest civilian award, awarded for the highest degrees of national service. This service includes artistic, literary, and scientific achievements, as well as "recognition of public service of the highest order." Unlike knights, holders of the Bharat Ratna carry no special title nor any other honorifics, but they do have a place in the order of precedence. Bharat Ratna roughly translates as 'Gem of India'.

The original specifications for the award called for a circular gold medal, 35 mm in diameter, with the sun and the Hindi legend "Bharat Ratna" above and a floral wreath below. The reverse was to carry the state emblem and motto. It was to be worn around the neck from a white ribbon. There is no indication that any specimens of this design were ever produced and one year later the design was altered.

The original statutes of January 1954 did not make allowance for posthumous awards (and this perhaps explains why the decoration was never awarded to Mahatma Gandhi), though this provision was added in the January 1955 statute. Subsequently, there have been ten posthumous awards, including the award to Subhash Chandra Bose in 1992, which was later withdrawn due to a legal technicality, the only case of an award being withdrawn.

While there was no formal provision that recipients of the Bharat Ratna should be Indian citizens, this seems to have been the general assumption. There has been one award to a naturalized Indian citizen — Agnes Gonxha Bojaxhiu, better known as Mother Teresa (1980); and two to non-Indians — Khan Abdul Ghaffar Khan (1987) and Nelson Mandela (1990). The awarding of this honour though, has frequently been the subject of litigation questioning the constitutional basis of such state awards.

Bharat Ratna Medallion : An image of the Sun along with the words "Bharat Ratna", inscribed in Devanagari script, on a peepul leaf.

The original specifications for the award called for a circular gold medal, 35 mm in diameter, with the sun and the Hindi legend "Bharat Ratna" above and a floral wreath below. The reverse was to carry the state emblem and motto. It was to be worn around the neck from a white ribbon. There is no indication that any specimens of this design were ever produced and one year later the design was altered.

The original statutes of January 1954 did not make allowance for posthumous awards (and this perhaps explains why the decoration was never awarded to Mahatma Gandhi), though this provision was added in the January 1955 statute. Subsequently, there have been ten posthumous awards, including the award to Subhash Chandra Bose in 1992, which was later withdrawn due to a legal technicality, the only case of an award being withdrawn.

While there was no formal provision that recipients of the Bharat Ratna should be Indian citizens, this seems to have been the general assumption. There has been one award to a naturalized Indian citizen — Agnes Gonxha Bojaxhiu, better known as Mother Teresa (1980); and two to non-Indians — Khan Abdul Ghaffar Khan (1987) and Nelson Mandela (1990). The awarding of this honour though, has frequently been the subject of litigation questioning the constitutional basis of such state awards.

Bharat Sanchar Nigam Limited or BSNL : BSNL or Bharat Sanchar Nigam Limited is India's largest Communication Service Provider (CSP), and seventh largest in the world. Previously known as DoT(Department of Telecommunications) when it was under federal government control, it became a corporation in 2000. BSNL operates across the length and breadth of India (except the metropolitan cities of Mumbai and New Delhi which is managed by MTNL) and commands over 45 million landlines and mobile connections. Since its corporatisation in October 2000, BSNL has been actively providing connections in both Urban and Rural areas and the efficiency of the company has drastically improved from the days when one had to wait for years to get a phone connection to now when one can get a connection in even hours. Pre-activated Mobile connections are available at many places across India. BSNL has also unveiled very cost-effective Broadband internet access plans targeted at homes and small businesses. BSNL aims to have 150—175 million active connections by the year 2010. With the frantic activity in the communication sector in India, the number will be easily achievable. Today, BSNL is the No. 1 Telecommunications Company and the largest Public Sector Undertaking of India with authorized share capital of $ 3977 million and networth of $ 14.32 billion. It has a network of over 45 million lines covering 5000 towns with over 35 million telephone connections. With latest digital switching technology like OCB,EWSD,AXE-10,FETEX,NEC etc. and widespread transmission network including SDH system upto 2.5 gbps, DWDM system upto 80 gbps,Web telephony,DIAS,VPN, Broadband and more than 400,000 data customers.

Bharata : Bharata, sometimes Bharatavarsha (Bharat or Bharatvarsha in Hindi) is the name in Sanskrit and many languages of India for the northern India. The Hindi form is also an official name of the Republic of India, and possibly the earliest name given to the nation. (Article 1 of the Constitution of India - 'India that is Bharat shall be a Union of States.'). The name "Bharata" is derived from either of two ancient Hindu kings named Bharata, though it is more commonly accepted that the name derives from that of the son of Dushyanta, whom the Mahabharata credits with bringing the whole of Bharatavarsha under his rule and securing the title of an emperor.

"Bha" in Sanskrit means knowledge or light, and "rat" is a verb for 'doing'. Bharat is therefore 'the one in search of knowledge.' Bharatavarsha also means The Land of Bharata, and The Cherished Land. The name Bharata means The Cherished One in Sanskrit. The name derives from the times of Vedic civilization after King Bharata, who first conquered all of the known world, which was duly named after him in his honor. Hence his descendents were called as the Bharatas. In all the classical and religious works of Hinduism, such as the Mahabharata and Ramayana, the Puranas and Upanishads, Bharat is the name used for what is today known as northern India. Note that in Vedic Sanskrit, the most important meaning of the word Bharata was the epithet of Agni as the deity of knowledge. King Bharata himself may have been named after the Vedic Goddess Bharati. Images of the Goddess describe her as bearing a trident and accompanied by a lion

Bharata Muni : Bharata Muni was an ancient Indian writer whose life has been dated variously from the 5th century BCE to the 2nd century. His best known work is the Natya Shastra, a theoretical treatise on Indian performance, including theater, dance, acting, and music, which has been compared to Aristotle's Poetics. The classical dance form Bharath Naty is codified in Natya Shastra. He classifies Indian theatrical forms in to 10 forms and drama(Natak) is just one among such forms. Other forms are Dima, Bana, etc....

Bharata Natyam : Bharata Natyam was the dance technique evolved in the South of India in Tamil Nadu and practiced in the temples of Shiva. It is a highly specialised science with a traditional background and rigid codes and conventions. Bharata Natyam skillfully embodies the three primary ingredients of dancing. They are bhava or mood, raga or music and melody and tala or timing. The technique of Bharata Natyam consists of 64 principles of coordinated hand, foot, face and body movements which are performed to the accompaniment of dance syllables.

For many centuries Bharata Natyam has been performed only by certain families in the district of Tanjore, these inheritors of the craft being known as 'Nattuvans'. The chief exponents of this dance were the Devadasis or temple dancers. They would perform the dance daily at the time of worship or on festive occasions.

It came to be patronized by the Rajas and princes. In course of time Devadasis started dancing in the royal courts and thus its religious sanctity was lost.

Bharata Natyam stands in the forefront of all the classical dance arts now prevalent in India, owing to its religious origin and its highly developed technique. It is the form of dance most akin to the code compiled by the sage Bharata Muni in his famous 'Natya Shastra'. The modern form of Bharata Natyam presentation is the arrangement of four Nattuvans of Pandanallur. They were the brothers- Ponniah, Chinniah, Vadivelu and Sivanandam, who lived in the eighteenth century. The Vidwan, Menaskshi Sunderam Pillay of Pandanallur, the greatest teacher of Bharata Natyam is a direct descendant of the four brothers.

It was Rukmini Devi Arundale, the celebrated dancer and scholar who took this Dance form out of the temple and gave it a new respectability. She started a school at Tiruvanmiyur, (the village just outside Madras) named Kalak-Shetra. The age-old, 'Gurukulam' system of education is still followed and many classes are conducted in sylvan surroundings. In the Nataraja temple-(temple of the dancing Shiva) at Chidambaram, poses of the classical Bharata Natyam are sculpted around the shrines and on the gate ways

Bharathanatyam : Bharathanatyam, the most famous classical dance of India originated in Tamil Nadu.

Bharathapuzha River : The Bharathapuzha, also known as the Ponnani or Nila, is a river in India in the state of Kerala. At 209 km, it is the second-longest river in Kerala after the Periyar.

Bharathidasan : Bharathidasan was a twentieth century Tamil poet and rationalist whose literary works handled mostly socio-political issues. His writings served as a catalyst for the growth of the Dravidian movement in Tamil Nadu.

In addition to poetry, his views found expression in other forms such as plays, film scripts, short stories and essays. He was mentored by Mahakavi Subramanya Bharathi (after whom he called himself "Bharathidasan"). But Bharathidasan, unlike Bharathi rarely used words derived from Sanskrit in his works; also Bharathidasan's works were more political.

Bharati Theertha Swamigal : Shri Bharati Theertha Swamigal is the Jagadguru and Shankaracharya of the Advaitic Sringeri Sharada Peetham. Born in Andhra Pradesh, he became a disciple of Shri Abhinava Vidya Theertha Swamigal and was later appointed as head of the Mutt.The mutt he heads,has a huge following among the Vedic Community. As a child in the mother's womb,he spread halo around her.When he was delivered,people felt that there was something extraordinary about the child.Even as a child,he was proficient in Sanskrit. He was deeply committed to learning the Vedas.

He requested his father not to burden him with Modern Education. He wanted to dedicate his life to Vedic Study. His father who allowed him to study the Vedas, was not sure if a dedicated study would be feasible. In any case the young Boy,impressed the Seer (Abhinava Vidya Theertha) of Sringeri,with his proficiency in Sanskrit,when he got an opportunity to meet him. The Guru decided to accept the Boy in the Veda Pathashala at Sringeri. His father agreed to send him there.Here he got opportunity to attend classes given by the senior seer himself.He excelled in his studies more than anyone else, and was known for his dedication to the principles of Brahmacharya.

His dedication did not go unnoticed and visitors to the mutt were charmed by the Boy. The seer was also pleased by the spiritual Boy. Thus it was no surprise when the Seer appointed the Boy as his successor.After initiation into Sanyasa, the young man meticulously followed the instructions of his Guru and impressed everyone with his Knowledge and Understanding. Swamigal spent huge amount time on meditation and was called as Tapas Chakravarty.

Swamigal is a quiet and non controversial person. In spite of being the head of one of the most prestigious mutts in India, he does not advertise himself or his organisation, but rather spends his time contemplating on God. He is a guide for all those who want to learn from him, and could be considered as one of the most knowledgable Vedantins living today.

Bharatiya Jana Sangh : The Bharatiya Jana Sangh (abbreviated BJS, and often known simply as the Jan Sangh) existed from 1951 to 1980, whereupon it was succeeded by the Bharatiya Janata Party, one of India's largest political parties. Its name is Hindi for Indian People's Alliance.

The BJS was started by Dr Syama Prasad Mookerjee (also spelt as Shyama Prasad Mukherjee) on 21st October 1951 at Delhi in consultation with the RSS. The symbol of the party in Indian elections was the lamp. In 1952 general elections to the Parliament of India, Bharatiya Jana Sangh had won three seats - Dr. Mookerjee being one of the winning candidates. The BJS would often link up on issues and debates with the right-wing Swatantra Party of Chakravarti Rajgopalachari. Its strongest parliamentary performance came in the 1967 elections, when the Congress majority was its thinnest-ever.

The BJS was ideologically close to the Rashtriya Swayamsevak Sangh, and derived most of its political activist base and candidates from the RSS ranks. The BJS was considered the political arm of Hindu Nationalism, with the RSS being the central base. The Vishwa Hindu Parishad, formed in 1967 would become the religious arm.

The BJS also attracted many conservative Congressmen who were disenchanted with the policies and politics of Jawaharlal Nehru and Congress socialists. The BJS's strongest constituencies were in Rajasthan, Gujarat, Maharashtra, Madhya Pradesh and Uttar Pradesh.

The BJS leadership strongly supported a stringent policy against Pakistan and China, and were averse to the USSR and political Communism in India. Many BJS leaders also inaugurated the drive to ban cow slaughter nationwide in the early 1960s.

In 1975, Indira Gandhi declared a state of Emergency, and threw many major opposition politicians in jail including the leaders of the BJS. In 1977, the Emergency was withdrawn, and elections were held. The BJS, joined forces with the Bharatiya Lok Dal, the Congress (O), and the Socialist Party, to form the Janata Party (People's Party). The Janata Party became the first Indian government not led by the Indian National Congress. Former BJS leaders Atal Bihari Vajpayee and L. K. Advani became the External Affairs (Foreign), and Information and Broadcasting Ministers respectively.

After the Janata Party's poor showing in the 1980 elections, the former Bharatiya Jan Sangh members left to form the Bharatiya Janata Party, which has been one of the three largest Indian political parties since 1989.

Bharatiya Janata Party (BJP) : The Bharatiya Janata Party (BJP), literally meaning Indian People's Party, created in 1980, is one of the two major national political parties in India. It projects itself as a champion of socio-religious cultural values of the country's Hindu majority, conservative social policies and strong national defense. Its constituency is strengthened by the broad umbrella of Hindu nationalist organizations, informally known as the Sangh Parivar (Family of "Sangh" organizations), where the Rashtriya Swayamsevak Sangh play a leading role. Since its inception, the BJP has been a prime opponent of the Indian National Congress. It has allied with regional parties to roll back the left-centrist tendencies formerly endorsed by the Congress Party, which dominated Indian politics for four decades. The ideological rallying cry of the BJP is Hindutva, literally "Hinduness," or cultural Hindu nationalism. BJP, in alliance with several other parties, led the Government of India between 1998 and 2004, under Prime Minister Atal Bihari Vajpayee and Deputy Prime Minister Lal Krishna Advani, its most senior leaders. It has done so as the leading party within the National Democratic Alliance, of which it remains a part even today, and leads the opposition.

Bharatpur : Bharatpur is a city in Rajasthan state of India. It was founded by Maharaja Suraj Mal in 1733. Located in Mewat region, Bharatpur was once an impregnable, well-fortified city, and the capital of a kingdom ruled by Jat maharajas. The trio of Bharatpur, Deeg and Dholpur has played an important part in the Jat history of Rajasthan. Located 50 km west of the city of Agra (the city of the Taj Mahal), it is also the administrative headquarters of Bharatpur District.

The town was named Bharatpur after Bharata, a brother of Lord Rama, whose other brother Laxman is the family deity of the erstwhile royal family of Bharatpur. The name 'Laxman' was engraved on the arms, seals and other emblems of the state.

The city and the fort of Bharatpur have been believed to be founded by Rustam, a Jat chieftain belonging to the Sogariya clan. With the decline of the mughal empire in the early 17th century, the Jats established a state in the Mewat region south of Delhi, with its capital at Deeg. Leaders like Gokula, Raja Ram, Churaman and Badan Singh brought the Jats together and moulded them into a force to be reckoned with.

Maharaja Suraj Mal was the state's greatest ruler; he made the state a formidable force in the region. Suraj Mal took over the site of Bharatpur from Khemkaran, a son of Rustam, and established it as the capital of his state. He fortified the city by building a massive wall around it.

During the British Raj, the state covered an area of 5,123 sq.km.; its rulers enjoyed a salute of 17 guns. The state acceded unto the dominion of India in 1947. It was merged with three nearby princely states to form the 'Matsya Union', which in turn was merged with other adjoining territories to create the present-day state of Rajasthan.

Bharti Telecom : Bharti Telecom is among India's largest mobile phone operator. With more than a million subcriptions, the company is one of the world's fastest growing telecom company. It offers its moblie services under Airtel brand and is headed by Sunil Mittal, one of India's richest man with a total worth of 2.6 billion $US.

Bharuch : Bharuch is located in Bharuch District, Gujarat. Bharuch was once a small village on the banks of the Narmada River. It was considered to be sacred among sages, and they would come to Bharuch and pray. Excavations near the banks of the river Narmada in Bharuch have revealed many archeological and architectural wonders, mostly temples. Later Bharuch was part of the Mauryas, the Guptas, and Rudrama. As part of the Sultanate of Gujarat, it was subsequently annexed by the Mughals, and finally by the British.

Bharuch has always been prosperous because of its location on the Narmada River. Although water tends to be scarce in Gujarat, one never finds difficulty in getting water in Bharuch. As a result of this, agriculture and other linked commercial activities have flourished in Bharuch. Bharuch is also a central stopping point for many villages spread around its boundaries such as Palej, Valan, Vareydiya, Kamboli e.t.c. People from these small villages come to Bharuch when they want to shop for new clothes, or make a major purchase. Lately a lot of retiring ex-patriots have been returning to Bharuch and building new houses giving the economy a boost.

Modern Bharuch is one of the most heavily industrialized areas, not only in Gujarat but in India as a whole, with many large chemical plants producing fertilizers, paints, dyes, cotton, textiles, and dairy products. Bharuch has also advantage of Gujarat's biggest Liquid Cargo TERMINAL

Bhaskara : Bhaskara (1114-1185), also called Bhaskara II and Bhaskara Acharya ("Bhaskara the teacher") was an Indian mathematician-astronomer. He was born near Bijjada Bida in Bijapur district, Karnataka, South India and became head of the astronomical observatory at Ujjain, continuing the mathematical tradition of Varahamihira and Brahmagupta. In many ways, Bhaskara represents the peak of mathematical and astronomical knowledge in the 12th century. He reached an understanding of calculus, astronomy, the number systems, and solving equations, which were not to be achieved anywhere else in the world for several centuries or more. His main works were the Lilavati (dealing with arithmetic), Bijaganita (Algebra) and Siddhanta Shiromani (written in 1150) which consists of two parts: Goladhyaya (sphere) and Grahaganita (mathematics of the planets).

Bhatiore : A region between in sub district Chiniot of District Jhang in Punjab Province of Pakistan is named as Bhatiore. The area is collection of villages, towns and wells. The reason behind the name of the village is that the area is populated by the famous Bhatti tribe, the major population and leading tribe of the area is Bhatti and also almost all the lands of the region is owned by them. The bhattis of the area seem to having been migrated from Bikaner and Jaisalmer as some villages are named as Jaisalwala, Maru Bhattian etc. Famous town of the area is Barana which is at the boundary of district Sargodha.Others villages and town names are Kot Sultan, Burhani Bhattian, Kanianwali, Kot Ameer, Ganja Bhattian, Inayatpur, Ghoriwala, Thatta Umra,Peer Panja, Gaushewala etc.

Bhatiyali : Bhatiyali is a traditional boat song of eastern Bengal, sung in a specific mode, noted for its long-drawn notes. In riverine Bangladesh, boatmen spent a lot of time in their boats. While sailing downstream, they had plenty of leisure to sing comfortably in the drawn out and elevated notes characteristic of the bhatiyali. In course of time, this song gained popularity particularly in mymensingh and sylhet districts.

At one time, there were five types of bhatiyali in Bangladesh. But some of these forms are extinct at present. The songs known as murshidi and bichchhedi are also forms of the bhatiyali. Strains of bhatiyali can be found in Bangla folk drama, especially in the form known as gazir gan.

In many instances, the word bhatiyali is used in a song to point out the note of a specific verse. Usually in 'Pala' or panchali, the first verse of the bandana or hymn is referred to as the ujan (upstream) and the second verse as bhaital (downstream), for example: 'In the east, I salute the sun god/ When the sun arises from one side, light penetrates all sides'.

Bhavai : Bhavai (Strolling Players) is a popular folk theatre form of Gujarat. Veshas(means costume) or Bhavai plays are also known as swang. The origin of Bhavai goes back to 14th Century.It is said that Hemala Patel's(a resident of a village called Unza) daughter Ganga was kidnapped by a Muslim Subedar. Their family priest Asait Thakar, a resident of Siddhapur, rushed to the subedar claiming Ganga to be his own daughter.Subedar asked Asait Thakar to eat with Ganga from the same plate to prove that she is really his daughter. Asait did that but for this he incurred the ire of his own caste men and was excommunicated as he had taken food with a low caste Ganga. He started earning his living by performing plays which later came to be known as Bhavai.

Bhavani : The Bhavani is a river of southern India, a tributary of the Kaveri. The river's headwaters are on the eastern slopes of Western Ghats range, in Malappuram district of Kerala state. The river flows northwest, into Tamil Nadu, draining the south slope of the Nilgiri Hills. It joins its main tributary, the Moyar River, which flows in from the northeast, where it drains the valley between the northern slopes of the Nilgiris and the southern slopes of the Bilgiri Hills. After joining the Moyar, the Bhavani flows due east, past the town of Sathyamangalam, joining the Kaveri at the town of Bhavani, The Sangameswarar Temple was built at the confluence of the two rivers, and is an important pilgrimage spot in southern India.

Bhavani Island : Located in Vijayawada at a distance of 4 km. from Vijayawada, the Bhavani Island is situated upstream of River Krishna close to Prakasam Barrage. It is a good picnic spot for nature lovers.

Bhavani River : The Bhavani is a river of southern India, a tributary of the Kaveri. The river's headwaters are on the eastern slopes of Western Ghats range, in Malappuram district of Kerala state. The river flows northwest, into Tamil Nadu, draining the south slope of the Nilgiri Hills. It joins its main tributary, the Moyar River, which flows in from the northeast, where it drains the valley between the northern slopes of the Nilgiris and the southern slopes of the Bilgiri Hills. After joining the Moyar, the Bhavani flows due east, past the town of Sathyamangalam, joining the Kaveri at the town of Bhavani, The Sangameswarar Temple was built at the confluence of the two rivers, and is an important pilgrimage spot in southern India.

Bhavnagar : Bhavnagar is a city in the Gujarat state of India. It is administrative Headquarter of Bhavnagar District. This sprawling industrial city was founded in the 1743 by Bhav Sinhji Gohil as a port in 1743. It is still a prominent trading post for cotton products. Bhavnagar's commercial importance is enhanced by its proximity with the Gulf of Cambay and the Arabian Sea.

The city offers vibrant shades of traditional Gujarati culture to the traveler. Bhavnagar is also a suitable stopover for the tourists who are venturing to the Jain temples at Palitana on the Shatrunjaya Hills, Sirohi and the Blackbuck National Park, Velavadar — the home of the famous Indian Blackbuck.

Bhelpuri : Bhelpuri is a snack synonymous with the beaches of Mumbai (Bombay). The snack is available all across India, and may be known by different names— Bhelpuri in Mumbai, Jhaal Muri in Kolkata.

Puffed rice forms the base of the bhel. Finely cut tomatoes, onions and chillies are added to this base. Chutneys may be added to give it a sweet or spicy flavour. Sev, a chick-pea based topping is sprinkled and garnished with coriander leaves. It is then served with toasted puris, (a deep fried wheat bread). The result is a sour/pungent/sweet tasting evening snack.

Bhera : Bhera is a town in the Punjab Province of Pakistan. It is located on the Jhelum River in Sargodha District, at Latitude 32.48 N, Longitude 72.92 E. Pop. (1901) 18,680. It is the terminus of a branch of the North-Western railway. It is an important centre of trade, with manufactures of cotton goods, metal-work, carving, etc. Bhera was founded about 1540 on its present site, but it took the place of a city on the opposite bank of the river, of far greater antiquity, which was destroyed at this period.BHERA is located on the mid of Lahore-Islamabad motorway (M2) at the left bank of river Jehlum near Southern Salt Range in District Sargodha. Before independence 1947, it was located in district Shahpur.

Bhikaji Rustom Cama : Bhikaji Rustom Cama (Madam Cama, Madame Cama) (September 24, 1861-August 13, 1936) was a prominent figure in the Indian Nationalist Movement. Bhikaji Rustom Cama was born Bhika Sorab Patel on 24th September, 1861 in Bombay (now Mumbai) into a large, well-off Parsi (Persian) family. On August 3, 1885, she married Rustom Cama, a wealthy, pro-British lawyer with a desire to enter politics.

In October 1896, the Bombay Presidency (as it was then known) was first hit by famine, and shortly thereafter by bubonic plague. Bhikaji joined one of the many teams working out of Grant Medical College (which would subsequently become Haffkine's plague vaccine research center), in an effort to provide care for the afflicted, and (later) to inoculate the healthy. She contracted the plague herself, but survived. Severly weakened, she set sail for Europe for subsequent medical care and recuperation in 1902. In London, she recieved word that her return to India would be prevented unless she sign a statement promising not to participate in nationalist activities. She refused, and remained in exile in Europe until shortly before her death in 1936.

While in London, she served as private secretary to Dadabhai Naoroji, the first Asian to be elected to the British House of Commons, and the first to publicly demand independence from Great Britain. In Paris she came in contact with other notable members of the movement for Indian sovereignty, and would come to clandestinely (in Holland) publish and distribute revolutionary literature for the movement. While in France, the British Government requested her extradition, but the French Government refused to cooperate. In return, the British Government siezed Cama's inheritance.

Bhikaji Cama is best known for having unfurled a "Flag of Indian Independance" on August 22, 1907, at the International Socialist Conference in Stuttgart, Germany. That flag, a slight modification of the Calcutta Flag, was co-designed by Cama, Veer Savarkar and Shyamji Krishna Varma, and would later serve as a template upon which the current national flag of India is based.

Bhil : Bhils are a tribal people of central India. They speak Bhil languages, a group of Indic languages. Bhils are a scheduled tribe in the states of Gujarat, Madhya Pradesh, Maharashtra, and Rajasthan in western and central India, as well as in Tripura in far-eastern India, on the border with Bangladesh. The ghoomar dance is one well-known aspect of Bhil culture. In feudal and colonial times, many Bhil were employed by the ruling Rajput in various capacities, e.g. as shikari because of their knowledge of the terrain.

Bhilai : Bhilai is the second-largest city in Chhattisgarh, India with a population of 553,837 (2001 census}. The Bhilai/Durg agglomeration is the largest in the state (923,559). The city is located 40 km west of the capital Raipur on the Howrah-Mumbai rail line, and National Highway 6. It is famous for the Bhilai steel plant, one of the largest in India. Nearby mines, connected to the steel plant by specially built rail lines, supply it with iron ore, dolomite, and manganese. In addition to steel, the plant manufactures railway sleepers, rails, construction materials, and other steel products. Other factories in Bhilai produce chemicals, acids, and gases.

The nearest big railway station is Durg, other railway stations being Bhilainagar, Bhilai Powerhouse, Kumhari and Bhilai-3. Bhilai is a known educational centre for sending large number of students to Indian Institutes of Technology. Delhi Public School has been exceptional in its standards of quality of education and leads the way for schools throughout the state. Formerly a small town, Bhilai grew rapidly in the decades following the construction of the steel plant. During 1990's and 2000's Bhilai has emerged as an excellent educational centre both and school and college level. 5 enginnering colleges have come up in and around the city contributing to the educational needs in technological fields for the new developing state.

Bhils : Bhils are a tribal people of central India. They speak Bhil languages, a group of Indic languages. Bhils are a scheduled tribe in the states of Gujarat, Madhya Pradesh, Maharashtra, and Rajasthan in western and central India, as well as in Tripura in far-eastern India, on the border with Bangladesh. Bhils are also settled in Tharparkar district of Sindh in Pakistan. The ghoomar dance is one well-known aspect of Bhil culture. In feudal and colonial times, many Bhil were employed by the ruling Rajput in various capacities, e.g. as shikari because of their knowledge of the terrain

Bhilwara : Bhilwara is a town in Mewar region of Rajasthan, India, 600 km from Delhi. It is the administrative seat of Bhilwara District. The major industry is textiles, with more than 400 manufacturing units in the town. There is also a huge cloth market. The main textile product is synthetic fabric used in trousers.

Bhima River : The Bhima River is a river in western India. The river originates in the forest of Bhimashnakr in Pune, and flows through the states of Maharashtra and Karnataka.It is a major tributary of the Krishna River.

Bhimber : The Bhimber district was carved out of Mirpur district in 1995. Prior to this it was a sub-division (Tehsil) of the Mirpur district. The district is bounded to Mirpur district in the northwest, shares borders with occupied Kashmir in the east. It is bounded to Pakistan in the west and south. Total area of the district is 1516 square kilometers and is divided in three tehsils. According to 1998-census total population of the district stands at 297,000 while its population according to 1999 projections is approx 303,000. The area is very rich in archaeological remains. Bhimber falls on the route that was followed by the Moghul rulers of India for their frequent visits to the Kashmir Valley.

Bhimbetka : Bhimbetka is a place in Madhya Pradesh where the earliest known traces of human life in India were found. Stone age rock shelters and paintings date back 9,000 years. The region is declared a World Heritage Site. Bhimbetka is one of the oldest sites in the world where petroglyphs have been found.

'Rock Shelters of Bhimbetaka' lie 45 km south of Bhopal, and are located at the southern edge of the Vindhyachal hills. Towards south of these rock shelters are successive ranges of the Satpura hills. The entire area is covered by thick forests and vegetation. The area has abundant natural resources like perennial water supplies, natural shelters, rich forest flora and fauna and bear significant resemblance to similar rock art site like Kakadu National Park in Australia.

As reported in UNESCO citation declaring Bhimbetaka as a World Heritage Site, Bhimbetka was first mentioned in Indian archeological records in 1888 as a Buddhist site – based on information gathered from local adivasis. Long thereafter, while V. S. Wakankar was traveling by train to Bhopal, he saw some rock formations of similar nature which he has seen in Spain and France. He visited the area along with a team of archaeologists and discovered several prehistoric rock shelters.

Since then, more than 700 such shelters have been identified, of which 243 are in Bhimbetka group and 178 in Lakha Juar group. Archeological studies revealed a continuous sequence of Stone Age cultures (from the late Acheulian to the late Mesolithic), as also the world's oldest stone walls and floors. Earliest paintings on the cave walls are believed to be of Mesolithic period. Broad chronology of the finds has been done, but a detailed chronology is yet to be created.

Bhimrao Ramji Ambedkar : Bhimrao Ramji Ambedkar (April 14, 1891—December 6, 1956) has been called the most prominent Indian Untouchable leader of the 20th century.

He was born in Mhow of Madhya Pradesh state in central India, the fourteenth child of parents who belonged to the very lowest stratum of Hindu society, known as Untouchables or Dalits.

He helped spark a revival of Buddhism in India, a movement which is now known as neo-Buddhism He was posthumously awarded the Bharat Ratna in 1990.

Bhimsen Joshi : Bhimsen Gururaj Joshi (born February 14,1922) is popularly known as Pandit Bhimsen Joshi is a renowned khyal Vocalist in Indian classical, or Hindustani music. A master of kirana stream of Hindustani, he spent his life performing, teaching, researching and Popularising it in India. He was awarded Padma Vibhushan, India's Second highest civilian Honour in 1999. He has done many songs in other forms of Indian music.

Pandit Bhimsen Joshi was born in a small town Gadag, in the Dharwad district of Karnataka in South India. In 1933, 11-year old Bhimsen Left his home on his own to learn singing through Guru -Shishya (Master-desciple) tradition. He spent three years in Gwalior, Lucknow and Rampur in North India trying to get a good master.

Bhimsen Joshi first performed live at 19. His debut album, a few devotionals songs in Kannada and Hindi,came out when he was 20. He lives and teaches music in Pune, India. Sawai Gandharva Sangeet Sammelan, An annual classical music festival in Pune, is his initiative. The notable awards Bhimsen received include Padma Shree, The Sangeet Natak Academy Award, Padma Bhushan Awards etc.

Bhind District : This is a district of Madhya Pradesh state in central India around Chambal region. The town of Bhind is the district headquarter. Bhind District is situated in Chambal region in the northwest of the state. It is bounded by Agra, Etawah, Jalaun and Jhansi districts of Uttar Pradesh state to the north and the east, and the Madhya Pradesh districts of Datia to the south, Gwalior to the southwest, and Morena to the west. The geography of the district is characterized by uneven ravines, plain fertile fields and scanty forests. The total area of the district is 4,459 km^2. The soil of Bhind is very fertile and is well drained by the Chambal, Kali Sind, Kunwari or Kwari,Pahuj and Baisali rivers and by an extensive canal system. Formerly there were four tehsils, Bhind, Mehgoan, Gohad and Lahar, but at present there are seven tehsils: Bhind, Ater, Mehgaon, Gohad, Lahar, Mihona, and Raun. The district is part of the Chambal Division.

Bhindawas Bird Sanctuary : Bhindawas Bird Sanctuary in district Jhajjar is around 15 km from Jhajjar town and is about 3 and a half hours drive from Delhi. The lake and the birds in it are the main attraction of this complex. The Sanctuary is spread over an area of 1074 acres which makes it considerably larger than the *Sultanpur Bird Sanctuary*. The peripheral embankment is man made and basically constructed to store the escaped water of Jawaharlal Nehru canal through an escape channel at the time of power failure of Lift Canal System. The Bhindawas lake is being used by the migratory and resident birds of about 250 species. The best time to visit is December-January when you can view the maximum number of birds.

Bhishma Ekadashi : Bhishma Ekadashi is dedicated to Bhishma the grand old warrior of Kurukshetra and the son of Ganga and Shantamu. This festival is celebrated on the eleventh day of the bright fortnight in the month of Magha. Only pious Brahmins and well-read Kshatriyas observe this day. As Bhishma died childless, the observers think that it was their duty to make libations of water to his spirit. Brahmins observe a fast, to perform puja to Bhishma and break their fast on Dwadasi, is the subsequent day by parajama a feast. Kshatriyas invite their priests and hear the story of Bhishma's life and give them provisions and money.

Bhishmaknagar Forts : Roing in Dibang valley district in Arunachal Pradesh is known for the historical fort of Bhishmaknagar named after the king Bhismaka located at the foot of the mountains between the Dikrong and the Dibang rivers. The Bhishmaknagar Fort which was first excavated in 1996-97, testifies to the penetration of the Aryan culture into Arunachal in the 4th century A.D. The fort built with clay bricks and embellished with pottery has an elongated semi circle shape extending over an area of about 10 sq. km. Accommodation is available at the circuit house and Inspection Bungalow at Roing. The nearest airport is in Dibrugarh (Assam) and the nearest railway station is Tinsukia. Buses are available from Sadiya (24 miles).

Bhitar Kanika National Park : Bhitar Kanika National Park in Balesore district in an area of 167sq.km is better known as a marine park. The park with its mangrove forests in the rivers Brahmani- Bhaitarani Delta and creeks, estuaries, back water, accreted land and mud flats was mainly established to protect the saltwater crocodile and other marine inhabitants of the region. It was notified as a Crocodile sanctuary in 1975 and a crocodile breeding centre has been established by the Orissa Government.

The park contains tidal swamp forests consisting of an abundance of mangrove, saltwater and brackish water mixed species such as Causarinas, Thespia, grasses like indigo bush etc. It is the second largest viable stretch of mangrove forest in the Indian mainland. The Fauna of the park include Olive ridley turtles (sea turtle), saltwater crocodiles, wild pigs, rhesus monkeys, leopard, wild boar, hyena, jungle cat, sambar, giant squirrel, water monitor, chitals, king cobra, python, fishes besides insects and other micro fauna. Birds found are strokes, ibis, white necked sea eagle and fish eagle etc. The best season for visiting the park is winter (November to February). The park situated along the Gahiramatha Coast is a haven for thousands of marine species especially the Olive ridley turtles which come here to lay eggs during the nights in winter. The giant Pacific Ridley sea turtles believed to come as far away as South America nest on the Gahirmatha Coast

Bhitarkanika Mangroves : The Bhitarkanika Mangroves are a mangrove wetland in India's Orissa state. The Bhitarkanika Mangroves cover an area of 650 km^2 in the river delta of the Brahmani and Baitarani rivers.

The Bhitarkanika Mangroves are home to 55 of India's 58 known mangrove species. The mangroves harbor one of India's largest populations of saltwater crocodiles, and Gahirmatha Beach, which separates the mangroves from the Bay of Bengal, is the world's most important nesting beach for Olive Ridley Sea Turtles. The wetland also hosts a large and diverse population of resident and migratory birds.

The Bhitarkanika Mangroves were Zamindari forests until 1952, when the government of Orissa abolished the Zamindari system, and put the Zamindari forests in the control of the state forest department. In 1975, an area of 672 km² was declared the Bhitarkanika Wildlife Sanctuary. The core area of the sanctuary, with an area of 145 km², was declared Bhitarkanika National Park in September 1998. The Gahirmatha Marine Wildlife Sanctuary, which bounds the Bhitarkanika Wildlife Sanctuary to the east, was create in September 1997, and encompasses Gahirmatha Beach and an adjacent portion of the Bay of Bengal. Bhitarkanika Mangroves were designated a Ramsar Wetland of International Importance in 2002.

Bhitarkanika National Park : Bhitarkanika National Park is a national park located in the Kendrapara District of Orissa in India. The park encompasses with an area of 145 km² of the Bhitarkanika Mangroves, a mangrove swamp which lies in the river delta of the Brahmani, Baitarani, and Dhamara rivers. The national park is surrounded by the Bhitarkanika Wildlife Sanctuary. Gahirmatha Beach lies to the east, and separates the mangroves from the Bay of Bengal.

The park is home to the Saltwater Crocodile (Crocodylus porosus), white crocodile, Indian python, black ibis, and darters. Olive Ridley sea-turtles (Lepidochelys olivacea) nest on Gahirmatha and other nearby beaches. The national park was created in September 1998 from the core area of the Bhitarkanika Wildlife Sanctuary, which had been created in 1975

Bhiwani : Bhiwani, a district in Haryana, India, has an area of 5099 sq. km. Situated between 28.19 deg. & 29.05 deg. north latitude and 75.26 deg. and 76.28 deg. east longitude, it has 442 villages with a population of 1.42 million. The district headquarters is the city of Bhiwani, which is around 124 kilometers from Delhi. The city, it is believed, was founded by a Rajput named Neem after his wife Bhani. The name Bhani later changed to Bhiyani and subsequently to Bhiwani. The city finds mention in Ain-e-Akbari and has been a prominent center of commerce since time of Mughals. Bhiwani is known for its numerous temples and therefore is also called the little Kashi a.k.a. Benares of India.

Other major towns in the district of Bhiwani are Dadri, Loharu, Tosham and Bawani Khera. Excavations (1968-73 and 1980-86) in the village of Mitathal in Bhiwani have unearthed evidence of pre-Harappan and Harappan (Indus Valley Civilization) culture in the area. Near the village of Naurangabad, about 10 km from Bhiwani, preliminary diggings in 2001 have revealed artifacts like coins, tools, sieves, toys, statues and pots up to 2500 years old. According to the archeologists the presence of coins, coin moulds, statues and design of the houses, suggests that a town existed here sometimes in the Kushan, Gupta and the Youdheya period till 300 BC.

Bhiwani district has also a very religious respect. It is called as "Chhota Kashi" because of the number of temples in the city. There are very famous temples in Bhiwani. Apart from this, some big industries are also here such as Bhiwani Textile Mills, unit of Grasim industries.

Bhojpuri : Bhojpuri is a Bihari language spoken in northeastern India in the western part of state of Bihar, the northwestern part of Jharkhand, and the Purvanchal region of Uttar Pradesh, as well as an adjoining area of southern plains of Nepal. Bhojpuri is also spoken in Guyana, Suriname, Fiji, Trinidad and Tobago and Mauritius and is often said to be the only Indian language to be spoken on all continents.

People's attitudes towards the Bhojpuri language have evolved over time, and most linguists agree it is not a dialect of Hindi, which is a widespread belief among speakers. The government of India is preparing to grant it statutory status of as national scheduled language.

Bhojpuri shares vocabulary with Sanskrit, Hindi, Urdu and other Indo-Aryan languages of northern India. Bhojpuri and several closely related languages, including Maithili and Magahi, are together known as the Bihari languages. They are part of the Eastern Zone group of Indo-Aryan languages which includes Bengali and Oriya.

There are numerous dialects of Bhojpuri, including three or four in eastern Uttar Pradesh alone. Some notable Bhojpuri personalities are the first president of India, Rajendra Prasad, Bollywood actors Amitabh Bachchan, Manoj Bajpai, and former Indian prime minister Chandra Shekhar.

Bhola Cyclone : The Bhola cyclone was a powerful tropical cyclone that made landfall in East Pakistan (now Bangladesh) on 13 November 1970. It is the deadliest known tropical cyclone of all time; an estimated 500,000 people lost their lives, mostly through drowning. On the night of 12 November a tropical cyclone in the Bay of Bengal was approaching the coast of East Pakistan. Winds believed to be in excess of 120 mph (190 km/h), combined with an exceptionally high storm surge of 15 to 20 feet (5 to 6 m), drove a tidal surge into the low lying, densely populated region in the early hours of the morning. The result was widespread flooding, with many people drowning in their sleep.

The official death toll was put at 500,000, with 100,000 people missing, making it the deadliest tropical cyclone on record. Many estimates put the figure higher. It is also one of the deadliest natural disasters in modern times, being comparable to the 1976 Tangshan earthquake and the 2004 Indian Ocean earthquake (due to uncertainty over death tolls, it may never be known for sure which of these natural disasters was the deadliest). The highest loss of life and destruction occurred on the low lying islands of the Ganges Delta south of Dhaka. The island and district of Bhola (where casualties may have exceeded 100,000) was particularly impacted, with the towns of Charfasson and Tazumuddin being devastated. The city of Chittagong was also badly affected.

The Bay of Bengal is particularly vulnerable to cyclone disasters. The next most comparable disaster in the area was the 1991 Bangladesh cyclone which killed over 140,000 people. Bangladesh Cyclobe 1991 : On the night of 29 April 1991 a powerful tropical cyclone struck the Chittagong district of southeastern Bangladesh with winds of around 155 mph. The storm forced a 6 meter (20 foot) storm surge inland over a wide area, killing at least 138,000 people and leaving as many as 10 million homeless. An area of persistent cloudiness, in part due to the monsoon trough, developed into a tropical depression on April 22 in the Bay of Bengal. The wind speed and overall size increased, with the depression becoming Tropical Storm 2B on the 24th. The entire wind field at the time encompassed nearly the entire Bay.

The tropical storm continued slowly northwestward, slowly strengthening to a cyclone-strength storm on the 27th. The cyclone moved between a high pressure system to its northwest and east, and as mid-level westerlies met up with the storm, the cyclone moved northeastward. The westerlies enhanced upper level outflow, and in combination with warm water temperatures the cyclone steadily strengthened to a major hurricane on the 28th. On the 28th and 29th, as the system increased its speed to the north-northeast, the cyclone rapidly intensified to a 160 mph Cyclone, the equivalent to a Category 5 hurricane. Late on the 29th, Cyclone 2B made landfall a short distance south of Chittagong as a slightly weaker 155 mph Category 4 Cyclone. The storm rapidly weakened over land, and dissipated on the 30th over southeast Asia.

Bhola Cyclone : The Bhola cyclone was a powerful tropical cyclone that made landfall in East Pakistan (now Bangladesh) on 13 November 1970. It is the deadliest known tropical cyclone of all time; an estimated 500,000 people lost their lives, mostly through drowning. On the night of 12 November a tropical cyclone in the Bay of Bengal was approaching the coast of East Pakistan. Winds believed to be in excess of 120 mph (190 km/h), combined with an exceptionally high storm surge of 15 to 20 feet (5 to 6 m), drove a tidal surge into the low lying, densely populated region in the early hours of the morning. The result was widespread flooding, with many people drowning in their sleep.

The official death toll was put at 500,000, with 100,000 people missing, making it the deadliest tropical cyclone on record. Many estimates put the figure higher. It is also one of the deadliest natural disasters in modern times, being comparable to the 1976 Tangshan earthquake and the 2004 Indian Ocean earthquake (due to uncertainty over death tolls, it may never be known for sure which of these natural disasters was the deadliest). The highest loss of life and destruction occurred on the low lying islands of the Ganges Delta south of Dhaka. The island and district of Bhola (where casualties may have exceeded 100,000) was particularly impacted, with the towns of Charfasson and Tazumuddin being devastated. The city of Chittagong was also badly affected.

The Bay of Bengal is particularly vulnerable to cyclone disasters. The next most comparable disaster in the area was the 1991 Bangladesh cyclone which killed over 140,000 people. Bangladesh Cyclobe 1991 : On the night of 29 April 1991 a powerful tropical cyclone struck the Chittagong district of southeastern Bangladesh with winds of around 155 mph. The storm forced a 6 meter (20 foot) storm surge inland over a wide area, killing at least 138,000 people and leaving as many as 10 million homeless. An area of persistent cloudiness, in part due to the monsoon trough, developed into a tropical depression on April 22 in the Bay of Bengal. The wind speed and overall size increased, with the depression becoming Tropical Storm 2B on the 24th. The entire wind field at the time encompassed nearly the entire Bay.

The tropical storm continued slowly northwestward, slowly strengthening to a cyclone-strength storm on the 27th. The cyclone moved between a high pressure system to its northwest and east, and as mid-level westerlies met up with the storm, the cyclone moved northeastward. The westerlies enhanced upper level outflow, and in combination with warm water temperatures the cyclone steadily strengthened to a major hurricane on the 28th. On the 28th and 29th, as the system increased its speed to the north-northeast, the cyclone rapidly intensified to a 160 mph Cyclone, the equivalent to a Category 5 hurricane. Late on the 29th, Cyclone 2B made landfall a short distance south of Chittagong as a slightly weaker 155 mph Category 4 Cyclone. The storm rapidly weakened over land, and dissipated on the 30th over southeast Asia.

Bhonsle : The Bhonsle or Bhonsale were a prominent Maratha clan who served as rulers of several states in

India. The most prominent member of the clan was Sivaji, the founder of the Maratha empire. His successors ruled as maharajas from their capital at Satara, although de facto rule of the empire passed to the Peshwas, the Marathas' hereditary chief ministers, during the reign of Shahu I.

In addition to the Bhonsle Maharajas of Satara, rulers of the Bhonsle clan established themselves at Thanjavur in Tamil Nadu in the 17th century, and at Nagpur and Kolhapur in modern-day Maharashtra in the 18th century. The Bhonsle of Thanjavur were descendants of Sivaji's half-brother Venkaji, while the Bhonsle of Satara and Kolhapur were descended from Sivaji's sons, Sambhaji and Rajaram.

After the British defeat of the Marathas in the Third Anglo-Maratha War in 1818, the Marathas were forced to accept British rule. The four Bhonsle dynasties continued as rulers of their princely states, acknowledging British sovereignty while retaining local autonomy. The states of Nagpur, Thanjavur, and Satara came under direct British rule in the mid-nineteenth century when their rulers died without male heirs; Kolhapur continued as a princely state until India's independence in 1947, when the rulers acceded to the Indian government.

Bhoota (or Kola) : This is a ritual dance, similar to Teyyam of Malabar Coast, typical of the South Kanara district of Karnataka.

Bhopal : Bhopal is a city in central India. It is the capital of the Indian state of Madhya Pradesh. Bhopal has earned the sobriquet City of 7 Lakes

Bhopal Agency : Bhopal Agency was an administrative section of British India's Central India Agency. The Bhopal Agency was formed in 1818 at the conclusion of the Third Anglo-Maratha War, and consisted of the princely state of Bhopal and the smaller princely states of Khilchipur, Kurwai, Narsingarh, Muhammadgarh, Pathari, and Rajgarh to the northwest of Bhopal. It was administered by an agent to the British Governor-General of India. In 1931 the two princely states of Dewas, known as junior and senior, were added to the agency, and in 1933 the state of Makrai was transferred from the Central Provinces and Berar.

After Indian independence in 1947, the rulers of these states acceded to the Government of India. All of the states but Bhopal were incorporated into the new state of Madhya Bharat, and Bhopal became its own state. Madhya Bharat and Bhopal were merged into Madhya Pradesh state on November 1, 1956.

Bhotiya : The Bhotiya, also known as the Bhutia, lived in the trans-Himalayan region that divides India from Tibet. In Uttaranchal, they are known as Bhotiya, rather than the common Bhutia. The word Bhotiya came from the word Bod, which literally refers to Tibet. The Indian government uses the word Bhotiya to refer to those who have traditionaly resided in the upper Himalayan valleys of Kumaon and Garhwal of Uttaranchal state. Those include the Shaukas of Kumaon and Tolchhas and Marchhas of Garhwal. Shaukas, further consist of two sub-groups, residing in two different river valleys. Joharis live along the Goriganga river valley in Munsiyari Tehsil of Pithoragarh district, while the Rungs live along the Mahakali river valley in Dharchula teshil and Darchula district of Nepal.

The Bhotiya speak languages belonging to the Tibeto-Burman family, although their dialects are mutually unintelligible to the Tibetans and Garwhalis. Owing to social process of Sanskritization, many of them have intermarried with the Aryans over the years. Most of the Bhotiya practice a combination of Tibetan Buddhism, Bön and Hinduism, although Hinduism is prevalent among the earlier semi-Aryan groups, while Buddhism is prevalent among the recent immigrant groups of purer Tibetan origin, such as the Jadh. Hindu gods such as the weather God Gabla, Runiya and Suniya, are worshipped to protect their animals from disease. Sidhuwa and Bidhuwa are worshipped as well to find lost animals.

Bhubaneswar : Bhubaneswar (in Sanskrit and Oriya, "The Lord of the Universe") is a city located on the eastern coast of India. Once the capital of ancient Kalinga, the city has a long history and is today a bustling centre for commerce and religious activity. Bhubaneswar became the modern capital of the state of Orissa in 1948, a year after India gained its independence from Britain. The city is inhabited by over a million people and maintains a high rate of population growth.

Bhuj : Bhuj is a town in Gujarat, India. Bhuj the capital of the former native state of Kutch is now the head quarter of the Kutch district. Bhuj was chosen by Rao Khengarji I as his capital in 1549. Bhuj, the major town of Kutch, is an old walled city- in the past the city gates were locked each night from dusk to dawn. You can lose yourself for hours in the intricate maze-like streets and alleyways of this fascinating town. There are walls within walls, attractive crenellated gateways, old palaces with intricately carved wooden pavilions, and striking, brightly decorated Hindu temples. Bhuj resembles much of India before the tourist invasion, and you're much more likely to come across that disarming hospitality which was once the hallmark of rural India. Unfortunately if there has been no monsoon, the picturesque lake remains dry. The epicenter of 2001 Gujarat Earthquake was near Bhuj. This earthquake, measuring 6.9 magnitude on the Richter scale, reduced Bhuj to rubble.

Bhujia : Bhujia or Aloo Bhujia—an indian spicy snack or farsan that is similar to fine chopped potato fritters. It is ussually used as a topping on various Indian meals but has now become popular to eat alone as a snack.

Bhupinder Singh Hooda : Bhupinder Singh Hooda (born September 15, 1947) is an Indian politician and the current Chief Minister of Haryana. Previously, he has been a Member of Indian Parliament (Lok Sabha) for four terms in 1991, 1996, 1998, 2004 and the Leader of Opposition in Haryana's Legislative Assembly from 2001 to 2004.

Ch. B.S. Hooda also served as the President of HPCC (Haryana Pradesh Congress Committee) from 1996 to 2001. For three consecutive Lok Sabha terms he entered Indian Parliament defeating Ch. Devilal another tall Jat leader in famous electoral battles fought in the Jat heartland of Rohtak in Haryana. Mr. Hooda is well known for leading various farmer movements in Haryana. He is from the Indian National Congress. He is also a Member of the Bar Council of Punjab and Haryana.

Bhurban : Bhurban is a small town approximately an hour drive (13 kilometers) away from Murree, Pakistan. One of the most picturesque places in the country, it is a tourist paradise with fauna, flora and a wide variety species of animals not found elsewhere in Pakistan. It is known for a nine hole golf course, which is golfer delight during summer season. Bhurban is infact name of the nearby forest. The village itself is called Rawat which is also headquarter of a Union Council of the same name. It is situated on all weather Murree Kashmir road at a height of about 6000 feet.

Bhutias : The Bhutias or Bhotias are people of Tibetan origin, who migrated to Sikkim, India and Bhutan some time after the 15th century. They migrated through Bhutan and they are very closely related to the main Bhutanese population, the Ngalop, who are sometimes classifed as Bhutia. In Northern Sikkim, where the Bhutias are the majority inhabitants, they are known as the Lachenpas or Lachungpas.

The language spoken by the Bhutias is Sikkimese, which is 65% intelligible with Dzongkha, the language of Bhutan. Most of the Bhutias practice Tibetan Buddhism or Hinduism, often practicing a mix of these religions, although a very small number have converted to Christianity. The Bhutia are spread out over Nepal, Bhutan, and in the northern West Bengal towns of Kalimpong and Darjeeling. Bhutia is also often used as a derogatory term, used by people of Nepali heritage to describe people with Tibetan features.

Bibhutibhushan Bandopadhyay : Bibhutibhushan Bandopadhyay was a Bengali novelist and writer. He is most well known for the epic Pather Panchali (The story of the road), made into the memorable film trilogy by Satyajit Ray. Bibhutibhushan was born on 12 September 1894 at his maternal uncle's house in Ghoshpara-Muraripur village, in the 24-Parganasof Bengal. His father, Mahananda Bandyopadhyay, was a sanskrit scholar and a 'Kathak', one who tells stories for a living.

Pather Panchali is considered to be Bibhutibhushan's masterpiece. He has 16 novels and over two hundred short stories to his credit. Bibhutibhushan's works are mostly concerned with the lives of people from rural Bengal. His writings come alive with vibrant and thoroughly normal characters from the countryside.Bibhutibhushan is, without doubt, one of the most important Bengali novelists that Bengal ever produce.

Bibi Mariam's Mosque : Bibi Mariam's Mosque and Tomb situated at Hajiganj locality in Narayanganj. The mosque is said to have been built by Nawab shaista khan, Mughal subahdar of Bengal (1664 - 1688) and ascribed to Bibi Mariam, presumably his daughter who lies buried close by. The mosque is of the three domed type, but has lost much of its original features through later repairs; especially the corner towers have been completely modernised. The eastern facade has usual three arched entrances—each opening under a half-dome, and the central one wider than the other two. The interior hall has simple lateral arches, but the reduction of the size of the side domes is achieved by thickening the side walls. The basal leaf decoration of the three domes and the battlemented merlons speak of the common style. The mosque has been repaired and renovated several times and extended; a verandah added on the east. It is now used as a Jami mosque.

Bibi Russell : Bibi Russell is a fashion designer and former international model from Bangladesh. Born in Chittagong, Bangladesh, she studied in London College of Fashion, earning a graduate degree in 1975. In the next five years, she worked as a model for different magazines including Vogue, Cosmopolitan and Harper's Bazaar. She also worked as a fashion model in fashion shows until 1994, working with Yves Saint Laurent, Kenzo, Karl Lagerfield and Giorgio Armani. Having returned to Bangladesh in 1994, Bibi opened Bibi Productions, her own fashion house, fusing indigenous Bengali cultural elements into her line. With assistance from UNESCO, she organized her first European fashion show in paris in 1996. As of 2004, her company employed 35,000 weavers in rural Bangladesh. Her enterpreneurship has earned her many awards. The Asiaweek magazine highlighted her as "one of the 20 people to watch in the millennium".

Bibi-ka -Maqbara : It was built around 1657-1661, in Maharashtra,by the last of the six great Mughal Emperors, Aurangazeb, for his wife, Rabia Durrani. Aurangazeb's mausoleum is far less ornamental, than Taj Mahal. The mausoleum stands in a square of 1,37,00 sq. meters. The monument is an excellent example of Persian Architecture. It's more attractive at night, when it's floodlit. It's open from sunrise to 10pm.

Bicholim : Bicholim is a town in the territory of Goa, and the headquarters of the consuelho (district) of the same name; the Consuelho of Bicholim, located in the north-east quarter is one of the seven that make up the Novas Conquistas or New Conquests, territories added to Goa comparatively latter than the first three of the Velhas Conquistas. The town is located about 30 kilometres from the capital Ponnjhe. It is in the mining heartland of Goa.

Bicolored Frog : The Bicolored Frog (Rana curtipes) is a species of frog found in the Western Ghats. This frog is not very active and has a very toad like disposition. The tadpoles of the species are black and form dense and compact schools in slow moving streams in forested areas.

Bidar : Bidar is a city in Karnataka state, India. It is the administrative seat of Bidar District. Bidar was the capital of the Bahmani Sultanate from 1425 until the sultanate's breakup after 1518. It then became the center of one of the five independent sultanates, known as the Deccan sultanates, that were the successor states to the Bahmani kingdom. The Bidar Sultanate was absorbed by the Sultanate of Bijapur to the west in 1619, which was in turn conquered by the Mughal emperor Aurangzeb in 1686. Bidar was part of the Nizam of Hyderabad's dominions from 1724 to 1948, when Hyderabad was annexed to India to become Hyderabad state. In 1956, Hyderabad was partitioned along linguistic lines, and Bidar district became part of Mysore state, later renamed Karnataka. Bidar city is known for its unique Bidri handicraft products. Manjra is one of the main rivers supplying driking Water for Bidar and Hyderabad cities.

Biddery Ware : Biddery Ware is the ware of tin, copper, lead, and zinc, made at Bidar, in India. The ancient and eye-catching craft of Bidri entered India more than 4000 years ago from the culture-rich Persians, Syrians and Iranians. Bidri craftsmen were patronized in the Mughlai courts and settled down to practice their craft in the fortress town of Bidar in Karnataka, giving the craft its name. It originated with the ornamentation of royal swords and other weapons, and was later applied to domestic use in items like cigar and cigarette boxes.

Behind the breathtaking beauty of Bidri lies hours of painstaking effort by the artisan. The original technique involved the inlaying of gold or silver on a steel or copper base. This method had its origins in Persia. However, the metal used for the base today is an alloy of zinc and copper. The content of zinc gives the alloy a deep black color. It is engraved or overlaid with silver or brass. After casting and moulding, the surface is filed smooth till it acquires the typical Bidri sheen. It is then temporarily blackened with copper sulphate solution and etched into a traditional design using a sharp iron tool. Silver wire or sheets are beaten into the designed grooves, making it stand out like the stars in the night sky. During the final oxidation process, the shiny surface is briefly heated and rubbed with a thick paste of ammonium chloride. The chemical is supposedly mixed with a special clay from the walls of the Bidar Fort. The final step is using groundnut or coconut oil to polish each item, which may be a vase, bangle, bracelet, goblet, ashtray, plate, Jewellery or box.

Bidhan Chandra Roy : Dr. Bidhan Chandra Roy (July 1, 1882 – July 1, 1962) was the second Chief Minister of West Bengal, India. He remained in his post for 14 years as a Congress Party candidate, from January 14, 1948 until his death in 1962. He was a respected physician and a renowned freedom fighter.

He was an alumnus of the Medical College Calcutta of the University of Calcutta. In India, the Doctors Day is celebrated on the date of his birth (and death) July 1 every year. The nation honored Dr. Roy with the Bharat Ratna on February 4, 1961. On July 1, 1962.

Bidhan Nagar : Once a swampy stretch of land on the eastern fringe of Calcutta, Bidhan Nagar, or Salt Lake as it is popularly called, is a well planned and well-to-do satellite township developed to accommodate the booming population of Calcutta, India. It is not to be confused with its namesake city in the United States. It is famous as one of the nicer places in the city and also a centre for the IT industry.

Bihar : Bihar is a state of the Indian union situated in the eastern part of the country. Its capital is Patna. Etymologically, the name Bihar derives from the Sanskrit Vihara which means abode. The Buddhist Vihara, which were the abode of the Buddhist monks, dotted the area in the ancient and medieval periods. To Bihar's north is the Kingdom of Nepal. On its other three sides Bihar is surrounded by the Indian states of Uttar Pradesh to the west, Jharkhand to the south and West Bengal to the east. Bihar lies in the very fertile Gangetic plains. Culturally, it is a part of the Hindi heartland of India.

Bihar People's Party : Bihar People's Party was a political party in the Indian state of Bihar, founded by Rajput strongman and former leader of the Samajwadi Krantikari Sena paramilitary faction Anand Mohan Singh. Singh had previously been a member of Janata Dal, Samata Party and All India Rashtriya Janata Party. He had been elected to Lok Sabha as a SAP candidate in 1996 and as a AIRJP candidate in 1998. The wife of Singh, Lovely Anand, was a high-profile leader of BPP. BPP merged with the Indian National Congress on February 28 2004.

Bihar-E-Sharif : Bihar-E-Sharif, also called Bihar Sharif, is a small town in Nalanda district, Bihar, India. It is headquarter of Nalanda district. The neighbouring places of tourist interest are Rajgir, Pawapuri and Nalanda. The town is mostly agriculture economy although a Railway coach factory is being built in Noorsarai. The own is well connected by railway to all the major cities e.g. Delhi (Shramjeevi Express, 2392) (Magadh Express, 2401), Patna(Many local and Express trains are available at regular interval), Calcutta, Kanpur, Lucknow, Allahabad, Varanasi etc. Politically this small town has given some famous politicians like George Fernades, Nitish Kumar and more.

Bihari : Bihari (1595-1664) was a hindi poet, who is famous for writing Satasai (Seven Hundred Verses). Bihari wrote poetry in shringar ras depicting the divine love of Krishna and Radha.

Bihu Festivals : The national festivals of the Assamese, irrespective of caste, creed or religion are the Bihus. It is secular in concept because it is intimately connected with agriculture. There are three Bihus that come off at various stages of cultivation of paddy, the principal crop of Assam. They are Bahag (Baisakh) Bihu, Kati (Kartika) Bihu and Magh (Magha) Bihu. Among the Bihus, spring festival called Bahag Bihu is the most important. The Bahag Bihu is also popularly called Rangali Bihu or the Bihu that cheers, while Magh Bihu is the Bhogali Bihu or the Bihu that one enjoys with food and drink. In between comes the Kati Bihu observed on the last day of Aswin, also called the Kangali or Beggars bihu, for there is nothing much to eat at this time.

Bijapur : Bijapur is a district headquarters of the Bijapur district in the state of Karnataka. Bijapur city is well known for the great architectures of histrorical importance built during the Adil Shahi dynasty. Bijapur City is the head quarters of the district and is located 530 km northwest of Bangalore.

The city established in the 10th-11th centuries by the Chalukyas of Kalyani was referred as Vijayapura (City of victory). The city came under the influence of the Khilji Sultanate in Delhi by the late 13th century. In 1347, the area was conquered by the Bahmani Sultanate of Gulbarga. By this time the city was being referred as Vijapur or Bijapur

Bijayananda Patnaik : Son of Lakshminarayan and Ashalata Patnaik, Bijayananda Patnaik was born in Cuttack, Orissa (India) on March 5, 1916. He studied Aeronautics at the Aeronautical Training Institute of India. He joined the Indian National Airways, where he was involved with the war effort from 1940 to 1942. He was thereafter imprisoned until 1945 due to his activism efforts with the Quit India Movement. Inspired by Mahatma Gandhi, Gopabandhu Das, and Madhusudhan Das, Patnaik dedicated himself to the Indian Freedom Movement.

Patnaik was closely associated with the Nepalese Democratic Movement since 1953 and he was also instrumental in assisting Indonesia with its bout for Independence from the Dutch in 1947. Using his piloting skills, Patnaik was able to fly Indonesian Prime Minister Sultan Sjahrir and staff to Singapore, and finally to Dehli where Sjahrir was able to meet Jawaharlal Nehru. Nehru affectionately called Patnaik "India's buccaneer". During his time in the Indian parliament, Nehru said of him, "Biju Patnaik has the courage, dynamism, and zeal to work. So there is no blunder in giving more aid to Orissa."

Patnaik was also the Chief Minister of Orissa from 1961 to 1963, as well as for a 2nd term starting in 1990 until 1995. He was also a prominent member of both the Lok Sabha and the Rajya Sabha. Patnaik's political ideals were centered in Socialism and Federalism. His strong advocacy for equal resources to all Indian states who needed such, made him a champion of his Oriyan constituents.

The projects which he was known to have spearheaded include the Port of Paradip, Orissa aviation centre, Bhubaneswar Airport, the Cuttack-Jagatpur Mahanadi highway bridge, and the Choudwar and Barbil industrial belts. He died in New Dehli on April 17, 1997 of cardio-respiratory failure.

Bijnor : Bijnor is a town, which is the district headquarters of Bijnor district of Uttar Pradesh state, India. Of the early history of Bijnor even after it passed under Muslim rule little is known with any certainty. The district was ravaged by Timur in 1399, and thenceforward nothing is heard of it till the time of Mughal emperor Akbar, when it formed part of the Delhi empire and so continued undisturbed, save for occasional raids, so long as the power of the Moguls survived intact. In the early part of the 18th century, however, the Rohilla Pashtuns established their independence in the country called by them Rohilkhand; and about 1748 the Rohilla chief Ali Muhammad made his first annexations in Bijnor, the rest of which soon fell under the Rohilla domination

Bijoy Dibash : Bijoy Dibash commemorates the day in 1971 (16 December) when ninety thousand troops of the Pakistan occupation army surrendered to the allied forces of Bangladesh and India at Suhrawardy Udyan in Dhaka. The day is observed with due solemnity and nationalistic fervour. The first ray of the morning is heralded with a 31 gun-salute. In capital Dhaka, there is usually a ceremonial military parade in which all uniformed services are represented. Hundreds of thousands of people gather at the National Parade Square to watch this parade. Floral wreaths are laid at the Jatiya Smriti Saudha (National Memorial Monument) at Savar near Dhaka in memory of those who sacrificed their lives for the liberation of the country

Bijoy Ketan Museum : Bijoy Ketan Museum established in memory of the War of Liberation, freedom fighters, and the heroes who got Gallantry Awards. The motto of the Bijoy Ketan Museum is: 'Honour the Past, Enlighten the Future'. The main markers of the museum are: historical background to Bangladesh, the military prison where Bangabandhu Sheikh Mujibur Rahman remained confined during Agartala Conspiracy Case. These have been named Hall of Fame. In addition, visitors can see exhibits like the original copy of the constitution of Bangladesh, the National Flag, the map, and the National Anthem imprinted on metal-plate. At the main gate, there is a sculpture of the seven vigilant freedom fighters, one of whom is a woman holding a Bangladeshi flag. This particular sculpture is also called Bijoy Ketan. Bangabandhu Museum is virtually a part of Bijoy Ketan Museum, although it has a separate name and is situated a few yards to the north of the Hall of Fame.

Biju Janata Dal : The Biju Janata Dal is a regional party of the Indian state of Orissa. It has its roots in the rickety Janata Dal, which formed several short-lived governments at the Centre. After splitting from Janata Dal, the BJD has participated in several ruling coalitions with the Hindu nationalist Bharatiya Janata Party both at the Centre and in Orissa. The BJD, however, was one of the main professedly secular parties of the National Democratic Alliance.

Biju Patnaik Airport : Biju Patnaik Airport (IATA: BBI, ICAO: VEBS) also known as Bhubaneswar Airport, Biju Patnaik Airport is situated in the city of Bhubaneswar. It is currently the only major airport in Orissa, India. It is named after the former Chief Minister of Orissa Biju Patnaik, who was also a famed aviator and freedom fighter. The runway length is 5850 ft. Runway elevation is 146 ft. The airports coordinates are 85° 49' 0" E, 20° 14' 0" N.

Bikaner : Bikaner is a city in north-western Rajasthan state in western India. It is the administrative headquarters of Bikaner District. It was formerly the capital of the princely state of Bikaner. One of the most famous landmarks of Bikaner is Deshnokh Temple, a temple where rats roam around freely, and spotting a white rat is considered lucky. The Bikaner city was founded by Rao Bikaji and it progressed from small place to big economical city of the western desert.The Gang canal now "Indira Gandhi canal has changed the area. The city has diversified in various industrial areas with global presence.Bikaner wool, Gypsum,Plastic of Paris and Bentonite are few minerals found in abundant aroung Bikaner.

Bikram Choudhury : Bikram Choudhury (born 1946) is the founder of Bikram Yoga, a copyrighted series of 26 hatha yoga postures that are performed in a hot (105 degrees Fahrenheit or greater) environment. Bikram is a disciple of Bishnu Ghosh, brother of Paramahansa Yogananda, (author of Autobiography of a Yogi). The Bishnu Ghosh guru lineage has focused on translating Eastern philosophies and practices into a language that is more closely attuned to the Western mindset than can be found within their original traditional Indian contexts.

Born in Calcutta, India, Choudhury won the National India Yoga Championship four consecutive years in his teens. As an adult he opened yoga schools in India and Japan, and in the early 1970s opened his first U.S. school near Hollywood, California. In the Nineties he began offering 9-week teacher certification courses, and certified instructors now number in the hundreds with franchised ("Yoga College of India") schools all over the world. Generically known as "hot yoga," Choudhury's style remains prominent as the one of the most popular methods of yoga done in a heated room.

Bilaspur : Bilaspur is a district of Himachal Pradesh state, India. It is famous for the manmade Govind Sagar Lake on the Sutlej River which acts as the reservoir for the Bhakra and Nangal Dam project. The road bridge on this lake at Kandraur is highest of its kind in Asia. Its headquarters are in the town of Bilaspur. The district has an area of 1,167 km², and a population of 340,735 (2001 census).

Bilaspur District was formerly a princely state of British India. The ruler acceded to the Government of India on October 12 1948, and Bilaspur was made an Indian state under a chief commissioner. The state of Bilaspur was merged with Himachal Pradesh on July 1, 1954, and became Bilaspur District. Administratively, the district is divided into three tehsils, Ghumarwin, Bilaspur Sadar, and Jhandutta. Jhandutta was created out of Gumarwin in January 1998. Naina Devi is a sub-tehsil of Bilaspur Sadar, and was created in January 1980.

Biligirirangan Hills : The Biligirirangan Hills, commonly called B R Hills, is a hill range situated in south-eastern Karnataka, at its border with Tamil Nadu in South India. The area is a Wildlife Sanctuary under the Wildlife Protection Act, 1973. The hills are in the Yelandur Taluk of Chamarajanagar district of Karnataka. The hills are contiguos with the Satyamangalam range southwards, in the Erode district of Tamil Nadu. It is 90 km from Mysore and 180 km from Bangalore. It is connected by road, one from Yelandur and the other via Chamarajanagar. The hills are located at the easternmost edge of the Western Ghats and support diverse flora and fauna in view of the various habitat types supported. A wildlife sanctuary of 322.4 km² was created around the temple on 27 June 1974, and enlarged to 539.52 km² on 14 January 1987. The sanctuary derives its name "Biligiri" from the white rock face that constitutes the major hill crowned with the temple of Lord Rangaswamy or from the white mist and the silver clouds that cover these lofty hills for a greater of the year.

Bimal Roy : Bimal Roy (July 12, 1909—January 7, 1966), nicknamed Bimalda, was one of the most successful Hindi film directors of all time. He is particularly noted for his 1955 work Devdas, which starred Dilip Kumar as the lead. Roy was born in Dhaka, Eastern Bengal, British India (now Bangladesh). Bimal Roy entered the field of cinema as a camera assistant. During this time, he assisted director P.C. Barua on the hit 1935 movie Devdas, starring K.L. Saigal. In the 1940s and 1950s Roy was part of the parallel cinema movement in post-war India. He was famous for his romantic-realist melodramas that took on important social issues while still being entertaining. He was a filmmaker of great and in-depth understanding of human strengths and weaknesses.

Biman Bangladesh Airlines : Biman Bangladesh Airlines is an airline based in Dhaka, Bangladesh. It is the national airline and operates domestic services and international routes to Asia, Europe and the United States. Its main base is Zia International Airport, Dhaka. Biman Bangladesh was established on 4 January 1972 and started operations in February 1972, when a Douglas DC-3 that had seen action in World War II was given to the company as a present by the Bangladesh Air Force. Soon after, a Boeing 707 and Fokker F27 Friendship aircraft joined the airline's fleet, allowing Biman to begin international flights.

In 1983 Biman acquired Douglas DC-10 aircraft, and subsequently other planes such as the Airbus A310, Fokker F28 and British Aerospace BAe ATP. On January 31, 2003, the airline received 2 Boeing 737s.

The airline is 100% owned by the Bangladesh government. However, the government is now planning to offer 40% of Biman to foreign airlines, with the intention that the buyer will assume management control of the carrier. A further 9% of the airline will go to employees.

Bimbisara : Bimbisara (ruled 544-491 BCE) was a king of the Magadha empire and belonged to Haryanaka dynasty. There are many accounts of him in the Buddhist Jatakas, since he was a contemporary of Gautama Buddha. He acquired Anga and placed it under the viceroyalty of Ajatashatru at Champa. He also strengthed his position by marriage alliances. His first wife was the daughter of the king of Kosala and sister of Prasenajit. The Kosali bride brought him Kashi village as dowry. This marriage also ended the hostility of Kosala and gave him free hand in dealing with the other states. His second wife, Chellana, was a Lachchhavi princess from Vishali and his third wife was a daughter of the chief of the Madra clan of Punjab. Tradition tells us that Bimbisara was imprisoned by his son Ajatashatru who is said to have starved him to death. This is reported to have taken place around 492 BC.

Bimbisara's Jail : King Bimbisara was imprisoned here by his impatient son and heir, Ajatashatru. The captive king chose this site for his incarceration. For, from this spot, he could see Lord Buddha climbing up to his moutain retreat atop the Griddhakuta Hill. There is a clear view of the Japanese Pagoda. The stupa of peace was built on the top of the hill.

BIMSTEC : BIMSTEC or Bay of Bengal Initiative for MultiSectoral Technical and Economic Coorperation is an international organisation involving a group of countries in South Asia and South East Asia. The member nations of this group are : Bangladesh, India, Myanmar, Sri Lanka, Thailand, Bhutan and Nepal.

The organisation was formed in Bangkok, Thailand, on 6 June 1997. Initially, its name was BIST-EC (Bangladesh, India, Sri Lanka, Thailand Economic Cooperation). At that time, Myanmar was an observer, but later joined the organization as a full member at a special ministerial meeting held in Bangkok on 22 December 1997. Consequently, the name of the organisation was changed to BIMST-EC. Nepal was granted observer status by the second Ministerial Meeting in Dhaka, Bangladesh in December 1998. Later, full membership has been granted to Nepal and Bhutan in 2003. During the first summit in Bangkok on 31 July 2004, the organisation's name was changed to its current name.

Binat Bibi Mosque : Binat Bibi Mosque is one of the first mosques in Bengal area; Bakht Binat, daughter of Marhamat built in 1454 during the rule of Sultan Mahmud Shah I. Binat Bibi's mosque is located in Narinda, Dhaka.It is square and single domed mosque with octagonal corner towers. Entrance is from east, north and south. The mosque measures 12' square internally. Pre-Mughal features included in the curved cornice, battlements.

Bindusara : Bindusara was the second Mauryan emperor (297—c.272 BC) after Chandragupta Maurya. The Greeks called him Amitrochates—the Greek word for the Sanskrit 'Amitraghata' (Slayer of Enemies). Bindusara inherited a large empire that consisted of what is now, North, Central and East India and the parts of Afghanistan and Baluchistan. Bindusara extended this empire to the southern part of India, as far as what is now known as Karnataka. He brought sixteen states under the Mauryan Empire and thus conquered almost all of the Indian peninsula (he is said to have conquered the 'land between the two seas'—the peninsular region between the Bay of Bengal and the Arabian Sea). Bindusara didn't conquer the friendly Dravidian kingdoms of the Cholas, Pandyas, and Cheras. Apart from these southern states, Kalinga (the modern Orissa) was the only kingdom in India that didn't form the part of Bindusara's empire. It was later conquered by his son Ashoka, who served as the viceroy of Ujjaini (Ujjain) during his father's reign.

Bindusara's life hasn't been documented as well as his father Chandragupta or his son Ashoka. The philosopher Chanakya served as prime minister during his reign. During his rule, the citizens of Taxila revolted twice. The reason for the first revolt was the maladministration of Suseema, his eldest son. The reason for the second revolt is unknown, but it could not be suppressed by Bindusara due to his untimely death, but was later crushed by Ashoka. Ambassadors from Syria and Egypt visited his courts. He maintained good relations with the Hellenic World. Unlike his father Chandragupta (who was a Jain), he believed in the Ajivika (an atheist and anti-Brahminical philosophy). Bindusara died in 272 BC (some records say 268 BC) and was succeeded by his son Ashoka the Great. Bindusara is known as "The Son of a Father and the Father of a Son" because he was the son of a great father Chandragupta Maurya and father of a great son Ashoka, the Great.

Bipin Chandra Pal : Bipin Chandra Pal was born on November 7, 1858 in Sylhet, (now in Bangladesh), in a wealthy Hindu Kayastha family. His father was Ramchandra Pal. He was a teacher, journalist, orator, writer and librarian who started the journal Bande Mataram.

He was one of the trilogy of the three Extremist patriots of the Indian National Congress who had fought and gave his life during Indian independence movement in the first half of the twentieth century. The other two were Lala Lajpat Rai and Bal Gangadhar Tilak. Together they were known as Lal-Bal-Pal.

They had advocated extremist means to get their message across to the British, like boycotting British manufactured goods, burning Western clothes made in the mills of Manchester and strikes and lock outs of British owned businesses and industrial concerns. He came under the influence of eminent Bengali leaders of his time such as Keshab Chandra Sen and Pandit Sivanath Sastri, and joined the Brahmo Samaj. He was imprisoned for six months on the grounds of his refusal to give evidence against Sri Aurobindo in the Bande Mataram sedition case.

Pal opposed Gandhiji's non-cooperation Movement of 1920. The first Congress session he attended was in 1886 as a delegate from Sylhet. He virtually retired from politics from 1920 though he expressed his views on national questions till his death on May 20, 1932.

Bir Bikrom : Bir Bikrom (literally, "Valiant hero" in Bangla) is the third highest gallantry award in Bangladesh.

Bir Protik : Bir Protik (Symbol of Bravery) is the fourth highest gallantry award in Bangladesh.

Bir Uttom : Bir Uttom (literally, Best Hero in Bengali) is the second highest award for individual gallantry in Bangladesh. Since independence of Bangladesh in 1971, 68 people have been awarded Bir Uttom.

BIRDEM : BIRDEM, the Bangladesh Institute of Research and Rehabilitation for Diabetes, Endocrine and Metabolic Disorders at Shahbag, Dhaka, Bangladesh is a 600-bed multidisciplinary hospital complex of the Diabetic Association of Bangladesh. BIRDEM has been recognised nationally and internationally as a centre of excellence for medical services and research. It has been designated as a WHO Collaborating Centre on Diabetes, Endocrine and Metabolic Disorders, as the only on of its kind in Asia. The late National Professor Md. Ibrahim is its founder.

Birju Maharaj : Pandit Birju Maharaj (b.1937) is perhaps the foremost exponent of the country's Kathak dancers belonging to the Lucknow gharana. Son of well-known Kathak dancer Achchan Maharaj and nephew and student of Shambhu Maharaj, Birju Maharaj made his mark in the arena when he received the coveted Sangeet Natak Akademi award at the age of 28.

He has mastered the various nuances of Kathak from Acchan Maharaj, Lacchu Maharaj and Shambhu Maharaj and developed his own unique style. In his own words, Birju Maharaj has likened Lacchu Maharaj and Shambhu Maharaj to the moon and the sun, and Acchan Maharaj to the sky. Combined they form his universe of Kathak. He has several honours and awards to his credit including the prestigious Padma Vibhushan (1986) by the government of India and the Sangam Kala Award (2000). At present Birju Maharaj heads the teaching faculty at Delhi's Kathak Kendra.

Birla Corporation Limited : Birla Corporation Limited, popularly known as Birla Corp is an Indian company based in Kolkata. It is the flagship company of the M P Birla group of companies. In 1919, Shri Ghanshyam Das Birla founded the Birla Jute Manufacturing Company. This company diversified and expanded and was renamed to its present name to reflect the change.

Birla Mandir : The Laxminarayan Temple of Delhi, populary known as Birla Mandir, is a temple built in honor of the Hindu goddess of wealth, Laxmi, and of her consort, Lord Vishnu – the Preserver of the Hindu Trinity. It is a temple with many shrines, fountains, and a large garden.

The temple attracts thousands of devotees on Janmashtami day, the birthday of Lord Krishna. The temple was built in 1622 by Vir Singh Deo, and renovated by Prithvi Singh in 1793. Since 1938, funds for further renovations and support have come from the Birla family.

Birla Planetarium : The Birla Planetarium is present at the center of Hyderabad city, on the small hill known as Naubat Pahad (in hindi). It was opened by the Late Mr. N.T. Rama Rao, on 8 September 1985. This planetarium displays and demonstrates the advances in science and technology. Visitors can tune in for daily sky shows in Telugu, Hindi and English languages. The show covers the various aspects of the Cosmos, Space and the galaxies of the Universe, the comets, the Hubble Space Telescope, Eclipses, the mysterious Unidentified Flying Objects (UFO's) and the recent clash of the Titans. The visitors are transported into a new world, as they watch a large dome of an open dark sky with full of shining stars looking down upon them. With excellent sound effects added upon them gives a feel of being in outer space.

Biryani : Biryani is a rice dish from the Indian Subcontinent, made from a mixture of spices, basmati rice, meat/vegetables, yogurt. There are many kind of biryanis and each kind has an uniqueness about it. From Kashmir to Kanyakumari, from East India to West India there are different varieties of the dish. It can be considered a casserole dish, as the ingredients are ideally cooked together in the final phase, and is time-consuming to prepare. Pre-mixed biryani spices from companies like ITC (under the brand name Kitchens of india), MTR etc. have become commercially available, which reduces the preparation time though the taste differs considerably.

Though there are several methods of preparing biryani, the Hyderabad Biryani is by far the most popular version. Historians claim that the earlier Nawabs of Hyderabad wore a matching turban for each variety of biryani. The Nizam's kitchen boasted of 49 kinds, which included biryani made from fish, quail, shrimp, deer, and hare. The Sindhi variant of biryani is very popular in Pakistani cuisine, and biryani of all types are eaten in all parts of Pakistan.

Bishkhali River : Bishkhali River is the continuation of the Kirtankhola and Nalchity rivers. The Arial Khan picks up the name 'Bhasani Char' as it enters into Bhasani Char of the Barisal Sadar Upazila. Similarly it changes her name as the Kirtankhola at 5 km north of Barisal town, as Nalchity in Nalchity Upazila (Nhalokati District) and as Sugandha in Jhalokati Sadar upazila. The Sugandha turns into Bishkhali after entering Jhalokati town. At this point, after creating a great meander the river flows south into the Bay of Bengal. The Bishkhali receives the water of the Madhumati and Katcha through the Kaukhali and the Gabkhan Khal (canal) joining with the river near the meander. The river maintains a connection with the Burishwar river system through the Bakdugh, Ayla, etc at the lower reach of Bamna upazila and falls into the Bay of Bengal through the mouth of the Baleswar-Haringhata at 13 km down of Patharghata.

The total length of the river is 96 km. The average width of the river from its origin to first 30 km is about 1 km and the rest is about 2 km. The average depth is about 16m. The river is fully influenced by tide and ebb. Water is collected at Betna, Bamna, Barguna and Patharghata stations to examine the salinity status of the river. It shows erosional tend ency and the towns and ports, eg Betagi, Anua, Bamna are under threat to its erosion. Bangladesh Water Development Board (BWDB) has constructed an Embankment to prevent flood and salinity. Deposition process and char (island) formation is active at various parts of the river. Some of the chars are under settlement and cultivation. The Badankhalikone and Khakdone, two of the offshoots of the Bishkhali are about to die due to lack of sufficient flow. Jhalokati, Betagi, Kathalia, Bamna, Barguna, Patharghata, Phuljhuri are some important places on the north bank of the river.

Biswa Ijtema : Biswa Ijtema ("World Congregation") is an annual congregation of the Tablighi Jamaat Islamic movement in Bangladesh. It is the 2nd largest Muslim religious gathering after Hajj, and attracts over 3 million people from around the globe. It is currently an annual event, and is held at Tongi, on the outskirts of Dhaka, the capital of Bangladesh. The first meeting was reportedly held in 1946 (although various sources indicate other dates for this).

The congregation takes place at an area comprising 160 acres of land (0.25 square mile). Devotees from approximately 80 countries, including the host country, Bangladesh, attend the three-day Ijtema seeking divine blessings from Allah. The Ijtema has been held every year since 1966 on the bank of the river Turag near Tongi. Maulana Elius founded the Tabligh movement in 1927 at Saharanpur of Uttar Pradesh, India and at the same time organized regional congregation or Ijtema. In course of time, Ijtema movement spread throughout the subcontinent and also influenced other regions. After the partition of Bengal in 1947, three Ijtema centres developed in three parts of the subcontinent - India, West Pakistan and East Pakistan. Biswa Ijtema at Tongi is the annual Tabligh congregation of East Pakistan. In addition to Tongi, Ijtemas are now held in Raiwind, Pakistan and Bhopal, India. However, in terms of popular attendance, the Tongi Ijtema is the largest of all these congregations.

Bizu Dance : This popular form of dance in Tripura is characteristic of the Chakma community. Bizu means 'Chaitra-Sankranti'. 'Chaitra-Sankranti' denotes end of Bengali calendar year. It is during this period when the Chakmas sing and dance to bid good-bye to the year just being ended and welcome the new year. The dance is beautifully orchestrated with the rhythm playing of what is known as 'Khenggarang' and 'Dhukuk' sorts of flutes. The Chakma women are fond of flower, which they often use in their hair. They also use metal ornaments.

B K S Iyengar : B.K.S. Iyengar, (aka Yogacharya B.K.S. Iyengar) born Bellur Krishnamachar Sundararaja Iyengar, December 14, 1918, in India, is founder of Iyengar Yoga and one of the most respected yoga teachers in the world.

Millions of students and followers around the world practice Iyengar Yoga. Iyengar has written a number of definitive yoga texts.

B.K.S. Iyengar was born into a poor Iyengar family. He had a difficult childhood. Iyengar's home village of Bellur, Karnataka, India, was experiencing an influenza epidemic at the time of his birth, leaving him sickly and weak. Iyengar's father died when he was 9 years old, and he continued to suffer from a variety of maladies in childhood, including malaria, tuberculosis, typhoid fever, and general malnutrition.

At the age of 15 Iyengar went to live with the famous yogi, Sri Tirumalai Krishnamacharya in Mysore. There, Iyengar began to learn asana practice, which steadily improved his health. Soon his childhood weaknesses were overcome. With the encouragement of Krishnamacharya, Iyengar moved to Pune to teach yoga in 1937. There his practice developed as he spent many hours each day learning and experimenting in various techniques. As his methods improved, the number of students at his classes increased and his fame spread.

In 1952, Iyengar met and befriended the famous violinist Yehudi Menuhin. Menuhin arranged for Iyengar to teach abroad in London, Switzerland, Paris and elsewhere. This was the first time that many Westerners had been exposed to yoga, and the practice slowly became well known. In 1966, Iyengar published Light on Yoga, an international best-seller. More than anything else, this book made yoga an international phenomenon. Iyengar Yoga soon became the most practiced form of yoga in Europe and America.

In 1975, Iyengar opened the Ramamani Iyengar Memorial Yoga Institute in Pune, in memory of his recently departed wife. He officially retired from teaching in 1984, but continues to be very active in the world of Iyengar Yoga, teaching special classes and writing books. Iyengar's daughter Geeta and son Prashant have become internationally acclaimed teachers in their own right.

Black Hat (Kali Topi) Dance : On Lossoong, the Sikkimese New Year Day, Black Hat (kali topi) Dance demonstrating the triumph of good over evil is demonstrated. This masked dance is also performed by male dancers mostly the Lamas. The dance revives the old story which narrates that about twelve centuries ago King Land-Darma was slain for suppressing Buddhism in Tibet. The king was slain by a Lama wearing a fantastic black robe lined with white and riding a white horse blackened with soot.

Black Mountain : A Mountain range and district on the Hazara border of the North West Frontier Province of Pakistan. On the western slopes and face of the Black Mountain, the leading Tribes inhabiting are the Hassanzais, Akazais and Chagharzais etc. While on some eastern slopes or face and spurs of the Black Mountain, the majority of the clans belong to the Swati Tribes like Madda khel, Kuchelai, Malkals, Sumla khel, Warozais Deshiwals, Tikriwals and Jahangiris etc. The Priari Syyads are also welknown clans of the Black Mountain. The Black Mountain itself has a total length of 20 to 25 m, and an average height of 8000 ft. It rises from the Indus basin near the village of Kiara upto its watershed by bruddur, thence it runs north west by north to the point on the crest known as Chittabut. From Chittabut the range runs due north, finally descending by two large spurs to the Indus again. The Britishers have sent more than four expeditions to subdue the Black Mountain Tribes due to the intrigues of Ata Mohammad Khan Swati and his sons, who was the Khan of Agror and Arsala Khan of Allai, against the British Governement.

Blackbuck National Park : Blackbuck National Park at Velavadar is situated in the Bhavnagar District of Gujarat state, India. Established in 1976 in the Bhal region of Saurashtra, the park is located around 72 km from the district headquarter city of Bhavnagar. Hugging the coasts of the Gulf of Khambhat on the south, it is spread over an area of 34.08 km^2, which was primarily a "vidi" (grassland) of the Maharaja of the princely state of Bhavnagar. On the northern side, it is surrounded by wastelands and agriculture fields. The National park has been classified as 4B Gujarat-Rajwada biotic province of semi-arid bio-geographical zone.

Flat land, dry grasses and herds of antelopes have always attracted visitors to this park which has a unique grassland ecosystem running a successful conservation program of the Blackbuck, the Wolf and the Lesser Florican (a bustard) among others. Considered to be an exclusive Indian species, the Lesser Floricans, which were free dwellers throughout the country, have their numbers plummeting in the recent decades almost everywhere in India. Today, the largest population has been sustained in this park.

Blasphemy Laws : The Pakistan Penal Code (PPC) and the Criminal Procedure Code were amended, through ordinances in 1980, 1982 and 1986 to declare anything implying disrespect to Muhammad, Ahle Bait (family of the prophet), Sahaba (companions of the prophet) and Sha'ar-i-Islam (Islamic symbols), a cognizable offence, punishable with imprisonment or fine, or with both.

Bobita : Bobita (also written as Babita) is a renowned Bangladeshi film actress. During the 1970s and 1980s, she was arguably the most popular actress in the country, and to this day, she enjoys a large popular following. She was born Farida Akhter, to an educated family that had its origins in the southern district of Jessore. She was notable for her good looks, which were in the classical Bengali mould. But she was also a highly talented actress, and her performances in films such as Taka Anna Pai, Shorolipi and Anarkoli were noted by the critics. Her acting gained the attention of the legendary Indian director Satyajit Ray. In 1973, Ray cast Bobita in Ashani Sanket, his film about the Bengal famine of 1943. Bobita appeared in the lead role of Ananga, the demure wife of the village doctor Gangacharan, who was played by long-time Ray favourite Soumitra Chatterjee.

Ashani Sanket was a great critical success and won the Golden Bear prize at the 1973 Berlin Film Festival. Bobita's performance was central to the film, and she became the first Bangladeshi actress to achieve widespread international acclaim. Two decades later, Bobita's younger sister Chompa also received international recognition for her performances in arthouse films such as Padma Nadir Majhi, but Bobita's achievement remains the more significant one.

Her acting career continues, though less vigorously than before. In 2002, Bobita won a National Film Award for Best Supporting Actress for her role in Hason Raja, Chashi Nazrul Islam's biopic of the famed Bengali folk-poet. She has also formed her own film production company and has expressed an interest in directing in the future. Bobita has campaigned actively on behalf of various social causes in Bangladesh. Notable among the causes she has supported are the campaign against throwing acid on women; the national immunization drive for children; and a support group for children who suffer from leukemia.

Boddemma Festival : The Boddemma festival commences nine days prior to the Batakamma festival and concludes on Mahalaya Amavasya. Bodemma is a worship of goddess Gauri. This is the festival of unmarried girls. The image of Boddemma is prepared with ant—hill earth in seven layers in the shape of a gopura. It is decorated with flowers, turmeric and Kumkum and placed in the courtyard which has been cleaned and decorated with designs. All the girls of that street gather around the Boddemma during the evenings and dance and sing, praying to Gouri for their early and successful marriage. This festival is a counterpart to Gobbillu, popular in coastal Andhra.

Bodhgaya : The village of Bodhgaya situated near the river Niranjana, 12km from Gaya in the state of Bihar isthe most important Buddhist pilgrimage centre and attracts Buddhists from all over the world. It is the place where Lord Sakyamuni (Gautam Buddha) entered into meditation after being moved by the sufferings of mankind and attained enlightenment.

The original 'Bodhi tree' or Pipal (Ficus religiosa)—the tree of awakening; was said to have been destroyed by Mauryan emperor Ashoka. The giant Bodhi Tree (Peepal) seen here is believed to have grown from the original Bodhi Tree under which, sitting on the raised red stone platform, 'vajrasila', Prince Siddharth meditated and finally attained Nirvana. The platform has a stone carving of his footsteps where the devout make flower offerings. Then there is 'Chaukramana', the Jewel Walk, where it is believed that the Buddha strolled while in deep thought and 'Animeshlochana' is the sacred spot where Buddha stood to gaze in gratitude at the Bodhi tree for a week.

The magnificient Maha Bodhi temple in Bodhgaya is an architectural amalgamation of many cultures. Originally believed to be small shrine erected by Emperor Asoka in the 3rd century B.C, temple was later restored in the 11th and 18th centuries. The temple bears the stamp of the architecture of the Gupta Dynasty and subsequent ages. On the walls of the temple, one sees Buddha carved in different aspects, and in the sanctum sanctorum, a colossal

Buddha, is seen touching the ground, which has mythological significance in the Buddhist lores. The temple has a 54 meters high pyramidical spire and an ornamental arch way at the entrance.

The temple carries inscriptions recording the visits of pilgrims from Sri Lanka, China and Mayanmar in the 7th and 10th Centuries A.D. Hieun Tsang, the Chinese traveller, also visited the temple in the 7th Century.

South of the temple 3 kms. away is a lake close to the village Mucharim. Muchalinda, the multi-hooded snake king guards the lotus in the gardens. The legend is that Muchalinda protected the Buddha against the thunder and rain sent by the asuras and demons, to disturb his meditation. As Gautama sat in deep meditation, Mara, Lord of Illusion, perceiving that his power was about to be broken, rushed to distract him from his purpose. The Bodhisattva touched the earth, calling it to bear witness the countless lifetimes of virtue that had led him to this place of enlightenment. When the earth shook, confirming the truth of Gautama's words, Mara unleashed his army of demons. In the epic battle that ensued, Gautama's wisdom broke through the illusions and the power of his compassion transformed the demons' weapons into flowers and Mara and all his forces fled in disarray.

Pilgrims from Tibet, Thai, Bhutan, Japan, China and Burma have built their own temples and monasteries in their own style of architecture. A 20 meters tall Buddha statue built in stone can be seen at the end of the road, beyond the Japanese temple. The archaeological museum here houses a collection of terracotta and stone statues of the Buddha dating to 1st cent. B.C. and also samples of carved railings with lotus motifs and designs. Bodhgaya is also famous for the various meditation courses offered by a number of institutes, usually during October - February in and around the town.

Bodhi Tree : Bodhi tree was a large and very old specimen of the Sacred Fig, located at the Mahabodhi Temple at Bodh Gaya (about 100 km from Patna in the Indian state of Bihar) under which Siddhartha Gautama, the spiritual teacher and founder of Buddhism later know as Gautama Buddha, arrived at Bodhi. The Bodhi Tree belongs to the Sacred Figs (Ficus religiosa), also known as Bo, Pipul (Peepal) or Ashwattha trees, which are sacred to Hindus, Jains and Buddhists. According to Buddhist belief, Siddharta Gautama meditated under this tree, mentioned as Ashwattha in the Tipitaka, when he achieved Nirvana. The word 'Ashvattha' is derived from the Sanskrit roots 'Shwa' meaning tomorrow, 'a' indicating negation, and 'tha' meaning "one that stands or remains". (The Hindu philosopher Shankaracharya interprets the name to indicate "One which does not remain the same tomorrow", such as the universe itself.)

The Sacred Fig currently growing at the Mahabodhi Temple is not the original specimen, but probably a direct clone descendant of it. This tree is a frequent destination for pilgrims, being the most important of the four holy sites for Buddhists. Another sacred specimen, also propagated from the original Bodhi tree, is the Sri Maha Bodhi in Sri Lanka, planted in 288 BC.

Bodo : Bodo is a Tibeto-Burman language spoken by the Bodo people of north-eastern India and Nepal. The language is one of the official languages of the Indian state of Assam, and is one of 22 scheduled languages given a special constitutional status in India. The language is officially written using the Devanagari script, although it also has a long history of using the Roman script. Some researchers have suggested that the language originally used a now-lost script called Deodhai.

Bodo Security Force (BSF) : The Bodo Security Force (BSF) was created in 1988, under the leadership of Ranjan

Daimary. The Bodo (community) group is based on the state of Assam in India. In 1996 a branch of the BSF created the Bodoland Liberation Tigers Force that became the Bodoland Army and finally, the National Democratic Front of Boroland (NDFB) the following year.

This organisation fights to get a sovereign Bodoland north of the Brahmaputra. It was very active during the 1990s. It consists of around 1,000 fighters. The NDFB is allied with the National Socialist Council of Nagalim (IM) and holds training areas in the South of Bhutan. Ranjan Daimary is its current leader. The flag of the NDFB is green with a yellow star on red background on the corner. These three colours are the national colours of Boroland.

Bodos : The Bodos, also called the Boros, are an ethnic community that is concentrated mostly in the north-western parts of Assam in India. They are said to belong to a larger classification of ethnicity called the Bodo-Kachari. The nerve center of the Bodos is the city of Kokrajhar.

The Bodos are the largest tribe of the Brahmaputra valley. They divided into a number of clans such as the Basumatary, Sargwary, Mushahary,Ishlary,Boro, Sibigri, Narzary,Dwimary, Goyari and Brahma. Though the numbers are in dispute, the census report from 1971 state the Bodos as being the 8th largest tribal group in India, with Bodo being spoken by about 0.8 million people.

The Bodo language is part of the Tibeto-Burmese family of languages. The tribe recently adopted the Devanagari script formally, although the Roman script has also been extensively used- particularly due to the influence of Christian missionaries in that region. According to some scholars, the Bodo language had a script of its own called Deodhai. **The Bodos are thought to have** introduced rice cultivation and silkworm rearing to the region. The traditional favourite drink of the Bodos is Zu Mai- Zu meaning beer, and Mai meaning rice. Rice is a staple of the Bodos and is often accompanied by a non vegetarian dish such as fish or pork. Bodos are traditionally non-vegetarians.

Weaving is another integral part of Bodo culture. Many families rear their own silkworms, the cocoons of which are then spun into silk. Bodo girls are taught to weave from a young age, and no Bodo courtyard is complete without a loom. Most women weave their own Dokhnas (the traditional outfit of the Bodo women) and shawls. The Bodos are also expert craftsmen in bamboo products. The Bodos practice a number of religions, with Bathou being the primary faith, along with Hinduism and Christianity.

Bogra : Bogra is a northern district of Bangladesh, in the Rajshahi Division. It is called the gateway to the north Bengal. It is an industrial city where many small and mid sized industries are housed. Bogra is also known for some historical sites including Mahasthangarh. So far the oldest archaeological site of Bangladesh, Mahasthangarh lies on the western bank of river Karatoya, about 12 km north of Bogra town, and is connected by a good metalled road. The site includes partly shibganj and partly bogra sadar upazilas of bogra district and lies between latitudes 24 50 N and 25 0 N and longitudes 89 15 E and 89 30 E. The spectacular site is an imposing landmark in the area, having a fortified, oblong enclosure measuring 1524m by 1370m with an average height of 5m from the surrounding paddyfields.

Boishakh : Boishakh is the first month in the Bangla Calendar used in Bangladesh and parts of India. Boisakh is also the first month in the Nepali calendar Bikram Sambat. The first day of Baishakh is celebrated as the

Pôhela Boishakh or Bangla New Year's day. The day is observed with cultural programs, festivals and carnivals all around the country. The day of Pôhela Boishakh is also the beginning of all business activities in Bangladesh and neighboring Indian state of West Bengal. The traders purchase new accounting books called 'Halkhata'. The accounting in the 'Halkhata' begins only after this day. The shops also offer sweets and other gifts to customers.

The month of Boishakh also marks the official start of Summer. The month is notorious for the afternoon storms called Kalboishakhis. The storms usually start with strong gusts from the north-western direction at the end of a hot day and cause widespread destruction. Baishakh is the month when many of the seasonal fruits, especially mango and jackfruit become available.

Bokaro Steel City : Bokaro Steel City, is the home of one of largest steel mills in India, and several other medium and small industries. It is the district headquarters of the Bokaro district. Situated in the Chhotanagpur Plateau, the vast rolling topography of the city is typical, strewn by graded valleys and winding streams. In this setting, within a short period of two decades, a new city with a strong multi-dimensional economic base, has blossomed into a regional urban centre of around 800,000 people drawn from different parts of the country, giving the city the character of Mini India.

Bolan : Bolan district is in the center of Balochistan province of Pakistan. The Bolan area remained under one district Kachhi until 31 December 1991. The Deputy Commissioner's office started functioning on 17 May 1992. It is now one of the four districts of Nasirabad division. The district is named after the historic Bolan Pass. The pass, 85 kilometres long, extends from Kolpur, the highest place in Bolan district with an altitude of 2,200 metres above sea level. The area included in the Bolan district is

8,036 sq. km. Tehsils and Mozas of the Bolan district are : Mach, Dhadar, Nari Bala, Sanni, Khattan, Bhag and Lehri. The population of Bolan districts in 2005 is estimated to be over 450,000. Muslims constitute over 99% of the population. Ther is a small Hindu minority in Bhag sub-division. The major Baloch tribes of the district are : Raisani, Domki, and Rind.

Bolan Pass : The Bolan Pass is a gap through the Toba Kakar Range of mountains on the border of Pakistan. Strategically located, traders, invaders, and nomadic tribes have also used it as a gateway to and from the Indian subcontinent. The British took the threat of a Russian invasion of India via the Khyber and Bolan Passes very seriously so in 1837, a British envoy was sent to Kabul to gain support of the Emir, Dost Mohammed. In February of 1839, the British Army under Sir John Keane took 12,000 men through the Bolan Pass and entered Kandahar, which the Afghan Princes had abandoned; from there they would go on to attack and overthrow Ghuznee.

Traditionally, the Brahui of the Raisani tribe are in charge of the law and order situation through the Pass area. This tribe is still living in present day Balochistan in Pakistan. In 1879 at the close of the Second Afghan War, the Treaty of Gandamak, the Bolan Pass was brought under British control; this was when the Sind-Pishin Railway was built by the British across the pass between Kandahar and Quetta.

Bolgatty Island : The Bolgatty Island is a short but inspiring boat ride away from Kochi. The commercial capital of Kerala is also blessed with monuments of great historic relevance. One such monument is the Bolgatty Palace. Set amidst lush, tropical greenery, this prestigious heritage hotel answers your quest for a holiday of quiet enchantment. One of the oldest existing Dutch palaces outside Holland, this quaint mansion was built way back in 1744 by a Dutch trader. In 1909 the palace was leased to the British and it served as their residency till 1947 when the British Raj came to an end in India.

Bollywood : Bollywood is the informal name given to the popular Mumbai-based Hindi language film industry in India. The name is a conflation of Bombay, the old name of Mumbai, and Hollywood, the center of the United States film industry. Though some purists deplore the name (arguing that it makes the industry look like a poor cousin to Hollywood), it seems likely to persist and now has its own entry in the Oxford English Dictionary.

Bollywood and the other major cinematic hubs (Tamil—Kollywood, Telugu—Tollywood, Bengali—also called Tollywood, Kannada, and Malayalam) constitute the broader Indian film industry, whose output is the largest in the world in terms of number of films produced and in number of tickets sold. Bollywood is a strong part of popular culture of not only India and the rest of the Indian subcontinent, but also of the Middle East, parts of Africa, parts of Southeast Asia, and among the South Asian diaspora worldwide.

Bollywood is also commonly referred to as "Hindi cinema", even though use of poetic Urdu words is fairly common. There has been a growing presence of English in dialogues and songs as well. It is not uncommon to see movies which feature dialogues with English words and phrases, even whole sentences. A few movies are also made in two or even three languages (either using subtitles, or several soundtracks.

Bolup : The bolup is a hat used by the Adi Gallong tribe of Arunachal. It is made by coiling lengths of cane to obtain a semi-elliptical bowl with a horizontal boat-shaped rim. The hat is extremely sturdy. A similar construction is used in hats made by other tribes of

Arunachal. The form and decorative elements vary, but the basic structure is similar. In some cases, there are thick strips of cane that are tied onto the head as extra protection. In other hats, dyed wool or feathers are used as decorative elements

Bom Jesus Basilica : The Bom Jesus Basilica is in Goa, India. The basilica holds the mortal remains of St Francis Xavier. It is just about 10km from the city of Panjim.

The church is located in Old Goa, which was the capital of Goa in the early days of Portuguese rule. This world heritage monument built in 1695 is a fine example of Jesuit architecture and has emerged as a landmark in the history of Christianity. It is situated in Old Goa, 9kms from the Capital Panjim. It is a world renowned church which contains the body of St. Francis Xavier; a pupil of the soldier–turned–saint, Ignatius Loyola (the founder of the Order of Jesuits), who died while on a sea voyage to China on December 2, 1552.

The following year, while transferring Francis Xavier's remains to Goa, in accordance with his wishes, it was found that the saint's body was as fresh as the day it was buried. This miraculous phenomenon attracts huge number of devotees from all over the world, especially during the public viewing of his body every ten years. The saint is believed to have miraculous powers of healing, and pilgrims would come from all over the country to offer prayers.

This church is one of the richest churches in Goa and is carpeted with marble flooring and inlaid with precious stones. Apart from the elaborate gilded altars, the interior of the church is simple. The church also holds paintings of St. Francis Xavier. The Tomb of St. Francis Xavier (1696) was the gift of the last of the Medicis, Cosimo III, the Grand Duke of Tuscany.

The tomb was carved by the 17th century Florentine sculptor Giovanni Batista Foggini. It took 10 years to complete. The casket containing his body is made of silver. The holy relics of the saint is displayed every 10 years during the anniversary of the Saint's death. The Feast is organised on 3rd December every year.

Bombay Dyeing : Bombay Dyeing (The Bombay Dyeing & Mfg. Co. Ltd., established 1879) is the flagship company of the Wadia Group, engaged mainly into the business of Textiles. Its current chairman is Nusli Wadia. Bombay Dyeing has been in news, apart from other things, for various controversied surrounding tussle with Dhirubhai Ambani of Reliance Industries Limited and with Calcutta based jutebaron Arun Bajoria.

Bombay Mix : Bombay mix is a traditional Indian snack, named after the city of Bombay, now called Mumbai. It consists of a mixture of spicy dried ingredients, including fried lentils, peanuts, gram flour, corn, vegetable oil, chickpeas, salt and spices.

In the United Kingdom, some supermarket brands of "Bombay mix" also contain sultanas or raisins, resulting in a sweet taste and less crunchiness. This is a departure from the authentic recipe. The Bombay mix served to customers of Indian restaurants and take-aways does not contain dried fruit. In the USA it is alternately and more often referred to as punjabi mix.

Bombay Natural History Society : The Bombay Natural History Society is the largest organisation engaged in conservation research in the Indian subcontinent. On September 15, 1883 eight residents of Bombay met in the then Victoria and Albert Museum and "constituted themselves as the Bombay Natural History Society. They proposed to meet monthly and exchange notes, exhibit interesting specimens and otherwise encourage each other

In 1911 R. C. Wroughton a BNHS member and forest officer organized a survey of mammals making use of the members spread through the Subcontinent to provide specimens. This was perhaps the first collaborative natural history study in the world and it resulted in the collection of 50,000 specimens in 12 years resulting in the identification of several new species, 47 publications and an understanding of biogeographic boundaries. Today the BNHS is headquartered in the specially constructed Hornbill House is Southern Mumbai. It is commonly known by its acronym, BNHS.

Bombay Stock Exchange : The Bombay Stock Exchange Limited (formerly, The Stock Exchange, Mumbai; popularly called The Bombay Stock Exchange, or BSE) is located at Dalal Street, Mumbai. Established in 1875, it is the oldest stock exchange in Asia. There are around 3,500 Indian companies listed with the stock exchange, and has a significant trading volume. As of July 2005, the market capitalization of the BSE was about Rs. 20 trillion (US $ 466 billion). The BSE SENSEX (SENSitive indEX), also called the BSE 30, is a widely used market index in India and Asia. As of 2005, it is among the 5 biggest stock exchanges in the world in terms of transactions volume. Along with the NSE, the companies listed on the BSE have a combined market capitalization of US$ 125.5 billion.

Bomdila : Bomdila is the headquarters of West Kameng district in the state of Arunachal Pradesh in India. Tourist attractions of Bomdila include Buddhist temples, craft centres, the district museum, and the sports complex. It is located at a height of 2430m to 2700m. Curry is one of the favorite native dishes in this region. Bomdila is largely inhabited by the Monpa and Sherdukpen tribes.

Bommalattam or Pavakkuthu : This is puppet dance in Tamil Nadu, and this art form is used to spread religious stories. Simple folk believe that it is auspicious to have this performance in their village and that its performance will ward off evil spirits/epidemics and bring prosperity. The main themes are the stories from the Ramayana, the Mahabharatha and the Bhagavatha. This show is manipulated by strings and iron rods suspended from above. The stage is so setup that the puppets alone are seen through an opening roughly about four metres in height. The puppets are moved by skilled and experienced players who stand behind, unseen by the audience. The puppets are tied to the player's hand with black strings which are not visible.

The performance usually begins at 10 pm. and is over by about 4 am, the following morning it is continued for a week or ten days. On either side of the stage big earthen castor oil lamps are placed. The screen is a big black cloth about three metres high. In front of this curtain, the puppet make their appearance. When the chandramati puppet and the dancing puppet appear, the manipulators behind the curtains have themselves to do all the bodily movements and dancing. Their legs and arms have full work. The scenes in which chandramati tears her garland to pieces and laments on the cremation ground are great attractions.

Bonda : Bonda ia a typical South Indian snack. The process of making Bonda involves deep frying Potato (or other vegetables) filling dipped in gram flour batter.

Bondla Wildlife Sanctuary : Bondla Wildlife Sanctuary is located in Northeastern Goa, India. The total area of this park land is 8 square km. It is a favourite destination for both tourists and school children. Known for the place to go and encounter a wide variety of animal life inculding: sambar deer, Indian Bison, peacocks and many species of snake.

Bongvum Festival : The Bongvum festival generally falls in the month of October every year after the major harvest and is observed only for a day in Nagaland. This festival may be best interpreted as the festival of Thanksgiving to the unseen Almighty God. Paangmo is another important event of the Phoms. It is celebrated in the month of November which stretches over three days.

October is the month of festivity which every Pochury anxiously awaits, ever year to celebrate their greatest festival Yemshe. Yemshe is the festival of welcoming the new harvest and blessings. All the Pochuries, young and old, rich and poor, celebrate this festival with great pomp and gaiety anticipating a good harvest. Originally the festival commences in the end of September but now Yemshe is celebrated on 5th October every year.

Bopa : The Apatani and Nishi tribes of Arunachal use coiled hats that fit close on to the head like a skull cap. The bopa is slightly conical in shape. These hats are decorated with twisted cane ropes, and a hornbill beak that is dyed red.

Border Roads Organisation : The Border Roads Organisation, also known by its acronym BRO, is a unique combination of officers from the corps of engineers of Indian army and Border Roads Engineering Service (BRES) officers from General Reserve Engineer Force (GREF) to maintain roads that serve the borders areas. The BRO contributes to the army's other duties and supplies units that are part of the defence forces. BRO's activities have helped to accelerate the economic development of the North and North Eastern border states. The roads construction teams have to deal with some of the harshest climate in the world. The BRO has some formidable hurdles, the icy Himalayan tops, the marshes of West Bengal, the deserts in Rajasthan. BRO undertakes road constructions and maintenance at high altitude in the hills. Some of the BRO roads area built as high as 6,000 metres above mean sea level.

The BRO was formed on 7 May 1960 with the Indian Prime Minister, Jawaharlal Nehru as the chairman of the Border Roads Development Board, as an inter-ministerial organisation. BRO is led by the Director General of Border Roads (DGBR), as it Executive Head, who is of the rank of Lieutenant General. The BRO is also provided a General Reserve Engineer Force (GREF), as the execution force under the Ministry of Surface Transport.GREF comprises of engineers from civil engineering, electrical & mechanical engineering disciplines from reputed engineering colleges after selection through Union Public Service Commission(UPSC)by clearing Engineering Services Examination at All India Level, administrative officers, supervisors and other trades of personnel. Its operations also run in Bhutan and Myanmar.

The Border Roads Organisation operates a network of over 34,306 km of roads and 16,601 meters of permanent bridges. BRO has operations in twenty two states including the Andaman and Nicobar Islands, a Union Territory.

Border Security Force (BSF) : The Border Security Force (BSF), established on December 1, 1965, is responsible for guarding India's land borders during peacetime and preventing trans-border crimes. It is a Central paramilitary force operating under the Union Ministry of Home Affairs. The Indian Union has a federal structure and is made up of several states, much like the United States. From independence in 1947 to 1965, India's international boundaries were manned by the Armed Police battalions of each Indian state sharing a border with a neighbouring country—with little co-ordination between the states. When Pakistan attacked Indian outposts on April 9, 1965, the inadequacies of the existing border management setup in coping with external armed aggression were exposed. The Central Government then sanctioned the formation of the Border Security Force (BSF)—a unified, centrally-controlled agency with a specific mandate to guard international boundaries. The BSF was seen in action in the Indo-Pakistani War of 1971 in areas where the army was thinly spread. A notable battle in which BSF troops gave a good showing was the Battle of Longewala in Western India.

In 1989, a violent Islamic insurgency, or Jihad, was initiated by Pakistan-sponsored militants in Jammu and Kashmir. The task of tackling the violence proved to be beyond the capability of the existing security apparatus, including the Jammu and Kashmir state police and the Central Reserve Police Force. The Central government then decided to bring in the BSF. Mandated since inception to guard India's external boundaries, the BSF ironically found itself burdened with the additional task of tackling insurgency within the country, along with the Indian army. After initially suffering heavy casualties to hit-and-run terrorist attacks by Jihadists, the BSF successfully set up an intelligence network in Jammu & Kashmir with the help of local civilians opposed to the Jihad. Steadily, the BSF reaped the rewards and successfully liquidated and arrested a large number of hardcore Islamic militants.

Among the BSF's prime successes in Jammu and Kashmir was the elimination of a Pakistani national known by his comrades as "Ghazi Baba" (rough translation: "killer of non-Muslims"). As the second-in-command of the Pakistani-based Islamic group Jaish-e-Mohammad, Ghazi Baba had masterminded the deadly suicide attack on the Indian parliament in New Delhi in December 2001—an event sometimes referred to as "India's 9/11". In August 2003, his highly secret hideout in Srinagar city was busted by the BSF and he was killed in the ensuing gun-battle.

Despite the BSF's success in a counter-terrorism role, many in the administration felt that this additional burden was leading to a dilution of the BSF mandate and degrading the force's ability to perform its primary role of guarding the country's borders. The Indian government has now decided to implement recommendations to use each security agency exclusively for its mandated purpose. Thus BSF battalions in Jammu and Kashmir are gradually being withdrawn from counter-insurgency duties and being sent back to guard the borders. They are being replaced by fresh CRPF units that have undergone specialized training in counter-terrorism. Currently the strength of the BSF is at around 165 battalions or 200,000 men.

Borith Lake : Borith Lake is a famous lake in the Northern Areas of Pakistan. Borith is a hamlet in the surroundings of the Borith Lake to the northwest of Hussaini, a village near Gulmit, Gojal, in the upper Hunza. The altitude of Borith is roughly 8500 feet above sea level. It lies Approximately 2 km to the north of Ghulkin, a saline body of water occupying a small hollow at an elevation of 2500 meters. The lake can be reached via a 2 km unpaved jeep route from Hussaini village, which lies adjacent to Ghulkin village. It is also accessible by a 2-3 hour trekking route directly from Ghuylkin, across the end of the Ghulkin glacier. The site is an important sanctuary for migrating wildfowl and is a must to be included in the itinerary of bird-watchers and nature lovers. To witness the large number of ducks arriving from the warmer parts of southern Pakistan, one should visit between the months of March and June. The birds rest here on their way northwards to the cooler waters of central Asia. Similarly, from September - November, the spectacle occurs in reverse with the onset of winter towards the north.

Borra Caves : The Borra Caves are located near Vishakapatnam, India. They are famous for millions of years old stalactite formations.

Botanical Gardens : The first Botanical Gardens in Andhra Pradesh, spread over 120 acres, when completed will have 19 sections (Vanams). Already open to public is the first phase, with the completion of 5 sections.

BRAC: BRAC, formerly known as the Bangladesh Rural Advancement Committee, is a non-governmental organisation based in Bangladesh. It is also the world's largest non-governmental organisation. After independence in 1971, the BRAC was established. Initially its main objective was to conduct relief and rehabilitation programmes. It continued to widen its activities and, in 1976, established a micro-credit programme.

At present it is prominent among the biggest NGOs in terms of development and micro-credit activities. BRAC began its micro-credit programme in 1976. Its current programme was initiated in 1990 and is known as the 'Rural Credit Project'. BRAC's other development activities include free informal education and heath and medical facilities for low-income people in rural areas. In 2002, membership of BRAC was approximately 3.9 million, with a total loan disbursement of about US$1 billion. In 2000 the cumulative savings of BRAC stood at US$65 million. In the same year it achieved a recovery rate of 98.4%. Currently, BRAC is the second largest micro-credit organisation in Bangladesh.

Brahma : Brahma, the creator, from the cosmological point of view is the Golden Embryo (Hiranyagarbha), the ball of fire, from which the universe develops. The icon of Brahma has four heads facing the four quarters and they represent the four Vedas, the four Yugas (epochs of time), and the four Varnas (divisions of society based on nature, nurture and vocation). There are four arms holding different objects and in different poses.

The objects usually shown are Aksamala (rosary), Kurca (a bunch of Kusa grass), Sruk (ladle), Sruva (spoon), Kamandalu (water pot} and Pustaka (book). The rosary represents time, and the water pot; the casual water, from which all creation has sprung. The Kusa grass, the ladle and the spoon being sacrificial implements, represent the system of sacrifice which means to be adopted by the various creatures to sustain one another. The book represents knowledge, sacred and secular. The poses of the hand (Mudras) are Abhaya (assuring protection) and Varada (granting boons). Saraswati is his consort. She is the goddess of knowledge and music. Hamsa (goose/swan) is his vehicle.

Brahma Sarovar : Dharmic religions lay emphasis on taking bath for internal and external purity. So most of the religious sites have water tanks/ponds or sarovar along with the temple/gurdwara. Amongst the holiest of the water tanks of India is the Brahma sarovar in Thanesar.

It is believed to be the cradle of civilization because Lord Brahma, the creator of universe conceived the earth here. It is believed that a dip in this sarovar bears the sanctity of performing Ashvamedha. The sanctity of the water tank finds mention in the memoirs of Al Beruni named Kitab-ul-Hind. The scholar was describing India in 11th century AD.

Today Brahma Sarovar has been renovated. It is 3600 X 1500 feet in size. Its important feature is holy seat of Lord Mahadev another name of Lord Shiva. Come solar eclipse and the tank tuns into a sea of humanity, because it is believed that to bathe here during the solar eclipse absolve one of all sins.

One of the most delightful occasions is the Gita Jyanti celebrations held in the last week of November or the first week of December. The tank presents breath-taking spectacle of Deep daan (ceremony of floating lamps in water) and Aarti organized on this occasion.

Brahmagupta : Brahmagupta (598-668) was an Indian mathematician and astronomer. He was the head of the astronomical observatory at Ujjain, and during his tenure there wrote two texts on mathematics and astronomy: the Brahma Sputa Siddhanta in 628, and the Khandakhadyaka in 665. If there is a person to be assigned the most important discovery in all of mathemeatics, finding of zero, that would be Brahmagupta.

The Brahmasphutasiddhanta, written circa 628 AD, is the earliest known text to treat zero as a number in its own right. It goes well beyond that, however, stating rules for arithmetic on negative numbers and zero which are quite close to the modern understanding. The major divergence is that Brahmagupta attempted to define division by zero, which is left undefined in modern mathematics. His definition is not terribly useful; for instance, he states that 0/0 = 0.

Brahmananda Saraswati : Brahmananda Saraswati (1870 - 1953) was born into a Brahmin family in the village of Gana, near Ayodhya in Uttar Pradesh, North India. At the age of nine he left home to follow a spiritual path of renunciation. At around the age of 14, in Uttar Kashi, he found his master, Dandi Swami Krishnanand Saraswati. Later, on his masters instructions, he retired to a cave, resolving not to emerge until he had attained enlightenment. In 1902 he was initiated into the order of "Sanyas" by his Master at the Kumbh Mela.

In 1941, after decades of silence, Swami Brahmananda Saraswati finally accepted an invitation to be first Shankaracharya (spiritual head) in 150 years of Jyotirmath in India. Adi Shankara, the great reviver of Vedic Sanatana Dharma, had four principle followers, Padma-Pada, Hasta-Malaka, Vartika-Kara and Trotaka who each established a monastery in the north, south, east and west of India. Jyotirmath is the northern monastery.

Swami Brahmananda Saraswati was guru of Maharishi Mahesh Yogi who became his devoted devotee shortly before his installation and later his personal assistant. The Transcendental Meditation programme and movement respect and revere "Guru Dev" as Paramguru.

Brahmaputra River : The Brahmaputra is one of the major rivers of Asia. In Sanskrit, it means "son of Brahma". It originates from Mount Kailash in the Himalayan mountains in western Tibet, in China and flows 2900km into the sea in the Bay of Bengal in Bangladesh. It is called Tsangpo in Tibet, Siang or Dihang in Arunachal Pradesh, Luit or Brahmaputra in Assam, and one of its main branches is called Jamuna in Bangladesh. Old sanskrit call it Lauhitya. The Bodos call this river Bhullumbutter, which some have suggested, has been sanskritised to Brahmaputra.

This river eventually meets the Ganges (called Padma in Bangladesh) and Meghna rivers to form the largest river delta in the world, most of which is in Bangladesh. It is one of the few rivers in the world that exhibit a tidal bore. Most Indian rivers bear the name of a female. But this one has a rare male name.

It is navigable for most of its length and the lower reaches are sacred to Hindus. The river is prone to catastrophic flooding in spring when the Himalayan snows melt.

Brahmaputra Valley Semi-evergreen Forests : The Brahmaputra Valley semi-evergreen forests is a tropical moist broadleaf forest ecoregion of eastern India. The ecoregion covers 56,700 square kilometers (21,900 square miles), which encompasses the alluvial plain of the Brahmaputra River in India's Assam state.

Brahmaputra-Jamuna River System : Brahmaputra-Jamuna river system is one of the three major river systems of Bangladesh. Brahmaputra-Jamuna and Old Brahmaputra, with their main tributary Tista, and a good number of small tributaries and distributaries constitute the largest floodplain of Bangladesh. Excepting for a small portion in the north, the entire floodplain lies within the pleistocene terrace regions. The floodplain and the Pleistocene terraces almost completely cover two of the six administrative divisions of the country, Rajshahi and Dhaka.

Brahmin : A Brahmin is a member of the Hindu priestly caste. The word is related to, but not to be confused with, the Hindu religious conception of the transcendent and immanent supreme soul, "Brahman". The word Brahmin is said to literally mean One who has realised or attempts to realise Brahman. The traditional duties of this caste include studying Hindu religious scriptures of Vedas and preserving them in memory and transmitting them orally to the next generation. Additionally, they were also the philosophers, contributing to Hindu Philosophy and religion. The priests of Hindu temples were also from this caste. In India, in ancient times they also served as spiritual advisors of Kshatriya Kings.

In the caste system Brahmins have been traditionally regarded as the highest order caste. They are usually vegetarian (but some eat meat) and some are not allowed to eat onions, garlic, leeks, mushrooms and some other foods. Currently, all produce that cannot be grown locally is forbidden. Brahmin tend to engage in education and learning-based activities rather than purely business pursuits. Some are also involved in military pursuits, the most notable of whom was Parashurama.

If a Brahmin is unable to perform the duties of his caste, svadharma, he can resort to duties of the other two castes (Vaishyas and Kshatriyas). So also, if the other castes show themselves worthy of being a Brahmin, they were accepted well by the society. In their ignorance, some Brahmin's believe that dalits are born into that caste according to their Karmas, but this view is clearly not sanctioned in any of the scriptures. Upper class and Brahmin opposition to the integration of dalits into Indian society is one of the reasons that life in India is difficult for them. The Opposition to this integration has come mainly from the Landlords, Landowning Brahmins, usually referred to as Thakurs' in North India, who feared a loss of labour force and rise of the so called 'lower castes'. It is to be noted that this segregation was never sanctioned by the vedas, which created the varna syatem only as a classification on the basis of the four major occupations, Intellectual and teachers, Warriors and Kings, Traders and Farmers, and Workers.

According to the Purusha Suktam, a famous vedic hymn, which cronicles the Birth of the world, and describes the Supreme Being(Brahman), Brahmins were born out of the mouth or head of Brahman, signifying the Intellectuals of the society (Brahmanosya mukhamaaseeth baahu rajanyah krutaha, Uuru tadasya yadvaishyah padbhyam shudro ajayath). The brahmins are mostly well integrated into society and today, can be seen in all occupations. However, major Brahmin-Dominated occupations are as Pujaris-Priests (Overseers of Rituals-Puja). Brahmin Priests are involved in all the rituals of the Hindu Religion.

Brahmo Samaj : Brahmo Samaj is a social and religious movement founded in Kolkata, India in 1828 by Raja Ram Mohan Roy. He was influenced by western thought and was one of the first Indians to visit Europe. He died in Bristol, England. The Brahmo Samaj movement thereafter resulted in the Brahmo religion in 1850 founded by Debendranath Tagore — better known as the father of Rabindranath Tagore. The popularity of the Brahmo Samaj grew as a result of the raising of a new class of educated Indians that resulted from the occupation of India by the British Empire. Its prime belief is that there is only one God. It rejected the Vedas, the caste system, polytheism, idol worship, and the belief in avatars.

1. The core principles of the Brahmo Samaj are:
2. There is only one God.
3. No created object is to be worshipped as God, and God alone is to be considered as infallible.

The Bengal Renaissance of the nineteenth century had among its luminaries a large number 1emerging from the Brahmo Samaj, Rabindranath Tagore being the foremost of them. Keshab Chandra Sen (1838–1884) and Protap Mazumdar (1840–1905) are some other notable members of the Brahmo Samaj.

Brahui : The Brahui are an ethnic group of about 2.2 million people with the majority found in Kalat, Pakistan, but also found in smaller numbers in neighboring Afghanistan and Iran. They are closely linked to the Baloch with whom they have substantially intermingled and whose cultural traits they have absorbed. Linguistically, they speak the Brahui language, which is a North Dravidian language, but due to its isolation from the other Dravidian tongues it has considerable Balochi vocabulary and even counting begins with Balochi numbers. There is no distinct indigenous script for Brahui; like Balochi it is written in Perso-Arabic alphabet. Brahui is spoken in the following areas: Merv area of Turkmenistan, Sindh, Zahedan and Zabol in Iranian Balochistan, southern parts of Afghanistan, Pakistan Balochistan and with the bulk in the Jhalawan region.

Brahui Language : The Brahui language is mainly spoken in Balochistan, Pakistan, although also in

Afghanistan and Iran by the Brahui. It reportedly has about two million speakers in Pakistan (1998), and a tenth that number elsewhere. In Pakistan it is mainly spoken in the Kalat region of Balochistan. Although it is a Dravidian language, it has been heavily influenced by other languages spoken in the area and shares few words with the Dravidian languages spoken in southern India and Sri Lanka

Brihadisvara Temple : The Brihadisvara temple (also spelled Brahadeeswarar temple) is an ancient Hindu temple located at Thanjavur in the state of Tamil Nadu, India. This 10th century CE temple, one of UNESCO's World Heritage Sites, is a brilliant example of the Dravidian style of temple architecture. The central temple known as the Periya Koil (Big Temple) stands within a fort, whose walls are later additions built during the 16th century. The vimana (main tower) of the temple is about 70 m high and is the tallest in the world.

The Brihadisvara temple was built by the great Tamil ruler, Rajaraja Chola I of the Chola dynasty. In the twenty-fifth year of Rajaraja Chola (1009–1010 CE), on the 257th day of the year, the king handed over the copper pot for the final decoration atop the Vimana. It weighed about 107 kg and was overlaid with gold plate of the weight of 292.5 Kalanju (nearly 13 kg). The main deity worshipped the temple is Siva, in the usual form of a linga.

The Sivalinga of Sri Brihadisvara is probably the grandest in existence. It is the largest Shiva linga in the world. This image was originally called Adavallan (Expert Dancer). Another name was Dakshina Meru Vitanken. Both the names occur in Thiruvisaipa as the names of the deity at Chidambaram. This possibly indicates that the Saiva creed derived its support at the time mainly from Chidambaram. Rajaraja Chola calls the image Rajarajeswaramudaiyar (The Lord of Rajarajeswaram). The tower over the shrine is named Dakshina Meru after the abode of Lord Siva at Kailasa.

A remarkable feature of the temple is the great Nandi (stone bull). The Nandi that figures at the entrance is immense in size (a popular belief is that it is growing by the day), and the ceiling of its enclosure is decorated with frescoes in the typical painting style of Thanjavur. The Nandi weighs 27 tonnes and is the second largest in the world.

Brihatpalayanas : The Brihatpalayanas were an ancient Indian Kingdom who were based in the modern state of Andhra Pradesh. They ruled Northern Andhra with Kodur in Krishna District as the Capital after the Ikshvakus around the third century AD. Jaya Varma was the only Brihatpalayana ruler. A princess of his family was married to the Andhra Ikshvaku king. His Kingdom included Musala Taluk as far as Gudivada, Kolleru and northern parts of Guntur. His capital was Koduru near Ghantasala in Krishna District. He gifted the village of Patur in Tenali Taluk to eight Brahmins. After his death the Ananda Gotrikas occupied his territory to the south of the Krishna river and the Salankayanas took his territory north of the river. mentioned.

Brita or Vrita Dance : It is one of the most important traditional folk dances of Bengal. It is performed by the barren women of Bengal, as a mark of gratitude to the God after their wish of conceiving a child is fulfilled. Quite often, this dance is performed after recovery from contagious diseases.

British East India Company : The British East India Company, sometimes referred to as "John Company", was a joint-stock company of investors, which was granted a Royal Charter by Elizabeth I on December 31, 1600, with the intent to favour trade privileges in India. The Royal

Charter effectively gave the newly created Honourable East India Company (HEIC) a 21 year monopoly on all trade in the East Indies. The Company transformed from a commercial trading venture to one which virtually ruled India as it acquired auxiliary governmental and military functions, until the Company's dissolution in 1858.

The East India Company flag changed over time. From the period of 1600 to 1707 (Act of Union between England and Scotland) the flag consisted of a St George's cross in the canton and a number of alternating Red and White stripes. After 1707 the canton contained the original Union Flag consisting of a combined St George's cross and a St Andrew's cross. After the Act of Union in 1800, that joined Ireland into the United Kingdom, the canton of the East India Company's flag was altered accordingly to include the new Union Flag with the additional St Patrick's cross. There has been much debate and discussion regarding the number of stripes on the flag and the order of the stripes. Historical documents and paintings show many variations from 9 to 13 stripes, with some images showing the top stripe being red and others showing the top stripe being white.

At the time of the American Revolution the East India Company flag would have been identical to the Grand Union Flag. The flag probably inspired the Stars and Stripes (as argued by Sir Charles Fawcett in 1937). Comparisons between the Stars and Stripes and the Company's flag from historical records present some convincing arguments. The John Company flag dates back to the 1600s whereas the United States adopted the Stars and Stripes in 1777.

Based in London, the company presided over the creation of the British Raj. In 1717, the Company received a royal dictate from the Mughal Emperor exempting the Company from the payment of custom duties in Bengal, giving it a decided commercial advantage in the Indian trade. A decisive victory by Sir Robert Clive at the Battle of Plassey in 1757 established the British East India Company as a military as well as a commercial power. By 1760, the French were driven out of India, with the exception of a few trading posts on the coast, such as Pondicherry.

The Company also had interests along the routes to India from Great Britain. As early as 1620, the company attempted to lay claim to the Table Mountain region in South Africa, later it occupied and ruled St Helena. The Company also established Hong Kong and Singapore; employed Captain Kidd to combat piracy; and cultivated the production of tea in India. Other notable events in the Company's history were that it held Napoleon captive on St Helena, and made the fortune of Elihu Yale. Its products were the basis of the Boston Tea Party in Colonial America.

Its shipyards provided the model for St. Petersburg, elements of its administration survive in the Indian bureaucracy, and its corporate structure was the most successful early example of a joint stock company. However, the demands of Company officers on the treasury of Bengal contributed tragically to the province's incapacity in the face of a famine which killed millions in 1770-1773.

British India : In 1600, Queen Elizabeth I accorded a charter, forming the East India Company to trade with India and eastern Asia. The British landed in India in Surat in 1624. Permission was granted by the ruling sovereign, Jehangir, to open up outposts in Calcutta and Madras. The British soon took advantage of their position by actively supporting the kingdoms militarily and gradually entering their politics. The Anglo-French wars of the 1700s, saw the British and the French fighting proxy wars on the behalf of the rulers. During the last of these wars, Robert Clive decisively defeated the French and greatly extended British rule. By early 19th century, the French were almost defeated and the British East India Company indirectly ruled most of India through puppet kings.

In 1857, an insurrection in the army sepoys ensued in the popular Revolt of 1857 (Sepoy Mutiny). This mobilised resistance, though short-lasting, was caused due to the widespread resentment due to British discriminatory and religious policies. As a result of this, India formally became a Crown colony. At the height of British power in the closing part of the 19th century, the British Empire stretched from Burma (now Myanmar) to Afghanistan, covering almost the entire undivided India consisting of modern day India, Pakistan and Bangladesh. Areas also under occupation were Bhutan (for a short period) and Ceylon, (now Sri Lanka). The British rule in India ended on August 15, 1947.

British Indian Army : The Indian Army was formed after the Indian Mutiny in 1857 by the British. Prior to this time the British East India Company had their own army units, paid for by their profits.

During the days of British rule, the Indian Army proved a very useful adjunct to British forces not only in India but also in other places, particularly during World Wars I and II.

British Physical Laboratories (BPL) : BPL is an Indian electronics company. The acronym stands for "British Physical Laboratories". It deals with consumer electronics (such as referigerators and washing machines), mobile networks etc.

In 1963, BPL founder and Group Chairman TPG Nambiar began manufacturing hermetically sealed precision panel meters in Palakkad, Kerala, under the name of British

Physical Laboratories. Having worked in the UK and USA, when he came back to India armed with a vision of pioneering the manufacture of superior quality electronic products, he dreamed of making BPL a household name.

Over the years, BPL's growth has been subject to constant challenges. The company was started at a time when the government had reserved many areas of business for the public sector. It had also virtually barred most entrepreneurs from entering other fields through reservations on licensing.

From 1980 onwards, when the industrial licensing was relaxed, BPL began manufacturing televisions and telecom equipment, demonstrating its potential and future business area. In the early 1990s, after globalisation and liberalisation of the Indian economy, competition entered the market. BPL retained its strong presence and growth rate. Strategic alliances with international companies provided the technology for them and set the standards of quality.

Using its experience of the market and the consumer, BPL concentrated on importing technology, improving product quality, innovations and manufacture of electronic products that enhanced the quality of life. After 37 years, BPL has metamorphosed from an entrepreneurial venture, into India's biggest consumer electronics company.

Broad Peak : Broad Peak (originally named K3) is the twelfth highest mountain on Earth. Broad Peak is part of the Gasherbrum massif and is about 8 kilometres (5 miles) from K2. Broad Peak was originally named K3 right after the naming of K2 but on closer inspection by a later party, it was discovered that the summit was over 1½ kilometres (1 mile) long, thus "Broad Peak". Broad Peak is known locally as Faichan Kangri. The literal translation of "Broad Peak" to Phalchan Kangri is not accepted among the Baltis.

Brocades : The brocades has a distinct style of weaving of silk satin cloth, gold brocading with coloured threads on the borders and in the lay technique in some cases. They carried traditional patterns of Popat Vel, stylized parrot flower border, jhardh, jhardh, flowering strub or tree motiff or the mango and ashorfi curcular gold coin. Today only simple Ashorfi brocade used in the rural areas is woven in Mehsana district of Gujarat.

Broghol : Broghol, also spelled Boroghil and several other ways, is a high mountain pass that crosses the Pamir and connects the Wakhan Corridor of Afghanistan with Chitral in Pakistan. According to the National Geographic Genographic Project, Broghol Pass appears to be the route used by the ancestors of all modern Western Europeans to reach Europe. Broghol is a relatively low pass, only 3,798 metres or 12,460 feet high. It was closed for about three months each winter because of snow, but for much of the rest of the year it was passable even for cart traffic. It is located at 37°00'N 73°26'E.

Broghol : Broghol, also spelled Boroghil and several other ways, is a high mountain pass that crosses the Pamir and connects the Wakhan Corridor of Afghanistan with Chitral in Pakistan. According to the National Geographic Genographic Project, Broghol Pass appears to be the route used by the ancestors of all modern Western Europeans to reach Europe. Broghol is a relatively low pass, only 3,798 metres or 12,460 feet high. It was closed for about three months each winter because of snow, but for much of the rest of the year it was passable even for cart traffic. It is located at 37°00'N 73°26'E. The area of Broghol is inhabited by Wakhi Tajiks and by Kyrgyz. The Broghol Pass is one of the four major mountain passes enter Chitral. The others are the Dorah Pass from Badakshan in Afghanistan, Shandur Top from Gilgit, and Lowari Top from Dir in Pakistan.

Buddha Purnima : Buddha Purnima is celebrated in May. Muslims celebrate Bakrid in the same month and Muharram is witnessed in June in remembrance of the Prophet Mohammed on his death anniversary. The full moon of Shravana is celebrated around August as Shravani Purnima, Rakhi Purnima and Raksha Bandhan. In the coastal areas it is celebrated as Narli Purnima to appease the sea gods. Fisher folk worship the sea and decorate their boats, sing and dance, and make offerings of coconut. Raksha Bandhan is celebrated on the same day in different parts of the state.

Buddhadeb Bhattacharya : Buddhadeb Bhattacharya (or Buddhadev Bhattacharya), born in 1944, has been the Chief Minister of West Bengal (India) since November 6, 2000. He is also a politburo member of the Communist Party of India (Marxist).

Born in 1944 in north Calcutta, the chief minister is the nephew of the revolutionary poet, Sukantya Bhattacharya. Soon after graduating from Presidency College in 1964, he joined the CPI-M as a primary member. Besides taking active part in the food movement, he also supported Vietnam's cause in 1968. As a result, he was appointed state secretary of the Democratic Youth Federation, the student wing of the CPI-M that is now known as the Democratic Youth Federation of India.

After becoming the chief minister Bhattacharya has liberalised Bengal's economy to some extent. He has attracted a lot of foreign investment in Bengal. Many new industries and IT related services have emerged under his leadership. He is generally seen as a Communist leader who is open to reforms. However, his opponents have criticized him for taking farmlands to build industries. Bhattacharya said in return, that these farmlands were not so productive and they will provide better jobs to many poor people.

Buddhism : Buddhism stands on three pillars: the Buddha; its founder, the Dhamma; his teachings and the Sangha; the order of Buddhist monks and nuns. Siddhartha, who was later known as the 'Buddha', the enlightened one, was the son of king Shuddhodana of Kapilavastu and his queen, Maya. He was born in 563BC on the Vaisakha Purnima day in the royal grove at Lumbini near Kapilavastu, Capital of the Sakyan republic. His family name was Gautama and he belonged to the Shakya clan. Hence he is sometimes called Shakyamuni (Shakya sage) or Shakyasimha (Shakya lion). Among his other epithets are Amitabha (infinite light) and Thathagata (he who has arrived at perfection).

Queen Maya died a week after delivering the prince. So the child was brought up by his step mother Gautami. At Siddharthas birth, the royal astrologer prophesied that he would one day become disillusioned with worldly pleasures and go forth as a mendicant in search of the wisdom that can overcome suffering.

The king, remembering the astrologers prophecy, tried to save his son from unpleasant sights. The king found for him a lovely wife, Yashodhara. Yashodhara bore him a son. He named his son Rahula (impediment). But the seeds of disenchantment had already sprouted in Siddhartha's heart.

As prophesied, Siddhartha saw the three signs of suffering: sickness, old age and death. These sufferings touched his heart and he left his palace on the night of the full moon in the month of Vaisakha, at the age of 29, to seek mental peace in the homeless life of an ascetic.

With a view to finding a true solution, the Buddha endeavored for full six years. During this period, he searched, scrutinized and examined in detail the prevalent schools of thought. He realised that wisdom could not be attained through self-mortification. At last, meditating under a tree near Gaya, he attained Bodhi (Illumination). Prince Siddhartha became the 'Buddha', the fully awakened one and the tree which had sheltered him came to be known as the bodhi tree.

After becoming enlightened, Gautama the Buddha could have immediately realised himself from the cycle of rebirths and attained 'Nirvana'; supreme liberation. But he decided to share his wisdom with others. His first sermon was preached in the Deer park at Saranath, near the ancient holy city of Varanasi. The five ascetics who had been earlier his colleagues became his first audience. Thereafter, for 45 years, the Buddha went about the country, from town to town, from village to village, disseminating the spiritual illumination for the benefit of suffering humanity. He attained 'Maha-Parinirvana' at Kusinara in 483 BC at the age of 80. Just before his death, when his favourite disciple, Ananda started weeping, the Buddha said "All component things must dissolve. Buddha can only point the way. Become a lamp unto yourself, work out your own salvation diligently". These were his last words.

Besides being a great spiritual teacher and preacher, the Buddha was also a great social reformer. The Buddha revolted against oppressive social laws, and proclaimed his new philosophy of liberty, equality and fraternity for the common welfare of all. Lord Buddha was considered as the creator of the virtues like individual liberty, tolerance, fellow-feeling, compassion, non-destruction of life (Ahimsa), moral character, benevolence, service and sacrifice.

Buddhist Gompa : Tawang Monastery or Gompa also known as the 'Galden Namgyal Lhatse', is a 400 year old Buddhist monastery of the Mahayana sect, built in the 17th century. It is situated at a height of 3500 meters or 10,000 ft at the Bhutan border. The monastery was founded by a monk, Mera Lama, a contemporary of the fifth Dalai Lama. It is a vast complex of 65 buildings—a treasure house of old scriptures, priceless images, painted tapestries, books and collection of gold lettered Buddhist scriptures.

The 'Parkhang' hall of the monastery houses the library which holds the rare hand written and block-printed Thankas or manuscripts of revered books like 'Tangym', 'Kangyur' and 'Sungbhum'. The other rare works of Buddhist literature include 108 gold-embossed manuscripts of the 'Teaching of Lord Buddha' and 225 volumes of the explanations of Buddha's teachings covered with specially designed moth—proof silk adorned with paintings. There is a towering 18 ft high gilded statue of the Buddha in the monastery complex. The Tawang Monastery is associated with the famous Torgva festival which is held in the eleventh Monpa month called the Dawa Chukchipah (i.e Dec-Jan as per the Buddhist). There is also a Craft Centre here producing fine woolen carpets of colourful designs.

Budhi Gandak : Budhi Gandak is an important river but the other river named the Gandak is a much bigger river originating from the Himalayas in Nepal. The Budhi Gandak originates From West Champaran near Ramnagar and Bagaha, passes through various districts of Bihar (East Champaran, Mujaffarpur, Samastipur, Khagaria) and flows into Ganges river near Khagaria/Manasi.

Budithi : There is a small village called Budithi in Central Srikakulam, a district in Andhra Pradesh. Here, life revolves around creating beautiful shapes out of alloys. The shapes range from the charmingly traditional to the elegantly modern. The art form expresses itself as traditional cooking utensils and also in forms that suit contemporary needs—like flower pots and planters. Usually made of brass, the objects have patterns that are geometric, with straight lines and curves forming simple and striking presentations. Floral patterns abound too.

Bugti : Bugti, is a Baloch tribe located in Balochistan, Pakistan. The Bugtis are divided into two clans Kalpars and Masuris. Bugti is a Baloch tribe of Rind (Arab) origin, numbering about 200,000, who are settled in hills to the east of the Sindh—Pishin railway, between Jacobabad and Sibi, with the Marris (a cognate tribe) to the north of them. Like the Marris, the Bugtis are physically a magnificent race of people, fine horsemen, good swordsmen and hereditary robbers. An expedition against them was organized by Sir Charles James Napier in 1845, but they were never brought under control till Sir Robert Sandeman ruled Balochistan. Since the construction of the railway, which completely outflanks their country, they have been fairly orderly.

Bugyals : Bugyals are high altitude alpine grass lands or meadows in Uttaranchal, India. They are locally referred as 'nature's own gardens'. They are flat and slopy carpeted with green grass and seasonal flowers. These provide an excellent grazing ground and pastures for tribal herdsman.At an elevation ranging between 3300 meters and 4000 meters, alpine meadows remain snow covered in winter. In the summer, the meadows burst into a multitude of beautiful flowers and grass. Tere are bugyals have been listed in Uttaranchal. Basins of Nanda Devi, Kedarnath, Gangotri and Bandarpunch have extensive meadows. Bugyals have very fragile ecosystem, so, need to be properly managed.

Bukka : Bukka (also known as Bukka Raya) was an emperor of the Vijayanagara Empire from the Sangama Dynasty.The early life of Bukka as well as his brother Hakka (also known as Harihara Raya) are relatively unknown and most accounts of their early life are based on theories. One such theory states that Bukka and Hakka were born from the Kuruba clan as well as commanders of the King of Warangal's army. After the King of

Warangal was defeated by Muhammad bin Tughlaq, he would capture both Bukka and his brother as prisoners and send them to Delhi were both were forced to follow Islam. Even so, Bukka and his brother eventually escaped and retained their Hindu traditions and founded the Vijayanagara Empire under the influence of the Brahmin sage Vidyaranya. Another account says that the brothers were instead in connection with the Hoysalas and were born from Karnataka near the Hampi territory, and that they were the successors to to the Hoysala sovereignty by natural process. Though the following may have been uncertain, either way Bukka and his brother were praised for their success in battle as well as the first rulers of the Empire.

Bukka, one of the most well-known of the Panchasangamas) as well as his brother Hakka founded the Hindu Vijayanagara Empire which reigned from the year 1336 and onwards. Under Bukka Raya's thirty seven year reign (according to Nuniz) the kingdom prospered and continued to expand as Bukka Raya conquered most of the kingdoms of southern India, continually expanding the territory of the empire. In the beginning of Bukka Raya's reign, Bukka desperately tried to destroy all hostile kingdoms so that he could strenghen the new empire, though initially he could not do anything as most of his forces were concentrated on fighting the Bahmanis.

Later on, Bukka conquered Madhura and extended his territory into the south all the way to Rameswaram. He would also defeat the Shambuvaraya Kingdom of Arcot and the Reddis of Kondavidu. In 1371, his son, Kumara Kamapna defeated the Sultanate of Madhura and conquered the territory in the penninusla south of Tungabhadra. Goa and the kingdom of Orissa (Orya) were also captured and Bukka forced the kingdoms of Ceylon and Malabar to have to pay tributes to him. During his reign Bukka would also have clashes with the Bahmani Sultans.

The first was during the time of Muhammad I and the other during the time of Mujahid. It is said that Bukka also sent a mission to China as well during his reign. Bukka however would later on die in about 1380 AD and was succeeded by Harihara II. It is also notable that under Bukka Raya's reign the capital of the Vijayanagara Empire established itself at Vijayanagara, on the south side of the river, which was more secure and defensive than their previous capitol at Anegondi. Even with the wars and internal conflicts, Bukka still managed to help support internal improvements for the city.

Bulbul Chowdhury : Bulbul Chowdhury (1919-1954) was a Bengali dancer and writer. He was born on 1 January 1919 in the village of Chunti under satkania thana of chittagong district. From childhood, Bulbul had been keenly interested in dance, music, painting, poetry and writing.

Bulbul Chowdhury used dance to express the ideas and aspirations of the new Pakistani nation. For this purpose he drew from common myths and legends, folk tales, and history. Most importantly, by showing that dance was part of the Muslim-Mughal tradition, he helped break down Muslim conservative attitudes and make dance respectable and popular. He died on 17 May 1954 at Calcutta. bulbul lalitakala academy was established in Dhaka on 17 May 1955 to carry on his work and in tribute to his contribution to dance and music.

Bull Temple : It is one of the oldest temple in the city and is built by Kempegowda, the founder of Bangalore. This typical Dravidian style temple has a mammoth, monolithic bull, 15ft high and 20ft long. It is made of gray granite polished with a mixture of charcoal and groundnut oil, in 1786. It is believed that it has grown in size since and now measures nearly 5 meters in height and 6 meters in length. The temple is dedicated to Nandi, the sacred bull. Visit—Daily 6- 8 PM, Entry is free.

Bulleh Shah : Bulleh Shah was a Punjabi Sufi poet, believed to have lived from 1680 to 1758.

As is a common practice in South Asian poetry, his poems include a signature line which contains his name. Bulleh Shah was settled in Kasur, now in Pakistan. His spiritual master was Shah Inayat Qadiri of Lahore.

Bundelas : The Bundelas are a Rajput clan who ruled several states in central India. The Bundelas of Bundelkhand trace their ancestry to Maharaja Hemkaran (Pancham Singh Bundela), who was driven from his kingdom by his younger brother. While in exile, he propitiated the Goddess Vindyhavasini, and with her assistance established a Kingdom at Mahauni in the Vindhya Range of central India. His descendants were known as the 'Vindhyalas', after the mountain range.

Beginning in the 14th century, the Bundelas moved south from the Vindhya Range into the Bundelkhand region, which now bears their name. In the 14th century Sahanpal Bundela captured Garhkundar, near Damoh from a Khangar king. The Bundela chief Rudra Pratap (ruled 1501-1531) founded the state of Orchha. He was succeeded by his son Madhukar. The Bundelas captured the city of Chanderi in 1586. Madhukar's son Virsingh Dev succeeded to the throne of Orchha, and Chanderi went to Madhukar's son Ram Sab. Virsingh Dev's son Jujhar Singh succeeded as ruler of Orchha, but was killed by the Mughal Emperor Shah Jahan in 1636, and Orchha was briefly annexed to the Mughal Empire, although it was later restored to the Bundelas. Bhagwan Rao, another son of Virsingh Dev, became ruler of Datia.

Bundelkhand : Bundelkhand is a geographic region of central India. The region is divided between the states of Uttar Pradesh and Madhya Pradesh, with the larger portion lying in Madhya Pradesh. Bundelkhand lies between the Indo-Gangetic Plain to the north and the Vindhya Range to the south. It is a gently-sloping upland, distinguished by barren hilly terrain with sparse vegetation, although it was historically forested. The plains of Bundelkhand are intersected by three mountain ranges, the Vindhya, Fauna and Bander chains, the highest elevation not exceeding 600 meters above sea-level. Beyond these ranges the country is further diversified by isolated hills rising abruptly from a common level, and presenting from their steep and nearly inaccessible scarps eligible sites for forts and strongholds of local kings. The general slope of the country is towards the northeast, as indicated by the course of the rivers which traverse or bound the territory, and finally discharge themselves into the Yamuna River.

Bundi : Bundi is a city of approximately 74,000 inhabitants in the Hadoti region of Rajasthan state in northwest India. It is of particular architectural note for its ornate forts, palaces, and baoris (stepwells), or water reservoirs. It is the administrative headquarters of Bundi District.

The town of Bundi is situated 36 km from Kota and 206 km from Jaipur. It is located at 25.30°N 75.35°E and an altitude of 515 m. The city lies near a narrow gorge, and is surrounded on three sides by hills of the Aravalli Range. A substantial wall with four gateways encircles the city.

In ancient times, the area around Bundi was apparently inhabited by various local tribes, in which the Meenas were prominent. Bundi and the eponymous princely state are said to derive their names from a former Meena tribal chieftain called Bunda Meena.

The Hadoti region in which Bundi stands takes is named for the Hada Rajputs, an offshoot of the Chauhan clan. The Hadas settled in the region in the 12th century and dominated the area for several centuries thereafter. Bundi was conquered by them in 1241 and nearby Kota in 1264. At one time, the Hada-ruled state of Bundi encompassed the present-day districts of Baran, Bundi, Kota, and Jhalawar.

The importance of Bundi state diminished over the years: as early as in 1579, it was deprived of the region which became Kota state; the alienated area included all of what later became Jhalawar state in 1838. However, Bundi state did remain an independent entity, if only nominally, up to and during the British Raj. After the independence of India in 1947, it became part of the Dominion of India (later the Union of India).

Burah : This is a macho martial dance in which men flourish their dangras (axes) in big open movements. Ballads telling of battles and legendary heroes are sung to the beat of the hulki (an hourglass-shaped drum).

Burha Talab : The city has many tanks out of which the Burha Talab is the largest lake in Chattisgarh and its beauty is enhanced by the existance of an island with gardens & trees in its midst.

Burig : The Burig, or Purik, are another group of Tibetan Muslims who live south of the Balti in Kashmir. Most of them live in Baltistan and Kargil, although significant numbers reside in Leh. Because they inhabit the higher reaches of the arid Himalayas, they depend on glacial runoff for irrigatation their crops. Barley, wheat, and millet are grown where water is sufficient, notably along small rivers. The hot summer temperatures also allow for a wide variety of fruits to be raised. Unlike the Dards and the Shina, the Burig are not nomads. They transfer their livestock from one grazing ground to another upon the arrival of autumn. During the summer months, they drive the cattle to alpine pastures, and all households own at least one female dzo, which is a cross between a cow and a yak. These animals produce milk. Most of them are Shia Muslims by religion, although significant Sunni Muslims and a small minority of Buddhists and Bön followers reside in isolated areas. Like the Balti, they spoke an archaic Tibetan dialect.

Buriganga River : Buriganga river is a tide-influenced river passing through west and south of Dhaka City. There is a traditional story behind naming it. In ancient times one course of the ganges used to reach the Bay of Bengal through Dhaleshwari. This course gradually shifted and ultimately lost its link with the main channel of the Ganges and was renamed as the Buriganga. The water levels during high and low tides in this river astonished the Mughals. The Buriganga originated from the Dhaleshwari near Kalatia. Its average width and depth are 400m and 10m respectively. This river is only 27 km long. The Turag has joined the Buriganga at Kamrangirchar of Dhaka City. In fact, the main flow of the Buriganga comes from the Turag. It meets with the Dhaleshwari at Munshiganj. The present head of the Buriganga near Chhaglakandi has silted up and opens only during floods, but the lower part is still open throughout the year. The downstream junction with the Dhaleshwari fluctuates from time to time according to changes in the position of the latter river; at present it lies about 3.22 km southwest of Fatullah. Its course by Dhaka is stable, fixed by the resistant clays marking the southern edge of the Madhupur tract.

The Buriganga is of great economic importance to Dhaka. It provides river connection by launch and country boats. Large steamers can no longer ascend the river in the dry season. In 1989, a bridge (the Bangladesh-China

Friendship Bridge) was built over the river for vehicles and pedestrians. In 2001, a second bridge over the river was also built at Babubazar for vehicles and pedestrians. Water pollution in the River Buriganga is as its highest. The most significant source of pollution appears to be from tanneries in the Hazaribagh area. In the dry season, the dissolved oxygen level becomes very low or non-existent and the river becomes toxic.

Burishwar River : Burishwar river is originates from the river Kirtankhola at Dapdapia of Bakerganj upazila under Barisal district in Bangladesh. It flows over Ranirhat, Khairabad, Bakerganj, Lebukhali, Alki, Mirzaganj, Karabunia, Ayla, Buraghata, Amtali and falls into the Bay of Bengal at Amtali upazila in Barguna district. Actually, the Burishwar is the downreach of the Arial Khan river and receives the main discharge from it. At the Tentulia confluence the Arial Khan creates a complex network system and one of these branches divides into two channels at Bakerganj. One arm named the Lebukhali flows through Patuakhali district and meets the Laukathi. The channel is very narrow. Another arm falls into the Bay of Bengal after receiving the names Bakerganj, Angaria, Katcha, Chighai and finally Burishwar. The Burishwar receives various small channels like the Subidkhali, Ayla, Gulishakhali, Pangasia (Golbunia), and Chargachhia on its course. The total length of the river is 158 km and is under tidal influence. There are meanders at some places of the river, which also shows an erosional tendency. Ranirhat, Bakerganj, Mirzaganj and Amtali are some important places on the banks of the Burishwar.

Burphu Dhura : Burphu Dhura is the Himalayan mountain peak situated in the Pithoragarh district of Uttaranchal, India.The altitude of the summit is 6,334 M.It is situated at the end ridge over the Kalabaland Glacier in the eastern part of the district, left to the Milam

Glacier.Kalabaland Dhura 6,105 M is situated to the west of this peak on the same massif.Burphu Dhura massif is the part of divide between Kalabaland and Goriganga valleys.This peak was first of all climbed to summit in 2000 from south on 27th September 2000 by Loveraj Dharmashaktu, Balwant Singh Kapkoti and Ramesh by an Indian team led by Wing Cdr S S Puri.The peak has two approaches-one from the Kalabaland glacier above the icefall and another from Burphu village in the Milam valley.

Burqa : A burqa (also burka or burqua) is a type of opaque veil sometimes worn in addition to a headscarf by Muslim women observing purdah.

Similar to a niqab, the burqa covers the wearer's entire face except for a small region about the eyes. A full burqa or Afghan burqa is a garment that conceals the entire body. The full burqa includes a "net curtain", which also hides the wearer's eyes. During the Taliban's reign in Afghanistan, women were required to wear a full burqa.

Women in some Muslim societies or subcultures wear burqa because of exegetic interpretations of the hijab. Standards for modest dress (sartorial hijab) for Muslim women and men vary greatly depending on the cultural context.

Burushaski : Burushaski (ISO/DIS 639-3 bsk) is a language isolate spoken by some 50,000-60,000 Burusho people in the Hunza, Nagir, Yasin, and parts of the Gilgit valleys in northern Pakistan. Other names for the language are Kanjut (Kunjoot), Khaguna, Werchikwar, Boorishki, Brushas (Brushias). Calvert Watkins, editor of the Indo-European etymologies in the American Heritage dictionaries, suggested that the word abel (apple), the only fruit tree reconstructed for Proto-Indo-European, may have been borrowed from a language ancestral to Burushaski.

Today Burushaski contains numerous loanwords from Urdu and a few from neighbouring Dardic languages such as Khowar and Shina, but the original vocabulary remains largely intact. The Dardic languages also contain large numbers of loan words from Burushaski.

Butta Bommalata : Marionette play is the oldest surviving art form in India. The marionette's or puppets are made of different materials. Butta Bommalu are made of bamboo, tamarind seed paste, paper, cattle dung or husk and hay. The figures are coloured according to the tradition and used for plays.

It is made up to waist only and hollow inside. The dolls are three to four times bigger than the human figures. A coloured cloth is tied around the doll at the waist that covers the player who enter into it. There is a hole in the doll at the navel through which the artiste can see the outside world. Figures of Siva and Parvati, Vishnu and Lakshmi, Garuda and Hanuman, Radha and Krishna are very common in Butta Bommalata. It is presented at festive gatherings, car festivals, marriage ceremonies, Navaratri celebrations, Ganesh immersion festivals and recently in election campaigns. These puppets are large enough to serve as full masks for men and women who dance to the rhythm of a Dappu or Mridangam.

Band, Dhole, Sonnayi are used as accompaniments in the Butta Bommalata. The troupe consist of at least ten members four of whom are in the puppets and dance, four who play instruments, one instructor and the troupe leader. This is only a dumb dance, accompanied only by the sounds of instruments.

Buxa National Park : The Buxa Tiger Reserve with an area of 759 sq.kms was established in the year of 1982-83 at the north eastern corner of West Bengal bordering Bhutan and Assam. The core area of 315sq.kms around the

Buxa Duar Fort was declared a National Park in January 1992. This park is located in eastern Dooars (rolling humid plains) at 2600 ft above sea level. The Dooars comprises of deciduous forests which are densely wooded and grasslands and is home to some of West Bengal's most varied flora and fauna.